Beyond the Binary

Beyond the Binary

Reconstructing
Cultural Identity in a
Multicultural Context

EDITED BY
TIMOTHY B. POWELL

RUTGERS UNIVERSITY PRESS
New Brunswick, New Jersey, and London

A substantially different version of chapter 5, "'One Hundred Percent American': How a Slave, a Janitor, and a Former Klansman Escaped Racial Categories by Becoming Indians" by Laura Browder, appeared previously in *American Indian Studies: An Interdisciplinary Approach to Contemporary Issues*, edited by Dane Morrison. New York: Peter Lang, 1997.

Library of Congress Cataloging-in-Publication Data

Beyond the binary : reconstructing cultural identity in a
   multicultural context / edited by Timothy B. Powell.
      p.   cm.
   Includes bibliographical references and index.
   ISBN 0–8135–2621–3 (cloth : alk. paper).— ISBN 0 –8135–2622–1
(pbk. : alk. paper)
     1. Group identity—United States. 2. Identity (Psychology)—
United States. 3. Pluralism (Social sciences)—United States.
4. Identity in literature. 5. American literature—19th century—
History and criticism. 6. American literature—20th century—
History and criticism. I. Powell, Timothy B., 1959– .
HM131.B475   1999
305.8'00973—dc21   98–30475
                                            CIP

British Cataloging-in-Publication data for this book is available from the British Library

Manufactured in the United States of America

For Jibreel

Contents

Part III   Mapping New Theoretical Territory

Acknowledgments

I WOULD LIKE TO THANK Rosemarie Garland Thomson who worked with me as a coeditor in the early phases of this project. Without her support this book would not have been possible. I would also like to thank the contributors to *Beyond the Binary* who believed in me in the tenuous early phases of the process and who worked extremely hard to make the book into something of which I hope that we can all be very proud.

I am extremely appreciative of the love and support of my family as well as my friends and colleagues at the University of Georgia: my parents, Bobbye Trout, Eve Troutt Powell, David Schoenbrun, Barbara McCaskill, Bryant Simon, John Inscoe, Miranda Pollard, John and Diane Morrow, Josh Cole, and Ron Miller. I would also like to especially thank Dana Nelson, Herman Beavers, and Houston Baker, who have provided me with guidance and strength. I am very grateful to Betty Jean Craige and the Humanities Center at the University of Georgia for a grant that allowed me time to work on this project.

Finally I would like to acknowledge the fine work of Leslie Mitchner, Brigitte Goldstein, Paula Kantenwein, and Marilyn Campbell at Rutgers University Press. My thanks also to the anonymous reader of the manuscript who provided thoughtful and very helpful suggestions. It has been a long and at times arduous journey; I have learned a great deal and I would like to thank the many unnamed though not unappreciated friends and colleagues who helped me along the way.

Beyond the Binary

| Introduction | Re-Thinking Cultural Identity |

TIMOTHY B. POWELL

CULTURAL STUDIES has reached a theoretical impasse. For the past twenty years, the central project of Cultural Studies has been to deconstruct the epistemological structures of Eurocentrism and to recover historical voices that were overlooked because of an entrenched ethnocentrism that privileged the elite, white, heterosexual, abled, male, European perspective. One of the most effective strategies in this initial phase of the cultural *deconstruction* of Eurocentrism was the identification of theoretical binaries such as Self/Other, Center/Margin, Colonizer/Colonized that helped scholars to delineate the inner workings of oppression and to establish a critical paradigm that would allow minority voices not only to be heard but to be esteemed as a critically important point of view.[1] It has become clear in recent years, however, that a binary form of analysis that collapses a myriad of distinct culture voices into the overly simplistic category of "Other" defined in relationship to a European "Self" is theoretically problematic. The time has come, therefore, to initiate a new critical epoch, a period of cultural *reconstruction* in which "identity" is reconfigured in the midst of a multiplicity of cultural influences that more closely resembles what Homi Bhabha has called the "lived perplexity" of people's lives and that more accurately reflects the multicultural complexities that have historically characterized "American" identity.[2]

This is not to say, however, that this initial phase of binary analysis was not terribly important and absolutely necessary. The emphasis that Cultural Studies placed on reconfiguring the canon to include "marginal" perspectives has led to a remarkable diversification of "American" identity. The progress that has been made in this direction is exemplified by the addition within

the last twenty years of such new MLA divisions as "Black American Literature and Culture," "Women's Studies in Language and Literature," "American Indian Literature," "Ethnic Studies in Language and Literature," "Gay
Studies in Language and Literature," "Asian American Literature," "Chicano
Literature," "Jewish American Literature," and "Puerto Rican Literature and
Culture." And yet, having proved an effective tool for dismantling Eurocentrism, this binary form of analysis has inadvertently replicated many of the
critical blind spots of the theoretical paradigm that it helped to displace. Instead of abandoning the theoretical structures of Eurocentrism altogether, the
cultural legacy of this binary analysis was the creation of new cultural centers
that, in turn, led to a period of "identity politics" characterized by a problematic quest for cultural "authenticity."[3] And while this new form of "identity
politics" did effectively empower an entire generation of cultural critics, the
problem was that, like Eurocentrism, the singular focus on trying to identify
new ethnic centers tended to collapse and oversimplify the historical complexities of black, white, Native American, Chicano, Asian American, gay
and lesbian, Puerto Rican, and women's cultures and the many points at which
these cultures intersected, overlapped, or else came sharply into conflict.

Beyond the Binary sets out to help implement this new phase of "cultural
reconstruction" by self-consciously moving beyond binary forms of analysis and
inventing new critical paradigms that will help scholars to theorize the fluidity, multiplicity, and intricate contradictions that characterize all forms of cultural identity. Rather than becoming embroiled in the hostile rhetorical battles
that continue to rage in the form of the Culture Wars, the essays presented
here are dedicated to a careful exploration of very specific situations and to
formulating new critical terminology that will allow for a more historically
accurate and theoretically sophisticated understanding of the unexplored complexities of cultural identity. More specifically, the goals of this collection are
to carry on this process of diversification by continuing to classify new forms
of cultural identity while working at the same time to bring this array of voices
into a dialogue that will reconfigure American Studies not as a series of distinct and disparate identities that are categorically separate but as a critical
site that will allow for the theorization of difference and conflict as well as
commonality and community.

A Brief Contemporary History of the Binary

The binary form of analysis that has dominated Cultural Studies for the last
two decades can be traced back to the writings of Frantz Fanon.[4] In works
like Black Skin, White Masks (1952) and The Wretched of the Earth (1961),
Fanon began the process of undoing Eurocentrism by using the critical binary

of Self/Other and colonizer/colonized to "help the black man to free himself of the arsenal of complexes that has been developed by the colonial environment."[5] Fanon's writings were of profound theoretical importance to Cultural Studies, for this formulation of Self and Other was adopted by a whole generation of scholars and helped open up the field up to postcolonial, Native American, Asian American, Latino, feminist, and gay and lesbian theorists.[6]

Henry Louis Gates's *"Race," Writing and Difference* (1985), for example, utilized the Self/Other theoretical paradigm to bring together a wide range of scholars in what is arguably the most important collection of essays from this period of Cultural Studies. Contributors included Edward Said, Houston Baker, Gayatri Spivak, Hazel Carby, Homi Bhabha, Jane Tompkins, Abdul JanMohamed, and Jacques Derrida. In the introduction, "Writing 'Race' and the Difference It Makes," Gates defined "texts written by the Other" as "that odd metaphorical negation of the European defined as African, Arabic, Chinese, Latin American, Yiddish, or female authors."[7] In this context the Self/Other binary served as a means of bringing together a wide range of scholars sharing a deeply felt ideological commitment to deconstruct the inherent biases of the Eurocentric canon. Although this critical revolution against Eurocentrism was necessary and successful, it eventually became apparent that the Self/Other theoretical model was deeply problematic. The critical penchant for identifying cultures as "Other" blurred meaningful historical and social distinctions between these unique forms of ethnic identity and, even more importantly, this binary critical framework implicitly relied on the very Eurocentric model that it was attacking—reducing these complex forms of cultural identity to being simply an "odd metaphorical negation of the European."

It is now possible to see, in looking back, that Gates's introduction contains within it the next step in the deconstructive process as well—the emphasis on "difference" that signaled a turn away from the white, European center. Writing about the importance of oral traditions in African American society, Gates notes that "in my own tradition, theorists have turned to the black vernacular tradition . . . to isolate the signifying black difference through which to theorize about the so-called discourse of the Other."[8] Thus, the vast array of scholars writing on such disparate topics as America, Africa, India, Spanish Moors, Native Americans, and black feminism that was held together in *"Race," Writing, and Difference* by what Gates calls the "so-called discourse of the Other" gave way to a singular focus on "difference" that would eventually lead to a much more monocultural approach to studying cultural identity. Three years later, for example, Gates published *The Signifying Monkey* (1988) in which he theorized, "Our goal must not be to embed, as it were Europe within Africa or Africa within Europe. . . . Rather, I have written this book to analyze a theory of reading that . . . has been generated from within the black tradition itself, autonomously." To do so, Gates concluded, was the "ideal way to confound a Eurocentric bias."[9]

This final step in the deconstruction of Eurocentrism led to the establishment of cultural centers on campus and a new generation of scholarship focused on exploring cultural identity in isolation. This phase of Cultural Studies, like the earlier ones, had both its distinct insights and its blind spots. On the one hand, scholars like Gates, Houston Baker, Gayatri Spivak, and Jane Tompkins produced detailed and insightful studies of African American, postcolonial, and women's literature and culture that radically changed the face of Cultural Studies. On the other hand, in the process of constructing new centers and searching to recover "authentic" historical voices that would reveal a racial past that had been "lost," a whole new set of theoretical problems arose. Identity politics, for example, created bitter academic battles about who would occupy the newly formed center or even who had a right to speak. This period of vicious infighting prompted Toni Morrison to write in the first chapter of *Playing in the Dark* (1992), "I do not want to encourage those totalizing approaches to African-American scholarship which have no drive other than the exchange of dominations—dominant Eurocentric scholarship *replaced* by dominant Afrocentric scholarship."[10]

In the midst of this final and often destructive phase of cultural deconstruction, several important theoretical works pointed the way beyond a binary form of analysis. In *Between Men* (1985) and *Epistemology of the Closet* (1990), Eve Kosofsky Sedgwick set out to demonstrate that "categories presented in a culture as symmetrical binary oppositions—heterosexual/homosexual, in this case, actually subsist in a more unsettled and dynamic tacit relationship." In the process of deconstructing the homo/heterosexual binary, Sedgwick helped to lay the foundations of Queer theory and to point the way to a new direction for Cultural Studies. "The appropriate place for critical analysis to begin," she writes in the introduction to *Epistemology of the Closet*, "is from [a] relatively *decentered* perspective."[11]

Another important work from the late 1980s that was to map out new critical territory for the 1990s was Gloria Anzaldúa's *Borderlands/La Frontera*. Anzaldúa's theoretical formulation of "a new *mestiza* consciousness . . . a consciousness of the Borderlands" called for a fuller understanding of the inherent complexities of cultural hybridity. "To live in the Borderlands," Anzald·a writes, "means you/are neither hispana india negra espanola/ni gabacha eres mestiza, mulata, half-breed/caught in the crossfire between camps/while carrying all five races on your back." And although Anzaldúa's text still falls into the obsession with authenticity in places—"I fear no betrayal on my part because, unlike Chicanas and other women of color who grew up white . . . I was totally immersed in [my culture]"—*Borderland/La Frontera*'s attempt to theorize a multiplicity of cultural influences signaled a turn away from the focus on studying cultural identity in isolation toward a more *multi*cultural theoretical framework.[12]

In the early 1990s cultural critics began to explore the theoretical possibilities of hybridity in more detail and to study the dialogic relation between different cultures. Toni Morrison's *Playing in the Dark*, for example, argues that "it may be possible to discover, through a close look at literary 'blackness,' the nature—even the cause—of literary 'whiteness'" and trained a new generation of scholars to see the Africanist presence in white, canonical writers like Melville, Hemingway, and Mark Twain.[13] Eric Lott's *Love and Theft* explored the interconnections between black and white cultures by carefully studying blackface minstrelsy and the exceedingly complex way in which African American culture influenced the white working class.[14] Likewise in *The Black Atlantic*, Paul Gilroy attacks what he calls "conceptual problems common to English and African American versions of cultural studies which . . . share a nationalistic focus that is antithetical to the rhizomorphic, fractal structure of the transcultural, international formation I call the black Atlantic."[15] Although all three of these scholars are still focused on the black/white binary, their work represents an important step forward in that it recognizes that these two cultures are neither isolated nor wholly distinct from one another by calling attention to the ways in which black and white society have mutually influenced one another in a complex and often deeply contentious manner.[16]

The next step is to reconstruct cultural identity in the midst of a *multiplicity* of cultures, in a theoretical matrix where there are no centers and no margins—a critical paradigm that will allow scholars to study the polyvalent nature of lived cultural identity. Unlike many other works on multiculturalism, *Beyond the Binary* does not advocate an ideological agenda or explicitly engage such political questions as affirmative action or racism. On the contrary, the essays included here are for the most part careful, analytic studies grounded in the historical complexities of individual instances of cultural identity that open outward into broader theoretical statements. This collection of essays sets out to accomplish the theoretical transformation of historically and culturally indistinct "Others" into fully constituted "Selves" and the expansion of the definition of "culture" to include not just issues of race, class, and gender but also sexuality, physical disability, transnationality, hybridity, and the complexities of Queer identity, as well as self-identification that does not conform to biological identification. The list of topics considered here is not meant to be exhaustive of the multiplicity of forms of cultural identity but rather is meant to be seen as a synecdoche that suggestively maps out part of a larger multicultural matrix that opens out beyond the margins of this collection. Nor does one coherent theoretical framework bind all of these scholars together—the binaries that these essays work to overcome include Self/Other, center/margin, colonizer/colonized, black/white, abled/disabled, straight/queer, and masculine/feminine. What all of the essays included here have in common is that they wrestle self-consciously with the limitations of binary analysis and are committed to initiating a new period of reconstruction in Cultural Studies.

Reconstructing Cultural Identity

Beyond the Binary is conceived as a dialogic narrative that unfolds over three distinct though interrelated sections. The first section of the book, "Extending the Boundaries of Cultural Identity," is dedicated to both exploring as yet unrecognized forms of "culture" such as physical disability and "freaks" and to productively complicating existing categories such as "black" and "queer" identity. The second section, "Exploring Cultural Self-Transformation," calls into question implicit assumptions about the fixed nature of "identity." The essays in this section problematize the notion that cultural identity is biologically determined by asking whether it is possible to choose one's racial identity or to empathize across the cultural borders of gender, race, and sexuality. Having destabilized received notions of both "culture" and "identity," the concluding section, "Mapping New Theoretical Territory," is devoted to inventing new terminology and new critical paradigms that will help scholars understand and articulate the inherently fluid and hybrid nature of cultural identity. The critical perspectives presented here have been carefully situated in dialogic relation to one another to construct a "relatively decentered whole" that cannot, therefore, simply be reduced to a sum of its parts.[17] In this sense the collection is meant to be read in its entirety, as a narrative made up of distinctly different voices whose richness depends as much upon its contradictions as upon its coherence.

Lennard J. Davis's essay "Nation, Class, and Physical Minorities," opens the book by exploring new critical territory and calling into question settled boundaries. Davis sets out to expand the borders of Cultural Studies by arguing that the Deaf, with their own distinct language and culture, need to be theorized as an "ethnic group" that constitutes a "nation within a nation." Davis argues against the general perception that "the disabled person is not of this nation, not a citizen in the same sense as the abled-body." Using Franklin Delano Roosevelt as a "national symbol of identity" at a historical moment when the "model of the able-bodied citizen was to be writ large on every WPA mural," Davis deconstructs the abled/disabled binary that works to exclude the physically disabled from the imagined community of the nation by demonstrating that disability lies at the very heart, even though it has been airbrushed out, of "American" history.

In "Strange Blood: Hemophobia and the Unexplored Boundaries of Queer Nation," Michael Davidson complicates this notion of nations within nations even more by uncovering the embattled position of hemophiliacs infected with AIDS within Queer Nation. Davidson exposes the "limits to the critique of identity waged in the name of Queer Nation" by illustrating the way in which "the borders of Queer Nation, while open to transgressions of sexuality are often closed to identities not constructed *through* sexuality." Having effectively deconstructed "Queer" identity, Davidson then works to reconstruct it by arguing for the "queering of hemophilia." In so doing, Davidson reintegrates hemophiliacs not only into Queer Nation but, in a larger context, back into "American" identity. He does this by delineating the history of the nation's obsession with "blood culture" from the miscegenation laws of the nineteenth century, to the way in which Thomas Sutpen's "grand design" is based on a Southern heroic ideal of uncontaminated blood, to Phil Donahue's awkward attempts to reintegrate hemophiliacs infected with AIDS into a problematic conception of "hetero-normalcy."

Like Michael Davidson, Heather Hathaway carefully analyzes the complexities within a "single" culture by examining the tensions between African Americans and Caribbean Americans in the 1920s. Focusing specifically on a "Special Caribbean Issue" of *Opportunity: A Journal of Negro Life* published by the National Urban League in November 1926, Hathaway demonstrates cultural differences "within the veil of race," calling into question the notion of a monolithic "black" identity and the tendency to see culture solely in terms of race. What Hathaway makes clear is that although an overriding racial essentialism "uniformly lumped African Americans and African Caribbeaners together in housing, employment, economic and sociological arenas, . . . significant differences, stemming largely from disparate national origins, caused friction between the two communities." Hathaway's argument is theoretically important in that it does not utterly deconstruct "black" identity or dismiss race as a meaningful factor in determining "culture" but rather complicates it productively. Conflicts between the two communities are articulated, as are the commonalities forged out of the "inexorable pressure" of racism in Jim Crow America.

In "Narratives of Deviance and Delight: Staring at Julia Pastrana, the 'Extraordinary Lady,'" Rosemarie Garland Thomson expands the existing discursive boundaries of "culture" by exploring the complicated role that "the hybrid construct of the sensitive monster" played in the formation of citizenship in Victorian America. Thomson offers a detailed analysis of the way in which Julia Pastrana, a Mexican Indian woman whose body was covered with thick black hair and whose dentition was unusually prominent, was exhibited as a freak in nineteenth-century American culture. Thomson demonstrates how the binaries of human/animal, civilized/primitive, and normal/pathological were used to create the "spectacle" of the "Marvelous Hybrid or Bear Woman." Explicating the way in which Pastrana's hybridity was used "to instruct, edify, and thus construct the middle-class canonical self," Thomson moves beyond these binaries by arguing that Pastrana was not simply excluded from "America" but was in fact integral to formations of national identity.

All the essays in the opening section demonstrate that the project to diversify "American" identity and to theorize the nation in the midst of dynamic multiplicity does not necessarily lead to balkanization or disunity, as critics of multiculturalism have often contended.[18] Rather, it reconstructs "America" by arguing forcefully and convincingly that this cultural diversity is integral to national identity and has always been a repressed part of the country's heritage.

The second section of this book, "Exploring Cultural Self-Transformation," wrestles with one of the most controversial and potentially important aspects of this new dynamic and multicultural conception of cultural identity—the possibility of overcoming biological determinism and the seemingly fixed borders of race, gender, and sexuality. In "'One Hundred Percent American': How a Slave, a Janitor, and a Former Klansman Escaped Racial Categories by Becoming Indians," Laura Browder documents how three very different authors used "fake" ethnic autobiographies to reimagine their cultural identity and escape the rigid black/white binary and attendant racism that have historically plagued American society. Browder demonstrates how Chief Buffalo Child Long Lance, who was born "black" but reinvented himself as an "Indian," played upon white stereotypes both to further his career in Robinson's circus and to demean Native Americans in his autobiography. Browder also delineates how James P. Beckwourth, who was born racially mixed (black and white), actually changed his cultural identity and became a chief in the Creek Nation. Browder's insights are important in that they demonstrate that cultural self-transformations are not merely a matter of whim—theoretical quandaries that if carried to their logical conclusion threaten to collapse into nihilistic absurdity by rendering "identity" utterly relativistic and therefore meaningless. Rather, such willed changes in cultural identity are historically real; in fact, many blacks and whites were not only fully accepted into Indian tribes but played important roles in Native American society. Moreover, Browder demonstrates how cultural transformation can be used as a way of escaping racism and America's fixation on the black/white binary. Forrest Carter, for example, a white southerner and author of George Wallace's infamous speech "Segregation now . . . Segregation tomorrow . . . Segregation forever," was able to use the genre of "fake" autobiography as a way, in Browder's words, "of leaving his racist reputation behind him . . . a way out of the black-white binary in which, ironically, he had trapped himself through his white supremacist politics."

Sharon P. Holland, in "From This Moment Forth, We Are Black Lesbians: Querying Feminism and Transgressing Whiteness in Consolidated's *The Business of Punishment*," takes Browder's argument one step further by exploring the issue of cultural self-transformation in her study of the attempt by members of the white, working-class thrash band Consolidated to reinvent themselves as black lesbians. Holland attacks the problem of "biology-is-destiny" in what she calls "new age feminism." Using Consolidated's notions of a "postmodern, postsubjective culture" that allows them to free themselves from their own biological whiteness and to transform themselves ideologically into black lesbians, Holland calls for "a theoretical paradigm appropriate to the multiple crossings performed in Consolidated's text." This notion that white working-class men could speak in the voice of radical black lesbian feminists obviously raises a plethora of difficult theoretical issues that go to the heart of rethinking identity in a multicultural context. In this sense Holland's exegesis serves as a wake-up call for both feminism and Cultural Studies, demanding the invention of new theoretical paradigms capable of articulating and understanding the highly permeable boundaries that exist between very different and often violently antagonistic cultures.

The final section of *Beyond the Binary*, "Mapping New Theoretical Territory," proposes new paradigms that will allow scholars to understand the theoretical intricacies of cultural hybridity more fully. David T. Mitchell's essay "The Accents of 'Loss': Cultural Crossings as Context in Julia Alvarez's *How the Garcia Girls Lost Their Accents*" opens this section, detailing the "always already hybrid nature" of cultural identity and the transnational character of "American" identity by charting the transformations of Alvarez's characters as they move back and forth between the Dominican Republic and the United States. Mitchell uses the term "multiperspectivity" to analyze the way in which Alvarez's novel is told from four different points of view within one family. This new paradigm productively complicates the critical tendency to study cultural identity in isolation by taking into consideration issues of gender, class, race, and multiple nationalities, delineating "the complex interplay of colliding ideological and political systems." In doing so Mitchell illustrates how Alvarez's novel explodes the binaries of home/exile, patriot/expatriate, and citizen/alien to reveal "the impossibility of locating a truly original homeland culture." Mitchell's essay contributes to the ongoing debate within Cultural Studies by demonstrating the theoretical shortcomings inherent in the search for "authentic" forms of cultural identity.

Timothy B. Powell's "Historical Multiculturalism: Cultural Complexity in the First Native American Novel" continues this line of inquiry by demonstrating how complicated "Cherokee" identity was in the lived historical perplexity following the Trail of Tears. Focusing on John Rollin Ridge's *The Life and Adventures of Joaquín Murieta* (1854), written by a survivor of Cherokee removal about the intense racial conflict in California following the Mexican American War, Powell demonstrates how the Self/Other binary collapses the cultural complexity of the novel by not fully engaging the ideological differences between the novel's Cherokee author and its Mexican American protagonist. In an effort to formulate a new critical paradigm that will allow for a more accurate and intricate appraisal of the myriad of competing cultures in mid-nineteenth-century California, Powell invents a new theoretical model that he calls "historical multiculturalism." This paradigm, grounded in historical complexity rather than political correctness, allows him to delineate how Ridge's novel combines formal elements of the historical romance from Anglo culture, the myth of the trickster figure from Cherokee culture, and the narrative structure of the *corrido* from Mexican American culture to construct a radically hybrid sense of cultural identity even as whites in California were working to exclude Mexican Americans from the rights of citizenship and to commit genocide against Californian Indians.

John Lowe's comparative analysis of humor in Irish, Creek, and African American cultures, "Newsprint Masks: The Comic Columns of Finley Peter Dunne, Alexander Posey, and Langston Hughes," also makes a constructive gesture toward the invention of new critical terminology. Lowe offers the model of the "'ethnic' kaleidoscope" as a paradigm that more accurately invokes America's culturally diverse heritage as an alternative to the assimilative sameness of the "melting pot" or the hermetic separatism of the "ethnic mosaic." Analyzing the "struggle to resurrect folk wisdom and ethnic values in the face of massive pressure to Americanize," Lowe studies the underappreciated role of humor in Irish, Greek, and African American cultures. Lowe's work is critically important in that he gives detailed descriptions of the specific cultural context of each writer without losing sight of the interrelations between the three different cultures, thus pointing to a new style of reconstructive, multicultural analysis.

Nicole Tonkovich's exegesis of Sui Sin Far's "Leaves from the Mental Portfolio of a Eurasian" deconstructs the binary assumptions that underlie critical constructions of Sin Far's nationality, gender, and genre to reconstruct a new theoretical model of "transnational identity." Mapping the middle ground between the binaries of the Occident and the Orient, between masculine and feminine identity, and between photography and autobiography, Tonkovich analyzes how Sin Far's work reveals the "imprecision of national, generic, and gendered classifications." In contrast to both Powell and Lowe, who are working to construct new conceptions of "American" identity, Tonkovich takes the reconstruction of cultural identity in a new direction by exploring Sin Far's claim to "have no national identity," demonstrating how Sui Sin Far's individual portraits "constitute a photomontage of a new transnational face."

Concluding the volume, Diane Price Herndl's "Miscegen(r)ation or Mestiza Discourse?: Feminist and Racial Politics in *Iola Leroy* and *Ramona*" offers a thoughtful dialogical response to many of the other essayists in the collection by sympathetically reconsidering feminist scholars' desire to locate "authentic" voices from the nineteenth century. By examining Helen Hunt Jackson's *Ramona* (1884) and Frances E. W. Harper's *Iola Leroy* (1892), Price Herndl analyzes the mixing of races and the mixing of forms in both novels. This literary and historical hybridity, Price Herndl argues, ultimately problematizes the feminist quest for a truly authentic voice from the past. Price Herndl, however, offers a caveat to the current critical focus on cultural hybridity by noting that "there [was] no *mestiza* option for either of these women . . . in the racially charged nineteenth century," that in the end the characters must choose one racial identity. Price Herndl's essay thus makes a trenchant point that should not be overlooked in the project to reconstruct cultural identity in a multicultural context: the sheer historical force of the black/white binary (for example, the one drop rule) is historically real and cannot, therefore, be ignored. Price Herndl concludes by offering a critically important alternative—inventing a new theoretical paradigm, "the *mestiza* reader," that will allow feminist and cultural critics of the late twentieth century to escape these rigid racial binaries and "work toward comprehending multiple, complex aims of nineteenth-century fiction."

This decentered dialogue of different critical and cultural voices is not meant to answer definitively the question of how Cultural Studies is to overcome the critical impasse of identity politics that has arisen in the wake of the deconstruction of Eurocentrism. Rather, this dialogue is constructed to be theoretically open ended—to encourage other scholars to continue expanding existing definitions of "culture" and to further complicate the present understanding of "identity" beyond overly simplistic binaries of center/margin and Self/Other. Most importantly, the intent of this many-voiced narrative is to bring the myriad of divisions within Cultural Studies back into contact with one another so as to reconstruct a new era of multicultural analysis that recognizes the historical existence of racism and separatism yet also acknowledges the hybridity and dynamic fluidity of cultural identity.

Notes

Special thanks to Priscilla Wald, Rosemarie Garland Thomson, Eve Troutt Powell, and Tricia Lootens for their careful reading of the manuscript and their suggestions.

1. I have used the term "cultural deconstruction" to make clear both its resonance with and its difference from "philosophical deconstruction." The two terms are not synonymous. Many of the deconstructionists (for example, Harold Bloom and Paul de Man) were not involved in the Cultural Studies movement. There were, however, explicit connections between the two movements. See, for example, Jacques Derrida, "Racism's Last Word," in *"Race," Writing and Difference,* ed. Henry Louis Gates, Jr. (Chicago: University of Chicago Press, 1985); Henry Louis Gates, Jr., *The Signifying Monkey: A Theory of African-American Literary Criticism* (New York: Oxford University Press, 1988); Gayatri Spivak, *In Other Worlds: Essays in Cultural Politics* (New York: Routledge, 1988).
2. Homi K. Bhabha, "Dissemination: Time, Narrative, and the Margins of the Modern Nation," in *Nation and Narration,* ed. Homi K. Bhabha (London: Routledge, 1990), 307.
3. For an example of the reinscription of new cultural centers of "authenticity" see Molefi Kete Asante, *The Afrocentric Idea* (Philadelphia: Temple University Press, 1987). For an interesting analysis of both the strengths and problems of identity politics see Wendy Brown, "Injury, Identity, Politics," in *Mapping Multiculturalism,* eds. Avery F. Gordon and Christopher Newfield (Minneapolis: University of Minnesota Press, 1996).
4. Any such brief historical overview as this one is, of course, distinctly limited. Binary analysis could be traced back as far as Plato's metaphor of the soul as a chariot drawn by one black horse and one white horse in *The Phaedrus.* I have chosen to begin with Fanon because of his central importance to cultural theorists working in the 1980s and 1990s.
5. Frantz Fanon, *Black Skin, White Masks,* trans. Charles Lam Markmann (New York: Grove Press, 1967), 30.
6. See Henry Louis Gates, Jr., "Critical Fanonism," *Critical Inquiry* 17 (spring 1991): 457–70.
7. Henry Louis Gates, Jr., "Writing 'Race' and the Difference It Makes," in *"Race," Writing and Difference,* ed. Gates, 2.
8. Ibid., 15.
9. Gates, *The Signifying Monkey,* xx.
10. Toni Morrison, *Playing in the Dark: Whiteness and the Literary Imagination* (Cambridge, Mass.: Harvard University Press, 1992), 8.
11. Eve Kosofsky Sedgwick, *Epistemology of the Closet* (Berkeley: University of California Press, 1990), 9–10, 1.
12. Gloria Anzaldúa, *Borderlands/La Frontera* (San Francisco: Spinsters/Aunt Lute, 1987), 77, 194, 21.
13. Morrison, *Playing in the Dark,* 9.
14. Eric Lott, *Love and Theft: Blackface Minstrelsy and the American Working Class* (New York: Oxford University Press, 1993).
15. Paul Gilroy, *The Black Atlantic: Modernity and Double Consciousness* (Cambridge, Mass.: Harvard University Press, 1993), 4.
16. For more explicitly political writings on multiculturalism see Wahneema Lubiano, "Like Being Mugged by a Metaphor: Multiculturalism and State Narratives," in *Mapping Multiculturalism,* ed. Gordon and Newfield; Lauren Berlant and Michael Warner, "Introduction to 'Critical Multiculturalism,'" in *Multiculturalism: A Critical Reader,* ed. David Theo Goldberg (Cambridge, Mass.: Blackwell, 1994); Man-

ning Marable, "Beyond Racial Identity Politics: Toward a Liberation Theory for a Multicultural Democracy," in *Beyond Black and White: Transforming African American Politics* (London: Verso, 1997).

17. The phrase "relatively decentered whole" is from Sedgwick, *Epistemology of the Closet.*

18. See Arthur Schlesinger, Jr., *The Disuniting of America: Reflections of a Multicultural Society* (New York: W. W. Norton, 1992).

Part I

Extending the Boundaries of Cultural Identity

Chapter 1

Nation, Class, and Physical Minorities

LENNARD J. DAVIS

*"It is true that deaf-mutes of
every country have no mother tongue."*
John Kitto, *Lost Senses* (1845)

PROBABLY NO BINARY has been more destructive to the possibility for human freedom than the "normal/abnormal" opposition. With a single sweep of some cultural Occam's Razor, race, class, gender, sexual preference, ability, nationality, ethnicity, and a host of other human variables have been simplified in the name of power. The Holocaust, colonization, racism, immigration restrictions, unequal distribution of wealth and power, the persecution of gays, the oppression of women, racial and ethnic warfare, to name a few of the evils of the past hundred years, were fueled by this simplistic binary opposition between normal and abnormal. The aim of this essay is to see how that binary, along with the variant binary "abled/disabled," used in establishing categories of disability, has operated in the process of national consolidation.

One category embodying the essence of the normal/abnormal binary is nationalism. Historically, and paradoxically, nationalism has been tied to both the institutionalization of and the eradication of ethnicity, tribalism, regionalism, and so on. One area never considered relevant to nationalism has been the area of disability. Disability has historically been seen as a personal problem, a palpable manifestation on the individual body of divine judgment, maternal or paternal culpability or neglect, and/or moral corruption. This personalization of disability has had considerable political consequences in making the issue of normalizing the body seem dependent on individuals rather than a consequence of collectivities. But in recent years a constructivist and civil rights view of disability has led to a newer notion that disability is a social and political issue, that a society at large defines the terms of whom it will consider disabled, and in that process defines those who are considered

17

legitimate members of a nation.[1] United States immigration laws, for example, particularly after 1924, clearly determined that certain categories of people with disabilities should not be allowed to become citizens.[2] It is important for any consideration of normalizing processes, particularly those linked to the body, to include this political dimension. In this essay, therefore, I would like to consider the ways that nationalism relates to and defines disability.

To place this argument in its historical context, let me begin with Marx, who, while not discussing disability per se, saw the body as essentially reified in the processes that came about as a result of the accumulation of capital in the eighteenth century. Marx's nostalgic retro-fit vision in the *Economic and Philosophical Manuscripts of 1848* saw an earlier period in which the body existed in sensuous relation to the world, inserted into that world and creating that world through labor. This vision, however romantic, seems to point to a kind of labor that was not easily distinguished from "life." The parameters of the body and its activities were seen as aspects of nature linked to the processes of natural activities and seasons.

One could go so far as to say that disability, in our sense of the word, could not exist in such a world. Of course impairments existed, but the impaired body was part of a lived experience, and in that sense it was functional. It was not defined strictly by its relation to means of production or a productive economy. By the mid nineteenth century, however, the body *an sich* became the body *für sich,* and the impaired body became disabled—unable to be part of the productive economy, confined to institutions, shaped to contours defined by a society at large. The disabled body became "abnormal."[3]

In this regard, it is possible to see how the disabled body came to be included in larger social and political constructions like that of the nation. We have only to consider the cliché that a nation is made up of "able-bodied" workers, all contributing to the mutual welfare of the members of that nation, to understand how this trope functions.

In order to discuss the way a concept of nationality fits into a concept of disability, it is first necessary to say what we mean when we speak of nations. It is commonplace to think of a nation as equivalent to various state or governmental groupings. But the question of nation has become vexed in recent years. As one political scientist puts it, "Where today is the study of nationalism? In this Alice-in-Wonderland world in which nation usually means state, in which nation-state usually means multinational state, and in which ethnicity, primordialism, pluralism, tribalism, regionalism, communalism, parochialism and sub-nationalism usually means loyalty to the nation." Walker Connor suggests that, as opposed to a governmental entity, nation should be defined as "a group of people whose members believe they are ancestrally related."[4]

This definition allows us to rethink nation as something perhaps divorced from a self-evident entity represented by the flag (for which it stands), an anthem, a collective will. The simplicity with which Edmund Burke speaks of "the men of England" or says, "The people of England know how little influence the teachers of religion are likely to have with the wealthy and powerful of long standing," shows us how powerful an idea is the homogenizing power of national hegemony, eliding as it does in this case the particularity of the Scots, the Welsh, the Cornish, and the Irish.[5]

The idea of a nation as a governmental entity is further refined by contemporary scholars like Benedict Anderson, Immanuel Wallerstein, Etienne Balibar, Hayden White, and Homi Bhabha, among others, who propose alternative ways of thinking about nationality. Anderson thinks of the nation as a manifestation of print culture. For him, the gradual honing of a group of people into readers of a common language creates the idea of a homogenous organization. So it was readers, "connected through print, [who] formed, in their secular, particular, visible invisibility, the embryo for the nationally imagined community."[6] Likewise, Homi Bhabha deconstructs nation and narrative, while Hayden White writes of histories as forms of fictive metanarrative that novelize a nation to itself.[7] Wallerstein prefers to downplay national entities, seeing them as aspects of a world capitalistic system, while Balibar sees nationalism as a self-constructing, destructive set of ideologies, always in a state of flux, but always defining power structures.

This reassessment of nationalism changes the discussion so that groups of people who see themselves bound by a common language, culture, and narrative are defined as nations or nationalities. This redefinition allows for ethnic and religious minorities to claim national identity, and even gender comes into play, as Sylvia Walby notes, since women must be seen as a distinct nationality within a nation.[8]

Perhaps one of the most concise definitions of nationality is to be found in a somewhat unlikely source—the writings of Joseph Stalin. His 1913 pamphlet entitled *Marxism and the National Question* outlined five features necessary for a group to consider itself a nationality: a common language; a stable community; a territory; economic cohesion; a collective psychology and character. Stalin stresses that nationality should not be thought of as something tribal or racial in nature, not something essentialist, but something constructed through history; inextricably connected to that construction is language.[9]

Nationality alone does not constitute nation, as we can see in the struggles that have taken place in Eastern Europe and the former Soviet Union. Nationality needs a political dimension. "A nation," Stalin refines, "is not merely a historical category but a historical category belonging to a definite epoch, the epoch of rising capitalism. The process of elimination of feudalism and

the development of capitalism was at the same time a process of amalgam-
ation of people into nations."[10] This historical agglutinizing of heterogeneous
peoples into the modern nation-state took place in the eighteenth century as
part of the process of increasing bourgeois hegemony, and by extension, the
process of consolidating the idea of nation and the ideology of nationality.

As Benedict Anderson and others point out, the consolidation of national
interests was very much involved with the enforcement of a common language
on a heteroglossic group of peoples. "Nothing served to 'assemble' related ver-
naculars more than capitalism, which within the limits imposed by grammars
and syntaxes, created mechanically-reproduced print-languages, capable of dissemination through the market."[11] The novel, according to Anderson, was
one step in the formation of national entities, yoking as it did images of national character, national language, and progress through structured time. And
Edward Said has taken pains to show how novels help construct national identities through normalizing imperialist attitudes toward "others" into narrative
form.[12]

In this essay, I want to observe some of the features of this hegemony as
it impacts on what I might call the nationality of Deafness and by extension
disability.[13] My aim is to show how the separation of disability from the category of nationalism has laid the ground for ableism by placing the onus of
impairment on the individual rather than on the collectivity.

The modern and postmodern redefinition of nation allows for groups of
people claiming a community, a language, a common history and culture to
assert themselves as nationalities. So ethnic and linguistic minorities may consider themselves nationalities, and although women cannot claim separate
nationality, they may consider themselves separately from the total national
identity. As Trinh Minh-ha says of women having to choose between ethnicity
and gender: "The idea of two illusorily separated identities, one ethnic, the
other woman . . . partakes in the Euro-American system of dualistic reasoning and its age-old divide-and-conquer tactics."[14] Fractionalized groups such
as women or the Deaf shared certain features of nationality during a period of
national consolidation in Europe in the eighteenth and nineteenth centuries.

At first blush, it might seem that deafness should be regarded as a social/
medical phenomenon and as such would have little to do with the issue of
nation and nationality. The issue of a common language is intricately involved
in the way the deaf were treated in the eighteenth and nineteenth centuries,
however, and parallels can be drawn from that experience and the experience
of other linguistically divergent groups in colonial settings.

Instead of calling the Deaf a nationality, one might consider them as occupying the place of an ethnic group. In fact, Connor notes that the term
"'ethnic' is derived from the closest equivalent to *nationem* in ancient Greek,

ethnos" and as such is quite close in meaning to *nation*.[15] Paul Brass places ethnicity within the realm of nationality and defines an ethnic group as "any group of people dissimilar from other peoples in terms of objective cultural criteria [language or dialect, distinctive dress or diet or customs, religion or race] and containing within its membership . . . the elements for a complete division of labor and for reproduction." And, Brass notes, "Ethnic identity is itself a variable, rather than a fixed or 'given' disposition."[16] By these criteria, the Deaf can be defined as an ethnic group or a nationality.[17] If an *ethnos* is defined as a culturally similar group sharing a common language, then the Deaf conceivably fit that category. So, by thinking of the Deaf this way, one can begin the process of politicizing the binary hearing/deaf or, on a larger scale, able/disabled.

The issue is by no means a simple one; the relationship between language and ethnicity is not monolithic. As Etienne Balibar points out, ethnicity is derived from two sources: language and race. "Most often the two operate together, for only their complementarity makes it possible for the 'people' to be represented as an absolutely autonomous unit."[18] However, language is also the first ethnic trait to go by the boards, since second-generation immigrants typically no longer bear the traces of their parents' accents or even their original language. In the United States, second- and third- generation Italian-Americans, Jews, or Germans, for example, now rarely speak their "native" tongues.

In the case of the Deaf, the issue of language presents itself as a defining structure of consciousness in quite a different way from the issues surrounding other disabilities. Unlike skeletal anomalies or mobility impairments, deafness is in some sense an invisible disability. Only when the Deaf person begins to engage in language does the disability become visible.

The deaf can be thought of as a population whose different ability is the necessary use of a language system that does not require oral/aural communication. Within a nation, they represent a linguistic minority. There are certainly other disabilities that involve a difficulty or inability to communicate (aphasia, autism), but none of these impairments imply the necessity for another language. While the blind have Braille, it is quite clear that Braille is not a language, but merely a way of transcribing whatever language the blind person may know. No one would claim that the blind have a language other than that of their mother tongue. As such, the Deaf can be thought of as a group defined by language difference.

This point perhaps needs some further elaboration. It is commonly thought that deafness involves the inability to use language properly. "Normal" Americans think that if only Deaf Americans could speak and understand English, there would be no problem for them or the larger community.

Thus, deaf people are schooled arduously in lip reading, speech therapy, and the activities associated with the oral/aural form of communication. However, it is precisely this focusing on the dysfunctionality of the deaf that constitutes a privileging of aural/oral system of communication. As Balibar writes, "The production of ethnicity is also the racialization of language and the verbalization of race."[19] Because we are interpellated as subjects by language, because language itself is a congealed set of social practices, the perceived dysfunctionality of the Deaf, according to the hearing world, is that the Deaf have another language system. That system challenges the majority assumption about the function of language, the coherence of language and culture. Consequently, the Deaf are, in a sense, racialized through their use of this system of communication. They are seen as outside the citizenry created by a community of language users and are therefore ghettoized as outsiders.[20]

Unlike other people with disabilities, also ostracized if not ghettoized, the Deaf have a community, a history, a culture; moreover, the Deaf tend to intermarry, thus perpetuating that culture. There is within the Deaf world a body of "literature" including written as well as signed works, a theatrical/choreographic tradition, academic discursive practices, pedagogic/ideological institutions, and so on. In this sense, the Deaf have created their own "nationalism" as a resistance to audist culture.[21] This level of social organization and resistance has not generally been the case with other physically impaired peoples, although political consciousness and organizing has increased dramatically among people with disabilities in recent years. A body of literature is beginning to develop around the area of disability studies, but the level of community that is part of the Deaf experience has not yet been achieved.

Ethnicity is, one can say, produced by a dialectical process in which a dominant group singles out a minority and ethnicizes it; reciprocally, minorities can ethnicize themselves in the course of trying to claim privileges and status from social elites. As de Vos says, ethnic identity is the "subjective, symbolic or emblematic use [by] a group of people . . . of any aspect of culture, in order to differentiate themselves from other groups."[22] If any aspect of culture can form the seed around which an ethnic community coalesces, certainly sign language can be regarded as such. Further, the formation of a group identity is both imposed from outside ("You are disabled: You are Deaf.") and from within ("We are Deaf!" "Deaf Power!"). So the site of ethnicity, as it were, is a contested one in a struggle for who will define the ethnicity of the group, who will construct it.

It is also possible to think of the Deaf as a race, that is, as a group carrying genetic information that affects physical traits and that can be passed down from generation to generation. One could argue that race is itself a product of imperialism—that considering a people a race based on some inherited trait was a concept that arose when it became necessary to think of humanity as divided into colonizer and colonized. To think of the Deaf as a race is clearly to follow a dubious line of reasoning, but one worth considering at least for the sake of argument. There are two senses in which the issue of racism can come into play here. The first fits in with Collette Guillaumin's insistence on a "broad definition of racism" that includes not just exclusion based on ethnic groupings but also exclusion on grounds of gender, class, sexual preference, and disability.[23] The second posits Deaf people themselves as constituting a race on the basis of inherited traits.

To think the latter, one must consider that there are two causes of deafness; one is genetic and the other is the result of disease or accident. If we focus on the former, we can trace lines of inherited deafness, as Nora Ellen Groce does in her study of deafness on Martha's Vineyard.[24] Since the trait for hereditary deafness is a recessive one, the idea of a deaf race is a bit farfetched. Many genetic traits, such as those for hair color, eye color, and skin color, are considered racial traits, however, because segregation or geographical isolation has forced those traits to remain within a specific population. As Immanuel Wallerstein suggests, "It makes little difference whether we define pastness in terms of genetically continuous groups (races), historical socio-political groups (nations) or cultural groups (ethnic groups). They are all peoplehood constructs, all inventions of pastness, all contemporary political phenomena."[25]

Discussions of race have to take into account the historical determinants of race. In other words, the very concept of race is historically determined and can be considered the product of a particular historical period of development. As Wallerstein points out, "*Race* was a primary category of the colonial world, accounting for political rights, occupational allocation and income [emphasis in original]."[26] Theories of race became elaborated during the period of greatest imperialism; indeed, it is hard to imagine a justification for imperialism without a theory of race. And it is no coincidence that the eugenics movement impacted directly on deaf people.

Eugenics further emphasizes the connection between disability and racism and targets disability as one prong in a series of binaries to be kept operative. As Etienne Balibar notes, "The phantasm of prophylaxis or segregation (the need to purify the social body, to preserve 'one's own' or 'our' identity from all forms of mixing, interbreeding or invasion) . . . are articulated around stigmata of otherness (name, skin colour, religious practices)."[27] The stigma of disability, of physical (and, in the case of deafness, inherited) traits, creates the icon of the other body—the disabled figure—an icon that needs to be excluded in a way similar to the exclusion of the body marked as differently pigmented or gendered.

This tendency toward prophylaxis, of course, is reciprocally one of the processes by which an ethnic group forms its own existence. In the process by which the Deaf were constructed as a group, institutionalized, and regulated, they perceived themselves to be such a group and acted as such. The very structures that are equivalent to what Althusser identified as the Ideological State Apparatus—educational institutions, associations, newspapers, language, and even the desire of Deaf people to form their own state—were pinpointed by eugenicists like Alexander Graham Bell as causes for alarm. Bell foresaw the development of these ideological apparatus as leading to "the production of a defective race of human beings [which] would be a great calamity to the world."[28] To avoid having a "deaf variety" of humans by discouraging intermarriage, Bell proposed abolishing residential schools, forbidding sign language education, and prohibiting the Deaf from teaching the deaf.[29] Logically, these steps are part of dismantling the culture of a non-national or indigenous people. They are also part of a discussion that creates binaries that link disability to race, nationality, and ethnicity.

Although a biological stigmata must be part of an antidisability discourse, it may be appropriate to consider the signification of such physical traits. In other words, there are allegorical meanings ascribed to deafness, blindness, lameness, and so on. As Balibar says, "Bodily stigmata play a great role in its [racism's] phantasmatics, but they do so more as signs of a deep psychology, as signs of a spiritual inheritance rather than a biological heredity."[30] Here, Balibar is speaking of Jews, whose physical appearance can often be indiscernible. Paradoxically, the more invisible the physicality of the Jew, the more dangerous the perceived infiltration. The mark of circumcision, for example, became one of the most hidden of "disabilities," particularly during a time when general circumcision of the male public was not the rule. To be a Jew then meant more symbolically than physically, although the symbolic and the physical were closely linked. Likewise, the deaf represented, among other things, the idea of moral and spiritual deafness, an inability to hear the word of God, to participate in reason and in life. Likewise, the blind were morally blind, and the lame were inept. The body illustrated those moral precepts to be avoided in the culture. If, as Balibar suggests, much of modern racism derives from early anthropology's tendency to classify with an aim of making distinctions between humanity and animality, then the deaf and the blind, as well as the mentally impaired and some of the physically deformed, will be seen as more animal, less human, than the norm.[31] Animals are "dumb"; they cannot hear language; they are morally deaf and blind. Thus the "normal" majority can, through this classificatory grid of binary oppositions, see itself as most properly human, as appropriate citizens, while those whose physicality distinguishes them are seen as non- or antinationals.

In order to continue the argument that the Deaf constitute a threat to ideas of nation, wholeness, moral rectitude, and good citizenship, I must rehearse what I have shown in my book *Enforcing Normalcy*. That is, first, that deafness appears in the eighteenth century as a discourse. By this I mean that before the eighteenth century there were individual deaf people or families of the deaf, or in urban areas even loose associations of the deaf, but that there was no discourse about deafness, no public policy on deafness, no educational institutions—and therefore the deaf were not constructed as a group. Since most deaf people are born to hearing families, the deaf did not see themselves as part of a community unless they were a part of an urban assemblage of the Deaf. It was only by attending the residential schools created in the eighteenth century that the Deaf became a community. The dramatic rise in the number of deaf schools in Europe—none in the beginning of the century and over sixty by the end—indicates the ground swell that made this new ethnic group self-aware.

The second point is that by the beginning of the nineteenth century there had developed a standardized language of the deaf that was transnational. That is, sign language had regional variations but was, for the most part, perceived by the hearing as a universal language. This language was disseminated through the deaf schools, and the teachers in these schools were themselves deaf. So an educational system evolved that consolidated the deaf into a linguistic and social community.

Thus, the Deaf became a new subgroup within each state throughout Europe; like Jews and Gypsies, they were an ethnic group in the midst of the nation.[32] Although their numbers were small, they amounted to a linguistic subgroup that increasingly perceived itself as a community with its own history and culture. By Stalin's criteria, all the Deaf lacked to claim nationhood were a territory and economic cohesion. One might indeed make a comparison with, for example, the Russian Jews, who were excluded from Stalin's definition of nationality because they lacked a territory, despite the fact that the Bund claimed national status for them.

Douglas Baynton shows us that by the nineteenth century, the Deaf were regarded as foreigners living within the United States, a kind of fifth column in society resisting nationalization. Baynton, quoting from the 1847 oralist publication *American Annals of the Deaf and Dumb*, describes the deaf not as afflicted individuals but as a "strongly marked class of human beings" with "a history peculiar to themselves." Baynton concludes that "deaf people were not so much handicapped *individuals* as they were a collectivity, a people—albeit, as we shall see, an inferior one." Thus, while the audist establishment initially constructed the deaf person as a model inhabitant of the Enlightenment, a citizen in the world of print culture, as I show in *Enforcing Normalcy* it came to see deaf people, particularly those with their "foreign" sign language, as an ethnic minority with a history and language that needed to be incorporated into the state and the nation. Educators were concerned that if deaf people "are to exercise intelligently the rights of citizenship, then they must be made people of our language." They insisted that "the English language must be made the vernacular of the deaf if they are not to become a class unto themselves—foreigners among their own countrymen." This was part of a larger argument for the suppression of sign language on grounds that it "isolated people from the national community."[33]

Pierre Desloges, a French deaf man who wrote in the late eighteenth century a defense of sign language against oralism, should be seen as defending his nationality from a hegemonic attempt to take away the native language of the Deaf. Desloges immediately made an equation between his deafness, his language, and his nationality when he wrote, "As would a Frenchman seeing his language disparaged by a German who knew at most a few words of French, I too felt obliged to defend my own language from the false charges leveled against it by [oralists like M.] Deschamps."[34]

The debate between oralism and sign is often seen as one that pits the hearing community against deaf standards, but I think the issue is sharpened if we think of it as a political attempt to erase an ethnic group. Like the ethnic groups who have lost their language and thus their existence as nationalities (the Cornish in the United Kingdom, the Frisians in Holland, the Sorbs and Wends of Eastern and Central Europe), the Deaf were in danger of being wiped out as a linguistically marked community.

The Deaf were not alone in this struggle. Groups like the Romanians had to establish their own press and print a grammar in 1780 to keep from being erased by the Transylvanians; so did the Bulgarians resisting the dominance of Greek Orthodox clerics in the eighteenth century.[35] Further, in dominant nation-states, foreigners and minorities, as well as the lower classes in general, were denigrated in cultural forms of symbolic production as a way of establishing national solidarity. One has only to think of hundreds of examples of French people being ridiculed in English literature of the period, particularly Captain Mirvan's excoriation of all aspects of Madame Duval's Frenchness in *Evelina* or Cimarosa's ridicule of an English suitor's accent and, tellingly, of a deaf father in the Italian opera *The Secret Marriage*. Telltale class-based accents are not acceptable either, as a nation attempts to create a standard, printed representation of the official language.[36]

The nexus of deafness, class, and nationality was put in its most extreme form when Jane Elizabeth Groom proposed in the 1880s that the deaf leave England and found a deaf state in Canada. Groom's reasoning was particularly related to class. She advocated founding a deaf state because the deaf in

England were poor and could not compete with the hearing in a tight labor market. The answer could not be revolution, but secession. (Incidentally, Groom's project was not an isolated event. There was another contemporary movement in the United States to found a deaf state in the West.)

The fact that some Deaf wanted to found a separate state is a strong enough argument for seeing them as a nationality or an ethnic group. It is more than possible to consider the flexibility of the concept of nationality and to see the way that the nation-state, in its formation in the eighteenth and nineteenth centuries, attempted to eliminate groups not normally thought of as minorities—women, gays and lesbian, linguistic subgroups—in an attempt to make one nation out of many.

I have been using the Deaf as a particular example to discuss the relationship of impairment to nationhood. I hope I been able to establish that the Deaf may indeed be thought of as a nation within a nation, or as an ethnic group, or a linguistic subgroup in a dominant and dominating society. Now I would like to muddy the waters somewhat by introducing the idea of class. There is a compelling relationship between disability in general and class. Mike Oliver in *The Politics of Disablement: A Sociological Approach* makes the point that "just as we know that poverty is not randomly distributed internationally or nationally . . . neither is impairment."[37] One expert notes that in the Third World, "Not only does disability usually guarantee the poverty of the victim but, most importantly, poverty is itself a major cause of disability."[38]

According to a United Nations report, 80 percent of the world's 500 million people with disabilities live in developing countries and are what one author calls "the poorest and most powerless people on earth."[39] If disability is reciprocally related to poverty and poverty in turn causes disability, since poor people are more likely to get infectious diseases, more likely to lack proper nutrition, and more likely to be injured in factory-related jobs and wars, then we have to see disability as intricately linked to capitalism and imperialism, or the latter-day version of imperialism that shifts factory work to Third World countries and creates poor and rich nations to facilitate a division of labor. Thus, the fire wall some might want to erect between disability and poverty collapses. Indeed, David Rothman, in his account of the development of the asylum in the United States, notes that in the colonial period the mentally ill were primarily seen as a category of the indigent. "The lunatic came to public attention not as someone afflicted with delusions or fears, but as someone suffering from poverty."[40] Later the first almshouses sheltered not so much the poor as the disabled poor. About half the population of the first such institution built in New York City was composed of people with physical or mental disabilities, including those with age-related impairments.[41]

Class is not absent even in the broad classification of disability. For example, in the case of people who use wheelchairs, paraplegics or quadriple-gics, we need to consider that among the approximately one million Ameri-cans in this category, class and race figure largely. Injury to the spinal cord through accident is one of the most common causes of paralysis, and this type of injury occurs disproportionately among young, working-class men. Particu-larly among the baby-boom generation, those wounded veterans who returned from Vietnam make up a large number of wheelchair users, and they were largely drawn from the working class. The chief cause of traumatic paraplegia and quadriplegia in American cities now are injuries sustained from gunshot wounds—and most of the people so injured are drawn from the lower classes, particularly from people of color. Contact sports, job injuries, and automobile accidents still tend to draw largely from young, working-class males.[42] So even "chance" and "accidents" fit a pattern involving class and race and thus nationalism.

Industrialization re-created the category of work, and in so doing re-created the category of worker. The very idea of citizenship came to be ideo-logically associated with this type of work. Various kinds of inclusions and ex-clusions in the category of nation were thus associated with work and work-related issues. Thus we see women initially bracketed out of the work force and into the domestic sphere in middle-class life, while proletarian fami-lies were redistributed into the factory orbit. In effect, the imperatives of in-dustrialism and capitalism redefined the body. "Able-bodied workers" were those who could operate machines and stand in assembly lines. The human body came to be seen as an extension of the factory. Ironically, this reciproc-ity between human and machine led to a conception of the mechanical per-fection of the human body. A strange paradox arises from the juxtaposition of the eighteenth-century notion that the human body was a divinely crafted machine and the increase of destructive acts against the human body in the form of factory-related mutilations following the Industrial Revolution. Thus the machine, like a latter-day Moloch, demanded human bodies and trans-formed them into disabled instruments of the factory process.

Friedrich Engels, in *The Condition of the Working Class in England*, describes this necessary chain of transformation. "A number of cripples gave evidence before the Commission, and it was obvious that their physical condition was due to their long hours of work. Deformity of this type generally affects the spine and legs." He cites a report by a Leeds physician, one Francis Sharp, who wrote,

> During my practice at the hospital, where I have seen about 35,000
> patients, I have observed the peculiar twisting of the ends of the lower
> part of the thigh bone. This affection I had never seen before I came
> to Leeds, and I have remarked that it principally afflicted children

from 8 to 14 years of age. At first I considered it might be rickets, but from the numbers which presented themselves particularly at an age beyond the time when rickets attack children, and finding that they were of a recent date, and had commenced since they began work at the factory I soon began to change my opinion. I now . . . can most decidedly state they were the result of too much labour. So far as I know they all belong to factories, and acquired this knock-kneed appearance from the very long hours the children worked in the mills.[43]

The report also mentions varicose veins, spinal distortions, and deformities of the limbs. Engels himself corroborates these observations. "It is easy to identify such cripples at a glance, because their deformities are all exactly the same. They are knock-kneed and deformed and the spinal column is bent either forwards or sideways." Miners are described as "either bandy-legged or knock-kneed and suffer from splayed feet, spinal deformities and other physical defects. This is due to the fact that their constitutions have been weakened and they are nearly always forced to work in a cramped position." Factory accidents contributed to this nineteenth-century version of negative body sculpting. Engels writes, "In Manchester, one sees not only numerous cripples, but also plenty of workers who have lost the whole or part of an arm, leg, or foot."[44] Engels records that there were 962 machine-related injuries in Manchester in 1842 alone.

If Engels gives us an insight into the way the body was perceived in the nineteenth century, it becomes clear that industrialization was seen as a palpable force in quite literally reshaping the bodies of the members of the body politic. Even the mind was seen as capable of being disabled by the stress of a capitalist society. In 1854 Edward Jarvis attempted to explain to a Massachusetts medical society how the tensions of the free market led to mental illness: "In this country, where no son is necessarily confined to the work or employment of his father, but all the fields of labor . . . are open to whomsoever will put on the harness . . . their mental powers are strained to their utmost tension; they labor in agitation . . . their minds stagger under the disproportionate burden." Jarvis notes that in precapitalist countries, "These causes of insanity cannot operate."[45]

Repeated references to diminished physical size, lack of robustness, delayed puberty, mental illness, endemic disease, and physical deformity led to a collective realization that the nation was in peril as a result of industrial practice. The deformed worker symbolized this. Likewise, the technical solution to this problem was the breeding of a better, more robust national stock. Thus, the eugenics movement came into existence as a way of repairing the

declining laboring stock of England and America, which the eugenicists saw
as resulting from a rapidly multiplying lower class and an influx of "foreign"
peoples with lower intelligence, less physical strength, and greater licentious-
ness than the natives.[46]

The relationship between disability and industrialization is a complex one.
The argument has been made that in a preindustrialized society, people with
impairments might more easily be part of the social fabric. Martha L. Edwards
argues that disability in ancient Greece did not limit the ability of men to
fight or engage in wars.[47] Although no utopia for the disabled or women, ancient Greek society acknowledged human physical variety and the possibility
of doing what one could given one's ability.

In a similar vein, J. Gwaltney describes the way that blindness was not
perceived as a disability in a Mexican village.[48] Other works describe how deaf
people were fully included in societies on Martha's Vineyard and in the Amazon in which most hearing members of the community could also sign.[49] Thus
the communal life and pace of rural society may not have constructed the
disabled body in the way that industrialized societies did.

> The blind and the deaf growing up in slowly changing scattered rural
> communities had more easily been absorbed into the work and life of
> those societies without the need for special provision. Deafness, while
> working alone at agricultural tasks that all children learned by
> observation with little formal schooling, did not limit the capacity for
> employment too severely. Blindness was less of a hazard in
> uncongested familiar rural surroundings, and routine tasks involving
> repetitive tactile skills could be learned and practiced by many of the
> blind without special training. The environment of an industrial
> society was however different.[50]

The demands of a factory system required another version of the body and
another version of time. "The speed of factory work, the enforced discipline,
the time-keeping and production norms—all these were a highly unfavourable
change from the slower, more self-determined and flexible methods of work
into which many handicapped people had been integrated."[51]

Another seemingly unlikely cultural event that connects disability with
national identity and class was the freak show that began in the middle of
the nineteenth century. Robert Bogdan makes the connection between physical disability and race when he discovers that not only were the obviously
disabled—the mentally retarded, the physically different—exhibited at freak
shows, but physically normal native peoples of colonized countries were also
grouped under the heading of "freaks."[52] As one press agent for the amusement world noted, "The Borneo aborigines, the head-hunters, the Ubangis,

and the Somalis were all classified as freaks. From the point of the showman the fact that they were different put them in the category of human oddities." These tribal peoples came from Oceania, Asia, Africa, Australia, South America, and the Arctic, but the notion of a racial difference put them in the same category as the disabled. As Bogdan says, "Showmen took people who were culturally and ancestrally non-Western and made them freaks by casting them as bizarre and exotic: cannibals, savages, barbarians."[53]

Some of those put on display were actual residents of the countries they were said to be from, but more often than not they were Americans whose relatives had earlier come from those foreign locations.[54] For example, in 1872, P. T. Barnum announced the appearance of four Fiji natives, including a princess, who were cannibals. As it turned out, the three men had been brought up as Christians and lived in California; the woman was African-American, a native of Virginia.[55] In this strange arrangement, people of color, disabled by society in so many ways, were transformed into non-Western natives who would then be seen as "freaks" and commodified as such.

The equation between people with disabilities and the non-Western worked both ways. Bogdan points out that beginning in 1850 and continuing through the 1940s, a pattern can be discerned in which "showmen constructed exhibits using people we would now call mentally retarded by casting them in an extreme form of the exotic mode."[56] Such people were made to seem as if they were representative of other races, or "missing links" in evolution. Two severely mentally impaired, microcephalic siblings from Circleville, Ohio, were exhibited as "Wild Australian Children" and said to be "neither idiots, lusus naturae, nor any other abortion of humanity, but belonged to a distinct race hitherto unknown to civilization."[57] Hiram and Barney Davis, each approximately three feet tall and mentally impaired, were billed as "The Astonishing Wild Men, From the Island of Borneo." Maximo and Bartola, two microcephalic children bought from their parents in Central America, were hawked as "The Last of the Ancient Aztecs of Mexico." Other microcephalics tended to be exhibited as Aztecs because of their small heads and facial features. In the case of William Henry Johnson, a fairly high-functioning, African-American microcephalic, the publicity projected this mentally retarded man as the "missing link" found in Gambia. Johnson, described as "What is It? or The Man-Monkey," was said to have been found in Africa "'in a perfectly nude state' roving through the trees like the monkey and the orangutan." His "keeper" is quoted as saying that "the formation of the head and face combines both that of the native African and the Orang Outang. . . . he has been examined by some of the most scientific men we have, and pronounced by them to be a *CONNECTING LINK BETWEEN THE WILD NATIVE AFRICAN AND THE BRUTE CREATION.*"[58]

What is most interesting about this is that the category of disability de-fines itself through an appeal to nationalism. The disabled person is not of this nation, is not a citizen, in the same sense as the able-bodied. That the freak show begins during the same period as medical statistics, eugenics, and restrictive immigration policies indicates a change in the way society thought about the physically different. In addition, discussions of disability always slide into discussions of race. The connection we have seen here between non-Western and disabled—both in the sense of the simple fact of non-Western culture being seen as "freakish" and in the glib elisions made between microcephalics, nonhumans, and the colonized world, show dramatically how closely race, nation, and physical identity are defined. One should also add that the people who were categorized as freaks, hoaxes or not, were drawn exclusively from the lower classes.

I want to end this discussion of nationality by looking at another disabled person, perhaps a kind of freak in this sense, who became a national symbol of identity. I am speaking of Franklin Delano Roosevelt.

The president of the United States has become more than a simple physi-cal entity; he has become an icon of the power and vigor of the country. Much public-relations time and effort is spent on making the man in office seem physically perfect and devoid of illness or disability. Countless photographs of the president golfing, jogging, romping on the beach emphasize his robust-ness and joie de vivre. Yet moments slip through the veil of well-being sur-rounding the president, and these moments are memorable in a disconcerting way. Recall Carter's collapsing during a running race or Bush's vomiting into the lap of the Japanese prime minister. Johnson's revealing his surgical scar was an unwanted reminder of his mortality. More profoundly, Eisenhower's heart attack and a series of assassinations and assassination attempts are re-minders of the physical vulnerability of the person in office.[59] When Reagan survived an assassination attempt, White House publicists covered up the ex-tent of his injuries and the pain of his quite lengthy recovery. The unwilling-ness to show the public the autopsy photographs of Kennedy stems from, among other possibly conspiratorial reasons, an impulse to prevent the na-tion from visualizing the president as having a wounded, mutilated body or being physically damaged. The simple binary—good president/bad president—collapses the physical body and the political effectiveness of head of state. In fact, Kennedy had what we could certainly call a disability—Addison's dis-ease. This debilitating and possibly life-threatening dysfunction of the adre-nal glands was consistently managed by those who controlled public relations around Kennedy. The back pain was romanticized as stemming from war wounds sustained when he was captain of PT 109. The president's rocking chair, used to alleviate the pain of his illness, was transformed into an evocative symbol associated with New England, the presidency, and the battle story. The fact that Kennedy was constantly medicated with painkillers and cortisone was erased, and even the telltale puffiness of Kennedy's face, a side effect of long-term cortisone use, was forgotten.

None of these attempts at management come close to the efforts surrounding Roosevelt's disability. Roosevelt himself was made into a symbol of triumph over a physical disability, and his own story was seen as paralleling America's recovery from and triumph over the Depression. Roosevelt's erect posture, with upturned face and jauntily held cigarette holder, was a symbol for America of hope, possibility, and recovery. Roosevelt's case is so interesting because he was the first president to be truly "mechanically reproduced" in Walter Benjamin's sense of the term. His was truly the first media presidency, with his time in office spanning the period of photography, photojournalism, radio, and television. Although radio was in a sense the primary medium, Roosevelt had to control the media of photography and film as no president before had needed to. In this sense, Roosevelt forged the national visual icon and aural identity of the presidency for the modern media.

This icon had to be seen as "one of us" and therefore not a cripple or a freak. Thus, of the hundreds of thousands of photographs and films of Roosevelt, spanning the period from 1928, when he became governor of New York, until 1945, when he died in office, there are only two photos extant showing him using a wheelchair. This archival evidence confirms the popular notion of Roosevelt—that he had contracted polio, went to Warm Springs to recover, and then went on to become president. As Hugh Gallagher notes, "Roosevelt's biographers have tended to treat his paralysis as an episode—with a beginning, a middle, and an end. By their accounts, Roosevelt gets polio, struggles through his rehabilitation, and then overcomes his adversity. End of chapter. The handicap is not mentioned again. It is viewed only as one of the stages through which FDR passes in preparation for the presidency."[60]

Because of a need to see the president's body as an extension of the nation's, the American people never had the facts about Roosevelt's polio. These, according to Gallagher's meticulously documented study, *FDR's Splendid Deception*, were that Roosevelt became, as a result of polio, a paraplegic who, after his illness, never was able to move his legs or stand without assistance. This fact was well known to Roosevelt's family and friends, one of whom wrote in 1921, "He's had a brilliant career as Assistant of the Navy under Wilson, and then a few brief weeks of crowded glory and excitement when nominated by the Democrats for the Vice Presidency. Now he is a cripple— will he ever be anything else?"[61] The writer of this letter expresses a common assumption—that disability and national leadership cannot combine.

Roosevelt was determined that people should not define him in this stigmatized role, and he managed the reception of his image so that he would not be thought of as fitting into the bad side of the abled/disabled binary. According to Gallagher, "From the very first, Roosevelt was determined not to be seen in a wheelchair unless absolutely necessary, and not to be lifted up stairs in view of the public." This desire not to be seen as visibly disabled points out an assumption that true nationalism is invisible, a degree-zero of existence, but that false nationalism can be seen. Thus we have "the alleged, quasi-hallucinatory visibility of the 'false nationals': the Jews, 'wogs', immigrants, Blacks. . . . racism thus inevitably becomes involved in the obsessional quest for a 'core' of authenticity that cannot be found, shrinks the category of nationality and destabilizes the historical nation."[62] Roosevelt saw that to be visibly disabled was to lose one's full nationality, which should be an invisibility, a neutrality, a degree-zero of citizenly existence.

FDR succeeded in convincing the world that he had beaten his disability. Will Durant's description of Roosevelt at the Democratic convention in 1928, written for *The New York World*, makes us see an upright Roosevelt. "On the stage is Franklin Roosevelt, beyond comparison the finest man that has appeared at either convention. . . . A figure tall and proud even in suffering."[63] Despite the rare mention of Roosevelt's disability, the president's image was so thoroughly controlled that the image remained the cigarette holder and not the wheelchair.

The sense of national identity associated with the president, with the almost sacred nature of his body and physical presence, was paramount. If in the post-Depression United States every citizen had to get to work and build a better future, if the model of the able-bodied citizen was to be writ large on every WPA mural, then the president had to embody normality, even if the efforts taken were Herculean to create this illusion. Since, as I have been asserting, the disabled are a kind of minority group within the nation, it would hardly do to have the president be a representative of that minority group. In the perverse logic that marks the political imagination of the United States, only an aristocratic WASP could embody the aspirations of the working classes; only a physically intact man could represent those who were crippled by the ravages of an economic disaster.

This contested battle of Roosevelt's disabled body continues. In 1995 a controversy arose over the construction of a memorial to FDR.[64] Disability-rights activists were appalled that none of the memorial's three sculptures and bas-reliefs would show Roosevelt with the wheelchair, crutches, braces, or canes that he used. The members of the memorial commission, headed by Senator Mark. O. Hatfield and Senator Daniel K. Inouye and including members of Roosevelt's family, opposed any such representation, arguing that Roosevelt's elaborate avoidance of public representations of his disability indicates his wish to be seen as intact and normal. When the memorial opened in 1997, after much controversy, some references to FDR's disability were included, but the essential design of the monument remained unchanged.

What resounds through this argument is the tenacity with which national images and identities are tied to notions of the body. More than half a century after Roosevelt's death, the specter of his "abnormal" body still needs to be exorcised so it will not haunt the nation's sense of its own wholeness and integrity.[65]

The stakes behind this battle are the stakes behind the simplistic equation involved in binary thinking. As I have tried to show, issues around disability involve much more than the neat division between normal and abnormal, abled and disabled. Further, the triad of race, class, and gender clearly needs to be opened up so that binarism, triadism, and any other geometric obsession partakes of the rich complexity in the world of oppression and domination. Too often discourses of liberation and progressivity participate unwittingly in categories of thought that serve another master. The task for scholars and activists is to resist those dominating categories, to go beyond the banalities of binarism, and to forge a complex destabilizing arrangement of knowledge linked to practice. This is no simple task, but, considering the alternative, there is really no choice.

Notes

1. See most recently James I. Charlton, *Nothing About Us Without Us: Disability Oppression and Empowerment* (Berkeley: University of California Press, 1998) and Leonard Cassuto, *The Inhuman Race: The Racial Grotesque in American Literature*, New York: Columbia University Press, 1997), 168–215.
2. For more information about this see Lennard J. Davis, introduction to *"Shall I Say a Kiss?" Love Letters of a Deaf Couple, 1936–1938* (Washington, D.C.: Gallaudet University Press, 1999).
3. For a detailed description of this process see Lennard J. Davis, *Enforcing Normalcy: Disability, Deafness, and the Body* (London and New York: Verso, 1996).
4. Walker Connor, "The Nation and Its Myth," *International Journal of Comparative Sociology* 33 (January/April 1992): 48.
5. Edmund Burke, *Reflections on the Revolution in France* (New York: Penguin, 1980), 200; ibid., 201–202.
6. Benedict Anderson, *Imagined Communities: Reflections on the Origin and Spread of Nationalism* (London: Verso, 1983), 47.
7. Homi Bhabha, *Nation and Narration* (New York: Routledge, 1990), and Hayden White, *Metahistory: The Historical Imagination in Nineteenth-Century Europe* (Baltimore: Johns Hopkins University Press, 1973).
8. Sylvia Walby, "Woman and Nation," *International Journal of Comparative Sociology* 33 (January/April):81–100.
9. Ironically, it was also Mussolini who said, "National pride has no need of the delirium of race." Cited in Alexander Stille, *Benevolence and Betrayal* (New York and London: Penguin, 1991), 22.

10. Joseph Stalin, *Marxism and the National and Colonial Question* (New York: International Publishers, 1934), 13.

11. Anderson, *Imagined Communities*, 47.

12. Edward W. Said, *Culture and Imperialism* (New York: Knopf, 1993).

13. I am following current usage and capitalizing "Deaf" when I want to refer to the social/political group and lower-casing "deaf" when I want to signal only the physical condition.

14. Trinh T. Minh-ha, *Women Native Other* (Bloomington: Indiana University Press, 1989), 104.

15. Connor, "Nation and Its Myth," 55, note 1.

16. R. Brass, *Ethnicity and Nationalism: Theory and Comparison* (London: Sage, 1991), 19; ibid., 13.

17. Harlan Lane makes a telling comparison between the colonization of Africans and the treatment of the Deaf.(*Mask of Benevolence*, 35–66) He particularly examines descriptions of both groups and shows how the deaf and the native are constructed in similar ways.

18. Etienne Balibar and Immanuel Wallerstein, *Race, Nation, Class: Ambiguous Identities* (London and New York: Verso, 1991), 96.

19. Ibid., 104.

20. Ironically, a study shows that approximately 50 percent of Americans are virtually illiterate in that they lack the skills necessary to write a simple letter or read a bus schedule (*New York Times*, 10 September 1993, A1). That would mean that the concept of a linguistic community exists in some kind of ideal form—at least at the level of writing and reading. One might better speculate on the degrees by which individuals are included or excluded from the ideal community of language users, rather than assume that all normal members of the community are users of language and all deaf are not.

21. It is worth remembering that nationalism is a two-edged sword. It cuts a broad cloth out of divergent peoples and creates the groundwork for imperialism and colonialism. However, nationalism in the Third World has been an important means of resisting domination by imperialist countries. See Simon During, "Literature—Nationalism's Other? The Case for Revision" in Bhabha, *Nation and Narration*, 138–153.)

22. George de Vos, "Ethnic Pluralism," in George de Vos and Lola Romanucci-Ross, eds., *Ethnic Identity: Cultural Continuities and Change* (Palo Alto, Calif.: Mayfield, 1975), 16.

23. Collette Guillaumin, *L'idèologie raciste. Genëse et langage actuel* (Paris: Mouton, 1972).

24. Nora Ellen Groce, *Everyone Here Spoke Sign Language: Hereditary Deafness on Martha's Vineyard* (Cambridge, Mass.: Harvard University Press, 1985).

25. Balibar and Wallerstein, *Race, Nation, Class*, 78–79.

26. Ibid., 189.

27. Ibid., 18.

28. Alexander Graham Bell, *Memoir upon the Formation of a Deaf Variety of the Human Race* (Washington, D.C.: Alexander Graham Bell Association for the Deaf, 1969), 41.

29. Ironically, all three steps have taken place. Deaf education was taken away from Deaf educators in the nineteenth century. Oralism was made official in the 1880 Congress of Milan. More recently, American educational policy has emphasized the mainstreaming of deaf children in hearing schools. This pattern coincides with an effort to nationalize other "non-national" populations by removing their own ideological apparatus.

30. Balibar and Wallerstein, *Race, Nation, Class*, 24.

31. Ibid., 56–57.

32. Indeed, the Nazis began the eradication of people with disabilities well before they began to exterminate Jews. Stan Schuchman, lecturing in 1996 on the Deaf and the Holocaust at the annual convention of Children of Deaf Adults, pointed out that deaf people were forced to wear armbands with three dots signifying deafness, just as Jews were forced yellow stars.

33. Douglas C. Baynton, "'A Silent Exile on This Earth': The Metaphorical Construction of Deafness in the Nineteenth Century," *American Quarterly* 44, no. 2 (June 1992): 22; ibid., 229; ibid., 217.

34. Pierre Desloges, *Observations of a Deaf Mute . . . .* in Harlan Lane, ed., *The Deaf Experience: Classics in Language and Education*, tr. Franklin Philip (Cambridge: Harvard University Press, 1984), 30.

35. Brass, *Ethnicity and Nationalism*, 30.

36. See Lennard J. Davis, *Resisting Novels: Fiction and Ideology* (London and New York: Routledge, 1987), chap. 5.

37. Michael Oliver, *The Politics of Disablement: A Sociological Approach* (New York: St. Martin's Press, 1990), 13.

38. L. Doyal, "The Crippling Effects of Underdevelopment," in *A Cry for Heath: Poverty and Disability in the Third World*, ed. O. Shirley (Rome: Third World Group and ARHTAG, 1983), 7.

39. Cited in Charlton, *Nothing About Us*, 8.

40. David Rothman, *The Discovery of the Asylum: Social Order and Disorder in the New Republic* (Boston: Little, Brown, 1971), 4.

41. Ibid., 39.

42. Robert F. Murphy, *The Body Silent* (New York: Norton, 1987; reprint, 1990), 139.

43. Friedrich Engels, *The Condition of the Working Class in England*, trans. W. O. Henderson and W. H. Chaloner (Palo Alto, Calif.: Stanford University Press, 1968), 171.

44. Ibid., 173, 280, 185.

45. Rothman, *Discovery of Asylum*, 115.

46. This argument is being made today again as if it were new thinking in three books: Richard J. Herrnstein and Charles Murray, *The Bell Curve: Intelligence and Class Structure in American Life* (New York: The Free Press, 1994); J. Phillippe Rushton, *Race, Evolution, and Behavior* (New Brunswick, N.J.: Transaction Publishers, 1994); and Seymour W. Itzkoff, *The Decline of Intelligence in America: A Strategy for National Renewal* (Westport, Conn.: Praeger, 1994). All of these works maintain that intelligence levels are declining because the underclass, poor and disproportionately of color, is dragging the "norm" down with its rapid reproduction of low intelligence and social dysfunctionality. The wonder is that anyone thinks these arguments are any more than the old eugenicist saws brought out with very little resharpening.

47. Martha L. Edwards, "Deaf and Dumb in Ancient Greece," in *The Disability Studies Reader*, ed. Lennard J. Davis (New York and London: Routledge, 1997), 29–51.

48. J. Gwaltney, *The Thrice Shy: Cultural Accommodation to Blindness and Other Disasters in a Mexican Community* (New York and London: Columbia University Press), 1970.

49. See Groce, *Everyone Spoke Sign Language*; also P. Farb, *Word Play: What Happens When People Talk* (New York: Bantam, 1975).

50. E. Topliss, *Provision for the Disabled* (Oxford: Blackwell, 1979), 11.

51. J. Ryan and F. Thomas, *The Politics of Mental Handicap* (Harmondsworth: Penguin, 1980), 101.

52. Robert Bogdan, *Freak Show: Presenting Human Oddities for Amusement and Profit* (Chicago: University of Chicago Press, 1988). See also Rosemarie Garland Thomson, ed., *Freakery* (New York: New York University Press, 1997).

53. Bogdan, *Freak Show*, 177.
54. The extent of the colonizing of these non-Western peoples included giving them names so that their "disabilities" might be identified. Thus the famous "Ubangi" women with artificially enlarged lips, reflecting a tribal practice of beautifying women by inserting increasingly large disks into their lips, turn out to be not "Ubangi" at all. These women were from the Congo, but the press agent for Ringling Brothers Circus, Roland Butler, was looking at maps of Africa and found an obscure district named Ubangi, several hundred miles from the tribe's actual location. The name sounded properly exotic, and so, in Butler's words, "I resettled them." This act of renomination also represented their own beauty practices as "freakish" disabilities. They were presented as "Monster-mouthed Ubangi savages" and as "Crocodile Lipped Women From the Congo" (ibid., 193–94).
55. Ibid., 183.
56. Ibid, 119.
57. Ibid., 120.
58. Ibid., 137.
59. Paul Tsongas's cancer became an issue that detracted from his candidacy in 1992. Although he tried to commandeer media coverage to show him swimming every day, he was unable to beat the perception that he was disabled by his disease. Dan Quayle's complications from phlebitis had to be given some spin and could not be "blamed" in his decision not to run for president.
60. Hugh Gregory Gallagher, *FDR's Splendid Deception* (New York: Dodd, Mead, 1985), 210.
61. Ibid., 28.
62. Balibar and Wallerstein, *Race, Nation, Class*, 60.
63. Gallagher, *Splendid Deception*, 67.
64. *New York Times*, 10 April 1995, A10.
65. More recently, President Clinton damaged his knee in a fall. The president and the media were quite comfortable with public photos of the chief executive using wheelchair, crutches, and cane. This public approach to a disability is clearly an advance, but one wonders how much of the display was possible because Clinton's disability was seen as temporary. Clinton also went public with his use of a hearing aid, although here again the device is one that is concealed in the ear canal, so that no visible sign appears that the president is hearing impaired.

Strange Blood: Hemophobia and the Unexplored Boundaries of Queer Nation

Chapter 2

MICHAEL DAVIDSON

In the late 1970s, the development of freeze-dried blood-clotting factors drawn from multiple donors dramatically affected the lives of persons with hemophilia.[1] Until this time, hemophiliacs had relied on transfusions from whole blood or cryoprecipitate (fresh frozen plasma) administered by a nurse or physician.[2] Such transfusions were both time-consuming and expensive, necessitating a ready supply of blood products and a clinical staff well versed in each patient's bleeding history and blood type. Since severe hemophiliacs require transfusions often—sometimes several times a week—patients need easy access to a clinic. Too long a delay following a bruise could result in joint bleeding or hematoma that would take weeks to dissipate. Hematomas are excruciatingly painful, and over time they cause severe cartilage and tissue damage to the joints, leaving many hemophiliacs crippled. In the case of bleeding to the cranial or neck area, delays in treatment could result in death. Without immediate blood transfusions, routine tooth extractions, nosebleeds, bumps, and bruises become life-threatening events. With the new freeze-dried product, hemophiliacs could infuse themselves at home, achieving a freedom they had not enjoyed before.

The miracle of factor concentrate was a boon to patients, doctors, and blood-product companies alike. Patients could keep vials of concentrate in their refrigerators to be used at the first sign of bleeding. Children were especially aided by this new technology since they could be transfused at home or at school and thus participate in most regular play activities. Whereas prior to the development of cryoprecipitate in the mid-1960s hemophiliacs seldom lived beyond the teenage years, they could now live a full life.[3] By using home transfusion as a prophylactic or preventive form of treatment, hemophiliacs could avoid joint or muscle bleeds, thus eliminating the attendant orthopedic problems that crippled so many severe bleeders. Doctors and hematologists could spend less time administering transfusions and devote more time to the residual effects of bleeding disorders. And, of course, the profits of blood product suppliers soared. A hemophiliac with severe Factor VIII deficiency will spend $60,000 to $150,000 annually for clotting factor alone, each vial of concentrate costing as much as $1,500. Any further complications such as injury or surgery can boost medical expenses for blood products to $500,000. Blood ceased to be a "gift," in Richard Titmuss's phrase, donated by disinterested individuals for the purpose of sustaining life, and became a product that earned high profits for its producers.[4]

As it turned out, the miracle of factor concentrate was a death sentence. In January of 1982 the Centers for Disease Control (CDC) in Atlanta received word of a fifty-five-year-old hemophilic male who was diagnosed with *Pneumocystis carinii* pneumonia, the most characteristic and fatal of the opportunistic diseases suffered by AIDS patients. Although his case could not be directly linked to AIDS, two more cases in the summer of that year were diagnosed, and all three patients died. When the CDC alerted the Food and Drug Administration (FDA) that what was then called GRID (Gay-Related Immune Deficiency) might be spreading through transfusions, the agency did nothing, fearing a panic that would severely diminish the blood supply. Since factor concentrate is distilled from thousands of donors, chances of infection for hepatitis had always been a risk. Now, with the added danger of HIV infection, blood could be lethal. Without any restrictions placed on them by the CDC or FDA, the major blood- product companies continued to distribute infected blood.[5]

In January of 1983, the National Hemophilia Foundation asked that screening procedures be adopted to discourage blood donations from high-risk groups, specifically homosexuals. It was not until 1985 that AIDS antibody screening tests were approved, and nationwide testing of blood began. Between 1980 and 1986, more than 60 percent of the nation's 20,000 hemophiliacs were infected with the HIV virus, and by 1988, 90 percent of all severe bleeders had been infected. With the advent of blood screening in 1985 and through the development of heat-treated and recombinant factor, exposure to HIV through transfusions dropped considerably. For the thousands of hemophiliacs who were infected with the HIV virus in the 1980s, this change offers little solace.

As a hemophiliac myself, I well remember the enthusiasm with which my doctors and clinical aids received the news of factor concentrate. I was instructed in the proper mode of home transfusion, given my precious bottles of powdered concentrate and infusion kit, and sent home to await my first bleed. Since I have a rather moderate form of Factor IX hemophilia (Christmas disease), I never had to use the concentrate during the years it was contaminated, but visits to the clinic in the mid-1980s revealed a profound change in the hemophilia community. Now in addition to the more recognizably crippled hemophiliacs I saw patients emaciated by various opportunistic diseases characteristic of persons with AIDS. Mailings from the various hemophilia organizations changed from being about new blood products and infusion therapies to information about HIV infection, AZT, hospice networks, AIDS hotlines, and, inevitably, memorial services. Persons with hemophilia who had been medically integrated into "normal" life were now ostracized from schools and businesses, their already fragile insurance policies cancelled and their access to life-sustaining blood products profoundly altered. Moreover, fears of AIDS contamination at the blood banks kept potential healthy donors away, thus diminishing the supply of fresh frozen plasma.

One of the psychologically most devastating effects of AIDS on the hemophilia community was its disruption of the codependent relationship between patients and the medical establishment. For obvious reasons, hemophiliacs had developed close ties with clinics, doctors, and pharmaceutical companies, and individuals often moved from positions as care receivers to positions as care givers, working within hemophilia organizations and clinics and serving on the boards of blood-product companies. Spouses and parents of hemophiliacs often became professional nurses or clinicians themselves through their intimate knowledge of blood infusion processes. If the National Hemophilia Foundation (NHF) was reluctant to criticize pharmaceutical companies in the early stages of AIDS, it was because these companies were regarded less as corporate entities than as members of the family, as interested in the health of their consumers as in that of their profits. As David Kirp observes, so dependant were medical specialists on their "pharmaceutical patrons" that it was not until 1994 that the World Federation of Hemophilia permitted public criticism of the drug companies.[6] As with other chronic diseases, patients developed long-term relationships with nurses and doctors, relationships cemented by the development of comprehensive care and family-oriented treatment. AIDS turned blood products into commodities and transformed medical professionals into antagonists. And after some delay, as I will point out, it turned hemophiliacs from patients into activists.

I rehearse this brief history to describe a multistage crisis in what I will call "blood culture," one based on the transmission and circulation of healthy blood. By speaking of a culture of blood I am contrasting those constituencies bonded by shared bodily fluids, tissues, and genetic codes to those based on family, racial, or even national characteristics. Among the latter, blood is often used as a metaphor that stands for racial characteristics—as in the infamous "one-drop rule" by which individuals with even the slightest trace of African heritage were automatically marked as black.[7] Since hemophiliacs—as well as other persons with genetically inherited diseases—share the blood of others, they are linked as a group in ways that defy traditional cultural markers. The fear of blood or bleeders (hemophobia), then, annexes phobias about other constituencies for which the penetration of the bodily envelope is perceived to transgress boundaries of racial or sexual normativity. Cultural identities are often based on binary terms (self/other, participant/observer, insider/outsider, hegemonic/subaltern), but one based on blood would have to be, in the most literal sense, fluid and porous.

The stages in this crisis within blood culture could be defined as follows. First, the infection of clotting factor dramatically halted what had been a forward-moving, optimistic narrative in hemophilia research.[8] Second, it marked a shift in AIDS discourse from narratives about a disease spread among "others" to one infecting "us."[9] If AIDS could be transmitted by blood (instead of sexual acts) then "we" heterosexuals were vulnerable to penetration. Finally, by bringing an exclusively male community of hemophiliacs together with gay males, AIDS redefined the nature of homosocial community and forced a reconsideration of sexual identities among heterosexual bleeders.[10] This latter stage has important implications, beyond AIDS, for current debates within queer theory and sexual politics. The politics of Queer Nation, as Lauren Berlant and Elizabeth Freeman have pointed out, involves a carnivalization of gender roles that contests fantasies of American national unity. But the borders of Queer Nation, while open to transgressions of sexuality, are often closed to identities not constructed *through* sexuality—identities that are interpellated into queer culture but which lack adequate documentation.[11] In this respect people with disabilities, including hemophiliacs and persons with AIDS, cross multiple borders, beyond those of sex and gender.

In each of these levels, public fear of tainted blood annexed earlier and national anxieties about infection, placing hemophiliacs in subject positions that had been occupied by immigrants, people of color, and sexual minorities. Hemophiliacs who had devoted their lives to integrating themselves into "normal" life now found themselves in clinics and support groups with nonmainstream, marginal groups. At the same time, by their proximity to a gay-marked disease, hemophiliacs were forced to create new positionalities in relation to their sexuality that contradicted their pursuit of normalcy. Such shiftings of identity suggest that designations for medically impacted minorities such as "disabled" or "handicapped" are inadequate to the social complexity of genetically inherited or chronic disease.[12] Furthermore, the blurring of medical and sexual binaries raises a problem for constructionist theory in that models of queerness based upon gender performance and theatricalization may have to accommodate subjectivities based upon the most essentialized of categories: genetics, epidemiology, and blood.

Cindy Patton observes that once "perceptions of HIV risk were linked to social deviance, literally anyone or any category of people deemed epidemiologically significant could be converted into nominal queers."[13] As an "epidemiologically significant" group, hemophiliacs were interpellated into homophobic, racist discourses for which they were ill prepared. Their political focus had traditionally been directed at medical research and health delivery systems, beginning with coagulation studies in the 1940s and the formation of the National Hemophilia Foundation in 1948.[14] Now, as "nominal queers," hemophiliacs had to confront a gendering process that had always attended their disease and that had resurfaced through homophobic responses to AIDS. What we might call the "queering of hemophilia" did not happen overnight through a Stonewall riot; it involved a gradual restructuring of a largely male homosocial culture and the support networks upon which it had been based.[15]

By speaking of hemophiliacs as "nominal queers" I am adapting Patton's phrase to describe figures who in acquiring AIDS iatrogenically (that is, through a medical procedure) also inherited discursive features of social Others. They became "high-risk" individuals whose sexual lives were scrutinized, whose employment was endangered, whose spouses became medical pariahs, and whose relationship to the blood-product industry upon which they depended became adversarial. In numerous cases they were subject to direct harassment, most famously in the case of the Ray family, whose hemophiliac sons were taunted at school and whose Florida house was burned down in a KKK-like attack, forcing them to relocate to another city. In more recent years and through contact with gay AIDS activists, hemophiliacs have developed an activist posture toward blood-product companies that sold infected blood, filing a class-action suit and sponsoring a congressional bill (the Ricky Ray Relief Act) that would provide compensation for HIV contamination.

This interpellation of hemophiliacs into gay culture was hardly a seamless process. With the entry of AIDS into their community many hemophiliacs closed the door to their medical closets in order not to be associated with gays or not to be subject to the same prohibitions that gay people with AIDS were facing. Many were resentful (wrongly as it turned out) of gay men whose sexual liberation had transformed their medical liberation into a nightmare. The media played up conflicts in between the two communities, creating what one commentator calls "hemo-homo wars."[16]

By serving as the "innocent victims" of a "gay plague," hemophiliacs became unwitting allies of the Religious Right in shoring up a homophobic agenda—not exactly a scenario designed to win friends among gay AIDS activists. In France, as David Kirp points out, Jean-Marie Le Pen's National Front used hemophiliacs as foils in its anti-immigrant, antigay policies, linking the French acronym for AIDS, SIDA, with "*Socialisme, Immigration, Déliquance, Affairisme.*"[17] The National Hemophilia Foundation's attempt to screen out homosexuals as blood donors in the early days of AIDS was regarded as scapegoating by various gay and lesbian groups. The screening of blood donors was linked by many gays and lesbians to racist practices of the nineteenth century. The San Francisco Coordinating Committee of Gay and Lesbian Services said that "donor screening was reminiscent of miscegenation blood laws that divided black blood from white blood and was similar to the World War II rounding up of Japanese Americans in the western half of the country to minimize the possibility of espionage."[18]

As I have already indicated, the role of hemophilia in AIDS discourse coincides with debates about family values and hetero-normalcy during the Reagan-Bush era. Hemophiliacs, by association with a "gay-related" disease, were subject to homophobia on the one hand and what one commentator has called "hemophobia" on the other. Cindy Patton quotes a hemophiliac who describes "the growing fear that hemophiliacs are dangerous to employ or to have in schools as 'hemophobia,' and speaks wryly of coming out of the 'clot closet.'"[19] If hemophilia means "love of blood," its phobic counterpart refers to the anxiety felt by health care workers, employers, teachers, and parents over the threat of infected blood. But hemophobia also taps a more ancient prejudice against bleeders—from Talmudic prescriptions against circumcision to warnings about Dracula to the Eugenics movement to germ theory and immigration reform.[20] As a specifically modernist trope, "hemophobia" resuscitates an earlier semiotics of the bleeder as aesthete or neurasthenic female, weakened by aristocratic privilege and threatening to democratic institutions. Bleeding disorders raise concerns about the porousness of boundaries, the vulnerability of the bodily envelope, the infection of bodily fluids—concerns that parallel phobias about sexual deviance and racial mixing. Hemophobia, in other words, represents the merging of two discourses—one of blood, the other of sexuality—in which anxieties about bodily boundaries in one are articulated through anxieties about gender binaries in the other.

Unfortunately, access to the origins of hemophobia is limited. Lacking an adequate cultural history of hemophilia we must turn to histories of race and sexuality to find analogues of cultural threat and moral panic based around blood. As I will suggest by reference to William Faulkner's *Absalom, Absalom!* anxieties about impure blood appear in even our most canonical literary sources, although like the fluid itself the subject lies beneath the skin. While I am not suggesting that hemophiliacs have been subjected to the same social opprobrium as blacks, gays, and lesbians, I am arguing that their relationship to homophobia and social othering has forced them to create a "medical closet" that, like the sexual closet, has had to be renegotiated in an era of AIDS. In a newspaper report, Ryan White, the Indiana hemophiliac boy whose HIV infection through blood products made him a poster boy for AIDS research, was called a "homophiliac," a journalistic slip of the typewriter whose implications I want to explore.[21]

Blood Culture

The division I have outlined between hemophilia and hemophobia is one anticipated by Michel Foucault in *The History of Sexuality*. Foucault describes a shift from a "society of blood," based on the divine right of the sovereign, to a "society of sex," based on the medicalization of the body in the late nineteenth century. In the case of the former, blood relations inform the maintenance of social order throughout every level of society. A monarch's authority is vested in a lineage established by blood, while citizens are willing to shed blood for the privilege of the sovereign's protection. Power, in a society of sanguinity, speaks "through blood; the honor of war, the fear of famine, the triumph of death, the sovereign with his sword, executioners, and tortures; blood was a reality with a symbolic function."[22] In a society of sex, on the other hand, power is based on maintaining the health of the larger social body, of which individual biology becomes the fetishistic focus. The policing of the body, the categorizing of its functions, ardors, and excesses, becomes the central concern of health and medicine. Hemophobia in this scenario would refer not only to a fear of bleeders but also to a fear of residual aristocratic features in the new scientific, rationalized society.

Blood and sex cultures meet in Bram Stoker's *Dracula,* a novel in which the vampire's need for fresh blood is often identified with sexual and racial perversions. Dracula's aristocratic appearance and behavior—pale skin, pallorous complexion, polite manners, elegant dress—become a monstrous perversion of eastern European refinement. As Judith Halberstam points out, he is also identified with anti-Semitic discourses of the late nineteenth century, linked to George Du Maurier's Svengali, Dickens's Fagin, and other representations of the predatory Jew. As such, Dracula marks an anxiety over "foreign" or "ethnic" insemination into Christian life that, as Halberstam says, "weakens the stock of Englishness by passing on degeneracy and the disease of blood lust."[23] Since Dracula drains the blood of others, he annexes anti-Semitic economic theories by which "true" economic value is weakened by usurious interest rates and in which the "liquidity" of capital is diverted into unhealthy investments. As a consumer of the healthy blood of citizens, Dracula contributes to eugenicist fears of national pollution and miscegenation. The health of the vampire depends, by an inverse logic, on the waning of empire, sapping vital fluids that could serve the national interest. And since Dracula's blood lust is gender blind, he is linked to homoerotic discourses, for which his effeminate and aristocratic qualities serve as markers.

A second narrative of the shift from sanguinity to sexuality is represented by the decline of the czars, a shift that, significantly, revolves around a hemophilic child. According to the well-known story, the young czarevitch Alexis Romanov is the answer to Russia's dreams, the long-awaited heir to the throne of Nicholas and Alexandra following the birth of four girls. But the visitation of hemophilia upon the child, through genes spontaneously mutated in his grandmother, Queen Victoria, alters the course of Russian history. In Robert Massie's now-canonical account, the "blessed birth of an only son" provided the mortal blow to the imperial state. "Along with the lost battles and sunken ships, the bombs, the revolutionaries and their plots, the strikes and revolts, Imperial Russia was toppled by a tiny defect in the body of a little boy. Hidden from public view, veiled in rumor, working from within, this unseen tragedy would change the history of Russia and the world."[24]

If we were to read Massie's romantic rhetoric through a Foucauldian optic we might see an alternative historical genealogy to his more elegiac version: the noble code of blood has been polluted, thinned by intermarriage with non-Russian subjects. Rasputin, vestigial remnant of archaic religious traditions, is engaged by Alexandra ("that German woman") as court advisor. Practicing the black arts of hypnotism and mesmerism he miraculously clots the czarevitch's blood, earning himself Alexandra's devotion and purchasing access to the inner court circle. His proximity to Alexandra leads to the public perception that he has become her consort; his sexual excesses among court ladies mime the degradation of royal blood in general. The restive proletariat, anxious to differentiate itself from the noble code of blood, focuses on the sexual activities of the royal family and on the absent body of the future heir. The overthrow of the Romanov dynasty replaces weak, feminized authority with the blood of the people in a bloodless coup. Scientific socialism replaces cosmopolitan aristocracy and the mystical religious traditions of the decadent Romanovs; Russian Moscow replaces European St. Petersburg.

Essential to this change is the restoration of racial and national purity, the repudiation of foreign forces and ethnicities by nationalist values of soil and folk. Foucault notes that a primary vehicle in the transition from blood to sex is the discourse of eugenics, the science of racial purity, which served in the formation of modern nation states. Founded by Francis Galton in the mid-nineteenth century in England and based on Darwinian theories of evolution, eugenics gained a powerful foothold in the U.S. as justification for

immigration reform, racial exclusion legislation, and antimiscegenation statutes. In many of its formulations and uses, genetic inheritance is figured
through the metaphor of blood. This linkage between genetic infection and
polluted blood is stated baldly by Robert Allen, Democratic congressman from
West Virginia, in 1922: "The primary reason for the restriction of the alien
stream . . . is the necessity for purifying and keeping pure the blood of
America."[25] Allen's reference to pure blood and uncontaminated bodily fluids resonates throughout racist discourses of the Progressive Era. One result
of such attitudes was the 1924 Immigration Act, signed into law by Calvin
Coolidge who, as vice president, declared, "America must be kept American.
Biological laws show . . . that Nordics deteriorate when mixed with other
races."[26] Although concern for pure blood lines had informed earlier debates
over immigration, beginning with the second wave of colonists to the New
World, it achieved a special importance in antimiscegenation legislation of
the Reconstruction years, the attempts to identify racial features through the
"one-drop rule" and in various germ theories in public health for which blood
was the dominant trope.

Blood provides one of the three colors of the national flag. As articulated
through eugenics discourse, it dominates what Lauren Berlant has called an
American national fantasy or imagined community. This national fantasy is
figured as an "anatomy" that links individual bodies of citizens with a corporate body of "embedded racial and gender inflections."[27] Blood, to adapt
Berlant's formulation, circulates through this national fantasy as a metaphor
of democratic possibility and potency that must be contained within the channels for which it is intended. Unlike the Russian national fantasy, with its
royal lineage of biologically linked leaders, the American version of national
succession must be based on the symbolic replacement of blood shed on the
revolutionary battlefield with the new blood of democratically elected leaders—
a kind of political transfusion that perpetuates the founding fathers' authority.

When blood is allowed to mix with other races, it threatens more than
the purity of the white race; it "pollutes" the exceptionalist character of the
American errand. For John Adams, slavery posed a threat to the Constitution because it threatened the normal orders of nature, defined as such by the
circulation of blood. In an essay on Shakespeare's *Othello*, written in 1835,
Adams says that the tragedy is not that the Moor kills Desdemona out of irrational jealousy but that her blood could be quickened by a Moor. "The blood
must circulate briskly in the veins of a young woman, so fascinated, and so
coming to the tale of a rude, unbleached African soldier."[28] As Alexander
Saxton points out, Adams feels that when Othello smothers his wife on stage,
audiences are denied the cathartic emotions of pity and terror proper to tragedy. Instead, their emotions "subside immediately into the sentiment that she

has her deserts."[29] Saxton relates Adams's reading of *Othello* to more general remarks on the ill effects of slavery as it was determining the growth and expansion of American interests in the 1830s. Events such as the annexation of Texas, according to Adams, had turned the Constitution into a "menstrous rag," a phrase joining misogyny to racism through the metaphor of blood as it was used to define national integrity and unity.[30]

The Brother Who Is Other

Founding fathers like Adams created more than a national imaginary of white succession; as in the case of Jefferson, they produced biological offspring from slaves whose stories were not incorporated into the national fantasy. The scandal of miscegenated blood is a topic to which numerous American literary works turn. Such works, as Russell Castronovo points out, are as much about blood as about race since both figure in the genealogical narrative of national purity. "Revolutionary 'blood' does not always follow predictable pathways and instead gets lost in questions of race and dismemberings of the fathers' law."[31]

One work that gathers together themes of patriarchal succession, racial purity, and sexual contamination most powerfully is William Faulkner's *Absalom, Absalom!*. The story of Thomas Sutpen's "grand design" to create a dynasty in Yoknapatawpha County is based on a southern heroic ideal of uncontaminated, white inheritance. Sutpen's project is doomed, not only because of his own lower-class roots in Tidewater Virginia but also by the potential presence of black blood in his own children. Prior to his arrival in Jefferson, Sutpen had married the daughter of a Spanish Creole woman while working as a plantation overseer in Haiti. Realizing that the presence of (real or imagined) African blood in her background would thwart his dynastic plans in the southern states, Sutpen leaves her and his young son behind. When that son, Charles Bon, turns up at college with Sutpen's son from his second marriage, the threat of miscegenated blood resurfaces. Furthermore, Bon's subsequent intention to marry Judith Sutpen, his father's daughter from that second marriage, adds incest to miscegenation in an ever-exfoliating cycle of familial pollutions. In order to prevent this tragedy of infections, Sutpen's son Henry kills Bon to preserve the patriarchal line.

Much of the novel's drama revolves around the "spot of negro blood" that may or not be carried by Bon into the Sutpen family. The details of Bon's racial background, his intentions toward Judith, his oedipal anxieties about his biological father—these issues are mediated by the various narrators who tell the story, all of whom have some personal stake in the historical meaning of Sutpen's design. We never learn definitively whether Bon has that fatal drop of blood, since he is never given a chance to narrate his own story. But it matters little; blood in this novel is not a biological or chemical agent but a discursive feature of a southern genealogical imperative. One's genetic or racial origin must be searched and codified, its origins subjected to the same scrutiny to which earlier Puritan preachers subjected the lives of New England saints. This speculative endeavor verifies Foucault's thesis concerning sexuality: that its medicalization during the nineteenth century creates it as a subject for speculation and discussion. The murder of Charles Bon is a futile attempt by his brother to stop not only the perpetuation of Negro blood but also the endless questioning of blood's contamination, its circulation as a sign within a racist society.

The element that links the various themes that I have adumbrated—blood culture, eugenics, hemophobia—is the role of Haiti in Sutpen's past. It is in Haiti that Sutpen earns the money that permits him to build his dynasty in the South and participate in the national fantasy. But that money is made on the backs of African slaves whose blood ultimately returns to "infect" Sutpen's dynastic plan. The tainted blood of Sutpen's Haitian sojourn is mixed with the moral taint associated with his megalomaniacal pursuit of southern respectability. Faulkner's narrator, Quentin Compson, describes Haiti as "the halfway point between what we call the jungle and what we call civilization, halfway between the dark inscrutable continent from which the black blood . . . was ravished by violence, and the cold known land to which it was doomed."[32] Although *Absalom, Absalom!* is usually seen as an epic of the rural South, it is equally a novel about the Caribbean, "a soil manured with black blood from two hundred years of oppression and exploitation."[33] Thus, while the narrative of racialized southern capital takes place in Jefferson, a second narrative of sexual and racial origins takes place in the "other" South of the West Indies. It is in this subsidiary narrative that Blood Culture, the dream of pure, white biological succession, supercedes American Culture.

Haiti not only provides Sutpen with offshore capital; it introduces an alternative sexual economy to the heterosexual code of southern homosociality. Bon is potentially black and potentially incestuous, but he is also regarded as feminine and aristocratic. To Quentin Compson's father, Bon is a kind of dandy, "the slightly Frenchified cloak and hat which he wore, or perhaps (I like to think this) presented formally to the man reclining in a flowered almost feminised gown, in a sunny window in his chambers—this man handsome elegant and even catlike and too old to be where he was, too old not in years but in experience, with some tangible effluvium of knowledge, surfeit: of actions done and satiations plumbed and pleasures exhausted and even forgotten."[34]

Although Mr. Compson does not speak of homosexuality, his indirect references to an "effluvium of knowledge" and obscure "actions done" and "satiations" suggest acts that have no referent, experiences without names. And as Mr. Compson often points out, Henry's interest in Bon is more than filial: "Yes, he loved Bon, who seduced him as surely as he seduced Judith."[35] As Barbara Ladd notes, Bon represents the "return of a tragic history to the American South—in the guises first of white creole decadence, then of blackness and in the form of retributive justice."[36]

Most commentators have noted the racial threat that Bon poses to Sutpen's dynastic ideal. What is less often observed is that Bon's feminization challenges the heterosexual lineage upon which that dynasty depends, a lineage stressed by the novel's title (Absalom as the firstborn, favorite son of David). This feminization threatens the novel's metaphorics of blood, rearticulating racial otherness as sexual unassimilability. The gendering of Bon as feminized aesthete turns a narrative about filiation into one of same-sex and (potentially) homosexual bonding among brothers. Henry's murder of Bon serves not only to eliminate the threat of African heritage in his family but also to stifle Henry's own homosexual desires for the brother who is other. Bon's Haitian background is no small feature in this series of transformations, just as the Caribbean plantation culture functioned as a site of racial danger and revolt throughout the antebellum period.

Absalom, Absalom! accesses an earlier version of American anxiety about germs and infection among immigrants, one that returns with AIDS. We could read Bon as the unassimilable hemophiliac, aristocratic, and feminine bearer of a "weak" or recessive gene through his mother, retainer of a "tragic" and aristocratic Europeanized past. His threat to southern patriarchal society, based on a genealogical principle among fathers and firstborn sons, is related to his combining two immigrant cultures: Creole (Mediterranean French and Spanish) and African (Haitian). In the media's treatment of AIDS, Haiti often functions as an "entry" point for the disease, the place where the disease originates or else the point of transition from Africa to the United States. In each case, AIDS comes from outside, entering the national body through "unprotected" borders. Haiti is a site for infected blood and acts that, like voodoo, challenge American Judeo-Christian identity. In the history of American national fantasy, Haiti functions as a colonial tinderbox where unspeakable revolt may fester and erupt. Furthermore those eruptions, like the revolt of Toussaint L'Ouverture, can serve as a moral proof for southern plantation owners that any failure of resolve in maintaining discipline among slaves could lead to disaster. As Faulkner makes clear, social revolt and chaos are carried in the veins as much as in the individual acts of ex-slaves.

"None of us up here have boyfriends"

The coalescence of blood, race, and sexuality in Charles Bon raises important questions about the integrity of blood as a marker of national identity. Although he is not a hemophiliac, Bon's threat to the postbellum South—and ultimately to Reconstruction America—is the fiction of racial and sexual pollution that will corrupt patrilineal descent. His identity is articulated through a cultural imaginary that includes figures at the heart of American romance from Poe and Hawthorne to Anne Rice and Jewell Gomez: feminized invalids, aristocratic recluses, and vampiric predators. Hemophiliacs have historically occupied a similar realm, threatening fixed gender codes in significant ways. Their vulnerability to physical trauma keeps them from participating in the normal indices of hetero-masculinity—contact sports, physically demanding work, regular working schedules. Their particular genetic configuration as males who receive a recessive gene through their mothers has traditionally identified them as sissies or mama's boys. As men who bleed internally on a regular basis, hemophiliacs share biological similarities with menstruating women; as men who depend on the blood of others, they occupy a passive or "receptor" position with respect to health delivery systems. As cripples and invalids they contest the American masculine cult of action and energy; that hemophiliacs are, in fact, obsessive risk takers and exercise addicts has not altered the pervasive image of them as emaciated invalids.

The gendering of bleeding disorders exposes the degree to which hemophilia is a cultural as well as a medical formation. As such it can be used as a lens by which to view normalcy and national health. Speaking of deaf persons, Lennard Davis notes, "[Disability] is not an object—a woman with a cane—but a social process that intimately involves everyone who has a body and lives in the world of the senses. Just as the conceptualization of race, class, and gender shapes the lives of those who are not black, poor or female, so the concept of disability regulates the bodies of those who are 'normal.'"[37]

Thinking of AIDS as a gay disease not only reinforces negative social attitudes toward homosexual men; it protects and reinforces the compulsory nature of heterosexuality. Within a national AIDS narrative, hemophiliacs played (unwittingly in some cases) an important role in securing an image around which legislation, research, and public policy could be made without having to engage issues of homosexuality and homophobia. Nationally recognized persons with AIDS (PWAs) like Ryan White or the Ray brothers were routinely brought out at public functions to serve as signs that the government was concerned. Yet this concern was expressed in ways that denied gays, Africans, spouses, and partners of PWAs and others infected with HIV the element of personhood. In its obituary for Ryan White in 1990, *Time* magazine claimed that White "first humanized the disease called AIDS. He allowed us to see the boy who just wanted, more than anything else, to be like other children and to be able to go to school"[38] The fact that that White "humanized" a disease that, by the time of his death, had already killed thousands of humans reinforces Paula Treichler's contention that AIDS is an "epidemic of signification" as well as a lethal disease, perpetuated as much by discursive markers as by the exchange of bodily fluids.[39]

Essential to the enforcement of normalcy among hemophiliacs has been the perceived threat to the family as a result of AIDS. Sander Gilman notes that press representations of hemophiliacs with AIDS show the child in the family setting, which contrasts radically with the imposed isolation of the gay man or IV drug user with AIDS. "The presence of the family serves to signal the 'normality' of the child and the low risk of transmission, in spite of the child's radical stigmatization."[40]

In the case of hemophilia there are institutional reasons for this identification of the bleeder with the family. The earliest medical support groups for hemophiliacs were based on children. The Crippled Children Services (CCS), established in the 1960s, served as advocates for hemophiliacs' orthopedic needs. Their efforts led in 1974 to passage of the Genetically Handicapped Persons Program (GHPP), which provided funding to families for blood products. The Bureau of Maternal and Child Health (MCH) was also formed by the U.S. Public Health Service to monitor federal funds relating to hemophilia. Much hemophiliac socialization was provided for children at special hemophilia camps that offered a positive environment for children whose medical exigencies could be easily accommodated and monitored. In most cases hemophilia advocacy efforts have been sponsored by parents of hemophilic children.[41] Since hemophilia was, until the 1970s, largely a pediatric disease, it is not surprising that early funding efforts should have been directed at children. Yet this association of hemophilia with children played into the New Right's family values agenda, even in the most innocuous cultural venues.

Nowhere is the discourse of normalcy within hemophilia better illustrated than by a *Phil Donahue Show* of 1 October 1993, during which HIV-infected hemophilic boys were interviewed along with their mothers. The absence of fathers on the show reinforced the genetic links between mothers and sons, leaving Donahue to serve as the all-purpose nongenetically linked dad to provide the "difficult" questions. In the give-and-take, Donahue stresses the boys' ordinariness by calling attention to how healthy they look or how active they are in school. Most significant for our purposes is that Donahue treats the boys' appearance on his show in the very terms of queer politics—as a coming-out narrative.[42]

DONAHUE: All right, what's going on here? Are you coming out today?

MR. BLAND: I came out when I . . . was on a panel in St. Louis with Jeane White *[mother of Ryan White]*, so . . .

. . . .

DONAHUE: *[to Eric Benz, age fourteen]:* You're fourteen and you're going public here for the first time, huh?

MR. BENZ: Yes.

DONAHUE: You're in a regular—you go to school every day and——

. . . .

DONAHUE: Josh Lunior—Accord, New York. You're twelve. You're in the sixth grade. Yes, you are HIV-positive. You went public this spring, huh?

MR. LUNIOR: Yeah.

DONAHUE: No longer a big secret.

"Coming out" or "going public" as a metaphor for hemophiliacs with AIDS is tolerated in this program because, as Donahue is at pains to emphasize, all of the boys are "normal."

MR. BLAND: I have full-blown AIDS now.

DONAHUE: You don't look full-blown sick to me.

MR. BLAND: You can't tell by looking, Phil.

DONAHUE: You can't? Well, how do you feel? Do you feel any symptoms? Don't you feel weak or—

MR. BLAND: No, I feel like a normal person

DONAHUE: You do? You look like a normal person . . . Very clear of eye.

This sort of banter is conducted with each of the boys. Donahue stresses the fact that despite their illness they don't "look" sick; they have "normal" friends and they all play sports. Speaking to Grant Lewis, age thirteen, Donahue asks, "How about your gang? Everybody understands and they're not, you know, looking at you, waiting for you to—" to which Lewis answers, "All my friends have been real supportive." Donahue concludes, "Really? And you lead a normal life? You play any sports?" The incessant references to sports throughout the interview suggest that it becomes the single indice for hetero-masculinity, as important for a boy's cultural assimilation as any biological factor.

Although the occasion for the boys' appearance on the show is hemophilia in the AIDS community, Donahue makes their heterosexuality a primary issue:

AUDIENCE MEMBER: Hi. Do any of you have girlfriends and do they—and what do they think of you?

. . . .

DONAHUE: . . . Sure, they do. They have girlfriends, boyfriends, and—
   Yes? And enemies, too, I'm sure.
PANELIST [off camera]: Boyfriends!
RANDY RAY: None of us up here have boyfriends.

Donahue's intentions may be to alert the public to the hostility faced by hemophiliacs with AIDS, but in order to do this he must differentiate the os-
tracism these boys have felt from that affecting homosexuals. "None of us up
here have boyfriends" is a given on this show, and Donahue reinforces the
joke by not mentioning the gay community at all, even though it makes its
covert appearance in his responses:

DONAHUE: You don't have any—nobody's starting to walk around you,
   you know, oh, you know, like you're—

Donahue's difficulty in completing his sentence, his inability to supply a word
for what the boys "have," testifies to the queerness of a dialogue in which disease and sexuality intermingle.

   What we see in the *Donahue Show* and other such public forums (congressional hearings, talk shows, public rallies) is an attempt to screen off persons with hemophilia as innocent victims whose normalcy as heterosexual
males must be preserved. Sexual Otherness is enacted as an inexpressible sentence, something you wouldn't want your son to complete. All of the tropes
of masculine normalcy—participation in sports, homosocial contacts with
other heterosexual males, interest in girls—are trotted out for the public to
consume. And it is the *consumption of hetero-normalcy* that is very much at
issue in the portrayal of hemophiliacs in AIDS discourse. Since AIDS is, above
all, a complex associated with wastage and loss, it challenges consumerist notions of economic health and productivity. The bleeder with AIDS is a double
specter of capitalist decay—a male unable to capitalize and retain vital fluids;
a sexual body infected by "foreign" and "unsafe" investments. Donahue's desire to produce normal boys out of infectious diseases is underwritten by an
economic scenario designed to reassure worried investors.

Queer Coalitions

In my introductory remarks I mentioned that the emergence of hemophiliacs
into AIDS discourse represented a crisis in queer identities as much as in he-
matology. I want to elaborate this point with reference to the status of the
hemophiliac body made visible through AIDS. The public "outing" of hemophiliacs in forums such as the *Donahue Show* illustrates the extent to which

AIDS demands an anatomy, preferably that of a young boy, around which to create public policy. Yet if hemophiliacs have become increasingly visible as they are enlisted in appeals for federal research funding, they remain invisible in AIDS discourse. I have already outlined some of the reasons for their marginalization among gay activists, but given the fact that among severe bleeders HIV infection reached almost 90 percent, it is hard to understand why they have not been more prominent in the debate. In primary books and essays about the culture of AIDS by Douglas Crimp, Paula Treichler, Cindy Patton, Simon Watney, Kenneth MacKinnon, Douglas Feldman and others, hemophilia is mentioned seldom, if at all.[43] In the index of Cindy Patton's otherwise excellent book, *Inventing Aids*, hemophiliacs are referred to as "blood product consumers"—as if their only identity as persons with AIDS is their economic dependency on a product. This is a disservice to persons whose lives were shattered by a debilitating and painful disease and then by AIDS. It also fails to recognize activists within the hemophilia community, some of them gay, who fought this very consumerist relationship and who forged coalitions between the gay and hemophilia AIDS communities.

The reasons for the marginalization of hemophiliacs in AIDS discourse may attest to the success of the normalization effort mentioned earlier. It may also suggest some limits to the critique of identity politics being waged in the name of Queer Nation. If the concept of queer was mobilized to call into question the identitarian character of post-Stonewall sexual politics, then its more radical implications would be accommodation a wider matrix of constituencies than those usually defined by "gay" and "lesbian." If so, these constituencies might include figures usually (but not exclusively) defined as heterosexual. Can a medical condition or disability be construed as queer? Can we know in advance what forms the linking of medical and sexual minorities will take? Is queer an identity or a set of practices? The answers to such questions must first appeal to the performative aspect of queer identities, the extent to which any individual occupies a position from which to subvert or carnivalize gender binaries. In addition, one would have to attend to the interpellative activity by which any individual is enlisted into a given zone of social pathologizing— the extent to which someone called "queer" recognizes herself or himself as the object of such a speech act. I have argued that in certain instances, hemophiliacs have been the subjects of such interpellations, both as feminized men and as medicalized Others. Yet hemophiliacs have also been interpellated into a heterosexist economy in ways that make their identification with queer politics difficult. What makes hemophiliacs as a group problematic for queer theory is their conflation of an essentialist discourse of blood and a constructivist discourse of feminized masculinity.

Judith Butler observes that the materiality of the body is not a base upon which ancillary performances can be hung, a prediscursive sex that predates gender. Even the most biological of conditions—the absence of a certain protein in red blood cells for example—comes in gendered form. If we cannot fix identities to a material body, we cannot fix "queer" specifically to gay and lesbian identities. If we do, we replicate the very binarist logic that queer theory deconstructs. Butler recognizes that "queer" has a history, and that this should be honored. Yet she understands that the term sometimes represents a "false unity of women and men." She observes, "Indeed, it may be that the critique of the term will initiate a resurgence of both feminist and antiracist mobilization within lesbian and gay politics or open up new possibilities for coalitional alliances that do not presume that these constituencies are radically distinct from one another."[44]

Among those "possibilities for coalitional alliances" would be figures whose material bodies have been the sites of normalizing discourses and who, in order to claim authority over their own bodies, have had to emerge from closets they never knew they inhabited. One could think of numerous groups similarly positioned: African Americans with sickle cell anemia (whose dependency on transfusions places them in a conditions analogous to hemophiliacs), deaf persons, the homeless, quadriplegics, the visually impaired, welfare "mothers" (insofar as persons on financial assistance are usually seen as women)—all such groups and persons occupy multiple positions in relation to gendered and socialized norms.[45] In the terms introduced earlier, they are nominal queers whose cultural marginality has been articulated through narrow venues of medical and social advocacy. And in most cases their social marginality to heteronormal society results from processes of gendering that feminize in order to disempower. At the same time, if these coalitions are going to place their new queerness in service to larger social goals, they must mobilize as much against homophobic and racist agendas as against the corporatization of medicine, social services, and health care.

The current "good news" about AIDS—the development of protease inhibitors in combination with AZT, the success of sex education programs leads to cautious optimism about a possible decline of the pandemic.[46] But these advances must be set against the high costs of combination therapies that limit access to such treatments to only a few. Gains made in restricting the spread of AIDS must be qualified by awareness of increasing federal and state initiatives curtailing the rights of gays and lesbians, denial of health care to immigrants, and attacks against public assistance to the poor—all in the name of family values. In a similar climate, hemophiliacs may breathe a collective sigh of relief that the safety of the blood supply has been assured and their vulnerability to AIDS through blood transfusions eradicated. But they must be wary of retreating into a "clot closet" where bleeding is treated strictly as a matter of genetics and medicine. The lesson we, as hemophiliacs, should derive from AIDS is that, as a syndrome, it is spread by more than bodily fluids; it is spread by prejudice and stereotype, paranoia and phobia, diseases over which science has little control. AIDS activists have made such categories the subject of a powerful social critique, but unless the boundaries of Queer Nation include citizens of Blood Culture, such a critique will remain a relatively sectarian affair.

Notes

In writing this essay I have been aided by conversations with Judith Halberstam, Steven Epstein, David Lloyd, Susan Resnik, and Bob Gluck, all of whose comments have been extremely helpful.

1. Factors are proteins manufactured in the body that are necessary for the blood to clotting. There are twelve factors, two of which—factors VIII and IX—are among those most commonly absent in hemophiliacs. The quantity of factor in the blood determines the severity of a bleeding disorder.
2. As in any area involving disabilities, nomenclature is a vexing question. In this essay I will refer alternatively to "hemophiliacs" and "persons with hemophilia," recognizing that within the community so defined, the latter term is preferred.
3. Cryoprecipitate was discovered in 1965 by Judith Graham Pool, working as a researcher at Stanford University. She noticed that in the process of thawing frozen plasma to obtain Factor VIII—a process known as "fractionating"—there was a thick residue left that was rich in Factor VIII. This factor-rich residue became cryoprecipitate, and its discovery led to the development of freeze-dried concentrates. On the history of cryoprecipitate see Susan Resnik, "The Social History of Hemophilia in the United States (1948–1988): The Emergence and Empowerment of a Community" (Ph.D. diss., Columbia University, 1994), 52–81.
4. Richard Titmuss's study, *The Gift Relationship: From Human Blood to Social Policy* (New York: Pantheon, 1971), is an important pre-AIDS look at the blood-distribution industry. Titmuss asks why people donate their blood to strangers. He concludes that blood donation involves a "gift relationship" that, unlike so many other transactions in capitalist societies, transcends market considerations. When blood donation becomes a matter of economic policy—when donors give only for profit—then social policy is divorced from moral considerations and leads "to an ideology to end all ideologies" (12).
5. The willingness of the major pharmaceutical companies to continue distributing blood products after their purity had been questioned has been the focus of numerous individual suits and one major class-action suit. The suit was filed against four blood-product companies (Rhone-Poulenc Rorer, Baxter Healthcare, Miles [now Bayer], and Alpha Therapeutic) and the National Hemophilia Associations, the latter of which, according to the *New York Times*, "falsely advised hemophiliacs in the 1980s that the H.I.V. risk in taking the products was minimal. It [the suit] says the foundation gave this advice because it was financially dependent on the manufacturers." "AIDS Suit Accuses Companies of Selling Bad Blood Products," *New York Times*, 4 October 4 1993, 18. The Supreme Court refused to reinstate an order by a U.S. district judge that would allow the hemophiliacs to file as a group. The Court ruled that a class action in a suit of this size could bankrupt the plasma-products industry.

6. David Kirp, "Look Back in Anger: Hemophilia, Rights, and AIDS," *Dissent* 44, no. 3 (Summer 1997): 66.

7. The "one-drop rule," as Lawrence Wright points out, is based on "a long-discredited belief that each race had its own blood type, which was correlated with physical appearance and social behavior. The antebellum South promoted the rule as a way of enlarging the slave population with the children of slaveholders." Lawrence Wright, "One Drop of Blood," *The New Yorker*, 25 July 1994, 48.

8. The most thorough study of this narrative is provided by Susan Resnik whose dissertation, "The Social History of Hemophilia in the United States (1948–1988)" is the only full-scale institutional history of hemophilia.

9. Cindy Patton has provided the most thorough study of the effects of such pronominalization as it affected research. She notes that the New Right and Moral Majority opposed funds for AIDS research since in their minds it was an "elective disease created by homosexuals who might just as well die off." See *Sex and Germs: The Politics of AIDS* (Montreal and New York: Black Rose Books, 1986), 69.

10. All three levels of this shift had profound implications for AIDS research. If the disease could be restricted to constituencies regarded as socially deviant—homosexuals, IV drug users, prostitutes—it could be ignored or, more insidiously, used as a moral lesson and even a genocidal corrective. Once AIDS touched the blood supply—and hemophiliacs in particular—the epidemic became general. Despite the fact that heterosexuals around the world had been dying of AIDS since the late 1970s, it was represented in the popular media as a gay-marked syndrome for which funding, healthcare and education need not be not a priority.

11. Lauren Berlant and Elizabeth Freeman, "Queer Nationality," in *Fear of a Queer Planet: Queer Politics and Social Theory*, ed. Michael Warner (Minneapolis: University of Minnesota Press, 1993), 193–229.

12. On the politics of disabilities, see Lennard Davis, *Enforcing Normalcy: Disability, Deafness and the Body* (London: Verso, 1995).

13. Cindy Patton, *Last Served? Gendering the HIV Pandemic* (London: Taylor and Francis, 1994), 19.

14. The Hemophilia Foundation was formed in 1948, but was renamed The National Hemophilia Foundation in 1959.

15. Hemophilia is X-linked, which means that the gene for the disease is passed on through the X chromosome. Since a male has both an X and a Y chromosome, there is a fifty-fifty chance that he will receive the hemophilia gene from a carrier mother. In women, the presence of a second X chromosome masks the effects of hemophilia on the other chromosome. Although there is a theoretical possibility of a female hemophiliac (in which the second X chromosome failed to mask the effects of the disease), there are no records of such a phenomenon. Hence, for all intents and purposes, hemophilia is a male disease.

16. A former executive director of the National Hemophilia Foundation interviewed by Susan Resnik describes the way these "hemo-homo wars" were conducted, "They (the media) tried to pit hemophiliacs against homosexuals. We were then approached by . . . right-wing groups to engage The National Hemophilia Foundation in this war against 'sin.' . . . I'm really proud of the role of the hemophilia community in resisting these demagogues in trying to exploit this horrible situation." Resnik, "The Social History of Hemophilia," 199.

17. Kirp, "Look Back in Anger," 69.

18. Randy Shilts. *And the Band Played On: Politics, People, and the AIDS Epidemic* (New York: St. Martin's Press, 1987), 220.

19. Cindy Patton, *Sex and Germs*, 23. In Andrew Puckett's mystery novel, *Bloodstains* (New York: Doubleday, 1987), the main character, Tom, is asked to investigate

the theft of blood from a transfusion center. Tom's task is made the more difficult due to his "haemophobia" or fear of blood. Whether referring to a phobia of blood or a fear of bleeders, the term is metonymically linked to homophobia by a series of displacements involving anxiety over penetration. In popular media representations of AIDS such as those on television shows of the 1980s like *Hill Street Blues* or *St. Elsewhere*, a standard AIDS scenario involved the threat of needle "sticks" from potentially infected blood. The drama that ensues involves the innocent nurse or policeman negotiating conflicting attitudes not only about infection but also about gays.

20. On hemophilia in the Talmud see Fred Rosner, "Hemophilia in the Talmud and Rabbinic Writings," *Annals of Internal Medicine* 70 (April 1969), 833–837; on hemophilia in early North America see Victor A. McKusick, "Hemophilia in Early New England: A Follow-up of Four Kindreds in Which Hemophilia Occurred in the Pre-Revolutionary Period," *Journal of the History of Medicine* 17 (1962), 342–365; on hemophilia in Eugenics see Daniel J. Kevles, *In the Name of Eugenics: Genetics and the Uses of Human Heredity* (New York: Alfred A. Knopf, 1985); on germ theory see Alan M. Kraut, *Silent Travellers: Germs, Genes, and the "Immigrant Menace"* (New York: Basic Books, 1994), and Joan Burbick, *Healing the Republic: The Language of Health and the Culture of Nationalism in Nineteenth-Century America* (Cambridge, U.K.: Cambridge University Press, 1994). Robert Gluck has reminded me that kosher dietary laws prohibit the eating of certain "bloody" parts of cows or chickens that have not been cleaned of blood.

21. In the *Ithaca Journal*,1 May 1986, White was photographed at a benefit for AIDS research; the accompanying caption reads, "Ryan . . . is a homophiliac [sic] who contracted AIDS through a blood transfusion." Quoted in Sander L. Gilman, "AIDS and Syphilis: The Iconography of Disease," *AIDS: Cultural Analysis, Cultural Activism*, ed. Douglas Crimp (Cambridge: The MIT Press, 1991), 105.

22. Michel Foucault, *The History of Sexuality*, vol. 1, *An Introduction*, trans. Robert Hurley (New York: Vintage Books, 1980), 147.

23. Judith Halberstam, *Skin Shows: Gothic Horror and the Technology of Monsters*. (Durham, N.C.: Duke University Press, 1995), 95.

24. Robert K. Massie, *Nicholas and Alexandra* (New York: Atheneum, 1967), 114. Massie was moved to write his book by his own son's hemophilia. Curiosity about his son's disease led him, as he says in his introduction, "to curiosity about the response of the parents of the boy who was the most famous hemophiliac of all," vii.

25. Quoted in Kevles, *In the Name of Eugenics*, 97.

26. Quoted in ibid., 97.

27. Lauren Berlant, *The Anatomy of National Fantasy: Hawthorne, Utopia, and Everyday Life* (Chicago: University of Chicago Press, 1991), 5.

28. Quoted in Alexander Saxton, *The Rise and Fall of the White Republic: Class, Politics, and Mass Culture in Nineteenth-Century America* (London and New York: Verso, 1990), 89.

29. Ibid., 89.

30. Ibid., 88.

31. Russell Castronovo, *Fathering the Nation: American Genealogies of Slavery and Freedom* (Berkeley: University of California Press, 1995), 3.

32. William Faulkner, *Absalom, Absalom!* (New York: Vintage, 1986), 202.

33. Ibid.

34. Ibid., 76.

35. Ibid.

36. Barbara Ladd, "'The Direction of the Howling': Nationalism and the Color Line

in *Absalom, Absalom!*" in *Subjects and Citizens: Nation, Race and Gender from Oroonoko to Anita Hill*, ed. Michael Moon and Cathy N. Davidson (Chapel Hill: Duke University Press, 1995), 357.

37. Davis, *Enforcing Normalcy*, 2.

38. "The 'Miracle' of Ryan White," *Time*, 23 April 1990.

39. Paula Treichler, "AIDS, Homophobia, and Biomedical Discourse: An Epidemic of Signification," in *AIDS: Cultural Analysis, Cultural Activism*, ed. Douglas Crimp (Cambridge: The MIT Press, 1991), 32.

40. Gilman, "AIDS and Syphilis," 105.

41. On hemophilia camps, see Resnik, "The Social History of Hemophilia," 135–37. See also "Hemophiliacs Lead Fairly 'Normal' Lives," *Antioch (Ill.) News Tribune,* 1 July 1993.

42. The dialogue excerpted here is from the *Donahue Show*, 1 October 1993, Multimedia Entertainment, Inc.

43. Douglas Crimp, *AIDS: Cultural Analysis, Cultural Activism* (Cambridge: The MIT Press, 1991); Cindy Patton, *Inventing AIDS* (New York: Routledge, 1990); Simon Watney, *Policing Desire: Pornography, AIDS and the Media* (London: Methuen, 1987); Kenneth MacKinnon, *The Politics of Popular Representation: Reagan, Thatcher, AIDS, and the Movies* (Rutherford, N.J.: Fairleigh Dickinson University Press, 1992); Douglas Feldman, *Culture and AIDS* (New York: Praeger, 1990).

44. Judith Butler, *Bodies that Matter: On the Discursive Limits of "Sex"* (New York: Routledge, 1993), 228–29.

45. On new coalitional alliances see Cathy J. Cohen, "Punks, Bulldaggers, and Welfare Queens: The Radical Potential of Queer Politics?" *GLQ* 3 (1997): 437–65. On AIDS activism in general see Steven Epstein, *Impure Science: AIDS, Activism, and the Politics of Knowledge* (Berkeley: University of California Press, 1996).

46. This optimistic mood is best represented by the 1996 International AIDS Conference in Vancouver, British Columbia. Articles in the *New York Times* (7 July 1996) and *Los Angeles Times* (4 July 1996) describe advances made in combination therapies as they were outlined by researchers at the conference. Both articles go on to point out that while AIDS may be contained in the United States, it is expanding in staggering rates in Africa, Southeast Asia, and the Middle East. Ninety percent of HIV infections are in the Third World, and the high cost of new drugs will place them out of the reach of most affected individuals.

"An Essential Friendship": African Americans and Caribbean Immigrants in Harlem

Chapter 3

HEATHER HATHAWAY

In November 1926, *Opportunity: A Journal of Negro Life,* the literary organ of the National Urban League, published a "Special Caribbean Issue." According to the opening editorial, the purpose of the special issue was to provide the *Opportunity*'s predominantly African American readers with a "wider and deeper acquaintance . . . with the large group of Negroes who have come to these shores, as millions of others have come, seeking a new economic and cultural freedom." In so doing, however, the magazine also sought to address an issue of even greater urgency—it sought to palliate the increasing hostility between African Caribbean immigrants and native-born African Americans in Harlem that emerged as a result of high levels of immigration during the early decades of the twentieth century. As *Opportunity* editor Charles Johnson stated, the unique edition of the magazine was expressly designed to cultivate "an essential friendship" between foreign- and native-born blacks based on the "conviction that friendships usually follow the knowing of one's neighbors."[1] This essay, in keeping with the overall purpose of *Beyond the Binary* to probe the intricacies of "American" identity, seeks to complicate the monolithic conception of blackness that has tended to dominate U.S. cultural studies by examining the historical roots of the often contentious relationship between African Caribbeaners and African Americans in Harlem.

When discussing "American" identity in terms of racial classifications, the binary most often in operation is that of black and white. As Maxine Hong Kingston's decidedly unhyphenated Chinese American protagonist, Wittman Ah Sing, in her novel *Tripmaster Monkey: His Fake Book* (1990) explains, the perception that generally governs in the United States is "that Americans are

61

either white or Black. I can't wear that civil-rights button with the Black hand and the white hand shaking each other," proclaims "Wit Man" (as his mother knowingly calls him). "I have a nightmare—after duking it out, someday Blacks and whites will shake their hands over my head. I'm the little yellow man beneath the bridge of their hands and overlooked" (307–308). Wittman/Wit Man/Whitman/Whit(e)man Ah Sing's observation exposes the limitations of as well as the exclusions inherent in the simplistic binary of black and white that pervades both popular and institutional cultures in the United States, and points toward the need to problematize other racial concepts that are equally vague, such as the even more general "people of color." Certainly, the ways in which race, class, gender, ethnicity, and nationality figure in questions of individual and group identity formation must be analyzed if we are truly to come to a more thorough understanding of meanings of "Americanness."

Although this essay contributes to that process by examining one under-studied aspect of difference within racial sameness, in so doing it risks establishing another binary that is as troubling as the one it seeks to dismantle. Indeed, by discussing "African Americans" and "African Caribbeaners" as seemingly discrete entities, this essay necessarily overlooks important issues of both region and nationhood, not to mention class, that require similarly rigorous scrutiny in order to understand the details of both differentiation and division that characterize the larger black American community. Moreover, when discussing the *migration* of multiple distinct national groups (for example, Jamaican, Haitian, Dominican, Puerto Rican, Cuban, Antiguan, Barbadian, and so on), attention should be addressed to the specific cultural frameworks, national identities, and historical contexts from which these migrations stem, as well as to the fundamentally re-creative process of nationhood that occurs upon arrival in new, and in most cases modern, environments. The act of migration itself is obviously disruptive not simply to geographic but also to sociocultural boundaries that engender a sense of national homogeneity. As cultural theorist Homi Bhabha argues in his analysis of the process of "DissemiNation," upon migration issues of national identity shift from "the 'selfhood' of the nation as opposed to the otherness of other nations" toward "the nation split within itself, articulating the heterogeneity of its population." This "barred Nation *It/Self*," Bhabha asserts, "alienated from its external self-generation, becomes a liminal signifying space that is *internally* marked by the discourses of minorities, the heterogeneous histories of contending peoples, antagonistic authorities and tense locations of cultural difference."[2] Thus, in some ways, the categories of "African American" and "African Caribbeaner" employed here are as inadequate as those of "Black" and "White"; according to this line of reasoning, any attempt at classification by race or nation, in fact, verges upon futility.

That said, we must begin *somewhere* and one logical place to do so, when seeking to understand more clearly the complexity of the postemancipation black American community, is at the historical moment when African Americans and African Caribbean immigrants to the United States first began to interact on a large scale. The foundations of the complex relationship between the two groups were laid during the "first wave" of Caribbean immigration to this country which took place roughly between 1900 and 1930.[3] Questions concerning the relationship between race, ethnicity, and nationality that emerged during this period continue to remain central in U.S. society as immigration from the islands has accelerated in the wake of political and economic turmoil. Grappling with the details of African Caribbean–African American relations during the "first wave" not only clarifies our understanding of constructions of "American" identity in the past but also valuably illuminates that same process in the present. Toward that end, this essay first provides a brief overview of the factors that stimulated a mass migration from the Caribbean to the United States between 1900 and 1930, then analyzes the reactions to this migration in terms of cross-cultural contact in Harlem, and finally focuses in detail upon the *Opportunity*'s "Special Caribbean Issue" in an effort to get a glimpse of how definitions of nation and race were narrated by members of both communities during the period.

The impact of Caribbean immigration on black life in Harlem between roughly 1890 and the stock market crash of 1929 was profound. While by 1930 the total number of first- and second-generation black immigrants living in the city constituted only 1.5 percent of the total black population, a review of the numbers arriving during such a short span of time suggests in part why the presence of the new arrivals appeared so momentous.[4] In 1899, 412 black immigrants entered the United States. In 1902 the number of newcomers doubled to 832; in 1903 that number rose to 2,174 and by 1907 doubled again to reach 5,633. From 1908 to 1924 between 5,000 and 8,000 African Caribbeaners immigrated to the United States annually, and by 1924 the numbers peaked at 12,243 arrivants entering during a twelve-month period.[5] By 1930, 177,981 foreign-born blacks and their children lived in the United States. Nearly all of these immigrants came from the "West Indies," the "non-Hispanic" Caribbean, and the majority settled in New York City.[6]

A variety of "push" and "pull" factors drove immigrants out of the Caribbean and toward the United States between 1880 and 1920. A considerable degree of regional migration occurred as people sought work on banana and sugar plantations in Cuba and the Dominican Republic, on the railroad in Costa Rica, and on dry docks in Bermuda.[7] The creation of the Panama Canal between 1906 and 1914, however, presented the largest impetus for Caribbean

migration toward the United States. By working on the Canal, many Caribbeaners were able to finance eventual moves north.[8] More significantly, the
transnational exchange of cultural products and commodities that occurred
between the two regions as a result of a large U.S. presence in Panama offered Canal workers glimpses of at least the material, if not necessarily the
social, possibilities presented by life under U.S. governance. All of these factors combined to result in the Canal serving as a temporary layover for many
U.S.-bound migrants.

But the Canal also introduced workers to the limitations of life in the
United States—namely those imposed by the strict codes of American racism. Black canal workers were discriminated against in terms of both job as-
signments and wages, and between 1906 and 1923 more than 20,000 of these
"pick and shovel" men died as a result of poor working and living conditions.[9]
As historian Irma Watkins-Owens has explained in her comprehensive study
of Caribbeaners in Harlem, *Blood Relations: Caribbean Immigrants and the
Harlem Community, 1900–1930*, while employment with the Canal project
did offer valuable wages, it also meant long hours, hard labor, and, perhaps
most importantly, since it was supervised by U.S. officials and marines, a rather
startling introduction to the strict forms of segregation practiced in the United
States. Jim Crow ruled the Canal Zone just as it ruled the American South,
but in an ironic reflection of the economic motivations underlying the Canal's
construction, the designations "colored" and "white" at all public facilities were
replaced by those of "silver" and "gold." Black workers, "regardless of their
actual skill, were designated 'unskilled' and paid in Panamanian silver balboas,
while white American" workers were routinely considered "skilled" and "paid
in gold."[10]

This classification system resulted, in part, from Panamanian discomfort
with racial designations as well as an importation of American modes of social organization. Categorizing workers by race was uncommon in the Republic of Panama and Colombia, and immigrant laborers, used to social hierarchies
based more on class, were unaccustomed to such stratifications; thus the "silver" and "gold" standards were established by U.S. officials.[11] But these labels, if superficially different from "colored" and "white," accomplished the
same purpose of entrenching a racial caste system. One observer during the
period noted that "very often a West Indian doing clerical work with a long
and good record is discharged to make room for some white ne'er-do-well.
When he complains to authorities he is often told: 'Well, we'll give you a job
as foreman over a gang in the shops. No matter what class of work you're doing you can't make any more than seventy-five dollars per month.'" Addition-
ally, American officials deliberately encouraged intraracial hostility in order
to prevent the formation of labor unions. The same observer described "a spirit

of hatred" as being "kindled among the islanders. . . . The Jamaican [is told] that because some Caucasian blood flows through his veins he is better than the Trinidadian. The Barbadian has been taught that because he is more nearly of pure Negro blood he is better than the mixed people of Jamaica. . . . Thus they go, ever fighting, ever hating each other. The Barbadian hates the Jamaican, the Trinidadian hates the Barbadian and the Jamaican hates them all."[12] On the Canal, then, white Americans used a time-tested method to insure their own hegemony. By introducing a binary U.S. system of racial hierarchy in which all whites were automatically deemed superior to all blacks, and then fomenting dissension among the blacks using national and class differences as fuel, white officials ensconced themselves in positions of economic and cultural authority.

Despite this rather harsh introduction to the "American way," many of these workers, tempted by the prospect of American riches and facing eviction and unemployment upon completion of the project, still sought the promise of prosperity offered by the "land of opportunity." Underscoring scholar Peter Linebaugh's suggestion that "the ship remained perhaps the most important conduit of Pan-African communication before the appearance of the long-playing record," Caribbean immigrants began the gradual and evolving process of transplanting island cultures to U.S. soil as they took to the sea.[13] Some took advantage of the newly established mail and shipping routes running between New York and the Isthmus by booking passage on these vessels; others traveled via United Fruit Company ships, which were carrying on a lucrative export business to major cities along the eastern seaboard.[14] All, like the members of the "Great Migration" of African Americans from the American South, were drawn to northern urban centers in the United States in search of the jobs and wealth resulting from the wartime economic boom.[15]

This massive black migration resulted in a dramatic convergence of peoples in New York City in particular, the consequences of which manifested themselves in singularly "American" ways. On one hand, as reflected in Jamaican immigrant and writer W. A. Domingo's description of New York in 1925, the United States did indeed appear to be a new type of "melting pot" for the dark-skinned peoples left out of Crèvecoeur's original conceptualization of the term:

> Almost unobserved, America plays her usual role in the meeting,
> mixing, and welding of the colored peoples of the earth. A dusky tribe
> of destiny seekers, these brown and black and yellow folk, eyes filled
> with visions of an alien heritage—palm-fringed seashores, murmuring
> streams, luxuriant hills and vales—have made an epical march from
> far corners of the earth to the Port of New York and America. They
> bring the gift of the black tropics to America and to their kinsmen.

> With them come vestiges of a quaint folk life, other social traditions,
> and as for the first time in their lives, colored people of Spanish,
> French, Dutch, Arabian, Danish, Portuguese, British and native
> African ancestry meet and move together, there comes into Negro life
> the stir and leavening that is uniquely American.[16]

Like so many white immigrant groups who had preceded them, foreign-born blacks contributed an internationalism to the American scene that made it, paradoxically enough, quintessentially "American." On the other hand, in an equally "American" manner, the presence of these immigrants also provoked hostility, nativism, and fear. As both newcomers from the South and the islands competed with native New York blacks for the same jobs, housing, and monetary rewards, considerable tensions arose.

These tensions infused all aspects of African American-African Caribbean interaction. Differences between the two groups in terms of educational background, employment status, class standing, and political affiliations, for examples, became grounds for potential discord. Under all lay the central fault line between racial similarity and ethnic and/or national differences. As Charles Johnson lamented, "Of the same blood and, in the United States of the same status with American born Negroes, [Black immigrants] represent vastly different social and political backgrounds, even among themselves. It is inevitable that [native- and foreign-born Blacks] should fail either to know or understand each other or to profit fully by the virtues of each other. And all the while, the single, inexorable pressure of race,—with a characteristic indifference to the disaffection between elements of minorities of the same class, proceeds on the assumption that being alike, they are the same" ("Caribbean Issue," 334).

But in nearly all ways but one, African Americans and African Caribbean immigrants were not "the same." In terms of educational background, for instance, immigration records show that 98.6 percent of black immigrants admitted in 1923 could read and write; a decade later the statistics held firm at 99.0 percent.[17] The educational structure on each island was modeled upon that of the local colonial power and was generally perceived by Caribbeaners to be superior to that offered in the United States; some immigrants, in fact, including the parents of politician Shirley Chisolm and singer-activist Harry Belafonte, sent their children back to the Caribbean to be educated. In her autobiography, *Unbought and Unbossed*, Chisholm reflects that "years later I would know what an important gift my parents had given me by seeing to it that I had my early education in the strict, traditional, British-styled schools of Barbados. If I speak and write easily now, that early education is the main reason."[18] Following elementary and secondary education, African Caribbeaners who could afford to often sent their children for additional schooling in England or France. In contrast, the strict enforcement of separate and un-equal public educational facilities for blacks in the United States created multiple barriers to the attainment of higher degrees for African Americans—and, perhaps more importantly, to the skilled and professional positions which these degrees helped secure.

Indeed, related to differences in educational background between the two communities were differences in work experience and skill levels as well. Sociologist Ira Reid, in his path-breaking 1939 study, *The Negro Immigrant: His Background, Characteristics, and Social Adjustment, 1899–1937*, noted that "distinctly out of proportion to the prevalence of such classes in the occupational schemes of the native-born Negro are the high proportions of [immigrant] workers who had been employed as skilled artisans, as bankers, agents, merchants, clerical workers in commerce and finance, and as professional persons."[19] In fact, Reid's research showed that between 1931 and 1935, of the roughly 50 percent of immigrants who reported occupations upon arrival, 40.4 percent identified themselves as industrial workers, 28.1 percent as laborers (with the skill level being unspecified), 17.6 percent as previously employed in commerce and finance, and 12 percent as professionals.[20] Upon arriving in the United States, many of these immigrants either relied upon money earned in the islands to set up small businesses, practiced their previous work in such skilled trades as carpentry, shoemaking, baking, or tailoring, or continued in the professions of medicine, dentistry, or law. Furthermore, immigrants who had become accustomed to social standings in their homelands based on class resisted being demoted upon immigration to less skilled positions simply by virtue of their race. Unaware that certain jobs were theoretically "unavailable" to them as blacks, Caribbean immigrants often sought and secured positions for which African Americans did not even apply, frequently using their British or French citizenship and the consulate of the "mother country" as arsenals against discrimination. While this pattern of adjustment to the United States often resulted in the provision of important services and the breaking down of certain employment barriers to the African American community, it also created a xenophobic competition for the scarce employment and compensation resources that were available to blacks in general.

A combination of financial standing and cultural institutions that facilitated immigrant prosperity in the "new world" also proved to be a source of intraracial tension. African Caribbean groups, and British "West Indians" in particular, developed associations of rotating credit in which individuals contributed a certain portion of their monthly incomes to a central fund that was then distributed to the members of the group on a rotating basis. This system of collective financing, rooted in African traditions carried first to the Caribbean and then to the United States, enabled members to obtain interest-free loans that fostered entrepreneurial activity within the community and also allowed black immigrants to remain independent of white lending institutions. For a variety of reasons related to the peculiarities of the institution of slavery in the United States as well as to the economic conditions with which African Americans were confronted upon emancipation, however, the community-based economic collectives and fraternal organizations that have commonly arisen among newly arrived immigrant groups did not develop in the native-born black community.[21] Thus African Americans were not only at the mercy of white bankers and financiers whose lending decisions were often racially based, but the native-born community felt that newly arrived immigrants were usurping commercial territory rightfully belonging to the local population.

A different type of territory was at issue between African Americans and African Caribbeaners in the realm of politics. Again in disproportionate numbers, Caribbean immigrants were active in the Harlem political scene, generally exhibiting a higher degree of radicalism than their native-born counterparts (as is reflected by the prominence of Caribbeaners in such organizations as the African Blood Brotherhood, the Socialist Speakers Bureau, and the Peoples Educational Forum). The key roles that Caribbean natives Cyril Briggs, Richard B. Moore, Hubert Harrison, Frank Crosswaith, W. A. Domingo—and most significantly Marcus Garvey, leader of one of the most powerful forces during this period, the Universal Negro Improvement Association (UNIA)—played in local politics, as well as Garvey's role in solidifying lines of ethnic difference within the black American community, are beyond the scope of this essay.[22] But it is important to recognize here that, as "minorities" within a "minority" in the United States, these activists did not necessarily have access to traditional political forums controlled either by white Tammany bosses or, to a limited degree, by members of the African American elite. In response, beginning around 1917 and continuing through the 1930s, Caribbean radicals developed a new means of educating their peers about political issues through street-corner speaking or the "stepladder forum."

Throughout the period Caribbeaners could be heard delivering political commentaries and intellectual presentations to listeners from atop stepladders perched on Harlem street corners. Historian Irma Watkins-Owens cites a *New York News* reporter's description of one forum led by the most famous of these speakers, St. Croix native Hubert Harrison, which suggests the cultural significance of these informal symposia:

> The Age of Pericles and Socrates in ancient Athens had nothing on
> the present age of Harlem in New York. Coming out of the "movies"
> between 137th Street and 138th Street on Seventh Avenue, we saw
> one of the biggest street corner audiences that we have ever met in

this block, which is famous for street corner lectures, and the subject was "Evolution." This was not a selected audience but the "run of the street," and their faces were fixed on a black man who stood on a ladder platform, with his back to the avenue and the passing buses and his face to the audience who blocked the spacious sidewalk. . . . And what was he talking about? . . . The theory of evolution, and its illustration in different lines of material and biological development—the Darwinian science of the evolution of life, and the Marxian philosophy of the evolution of capitalism—and a possible development from capitalism to a state of communism.[23]

Intellectual issues and radical politics were often skillfully integrated in these speeches, which were designed to move listeners toward a more committed activism in the quest for racial equality. But the popularity of African Caribbean speakers, combined with the factors of foreign birth and a socialist-grounded distance from the political mainstream, led African American leaders to perceive the immigrant/orators as threats. Jamaican-born author Claude McKay, himself an insider to both groups, described a "sharp struggle for place and elbow room" as having been waged between the educated classes of immigrant and native-born blacks during the period. Indeed, members of W.E.B. Du Bois's "Talented Tenth" were convinced of their own authority to "represent the race" to the larger white populace and, according to McKay, "resent[ed] the aggressiveness of the foreign-born Negroes, especially in politics."[24] In this venue in particular, ethnic and national differences between African Americans and African Caribbeaners became vital issues for the black American community overall as intraracial tensions led, at times, to the fragmentation of united black efforts toward obtaining equal rights for the race as a whole.

The tensions between the two communities that stemmed from key differences in educational practices, employment opportunities, class status, and political views, not to mention additional strains surrounding religion, language, and citizenship, amply illustrate that the two black groups in the United States were indeed *not* "the same," despite the perception of outsiders to the contrary. Not surprisingly, in fact, the very merging of the two groups within the clearly defined and relatively closed boundaries of Harlem resulted in the common pattern of each group identifying itself based on its opposition to the "other." Ethnic theorist George Devereux has explained how the process of ethnic identity construction involves "two symmetrical specifications": the determination that "(1) A is an X" (for our purposes, so-and-so is a Caribbeaner) is necessarily predicated upon the knowledge that "(2) A is not a non-X" (so-and-so is not, in this instance, an African American). The identification of self is fundamentally linked to one's awareness of one's difference from an other. Devereux continues, stating that "specifications as to what constitutes ethnic identity develop only after an ethnic group recognizes the existence of others who do not belong to the group. At the start, these specifications may conceivably include only certain real (racial, cultural, personality) traits of the group. But it is almost inevitable that these distinguishing traits will eventually acquire also evaluative connotations."[25] The experience of African Americans and African Caribbeaners in Harlem provides a valuable case study of this process in action. The act of migration forced the two groups to interact within a closed space; each group, in an effort to distinguish itself from the other, defined itself in relative opposition to the other; soon, the "real" differences that loomed large between African Americans and Caribbeaners acquired "evaluative connotations" as they became codified into rigid sets of reciprocal stereotypes.

Ira Reid interviewed members of both communities between 1935 and 1939 and catalogued the most common stereotypes held about Caribbeaners during the period. A desire to save money, acquire property, or open a business fostered the popular stereotype that Caribbeaners were stingy, "craftier than the Jew, and not to be trusted in financial matters."[26] Previous education in the islands or the pursuit of higher education in the United States contributed to the belief that immigrants were "intellectual prigs" and perceived themselves to be "smarter" than native-born blacks.[27] Distinguishing oneself by accent or nationality before race led to charges that Caribbeaners felt "superior to the native-born Negro" as well as to the criticism that they were "so British . . . that [they didn't] have time to be [themselves]." An emphasis on class rather than race as an index of status, inherited from the social structures on many Caribbean islands, perpetuated the belief that the newcomers "lacked race-pride." At the same time, however, high levels of political radicalism led to charges of "troublemaking" with whites and paradoxical perceptions that African Caribbeaners were "too race conscious." Involvement with other immigrants in the form of fraternal and community organizations provoked resentment about the "clannishness" of Caribbeaners. Finally, expressing the same blindness that was directed toward their own community by whites, African Americans during the period tended to believe that "all the foreigners were just alike."[28]

Caribbeaners held comparable and converse stereotypes about African Americans. Second-generation Barbadian immigrant Paule Marshall recalls being aware of these biases in her parents: "It seems to me from what I observed as a child that the West Indian woman considered herself both different [from] and somehow superior [to the African American woman]. From the talk which circulated around our kitchen it was clear, for example, that my mother and her friends perceived of themselves as being more ambitious than black Americans, more hard working and in terms of the racial question, more militant and unafraid in their dealings with white people."[29] Caribbeaners during the period generally viewed African Americans as less educated, less industrious, and less willing to challenge designations of second-class citizenship determined by race alone. At the same time, however, revealing again the paradoxes of such biases, Caribbeaners believed African Americans to be overly preoccupied with racial slights and barriers.[30] Because of the perception that African Americans were a "keepback" to immigrant advancement, intermarriage among members of the second generation was strongly discouraged. Adam Clayton Powell, Jr., recalled that in the 1930s, "the same feeling the average white bigot had when a Catholic married a Jew was the experience of Harlem Town when a West Indian married an American black."[31]

By 1926 intraracial relations had become so strained that the leaders of the National Urban League, a nonprofit organization founded in 1910 to promote better relations between blacks and whites, felt compelled to publish the "Special Caribbean Issue" of the *Opportunity* in an effort to intervene in the increasingly contentious relationship that had developed within the black community itself. An analysis of the edition, however, suggests that even within the context of this deliberate effort to unify blacks, classifications based on binary constructions of "foreign" and "native," of "self" and "other," were extremely difficult for the contributors—African Caribbean and African American alike—to overcome.

Charles Johnson's opening editorial explained the purpose of the edition and provided a microcosm of the concerns that framed its inception. First Johnson established that the goal of the special issue was to discuss "questions dealing with the Caribbean countries and their sons now living in the United States" in order to familiarize the *Opportunity*'s largely African American readership with the newcomers. To that end, the special issue consisted of a series of articles, the majority of which were written by prominent Caribbean immigrants, that provided factual information about Caribbean history, geography, and arts.[32] Upon identifying this objective, Johnson emphasized that underlying this goal was a desire to improve relations between the two groups whose association had been hindered by misunderstanding: "This well selected group [of Caribbeaners] posited in the midst of a large and varied Negro population has brought its questions and difficulties. The situation has encouraged snobbishness and jealousies, resentment and group selfishness. The American Negro who dislikes West Indians and applies to them offensive names, can be matched by the West Indian who can outlaw a fellow countryman for associating too much with American Negroes." Johnson praised the immigrant group, which, "however small in number, has made itself felt" by "provid[ing] business and professional men and a substantial group of workers," and he asserted that African Caribbeaners had much to contribute not simply to intraracial culture but to interracial interactions as well. "The present foreign Negro population is closely selected," he stated. "Their interests are keen, as their preponderance at most of Harlem's forums and the libraries indicate. And among the more intellectual ones, the play of their minds against the peculiar angles of North American race situations, offers, for the American born Negro an invaluable stimulation." But most importantly, Johnson claimed, although significant "social and political" differences divided African Caribbeaners even from one another, it was imperative that they and African Americans forge an "essential friendship" precisely because of the "inexorable pressure" of race that bound the two groups indelibly to one another.

Perhaps nowhere else are the tensions surrounding these differences more apparent than in the subtext and context of the article contributed by Jamaican immigrant and journalist, W. A. Domingo—an article whose interest lies less in what it says than in what it does not say. As the first item following Johnson's editorial and titled simply "The West Indies," this flagship essay was clearly intended to offer that "wider and deeper acquaintance" with the Caribbean about which Johnson spoke in his opening comments. To this end, Domingo sketched a brief history of the Caribbean from the colonial period to the present. He described the conquest and development of slavery, reported on geographic and demographic characteristics of the region, outlined the islands' political, economic, and educational structures, and commented briefly upon race relations. He also discussed Caribbean relationships with both Great Britain and the United States. Throughout this overview Domingo was careful to emphasize the significant differences among the nations that make up the region, seeking implicitly to break down the simplistic conception of "the West Indies" (or more recently "the Caribbean") that gripped American thinking about the area.

What is unusual about Domingo's contribution to the special issue, however, is the absence of more explicit references to the specific topic at hand— African Caribbean–African American relations. Domingo's only nod in this direction can be found in the closing two sentences of his essay, in which he stated that, "by virtue of the presence of thousands of West Indians in the United States, a bond is being forged between them and American Negroes. Gradually they are realizing that their problems are in the main similar, and that their ultimate successful solution will depend on the intelligent cooperation of the two branches of Anglo-Saxonized Negroes" (342). Domingo's relative silence on the matter is most surprising because of the piece he had contributed just one year earlier, "The Gift of the Black Tropics," to Alain

Locke's hallmark 1925 anthology, *The New Negro*, in which he confronted head-on the topic of the special issue by discussing not the "West Indies" but rather West Indians in the United States.

Early in the 1925 essay Domingo drew attention to how reductive conceptions of race in this country posed unique problems for black immigrants: "Divided by tradition, culture, historical background and group perspective, these diverse peoples are gradually hammered into a loose unit by the impersonal force of congested residential segregation. Unlike others of the foreign-born, black immigrants find it impossible to segregate themselves into colonies; . . . they are inevitably swallowed up in Black Harlem."[33] While differences in ethnic or national origins, language, or religious practices were perceived by the native-born white community as features that distinguished white immigrants both from one another and from themselves, racial similarity alone served as the criterion for a blind association of African Caribbeaners to African Americans upon the black immigrants' arrival. But, Domingo continued, the native-born black community subsequently fell victim to similarly simplistic classifications: "To the average American Negro, all English-speaking black foreigners are West Indians, and by that is usually meant British subjects. There is a general assumption that there is everything in common among West Indians, though nothing can be further from the truth. West Indians regard themselves as Antiguans or Jamaicans as the case might be, and a glance at the map will quickly reveal the physical obstacles that militate against homogeneity of population; separation of many sorts, geographical, political, and cultural tend everywhere to make and crystallize local characteristics" ("Caribbean Issue," 343). Even from within the veil of race, Domingo claimed, blindness persisted: the presence of one false dichotomy—that of black and white—facilitated the development of another—that of "West Indian" and African American.

These gulfs between self and other, however, proved impossible for even Domingo to bridge. While this is perhaps neither surprising nor, on the surface at least, terribly ominous, the history of tension between African Caribbeaners and African Americans, combined with the pattern of ethnic identity construction based on opposition that seems to be at play in this instance, made the rhetoric of "Gift" implicitly condemnatory and confrontational. As Werner Sollors has argued, ethnicity is not a thing in itself but is rather a relation based on contrast.[34] This sense of ethnicity as rooted in contrast is illustrated throughout "Gift" as Domingo repeatedly attributed positive characteristics to African Caribbeaners, attributions that stood in juxtaposition to his notable silences about African Americans. In this particular context, whatever qualities Domingo ascribed to African Caribbeaners implied the contrary about African Americans.

Describing African Caribbean employment circumstances in the United States, for example, Domingo stated in "Gift" that, "coming from countries in which they had experienced no legalized social or occupational disabilities, West Indians very naturally have found it difficult to adapt themselves to the tasks that are, by custom, reserved for Negroes in the North." Continuing, Domingo made inferences about levels of ambition and industry between African Caribbeaners and African Americans that grew increasingly problematic: "Skilled at various trades and having a contempt for body service and menial work, many of the immigrants apply for positions that the average American Negro has been schooled to regard as restricted to white men only, with the result that through their persistence and doggedness in fighting white labor, West Indians have in many cases been pioneers and shock troops to open a way for Negroes into new fields of employment" ("Caribbean Issue," 345). Implicitly, this statement argued that African Americans were unskilled at trades, had little contempt for body service and menial work, were resigned to white-constructed barriers of segregation, and were neither "persistent" nor "dogged" in confronting white labor.

Domingo continued, referring to the behavior of Caribbean immigrants as evincing a "freedom from spiritual inertia," and went on to say that this quality allowed Caribbeaners to be especially enterprising. Becoming more explicit, Domingo claimed that "while American Negroes predominate in forms of business like barber shops and pool rooms *in which there is no competition from white men*, West Indians turn their efforts almost invariably to fields like grocery stores, tailor shops, jewelry stores and fruit vending *in which they meet the fiercest kind of competition*. In some of these fields they are the pioneers or the only surviving competitors of white business concerns [emphasis added]."[35] In terms of worship, Domingo described African Americans as being "inclined to indulge in displays of emotionalism that border on hysteria" while African Caribbeaners, "in their Wesleyan Methodist and Baptist churches maintain . . . all the punctilious emotional restraint characteristic of their English background."[36] He concluded the essay with a statement that can be considered at best a firm pronouncement of patriotism and at worst as bordering on vaingloriousness: "The outstanding contribution of West Indians to American Negro life is the insistent assertion of their manhood in an environment that demands too much servility and unprotesting acquiescence from men of African blood. This unwillingness to conform and be standardized, to accept tamely an inferior status and abdicate their humanity, finds an open expression in the activities of the foreign-born Negro in America" whose "dominant characteristic" is that of "blazing new paths, breaking the bonds that would fetter the feet of a virile people."[37] In the heated political and cultural moment in which Domingo wrote, to argue that African Caribbeaners were "insistent[ly] assert[ing] . . . their manhood" was to more than suggest that African Americans were not. To praise African Caribbeaners for refusing "to accept tamely an inferior status and abdicate their humanity" was to intimate that African Americans did not. To assert that the "dominant characteristic [of African Caribbeaners] was that of . . . breaking the bonds that would fetter the feet of a virile people" was to insinuate that African American could not do this for themselves.

Granted, the objective of "Gift" was to highlight for readers of *The New Negro* the contributions African Caribbeaners were making to black American culture. Indeed, it is not insignificant that Locke, in his effort to redefine the image of the black for the twentieth century, chose to include not simply the essay by Domingo but also additional pieces by Puerto Rican Arthur Schomburg, British Guianan Eric Walrond, and Jamaican Claude McKay, suggesting that in Locke's mind, at least, foreign-born blacks were vital elements in the development of the "New Negro" as a cultural force. But the very different goals of the *Opportunity* edition, combined with the inflammatory rhetoric of "Gift," make it clear why Domingo's contribution to the special issue could not echo his earlier work.

Although Domingo's informative but more benign article in the *Opportunity* set an optimistic tone by ending on a note of resigned if not hopeful conciliation for African Caribbeaners and African Americans, the piece that concluded the special issue suggested that relations between the two groups still had a long way to go. The final word on the topic, contained in a "Symposium" on "West Indian-American Relations," consisted of a dialogue between Jamaican immigrant Ethelred Brown, a prominent religious leader in Harlem, and African American Eugene Kinckle Jones, executive secretary of the National Urban League. Brown began by attributing "responsibility for the unsatisfactory relations of the past . . . in almost equal measure" to "both parties in the conflict," but closed with the assertion that the prospect of eradicating these tensions rested firmly on the shoulders of African Americans: "If the Americans will but remove the last lingering remains of misunderstanding, suspicion and jealousy, forget as much as possible the accident of geographical origin, and show more of the spirit of the kindly host, I am strongly of the opinion that in a few years the relations . . . will have become . . . genuinely cordial and . . . mutually helpful." Jones's response was less imputative but no more promising in its vision of the potential for collaboration over important political, social, and cultural issues: indeed, he cited the cooperation of the two groups only in a recreational realm—in the development of the American Tennis Association—as providing "the best example of the possibility" of "good fellowship" between African Americans and African Caribbeaners. Placing perhaps too much faith in mere symbols of conciliation rather than suggesting actual tools for healing, he expressed his firm belief that the special issue itself would be "most effective in cementing the good will between Negroes of whatever place of birth" ("Caribbean Issue," 356). A full decade after the publication of the special issue, however, the National Negro Congress felt obligated to "go on record as condemning any form of discrimination practiced against foreign-born Negroes in the United States, . . . as opposing any attempt at deporting . . . or dropping them from relief; . . . as seeking to bring about a better relationship between the foreign-born and native Negroes; . . . [and] as supporting foreign-born Negroes in their struggle for economic and political freedom in their respective homes."[38] Clearly, the tensions of the previous years had not fully abated.

The "essential friendship" the special issue was intended to foster was indeed difficult to forge during the "first wave" of Caribbean immigration to the United States. Due to an overriding racial essentialism that pervaded both popular and institutional cultures during the period, African Americans and African Caribbeaners were uniformly lumped together in housing, employment, economic, and sociocultural arenas. But significant differences, stemming largely from disparate national origins, caused friction between the two communities. These differences both became more pronounced and acquired value connotations within the closed geographic and social space that the groups were forced to share, leading each to define itself in binary opposition to the other.

But by definition, binaries are not inherently oppositional, and it would be historically inaccurate to present the two communities investigated here as always standing in antagonistic relation to one another. As subsequent newcomers have arrived on U.S. shores, the relations between African Americans and African Caribbeaners have developed, shifted, and at times improved, possibly proving true the *Opportunity* staff's conviction that familiarity breeds friendship. Contemporary African Caribbean immigrants, for example, exhibit a range of responses to the American racial system. Some identify themselves most prominently as Americans; others continue to see themselves as ethnic Americans in a way that, like members of the first wave, establishes a distance between themselves and African Americans; still others conceive of themselves first and foremost as immigrants in a way that does not engage American racial and ethnic categories at all.[39] Similarly, changes in the political dynamics of blacks and whites have also affected the relationship between African Americans and African Caribbeaners, illustrating that, as Paul Gilroy has noted, "homogeneity can signify unity but unity need not require homogeneity."[40] When a twenty-year-old Trinidadian man was murdered by a mob of white teenagers in the Howard Beach section of Queens in 1986, African Americans and African Caribbeaners rallied together to challenge systems of racism and oppression. Jesse Jackson's 1988 presidential bid provided another occasion for intraracial unity as blacks of a variety of ethnic and national backgrounds joined other members of the Rainbow Coalition to place the concerns of people of color in the national political spotlight.[41] More recently, second-generation Jamaican Colin Powell was supported by native-born and immigrant blacks alike as capable of "representing" not merely "the race" but the nation as a whole as a leading prospect for the 1994 presidential election. Clearly, African American and African Caribbean cultures, like all cultures, modified and will continue to modify one another, particularly in the hybridizing space of the city in which the two communities are still concentrated. With each new wave of immigration, the dramas of association and dissociation that began during the first stage of contact will continue to shape and be shaped by the complexities of racial, ethnic, and national identity formation in the United States. The one constant of which we can be certain, however, is that "black foreigners," and African Caribbeaners in particular, will continue, as Domingo first stated in 1925, to remain "considerable factor[s] and figure[s]" in the changing nature of the American social fabric.

Notes

I would like to thank my colleagues and friends Timothy Powell, Nigel Rothfels, Anthony Peressini, and Werner Sollors for their insightful comments on and assistance with this essay.

Note on terminology: The term "West Indies" derives from the name applied to the Caribbean region upon colonization by the Spanish. Because of the colonialist connotations of "West Indian," Caribbeaners in New York prefer to be designated by the term "Caribbean." I use the term "African Caribbeaner" to refer to black immigrants from the region, "African American" to refer to blacks born in the United States, and the term "black Americans" to refer the entire black population, foreign- and native-born, residing in the United States.

1. Charles S. Johnson was an African American sociologist who played a pivotal role in the Harlem Renaissance through his position as the Urban League's national director of research and investigations and editor of the *Opportunity*. Johnson, "A Caribbean Issue," *Opportunity: A Journal of Negro Life* 4 (1926): 334. All subsequent references will be cited parenthetically as "Caribbean Issue" in the text.
2. Homi K. Bhabha, "Dissemination: Time, Narrative, and the Margins of the Modern Nation," in *The Location of Culture* (New York: Routledge, 1994), 148.
3. For more information on the three "waves" of Caribbean immigration see Philip Kasinitz, *Caribbean New York: Black Immigrants and the Politics of Race* (Ithaca, N.Y.: Cornell University Press, 1992), 23–32.
4. Ibid., 24. First-generation immigrants are those who actually migrate from a home to a host country; second-generation refers to the children of these immigrants who are born in the host country.

5. Ira De A. Reid, *The Negro Immigrant: His Background, Characteristics and Social Adjustment, 1899–1937* (1939; New York: Arno and the New York Times, 1969), 31–32.

6. Kasinitz, *Caribbean New York,* 24–25. Large groups of black immigrants were also concentrated in Massachusetts and Florida.

7. Irma Watkins-Owens, *Blood Relations: Caribbean Immigrants and the Harlem Community, 1900–1930* (Bloomington: Indiana University Press, 1996), 13.

8. Author Paule Marshall, a second-generation Barbadian whose parents migrated to Brooklyn during this period, describes well the cultural significance of "Panama money": "This was the name given to the remittances sent home by fathers and sons who had gone off to work building the Panama Canal. My Mother, for example, came to the 'States' on money inherited from an older brother who had died working on the Isthmus. 'Panama Money'—it was always spoken of with great reverence when I was a little girl." Marshall, "Black Immigrant Women in *Brown Girl, Brownstones,*" in *Female Immigrants to the United States: Caribbean, Latin American and African Experiences,* ed. Delores M. Mortimer and Roy S. Bryce-Laporte (Washington, D.C.: Smithsonian Institution, 1981), 5.

9. Dawn Marshall, "A History of West Indian Migrations: Overseas Opportunities and 'Safety-Valve' Policies," in *The Caribbean Exodus,* ed. Barry B. Levine (New York: Praeger, 1987), 15–31. British Guianan immigrant Eric Walrond also wrote an extensive although as yet unpublished manuscript on the building of the Panama Canal, and depicted aspects of this issue in his novel *Tropic Death* (1926), which, incidentally, is reviewed by Waldo Frank in the special issue of *Opportunity.*

10. Watkins-Owens, *Blood Relations,* 14.

11. Reid, *The Negro Immigrant,* 68.

12. Ibid., 69–70; quoted from original article by Harvey T. Patterson, "American Democracy in the Canal Zone," *The Crisis* 20, no. 2 (June 1920):83–85.

13. Peter Linebaugh, "All the Atlantic Mountains Shook," *Labour/Le Travailleur* 10 (autumn 1982): 87–121; cited by Paul Gilroy, *The Black Atlantic: Modernity and Double Consciousness* (Cambridge, Mass.: Harvard University Press, 1993), 13.

14. Watkins-Owens, *Blood Relations,* 18.

15. For further information see Joe Trotter, *The Great Migration in Historical Perspective: New Dimensions in Race, Class, and Gender* (Bloomington: Indiana University Press, 1988); Carole Marks, *Farewell—We're Good and Gone: The Great Black Migration* (Bloomington: Indiana University Press, 1989).

16. W. A. Domingo, "The Gift of the Black Tropics," in *The New Negro,* ed. Alain Locke (1925; New York: Atheneum, 1992), 341.

17. Reid, *The Negro Immigrant,* 84.

18. Shirley Chisholm, *Unbought and Unbossed* (New York: Houghton Mifflin, 1970), 8.

19. Reid, *The Negro Immigrant,* 83.

20. Ibid., 244.

21. For a more detailed discussion of West Indian entrepreneurial practices see Aubrey W. Bonnett, "Structured Adaptation of Black Migrants from the Caribbean: An Examination of an Indigenous Banking System in Brooklyn," *Phylon* 42, no.4: 346–355; for a discussion of the absence of these systems in the African American community, see Ivan H. Light, *Ethnic Enterprise in America: Business and Welfare among Chinese, Japanese, and Blacks* (Berkeley: University of California Press, 1972), 19–44.

22. For a thorough discussion of Caribbean political involvement in Harlem see Watkins-Owens, *Blood Relations,* 75–111. She also provides an important analysis of the ways in which Garvey's presence served to heighten ethnic consciousness

in Harlem (Watkins-Owens, *Blood Relations*, 112–126). For a complementary study of the political radicalism of more recent immigrants see Kasinitz, *Caribbean New York.*

23. *New York News*, 28 August 1926 as quoted by Watkins-Owens, *Blood Relations*, 94.

24. Most basically, the "Talented Tenth" was the phrase Du Bois used to refer to the top ten percent of the race who were, he felt, most equipped by virtue of education and background to lead their peers into the twentieth century. See Du Bois, "Of the Training of Black Men," chap. 6 in *The Souls of Black Folk* (1903); Claude McKay, *Harlem: Negro Metropolis* (New York: Dutton, 1940), 132.

25. George Devereux, "Ethnic Identity: Its Logical Foundations and its Dysfunctions" in *Theories of Ethnicity: A Classical Reader*, ed. Werner Sollors (New York: New York University Press, 1996), 397.

26. Reid, *The Negro Immigrant*, 108. This comment, of course, reflects another equally dangerous stereotype: the widespread Western preoccupation with and fear of the figure of the Jew as merchant and lender combined with African Caribbeaner entrepreneurial success to cause the latter to be labeled "black Jews."

27. Ibid., 107. See also Barbara Christian, "Black, Female, and Foreign-born: A Statement," in *Female Immigrants*, ed. Mortimer and Bryce-Laporte, 175.

28. For the full catalogue of stereotypes discussed here see Reid, *The Negro Immigrant*, 107–108.

29. P. Marshall, "Black Immigrant Women in *Brown Girl, Brownstones*, 8.

30. Mary C. Waters notes the persistence of many of these stereotypes among members of the current second generation in "Ethnic and Racial Identities of Second-Generation Black Immigrants in New York City," in *The New Second Generation*, ed. Alejandro Portes (New York: Russell Sage Foundation, 1996), 173.

31. Jervis Anderson, *This Was Harlem: A Cultural Portrait, 1900–1950* (New York: Farrar Straus Giroux, 1982), 303. For a fictional depiction of this, as well as other patterns of immigrant adaptation to the United States, see Paule Marshall, *Brown Girl, Brownstones* (1959; Old Westbury, N.Y.: Feminist Press, 1981).

32. In addition to those articles discussed at length in this essay, the contents of the "Special Caribbean Issue" included pieces by Lucius J. Malmin, judge of the District Court of the U.S. Virgin Islands, and Caspar Holstein, St. Croix native and Harlem businessman, which critiqued the United States purchase of and presence in the Virgin Islands in 1917 but did not address substantively the role of Virgin Islanders in New York. A. M. Wendell Malliet, editor of the *West Indian Statesman*, provided a survey of "Some Prominent West Indians" in England, the Caribbean, and the United States, and Arthur A. Schomburg, founder of the central archive on black studies in this country, the Schomburg Center for Research in Black Culture, allowed the publication of excerpts on "West Indian Composers and Musicians" from an album he had been compiling of historical sketches and essays. Waldo Frank reviewed British Guianan (and *Opportunity* business manager) Eric Walrond's novel, *Tropic Death*, and Claude McKay contributed three poems ("Desolate," "My House," and "America in Retrospect"). The *Opportunity* also continued its regular features on the arts ("The Ebony Flute"); the "Survey of the Month," which described recent events and people of importance in the black community; an editorial section ranging from a discussion of the cotton market to the rise in lynchings; and "Our Book Shelf." Although the texts reviewed in "Our Book Shelf" were all international in focus, none of the regularly featured sections was overtly devoted to Caribbean American concerns.

33. Domingo, "Gift of the Black Tropics," 341–42.

34. Werner Sollors, "Ethnicity," in *Critical Terms for Literary Study*, ed. Frank

Lentricchia and Thomas McLaughlin (Chicago: University of Chicago Press, 1990), 288.

35. Domingo, "Gift of the Black Tropics," 345.
36. Ibid., 347.
37. Ibid., 349.
38. Reid, *The Negro Immigrant*, 108–109.
39. Waters, "Ethnic and Racial Identities," 178.
40. Paul Gilroy, *Small Acts: Thoughts on the Politics of Black Cultures* (New York: Serpent's Tail, 1993), 2.
41. Kasinitz, *Caribbean New York*, 247–248.

Narratives of Deviance and Delight: Staring at Julia Pastrana, the "Extraordinary Lady"

Chapter 4

ROSEMARIE GARLAND THOMSON

To go beyond the binary categories that currently inform the way we imagine social formations such as race and gender, we need to focus on the tensions and complications within those seemingly discrete divisions that structure identity. While structuralism naturalized the binary systems that we use to interpret the material world, poststructuralism challenged binarism's claims by providing the theoretical rationale with which to accomplish such conceptual moves as positing third terms and interrogating boundaries, as well as identifying gaps and fissures. Nevertheless, I think we are often unsure how such abstractions are manifest in the actual social relations that cultural and literary texts refer to and shape. In our efforts to respect the social goals of such politicized forms of criticism as multiculturalism, feminism, and identity-based studies, we confront the problem of how both to claim and to interrogate the very identities upon which racial, gender, and ethnic categories depend. We often falter between the seemingly contradictory impulses to apply poststructuralism's critique of identity and to affirm identity for the purposes of recognizing diversity and challenging the notion of the universal subject.[1] In other words, we need to question the assumption that identity categories such as race and gender are self-evident, mutually informing binary systems which definitively distinguish male from female, black from white, while at the same time being careful not to dissolve these very categories that form the basis for political communities and undergird personal identity.

My own work, for example, examines how social relations construct the bodily differences we call "disability." I argue that disability is a representational system rather than a natural state of bodily inferiority. Disability, I assert, is a culturally fabricated narrative of the body, similar to the fictions of race and gender. By viewing disability as a comparison of bodies that legitimates the distribution of resources, status, and power within a biased cultural and architectural environment, I aim to reconceive disability as a minority discourse rather than a medical one. Nevertheless, I simultaneously want to claim that "disabled" is a valid social identity, a source of community, and a foundation for political praxis. In short, my challenge is to affirm disability as a politicized identity without reinscribing or naturalizing the category.[2] My goal is to contest entrenched assumptions that disability is a property of inherently flawed bodies or personal pathology and to resituate it within the template of identity politics. Yet, the more I theorize the social identity of disability, of course, the more elusive and insubstantial the category itself becomes. Disability is a fiction both oppressive and useful. Recognizing the ambiguities of disability as a category of analysis and identity has led me to probe the discursive and material practices that traffic in binary categories such as disabled and nondisabled, normal and abnormal, or self and other.

I am most interested in investigating social practices that expose the complexities, resistances, and histories of the representational systems that govern our understanding of the material world. Analyzing social practices, as Michel Foucault's work suggests, can reveal what we make of human variation, of the bodily differences to which we tether identity, community, and subjectivity. Such institutionalized, received systems as race, gender, and disability structure human variation into binary identities that are both policed and hardened by a matrix of social practices that tend to reduce the complexities of embodiment and its interpretations. Nevertheless, some of the social practices that produce subject positions from the raw material of human differences yield a great deal of complexity under scrutiny. One such practice, I will contend here, is the particular social ritual that I call staring.

Staring is a highly structured genre of social relations that produces the narrative of human bodily variation we now call "physical disability" or "congenital deformity," although the vocabulary used to describe these physical variations changes over time.[3] The cultural work of staring is to normalize the viewer by abnormalizing—indeed, spectacularizing—the body on view, fixing it in a position of difference. Yet, even as staring attempts to enforce difference, an analysis of its dynamics suggests how seemingly firm identity categories inflect and intrude upon one another. Indeed, what sustains staring are the very entanglements and contradictions of the identities it works at creating.

The particular manifestation of staring I analyze here is the exhibition of Julia Pastrana, whose display for profit and entertainment followed the conventions of popular nineteenth-century American freak shows. Rather than focusing on the body that staring foregrounds, I instead will explore the matrix of spatial, visual, and textual rhetorics that compose the narratives of the body that staring produces. Because displays such as Pastrana's were such intensely mediated, conventionalized, and exaggerated forms of staring, they serve as especially vivid instances from which I can coax the complex and often contradictory narratives of bodily difference that staring generates. My aim here is twofold: first, to excavate the ways that Pastrana's display at once enforces and challenges the lines between the self and the other, the human and the nonhuman, the ordinary and the extraordinary that such spectacles rely upon; and, second, to suggest how discursive systems such as race, gender, humanness, and normativity intertwine in the social practices that constitute them. What this examination ultimately reveals is that practices such as staring, which are designed to create otherness, always complicate and often supersede the binaries upon which they are founded.

The History of Julia Pastrana

On 1 December 1854, Julia Pastrana, a hirsute Mexican Indian woman, was exhibited in New York's Gothic Hall on Broadway, where she was billed as a "Marvelous Hybrid or Bear Woman." The theater chronicler George C. D. O'Dell found the display of this "semi-human being" a "delight," noting in his journal that she was "somewhat between an human being and an ourang-outang." O'Dell's description of Pastrana captures the essence of most all explications of her extraordinary body: "The eyes of this lusus natura [sic] beam with intelligence, while its jaws, jagged fangs and ears are terrifically hideous. . . . Nearly its whole frame is coated with long glossy hair. Its voice is harmonious, for this semi-human being is perfectly docile, and speaks the Spanish language."[4] O'Dell interprets Pastrana's body as a contradiction, a *lusus naturae* or joke of nature, designed by a fanciful and omnipotent God to delight and discomfort those who imagine themselves as unambiguously human by confounding their understanding of the natural world. O'Dell, like Pastrana's other spectators, viewed her as incongruity incarnate, as simultaneously "intelligen[t]" and "hideous," as "docile" while speaking Spanish through "jagged fangs." She seemed, in short, at once recognizably human and utterly alien. Pastrana's numerous stage sobriquets in her wide exhibition throughout the United States and abroad suggest the discordant readings her body prompted. She was billed variously as a "Nondescript," "Misnomer," "Bear Woman," "Baboon Lady," "Ape Woman," "Hybrid Indian," "Extraordinary Lady," and "The Ugliest Woman in the World." Naturalists, scientists, aristocrats, stage fans, and ordinary people flocked to see her and paid to make her famous. What emerges most clearly from even a brief review of Pastrana's

Image of the embalmed body of Julia Pastrana emphasizes the feminine through dress and removal of upper eye teeth and incisors. She died in Moscow in 1860 after giving birth to a child. Both bodies were preserved and exhibited. *Photo Anthropolocital Institute, London.*

history is the compelling interpretive occasion her body provided to her enthralled fellow human beings.

The facts of Pastrana's short life are few, but the narratives of her excep-
tionality are sundry and highly elaborated. She appears to have been born in
1834 and belonged to a so-called Root Digger Indian tribe in the Sierra Madre
Mountain region of Mexico. Her entire body was covered with thick, black
hair and her dentition was unusually prominent. As a young woman, she apparently left the mountains to serve in the household of the governor of the
state of Sinaloa, perhaps as a curiosity. Like many people whose bodies were
atypical, she was recruited by one of the eager entrepreneurs who trafficked
in unusual bodies for the burgeoning market in what the nineteenth century
called "freaks."

By 1854, Pastrana had been appropriated as a profit-making exhibition
and was being proclaimed as one of the greatest marvels to be seen on stage.
She went on tour in New York, Boston, and Baltimore and made her debut
in London in July 1857 as "the Wonder of the World." Like all people whose
bodies were commodified for these exhibitions, Pastrana was overseen by a
manager who closely regulated her social interactions, controlled the considerable profits, and, in this case, apparently married her as well. Her manager/
husband, Theodore Lent, displayed her throughout Europe in performances where
she sang, danced, submitted to examinations, and appeared at staged social
functions.

In 1860, while in Moscow, Pastrana died shortly after childbirth, during
which she delivered a son who inherited her hirsuteness, but who died shortly
after birth. Lent apparently sold both bodies to Professor Sokolov of Moscow
University's Anatomical Institute, who embalmed them. The process was so
successful that Lent repurchased both bodies and continued to exhibit them.
By February 1862, Pastrana's body, along with her baby's, now billed as "the
Embalmed Female Nondescript," were being viewed again in London, often
by those who had seen her live performance only a few years earlier. Pastrana's
singular body, augmented now with her son's, continued to circulate on public exhibition in various museums (such as the Prater in Vienna), in circuses,
before royal families, and in amusement parks for well over one hundred years.
In 1972, Pastrana's body toured the United States with a traveling amusement
park called the Million Dollar Midways. Because public and religious objec-
tions have now rendered Pastrana's display an embarrassment, her embalmed
corpse has been retired to the basement of the Institute of Forensic Medicine
in Oslo, where it is studied by medical experts whose careers benefit from the
exhibition of Julia Pastrana's extraordinary body.

Freak Shows in Victorian America

Julia Pastrana's exhibition was an early manifestation of the prolific freak shows that in the second half of the nineteenth and the early part of the twentieth centuries capitalized upon and institutionalized the ancient practice of displaying monsters and prodigies as forms of religious augury. The prodigious body—whether the fanciful hybrids of myth, such as centaurs, satyrs, or minotaurs, or the congenitally deformed newborns who were imagined as tokens from the gods—has obsessed humankind since antiquity. As the narrative of the natural world shifted from one of divine determination to secular explanations, early science viewed exceptional bodies as indices to the order of things and as sources upon which to hone medical expertise. Early scientists and philosophers kept cabinets of curiosities full of items like shark's teeth, shrunken heads, and bottled fetuses that they regarded with a mixture of awe and mastery. Irregular bodies continued to be interpreted as exegeses of the divine and natural orders by figures as respected as Cotton Mather and John Winthrop well into the eighteenth century. At the same time, these extraordinary bodies were commercialized at public fairs and on streets by monster mongers who charged for viewings, and they were narrativized in monster ballads that offered morals drawn from the wondrous bodies.[5]

In Victorian America, the variegated but united discourse of the freak show interwove a number of now-discrete disciplines and specialized practices, such as ethnography, anthropology, museum culture, anatomy, embryology, taxidermy, circuses, musical reviews, and educational lectures. Nonetheless, these disciplines can be sorted into two broad, competing, yet intertwined cultural discourses that controlled the extraordinary body and would eventually become distinct. They were entertainment—a popular, commercialized discourse—and science—the more elite, authoritative narrative of such bodies. The entertainment discourse trafficked mainly in the rhetoric of the marvelous and wondrous, while science enlisted the logic of rationality, mastery, authority, and pathology. By 1841, P. T. Barnum's early entertainment industry had institutionalized the once-itinerant practice of showing monsters in inns and on streets into his American Museum, which aspired to middle-class status with temperance tracts, appeals to education, entrepreneurship, and other gestures toward bourgeois respectability. By 1832, science, too, had institutionalized its preoccupation with monsters by formulating teratology, the study of monsters. Teratology endeavored to harness the ancient power of the prodigious by creating pigs with cleft palates and elaborate taxonomies of physical deviation. The meanings imposed upon the unsettling bodies of freaks were articulated through many of the emerging discourses fundamental to nineteenth-century culture: not only science and entertainment, but pathology, sentimentality, anthropology, gender, and beauty became templates that attempted to order these startling bodies. The showman, the entrepreneur, the curator, the professor of science, the impresario, the writer, the teratologist, the prestigious, the most ordinary of citizens, and even Queen Victoria, responded with wonder and delight in the communal articulation of embodied identity that was the freak show.[6]

The immensely popular displays of freak figures such as Julia Pastrana were an aspect of a larger culture of exhibition that developed as a part of nineteenth-century America's concern with appearances. The secularizing, mobile, rapidly changing social order, dominated increasingly by market economics, individualism, and a developing mass culture engendered both a trust in and an anxiety about how things looked. With the stable indices of a fixed social hierarchy eradicated by democracy, the shifting social and economic ranking promised by an egalitarian order demanded some sort of display, even within an ever more subtle and inconstant system of signs. Consequently, looking for an ever-changing meaning, status, and truth in external appearances became a challenge and an obsession. Americans were enthralled with looking: museums, circuses, grand expositions, photographs, freak shows, parades, theater, and department store displays flourished as early glimmerings of what Guy Debord would later call the society of the spectacle in advanced capitalism.[7] The *flâneur*, a peripatetic consumer of ceaseless images, became a figure in American life.[8] Since traditional structures such as kinship, titles, geography, guilds, official costuming, and other denotative particularizations no longer clearly marked one's position in society, the body became a major referent of social identity. As commodities came to index the equality and happiness that Enlightenment conceptions of both self and nation bestowed and authorized, the body itself became a commodity.[9] Fashion, manners, and appearances became the variable registers of position and identity as the newly decontextualized body took on the burden of signification left by the demise of a formally and rigidly classed society. This insecurity of signs fueled the nineteenth century's fascination with the exhibition of freaks, with recognizing the self in and against displays of bodies whose particularities were embellished through hyperbolic, sensationalized performance.

The Dynamics of Staring

My contention is that Pastrana's exhibition imposed upon her body the cultural meanings her historical moment required. America's preoccupation with appearances and anxieties about identity in the unstable sign system that was modernity partly fueled the public interest in displays of extraordinary bodies. This ritualized form of staring explored the somatic boundaries of what counted as human and as ordinary at a time when new rights, demands, and privileges were imagined as due to that category of person. At the time Pastrana was being displayed, the terms of citizenship for newly democratized nations were taking shape and being contested: the franchise and the rights it represented had been expanded in Jacksonian America; slavery forced a consideration of what constituted the human; and the woman's suffrage movement began pressing for a more universal conception of the citizen. In such an historical context, the stakes of what was included and excluded in the human category were high and under debate. Popular displays such as Pastrana's were both a manifestation of and an occasion for this debate. The spectacle of Julia Pastrana compelled her audiences by enacting a complex iconography of self and other that at once installed and sabotaged the borders of human identity.

Staring is structured seeing. It enacts a cultural choreography between a disembodied spectator and an embodied spectacle that attempts to verify norms and establish differences. Staring is a mediation between viewer and viewed that exaggerates particularity by turning the visible body into a series of theatrical props, gestures, or poses imbued with hyperbolic significance. For instance, the conventions of staring literally spotlighted differences and incongruities such as Pastrana's "jagged fangs," the "hideous" yet "intelligent" face, the "long glossy hair" covering the body, the "harmonious" voice.[10] Moreover, the display was always sensationalized and exaggerated by jarring contrasts and perplexing contradictions: Pastrana's hirsute face was set off with feminizing hair ribbons; her singing emphasized the distorted dentition; this apparent lady was covered with thick, black hair.

Staring thus produces narratives of the body such as the deviant, the delightful, the marvelous, the primitive, the exotic, the alarming, or the pathetic. As a kind of cultural didacticism where an array of scripts, roles, and positions can be writ large, staring struggles to establish a border between the canonical body of the citizen and the iconoclastic body of the freak as stable signifiers of identity and cultural legitimacy. Staring at Pastrana rendered her singular body into territory at once foreign and familiar, offering viewers an arena of self-contemplation for the price of a ticket.

Although Pastrana's presentation magnified contradiction and confused categories, the choreography of staring that structured the relationship between Pastrana and her viewers was rigidly prescribed and monitored. For example, the mediating "printed history" that accompanied Pastrana's exhibition explicitly instructs her viewers about their appropriate roles, entitlements, and expectations in the dynamic. The spatial conventions that controlled the visual dynamic between spectator and object of speculation created the nonreciprocal relationship of the stare. The visual nature of the stare, mediated by the conventional show language, enforces distance, precluding the more intimate exchange of touch or dialogue. Pastrana was on a stage or in some other highly controlled setting whenever audiences saw her.[11] Staring grants all perspective and agency in the relationship to the starer, who sees, moves, defines, judges, names, responds, and desires. The pamphlet accompanying Pastrana's exhibition directs the staring relationship by setting up a rhetorical "we" that fuses showman, audience, and prospective viewers into a single normative perspective that looks, advances, experiences, and testifies:

> Language fails us, when we attempt to depict the mingled sensations that filled our minds, at *even a first sight* of Miss Julia Pastrana. A *closer inspection* struck us with awe; a *lengthened interview* created astonishment unbounded; and a *minute examination*, compared with the printed history of her in our hands, which we purchased there, including an intense attention to her various entertaining performances (referred to in the above advertisement), so inspired us with amazement and delight, that, "*Strangely-formed Being!*"—"*Singular-looking Creature!*"—"*Wonderful Curiosity of Nature!*" and other ejaculations manifesting the excitement we were under, involuntarily escaped from our lips, and which were no sooner overheard by the spectators nearest to us, but they were caught up and responded to in a similar strain by every lady and gentleman present; so extraordinary and fearfully wonderfully they deemed the "Nondescript," that their eyes feasted upon.[12]

This narrative choreographs the participants so that Pastrana is the passive object upon whom the viewer advances from "first sight," to a "closer inspection," to a "lengthened interview," and finally to a "minute examination." With each move closer, the starer responds with increasing intensity, from "sensation," to "astonishment," to "amazement," "delight," and "excitement." Here is the rhetoric of wonder, designed to evoke what Stephen Greenblatt has called "exalted attention." [13] While this trajectory is one of arousal and fulfillment, designed primarily to get viewers' money, it is also one of license, in which the viewer is not only satisfied but empowered as an epistemological authority. The exhibition is an occasion for the onlooker to "feast" upon privileged knowledge. Thus the hyperbolic show language enlists a no doubt profitable synesthesia in which the eye that looks becomes the mouth that "feast[s]." The spectacle of Pastrana, the "Nondescript," becomes here a visual form of cannibalism in which the ordinary spectator consumes the ancient, wondrous power of the extraordinary body. In doing so, the spectator becomes—by contrast to the spectacle—a comfortingly normal, nonparticularized subject of modernity.

Pastrana's body functioned as a text intended to unsettle the onlookers' world view even as they tried to find a reassuring coherence about the order of things, their place in that order, and what human identity might be. Grasping the truths embedded in appearances was the compelling challenge that such displays offered onlookers, driving them in huge numbers to the exhibitions.[14] By describing Pastrana as a "Nondescript," a species neither previously nor easily classified in natural history, and a "Misnomered," the promotional material suggested that she was a category dilemma.[15] Applied to many other freaks as well, the term "Nondescript" lifted Pastrana out of the coherent empiricist scheme that cataloged and ranked living things and flung her into a tantalizing realm of ambiguity where onlookers could either anxiously or sanguinely hone their personal authority as interpreters of the material world. The scientific taxonomies she eluded depended upon empirical observation and predictable reoccurrence that the staring dynamic set up by the freak exhibition replicated and parodied, investing the spectator with the authority of the observer. Indeed, the fundamental dynamic of Pastrana's display was to expose her body as the object of observation and interpretation while eclipsing the observer who has the power to define.[16] By framing her as "Nondescript" and "Misnomered" within some natural order, her publicists invited viewers to define her in relation to themselves and to appropriate her to verify their imagined arrangement of the world and their place within it.

The ultimate aim of this nineteenth-century obsession with classification was to justify a political, economic, and moral hierarchy anchored to the supposed truth of the body. This hierarchy posited the figure of a certain type of Anglo male as superior to all living things and the legitimate heir to power and privilege. Such an ontological blueprint of status depended upon establishing discrete categories authenticated by the material differences we call species, race, and gender. Pastrana's body confused in several ways a number of the orthodox categories of being upon which the social structure was hung. Driven by profit, her exhibitors employed conventions of staring to heighten this confusion. Visual, spatial, and linguistic rhetorics sharpened the ways her body seemed to upset established taxonomies, at once casting the whole system into doubt and demanding explanations that could restore its legitimacy. Pastrana's body and its presentation troubled several oppositions fundamental to the accepted social order, thereby challenging its coherence, refuting its logic, sparking debate, firing anxiety—and all the while making Pastrana's handlers rich and Pastrana herself famous.

The conventions of the stare, I want to suggest now, recruited Pastrana's body in order to question five foundational cultural oppositions that structured the nineteenth-century social order. They are the interrelated oppositions between human/animal, civilized/primitive, normal/pathological, male/female, and self/other.

The Human/Animal Opposition

First, the exhibit of Pastrana's body queried the traditional ontological border that divided the human and the animal into mutually exclusive categories. Narratives from Genesis to the Great Chain of Being to Darwin had long sought to establish a natural order that elevated "man" above animals and differentiated them absolutely. The dominion Genesis promised to "man" over what he imagined to be the world required a distinct and hierarchical relation between man and beast. The idea of the natural rights of man that animated American democracy hinged upon who might be included in the definition of a citizen. Democracy's suggestion that simple humanity might be the criterion for citizenship threatened the established order by implying power sharing among all humans. Consequently, much nineteenth-century science devoted itself to policing the category of the human by questioning the full humanity of women and people of color in order to justify exclusionary practices such as slavery and limited enfranchisement that persisted in a supposedly egalitarian order.[17] Debate raged as abolitionists, suffragists, and Christian reformers equated the human and the citizen in their arguments for expanded political rights.

Pastrana's exhibition capitalized on this broadly and anxiously contested relation between the human and the citizen by presenting her as a "Hybrid Indian," a creature part human and part beast. Such show sobriquets as "Bear Woman," "Baboon Lady," and "Ape Woman" enlist her hirsute body in a fantasy of species fusion that harkens back to early interpretations of prodigious bodies.[18] One of the souvenir pamphlets accompanying her show, for example, describes her as having "the face of a Baboon—the body and limbs of a Woman—the skin of a Bear, and other strange formations."[19] This reading of Pastrana as a hybrid of animal an human refers to a prescientific belief that explained the unsettling appearance of singular bodies like Pastrana's as the result of unnatural unions between animals and humans. For instance, some of what we now call dermatological disorders produced narratives of fish people; the occasional extremely hirsute person such as Pastrana was taken as the offspring of furry creatures and humans; other unusually formed newborns were imagined as the progeny of pigs—a frequent disguise of the devil—and sinners. Indeed, humankind's sense of being above animals in the natural order was apparently so fragile and a strict boundary between persons and animals so essential to man's sense of a privileged identity that bestiality—which was thought to produce hybrids—became a capital offense in England in 1534.[20] The sensationalized entertainment conventions that directed Pastrana's exhibition appealed to this earlier, vanished era of superstition by exploiting the once popular suspicion that animals and humans could interbreed, kindling in audiences both the anxiety of identity and the wonder of the miraculous. The souvenir book of her "curious history" details, for example, "Her Remarkable Formation, and Mysterious Parentage, and how she was discovered in a cave, suckled by her Indian Mother, DWELLING ONLY WITH BABOONS, BEARS, AND MONKEYS." This titillating narrative suggests bestiality between the "Indian Mother" and the animals at the same time that it recruits the excitement and awe of the enigmatic. Narrating Pastrana's anomalous body as a "world's wonder" and a "nondescript," turned her into a mysterious marvel that would delight, amaze, and instruct. With this strategy, exhibitors could seduce viewers by assuaging potential anxieties about identity that hybridity might evoke and at the same time appealing to the viewers' authority to solve the mystery of her classification for themselves.[21]

Pastrana's exhibition appealed simultaneously to the ancient traditions of the wondrous and to the newest narratives of science. In addition to summoning the image of the hybrid marvel, extremely pronounced dentition and the black, coarse hair that covered her entire body were used to invoke the emerging scientific discourse of evolution by seemingly validating a troubling cousinship between humans and apes. Pastrana's whole tribe ostensibly closely resembled bears and orangutans. One doctor who supposedly examined Pastrana gestures toward crude evolutionary thought by testifying, for example, that "from her uncouth gait . . . it may be conjectured that the mysterious animal moves as if an elongation of the spinal column should have taken place, producing a tail, which in consequence of humanity predominating, has been denied."[22] Hybridity in this account, then, has produced a monster who is abnormal rather than marvelous, one with an "uncouth gait" who is arrested in evolutionary progress between the beast and the human.

Although I could find no extant advertising actually using the term in reference to her, Pastrana is an early prototype of the abundant "missing link" figures, popularizations of Darwinian thought that flourished in exhibits throughout the century.[23] Under the banner of popular entertainment, the rhetoric of the marvelous, and the authority of the evolutionary, then, the pressing question of who was human enough to be granted the natural rights democracy promised could be posed. And the answer was implicit in the presentation: entertaining and compelling as she might be, the "hybrid" figure before the viewers confirmed by contrast and with the testimony of her "semi-human" body their status as fully human and therefore legitimate citizens. The audience must have gone away satisfied.

The Civilized/Primitive Opposition

Besides querying the border between the animal and the human, Pastrana's exhibited body occasions an exploration of the distinction between the civilized and the primitive, an element of racial discourse inflected by science that underpinned the then emergent narrative of self and other we now call anthropology. Because the display of monsters and freaks offended the sensibilities of an increasingly rigid and influential bourgeois respectability, the shows sought legitimacy under the guise of education by invoking the increasingly elite discourses of science and medicine.[24] The narrative pamphlets assure prospective audiences that "she has appeared in all the principle cities and towns, exciting the greatest curiosity, especially among the medical faculty and naturalists."[25] In the nineteenth century, however, ethnography and monster displays had not fully bifurcated into high and low culture as they have today.[26] Medical men and naturalists participated in exhibiting her and wrote about her in their publications and memoirs. The souvenir pamphlets accompanying Pastrana's exhibition recruited men of science to authenticate her and mobilized the language of ethnology to lend authority to the often fraudulent biographies that explained her unusual embodiment.

The pamphlets offered a racist, proto-Darwinian ethnography of Pastrana's "semi-human" tribe, the "Root-Digger Indians" that casts them as primitives whose practices are opposed to those that mark a civilized society. In the authoritative, ostensibly objective language used by nineteenth-century ethnographers, the pamphlets describe her "race" or "tribe" by detailing its supposed diet of "grass-hoppers, snails, and wasps," elaborately prepared by drying, pulverizing, and mixing them with berry pulp before being eaten. Besides subsisting on gathered foods repugnant to the Western imagination, the "male digger never hunts, but usually depends on the exertions of his squaw" to provide food. Such a practice clearly suggests unmanliness and ineptitude according to bourgeois conceptions of male breadwinners. A final testimony to these Indians' uncivilized state is their violation of the middle-class disciplinary codes of labor, thrift, and cleanliness—practices that constitute virtue in the Western self: "They get their food daily, and never lay up anything. They have no cause to labor," readers are assured, and "of all the Aborigines . . . the Digger Indians are certainly the most filthy and abominable." They even eat with their hands while displaying "great relish."[27] Such ethnographic descriptions simultaneously validated the civility of even the most humble or socially insecure viewer by offering an authoritative, contrasting narrative of unequivocal primitivity that served to bond together citizens both high and low in a comforting fantasy of shared culture, equality, and resemblance.

In opposition to but alongside of ethnographic discourse was the embellished language of wonder, designed perhaps to draw in those readers whose repugnance had overcome their curiosity. Maintaining a balance between intriguing and disgusting the bourgeois sensibility was any freak show's rhetorical challenge. Barnum used temperance and family values; all the shows appealed to education and science. If the show were to make its audiences more civilized, it had to be careful not to allow them to develop a crude interest in the barbaric. An appeal to myth, wonder, and—most important—progress mitigated the coarseness of the primitive that the show created. Although the "Digger Indians" in general lived a supposed prelapsarian existence of innocence, nakedness, and plenty that may have romanticized the savages, the Diggers' only purpose was to provide a scenic background for the wondrous emergence of Julia Pastrana herself, the figure audiences paid to see. Pastrana is billed as a marvelous anomaly differentiated from the routine pack of primitives: she is "the Extraordinary Lady just imported from the regions of wonder."[28]

The narrative of the prodigious Pastrana affirms the march toward evolutionary advancement that Westerners were imagined to lead. The Root Diggers from whence Pastrana sprang are barely differentiated in body and manners from animals in the journey toward civilization. Being "endowed with speech, which no monsters have ever possessed," the Root Diggers are "a kind of link between the man and the brute creation." Pastrana, however, appears as the wondrous exemplar of civilization's sway over the primitive. In a doubled confusion of boundaries, one pamphlet claims that Pastrana is herself a hybrid between the semi-brute Diggers and a civilized woman. Having proved "capable of being cultivated and improved," Pastrana differs from her tribesmen physically, intellectually, and culturally because of her exposure to civilization.[29] After a detailed description of her simian body, a pamphlet asserts that she is "good natured, sociable, and accommodating," in contrast to her tribesmen, who are "very spiteful and hard to govern." She "can speak the English and Spanish languages—dance, sing, sew, cook, wash, iron—these latter accomplishments being acquired, of course since her introduction into civilized life, having been recovered from a state of nature when she was very young."[30] Pastrana's introduction to civilization has also made her larger than her tribesmen, and she now "eats the same food as any other person, and speaks the English language."[31] It is her ultraprimitive hirsuteness and dentition juxtaposed with her civilized demeanor that make her singular and wondrous. In this narrative of progress toward a state of civilization, then, Pastrana's exploitation becomes a salvation; her colonization becomes a conversion; and her display becomes a testimony.

The Normal/Pathological Opposition

The authoritative discourse of medicine, an increasingly elite cousin of science, also framed Pastrana's body as a taxonomical enigma. The entertainment rhetoric recruits the authority of medicine, dovetailed with a hint of the marvelous, as in Dr. Alex B. Mott's 1854 "Certificate" of Pastrana's examination: "She is therefore a Hybrid," Mott concludes, "wherein the nature of woman predominates over the brute—the Orang Outang. Altogether she is the most extraordinary being of the day."[32] While the show language tends to blend wonder and science, the medical discourse about Pastrana purges all vestiges of awe. Detailed observations expressed in dispassionate, elite, specialized jargon characterize Pastrana as abnormal. Some of the exhibition pamphlets begin using the language of abnormality. One testimony, for example, from Samuel Kneeland of the Boston Natural History Society pathologizes her "anatomical conformation" and "abnormal growth of hair," apparently vouching for her singularity by concluding that "there is no admixture of Negro blood."[33]

In contrast to show narratives, the medical discourse banishes wonder and sensationalism for a detached and restrained detailing of Pastrana's body. The esteemed British medical journal *The Lancet*, for example, trades the marvelous for the "peculiar" in its delineation of her: "Her face is peculiar: the alae of the nose are remarkably flattened and expanded, and so soft as to seem to be destitute of cartilages; the mouth is large and the lips everted—by an extraordinary thickening of the alveolar border of the upper jaw in front—below, by a warty hard growth arising from the gum."[34] Similarly, the popular *Anomalies and Curiosities of Medicine*, compiled by the distinguished doctors George M. Gould and Walter L. Pyle, presents Pastrana as having "defective dentition" and "pronounced prognathism."[35] Gould and Pyle's book has the format and style of an encyclopedia or textbook, even though a majority of the information and illustrations comes unacknowledged from freak shows. Thus, the entertainment discourse parades its collaboration with medicine in Pastrana's exhibition, whereas the medical discourse suppresses the fact that doctors were actually attending the shows to examine Pastrana. What we see here, then, is the incipient demise of the freak show as the legitimate articulator of the extraordinary body and its replacement by the discourse of medical pathology.

Pathology transforms hybridity into abnormality. It converts the freak to the specimen. Whereas the spectacle of the freak exhibit tries to expand the possibilities of interpretation through sensationalism and exaggeration, the spectacle of the specimen attempts to contain those possibilities through classification and mastery. The remarkable exhibition of Pastrana's body from 1860 through 1993 illustrated this discursive shift from prodigy to pathology more strikingly than did most of her fellow freaks. After her death in 1860, her embalmed body circulated for over one hundred years as either a medical specimen or a side show, depending upon the context of its presentation. As freak shows became increasingly unacceptable to middle-class sensibilities, the

construction of Pastrana as pathological eventually predominated. The narrative of Pastrana as wonder, however, has not been easily subdued.

The most intense pathologizing of Pastrana's body, both discursively and
materially, occurred in 1860, when she and her dead child were embalmed
by Dr. J. Sokolov of Moscow University. His detailed account of that procedure, published in an 1862 issue of *The Lancet*, is a pathology report. The article contains by far the most comprehensive description of Pastrana's body,
including precise measurements and weights of every part of her anatomy, from
her little finger to her "pelvicular diameter."[36] In graphic and repugnant detail, Sokolov narrates the complete process of embalming both mother and
child, exhaustively noting the colors, smells, textures, and extent of the de-
composition against which he raced. In addition, he provides the particulars
of Pastrana's difficult childbirth and the subsequent deaths of both mother and
child, including diagnoses, dates, times, and names of the accoucheurs in at-
tendance. The report includes as well an indignant explanation of how the
American consul and Pastrana's husband/manager legally procured the bodies, which "well deserved a place among the rarities of the [Anatomical
Institute's] museum," affirming that "wherever they may be they have a claim
upon the scientific world."[37] Sokolov's account is essentially an autopsy report that does not invoke a single trace of Pastrana's or her son's humanity.
Both become absolute specimens in this narrative. The only subjectivity that
emerges is his pride of craftsmanship in restoring the semblance of life to dead
flesh. But no matter how objectifying is this discursive frame, it nevertheless
does not reach far enough to contain Pastrana's compelling violation of the
order of things.

After being embalmed, Pastrana—in a Russian dancer's dress and with
her tiny hirsute son on an elevated platform beside her—became a spectacle
once again in tawdry side shows, exhibition halls, traveling circuses, and museums as prestigious as the Prater in Vienna. The famous British naturalist
Francis T. Buckland, who saw her body exhibited at 191 Piccadilly in London, reinvokes a vestige of awe by describing her in a section on human mum-
mies in his 1888 *Curiosities of Natural History*: "The face," he notes admiringly,
"was marvelous." At the same time, his recollection "of seeing and speaking
to this poor Julia Pastrana when in life" restores her semi-humanity, her position midway between the human and the other.[38]

The Male/Female Opposition

Staring at Julia Pastrana captivated audiences by violating more than only the
human/animal, the civilized/primitive, and the normal/pathological boundaries. As if to confound the anxious nineteenth-century preoccupation about

distinctions between men and women that underpinned the ideology of separate spheres, both the entertainment and the scientific discourses highlight gender transgression in their framing of Pastrana's body. For example, a characteristic medical report detailing her body that appears in *The Lancet* depends upon gendered traits as a map with which to make sense of her body. She is described as

> a female whose main peculiarity consists in her possessing hairs nearly all over the body, and more especially on those parts which are ordinarily clothed with hairs in the male sex. . . . She has a large tuft of hair depending from the chin—a *beard*, continuous with smaller growths on the upper lip and cheeks—moustache and whiskers. . . . Indeed, the whole of the body, excepting the palms of the hands and the soles of the feet, is more or less clothed with hairs. In this respect she agrees, in an exaggerated degree, with what is not very uncommonly observed in the male sex.[39]

Pastrana's hirsuteness becomes here not the mark of an ape but the mark of a man. The journal then goes on to juxtapose these signs of the masculine with "other respects" in which Pastrana "agrees with the female. Her breasts are remarkably full and well-developed. She menstruates regularly. . . . The voice is that of a female."[40] The same body that merged the human and animal in one register here confuses the male and female. This gendered reading of her body creates her as a hermaphrodite, an imagined ontological category that populated late-nineteenth- and early-twentieth-century freak shows.[41] Indeed, both the medical and show rhetorics conflate Pastrana's multiple atypical bodily characteristics into a single transgression of gender: she is "a bearded woman."[42] Gender expectations become the template that renders her extraordinary by placing her outside the system.

The entertainment discourse of staring visually narrativized Pastrana's body as a gender trespass as well. In the onstage part of her exhibition (the offstage portion being medical examinations), she performed the theatrics of femininity by dancing the popular Pepita, doing Highland flings, and singing "Mexican songs in a quiet, sad voice like the Creoles."[43] Her costuming included roses, ribbons, elaborate headdresses, and the Russian dancer's dress she wore after she was embalmed. Such hyperbolically feminine attire contrasted with her supposedly masculine face to create the disconcerting, illusory visual fusion of male and female. Francis T. Buckland, who examined her in life and in death, summons the language of gender to interpret Pastrana as a hybrid of the beautiful, elite lady and the bearded monster:

> Her eyes were deep black, and somewhat prominent, and their lids had long, thick eyelashes: her features were simply hideous on

account of the profusion of hair growing on her forehead, and her
black beard; but her figure was exceedingly good and graceful, and her
tiny foot and well-turned ankle, . . . perfection itself. She had a sweet
voice, great taste in music and dancing, and could speak three
languages. She was charitable and gave largely to local institutions
from her earnings.[44]

Here Buckland is at once attracted and repulsed by Pastrana's seeming fusion
of the "hideous" and "perfection itself." Using the gender system as a template
to interpret her physical traits, Buckland reads her body as a wondrous merger
of the male and female that enhances rather than dilutes each identity.

This merger produced a figure both grotesque and compelling to Buckland.
The show narratives capitalized upon this response, heightening the anxious
fascination with gender confusion in order to draw customers. The textual presentation of Pastrana challenged the viewers' understanding of what they imagined to be natural and immutable gender differences that structured their own
identities as men and women. But if Pastrana's exhibition provoked discomfort, it also assuaged the uneasiness it incited about themselves and their place
in the world. One account, for example, tells about a ball in Baltimore that
Pastrana supposedly attended, where she provided "a very genteel young man
in citizen's dress" an opportunity to demonstrate a kind of heroic civility despite the discomfort that her gender trespass aroused. The highly embellished—
and probably fictional—story presents an ultrafeminized, Cinderella-like
Pastrana costumed in "a blue dress, trimmed with silver lace, white kid gloves,
black satin slippers, bracelets, watch, and splendid set of Jewellery, including
a diamond ring, which had just been made a present to her [sic]." The reader—
and prospective audience member—is assured that "had [Pastrana's] face been
screened from observation" her femininity would have made her "'the cyno-
sure of all eyes'" at the ball. The archetype of bourgeois ladyhood, Pastrana
waltzes gracefully and adeptly "by some *natural* intuition," inspiring a "handsome gallant" [to run up] to Miss Julia with considerable eagerness." But when
the couples face one another to dance, "the young gentleman" is overcome
momentarily by "fright or some other undefined emotion . . . and exhibit[s] a
degree of embarrassment strangely at variance with his character." Nevertheless, he recovers in a "creditable manner" and the ball proceeds gaily with him
as its hero.[45]

The story leaves the source of his discomfort unnarrated, stressing only
the severity of his response to Pastrana's transgressive face and his "genteel"
recovery. This vignette assures the reader that he can maintain bourgeois de-
corum and self-control, literally in the face of this shocking violation of what
he imagines as a world discretely ordered into male and female. Pastrana's exhibition, then, becomes a kind of test of the (male) spectator's capacity to

absorb the instability of categories that structure self and world, to create "an enchanting occasion," where he masters his insecurity despite the "fright" and discomfort such ambiguity kindles.[46] This narrative of spectatorship thus instructs the viewer how to respond to the assault on his world view that Pastrana represents. So while Pastrana may seem to be the focus in the dynamic of staring, closer scrutiny of this encounter reveals that the rhetorical purpose is to verify the viewer's vision of himself.

The Self/Other Opposition

This affirmation of the viewer produced by Pastrana's exhibition is nowhere clearer than in the sentimental discourse of self and other that characterized Pastrana's display. In this relational choreography, the response Pastrana elicits from her onlookers defines them, ultimately placing them in the order of things that she seemingly so upsets. Coached by the promotional material, the spectator could expect a thrilling, even delightful, excursion through a disintegration and reintegration of his or her sense of self within the social order in Victorian America. This is perhaps what the audience was paying for. As I have already suggested, Pastrana's presentation as semihuman legitimated the status of her onlookers as fully human and thus potential citizens in a democratic order. But it was the sentimental discourse of self and other deployed in Pastrana's display that established precisely what kind of citizens her viewers might be. In short, the exhibition of Pastrana was an occasion upon which spectators could verify their position in the hierarchy of citizenship that was solidifying in nineteenth-century America.

Sentimentality was one element in nineteenth-century discourse that increasingly differentiated the bourgeoisie from the working classes. The sentimental was part of a rhetoric of upward social mobility registering the refined sensibility, genteel manners, and sense of stewardship that characterized emergent middle-class respectability.[47] Public exhibitions such as Pastrana's were effective vehicles for sentimentality, which rescued what the solidifying middle class took as the vulgar and offensive practice of exhibiting monsters from its slide into low culture and transformed it into the burgeoning business of freak shows and dime museums. In terms of bourgeois taste, such exhibitions moved from the crude to the refined and back again to the vulgar on exactly the same historical trajectory as the rise and fall of sentimental discourse. By the 1860s Barnum was courting Queen Victoria and charming the world with Tom Thumb, but by 1923 one writer condemned him for the "complete indifference to the semi-humanity or sub-humanity of the horrible creatures that he often exhibited," insisting that "a nature with a shred of sensitiveness would have recoiled from the public display of these monstrosities and the sickening morbid curiosity they fostered."[48] What made spectacles such as Pastrana's exhibition acceptable and profitable was their suitability to sentimental discourse, the exercise of which was a major marker of bourgeois status in Victorian America.

Sentimentality was the production and demonstration of a certain affect that structured a social relationship between the person who could show fine feeling and the one who could induce it. Pity, the primary sentimental affect, was the genteel response that often characterized relations between the bourgeoisie and the poor, the disabled, and the primitive. Pity is repugnance refined: the other becomes sympathetic rather than brutish in the service of cultivating a bourgeois self. The sentimental relationship is nonreciprocal as it elevates the self to a position of stewardship over the other. Pity thus defines its object even as it depends upon that object for its enactment. In other words, pity needs an incitement to which it must respond. Julia Pastrana's immense popularity, along with that of her fellow freaks, may be explained by her function as an anchor for the respectable sentiment of pity that the newly solidifying middle class needed to display and that its aspirants needed to perfect.[49]

Such an appeal to the ennobling emotion of pity is rather shamelessly exploited in the promotional material for Pastrana's exhibition. One account of her display insists that "there is nothing in her appearance in the least calculated to offend the sensibilities of the most fastidious, whether viewed, socially, morally, or physically. A feeling of pity, rather than of repugnance or antipathy is generally experienced in the bosom of all who pay her a visit."[50] Here pity keeps the onlookers "fastidious," delivering them from an interest in the lurid and from the "morbid curiosity" that such shows were often later accused of pandering to.

Similarly, Otto Hermann, who saw Pastrana's embalmed corpse on display in Vienna after ostensibly interviewing her in life, vows in his memoir, "I felt tremendous pity for this thing who could no longer see or hear, feel joy or pain, or my sorrow. I remembered her smiling face saying [of her manager/husband] 'He loves me for my own sake.'"[51] The ground for Hermann's pity is what he imagines as Pastrana's capacity for the same human emotions he feels. Even though he recognizes that "poor Pastrana was known for her ugliness," Hermann's interest in her supposedly transcends any fascination with the disturbing differentness of her body or with its violation of the gender order. Indeed, Hermann differentiates his stare from both the medical gaze, which he says "was fascinated with Julia," and the vulgar stare: "To the world, she was nothing more than an aberration, something grotesque that was paraded before others for money and trained to do tricks like circus animals. For those few who knew her better, she was a warm, thoughtful, capable being with a big heart. They knew her sorrow at being on the fringe of society, not part of it, of not knowing the normal joys of family, home, love."[52] Hermann uses sentimental rhetoric to suggest here that the state of total otherness Pastrana's "grotesque" bodily "aberration" creates for "the world" could be inflected and thus redeemed by affective properties imagined as "normal," as exclusive to the self, such as "a big heart" and being "warm" and "thoughtful." Thus, Hermann envisions Pastrana as pitiful rather than repulsive because she is like him emotionally, if not physically. By projecting the self onto the other in this manner, Hermann finds verification of his own humanizing sentiments in Pastrana. His ability to pity Pastrana makes him more sensitive and culti-vated, more bourgeois, than the other base spectators who constitute "the world."

Sentimentality thus hybridizes the self and the other by positing an ex-change of feeling so that the other inspires elevating and humanizing sensi-bilities in the self, which then projects those sentiments back onto the other. This sentimental economy merges identification through pity with differen-tiation through otherness to produce Pastrana as the hybrid construct of the sensitive monster, whose role it is to instruct, edify, and thus construct the middle-class canonical self. The starers become better people, citizens higher on the ladder of bourgeois respectability, through viewing Pastrana.

Sentimental discourse, like the others discussed here, leashes spectator and spectacle together in a performance of identity that compels, delights, troubles, and affirms by confusing categories and blurring boundaries. Yet the ritual and highly stylized quality of that performance seals it off from ordi-nary experience, and the commercial nature of the encounter demands that it serve the viewer. In the end, for all the ambiguity that staring introduces, it gestures in a conciliatory, almost nostalgic way toward affirming the bound-aries that organize the order of things: "Go and see Julia Pastrana, the 'Non-descript,'" a souvenir pamphlet instructs, "and learn wisdom, subdued by becoming humility. Go and endeavor to realize where man's bestial attributes terminate and where those that are *Divine* begin!"[53] It was perhaps this at once sentimental and comforting suggestion that one might be able to determine a line between the "bestial" and the "*Divine*" self that drew viewers to Pastrana. Yet her startling body invariably exceeded the binary discourses that audiences were invited to try to impose upon it. Staring at Julia Pastrana went beyond the binary. The exhibition was not about her; rather, it was about who her spectators imagined they were.

My point in probing the spatial and textual discourses that made up Julia Pastrana's exhibition is to show how actual social practices manipulated and complicated the binary cultural categories in which they trafficked. In the case of Pastrana, as well as her fellow freaks, the staring orchestrated by her handlers provocatively challenged the fundamental binaries upon which the social order relied, intensifying anxieties in the viewers. By destabilizing traditional binary categories of identity such as human/animal, civilized/primitive, normal/pathological, male/female, and self/other, staring at Julia Pastrana mobilized the viewers' fears and concerns to create the obsessed fascination that drove profits. So although the freak show seemingly depended upon an absolute distinction between the freak and the patron, the looked-upon and the looker, it in fact relentlessly contested those boundaries in order to perpetuate itself and to make money. But, of course, while it made money, the freak show also made meaning: in an age of mechanical reproduction, social instability, and economic transformation, it disseminated narratives of human bodily variation that pandered to the sociopolitical concerns of the historical moment. Thus, by analyzing specific social practices that invest the body with meanings, especially such highly ritualized and hyperbolic performances as freak shows, cultural studies can trace more complexly the processes that socially mark human bodies, consequently revealing more fully the operations of such representational systems as race, gender, ethnicity, and disability.

Notes

1. Betsy Erlikka, "Ethnicity, Literary Theory, and the Grounds of Resistance," *American Quarterly* 47, no. 4 (December 1995): 563–94.
2. For example, see Rosemarie Garland Thomson, *Extraordinary Bodies: Figuring Physical Disability in American Culture and Literature* (New York: Columbia University Press, 1997); *Freakery: Cultural Spectacles of the Extraordinary Body*, ed. Thomson (New York: New York University Press, 1996); and Thomson, "Redrawing the Boundaries of Feminist Theory," *Feminist Studies* 20 (fall 1994): 583–95.
3. "Disability" is defined here as the broad socially constructed identity category or representational system that assigns meaning to bodies that function or appear to be atypical or to differ from some culturally established norm. Thus, a wide range of unusual or stigmatizing traits or bodily characteristics might be interpreted as marks of disability.
4. George C. D. Odell, *Annals of the New York Stage*, vol. 6, 1850–1857, reprint (New York: AMS Press, 1970), 413.
5. For a history of the displays of monsters and freaks, see *Freakery*, ed. Thomson, especially chaps. 1 and 10; Robert Bogdan, *Freak Show: Presenting Human Oddities for Amusement and Profit* (Chicago: Chicago University Press, 1988); Leslie A. Fiedler, *Freaks: Myths and Images of the Secret Self* (New York: Simon and Schuster, 1978); Richard D. Altick, *The Shows of London* (Cambridge, Mass.: Belknap Press, 1978); John Block Friedman, *The Monstrous Races in Medieval Art and Thought* (Cambridge, Mass.: Harvard University Press, 1981); Dudley Wilson, *Signs and Portents: Monstrous Births from the Middle Ages to the Enlightenment* (London: Routledge, 1993); Kathryn Park and Lorraine Daston, "Unnatural Conceptions: The Study of Monsters in Sixteenth- and Seventeenth-Century France and England," *Past and Present: A Journal of Historical Studies* 92 (August 1981): 20–54; Frederick Drimmer, *Very Special People* (New York: Amjon Press, 1983); Michael P. Winship, "Prodigies, Puritanism, and the Perils of Natural Philosophy: The Example of Cotton Mather," *William and Mary Quarterly*, 3d ser., L1, no. 1 (January 1994) 92–105.

6. Neil Harris, *Humbug: The Art of P. T. Barnum* (Boston: Little Brown, 1973) and A. H. Saxon, *P. T. Barnum: The Legend and the Man* (New York: New York University Press, 1989).

7. Karen Halttunen, *Confidence Men and Painted Women: A Study of Middle-Class Culture in America, 1830–1870* (New Haven, Conn.: Yale University Press, 1982); Robert Allen, *Horrible Prettiness: Burlesque in American Culture* (Chapel Hill: University of North Carolina Press, 1991); Rachel Bowlby, *Just Looking: Consumer Culture in Dreiser, Gissing, and Zola* (New York: Methuen, 1985); Jonathan Crary, *Techniques of the Observer: On Vision and Modernity in the Nineteenth Century* (Cambridge, Mass.: The MIT Press, 1990); Guy Debord, *The Society of the Spectacle* (Detroit: Black and Red, 1983).

8. Susan Buck-Morss, "The Flâneur, the Sandwichman, and the Whore: The Politics of Loitering," *New German Critique* 39 (fall 1986): 99–140.

9. See Jean Baudrillard, *Simulations*, trans., Paul Foss (New York: Semiotext(e) Inc., 1983) for discussion of the circulation of signs in modernity.

10. Odell, *Annals of the New York Stage*, 413.

11. In fact, because people could be required to pay to glimpse a freak, managers did not allow freaks to go about freely or to have nonpaying relationships.

12. *Curious History of the Baboon Lady, Miss Julia Pastrana*, pamphlet, Harvard Theater Collection, 5. Hereafter cited as HTC.

13. Stephen Greenblatt, "Resonance and Wonder" *Exhibiting Cultures: The Politics and Poetics of Museum Display*, ed. Ivan Karp and Steven D. Lavine (Washington, D.C.: Smithsonian Institution Press, 1991), 82.

14. Harris, in *Humbug*, argues that the attraction of freak shows was that they challenged audiences to recognize fakes or "humbugs."

15. *Miss Julia Pastrana, the Misnomered Bear Woman*, pamphlet, 1855, New York Public Library. Hereafter cited as NYPL.

16. Although this dynamic is similar to the panoptic surveillance paradigm described by Michel Foucault in *Discipline and Punish: The Birth of the Prison*, trans. Alan M. Sheridan-Smith (New York: Pantheon, 1973), its effect is less disciplinary than definitive. The difference is that onlookers were invited to appropriate bodies such as Pastrana's as texts upon which they could project their fantasies, anxieties, and needs. The freak exhibition dynamic, then, is more like the gaze as elaborated in feminist film theory.

17. Stephen Jay Gould, *The Mismeasure of Man* (New York: Norton, 1981).

18. HTC, 2; NYPL.

19. HTC, 1.

20. Keith Thomas, *Man and the Natural World* (New York: Pantheon, 1983), 135.

21. HTC, 2.

22. NYPL. Because so many of the accounts of Pastrana and other freaks are found in surviving ephemeral promotional material, it is impossible to know whether the statements supposedly made by doctors and other authorities who examined the freaks are authentic. Nevertheless, it is the cultural concepts that frame the freaks' bodies for public view rather than the authenticity of these statements that are useful for this analysis.

23. For a discussion of "missing links" figures, see James W. Cook, Jr., "Of Men, Missing Links, and Nondescripts: The Strange Career of P. T. Barnum's 'What Is It?' Exhibition" in *Freakery*, ed. Thomson, 139–157.

24. Bruce A. McConachie, "Museum, Theater and the Problem of Respectability for Mid-Century Urban Americans," in *The American Stage: Social and Economic Issues from the Colonial Period to the Present*, ed. Ron Engle and Tice L. Miller (New York: Cambridge University Press, 1993), 65–80.

25. HTC, 8.

26. Ibid. For examples of the conflation of ethnography and show business, see Phillips Verner Bradford and Harvey Blume, *Ota Benga: The Pygmy in the Zoo* (New York: St. Martin's Press, 1992), and Christopher A. Vaughan, "Ogling Igorots: The Politics and Commerce of Exhibiting Cultural Otherness, 1898–1913," in *Freakery*, ed. Thomson, 219–33. For a discussion of the bifurcation of culture into high and low, see Lawrence W. Levine, *Highbrow/Lowbrow: The Emergence of Cultural Hierarchy in America* (Cambridge, Mass.: Harvard University Press, 1988).

27. HTC,6–7.

28. Ibid., 5.

29. NYPL, 2.

30. HTC, 7.

31. NYPL, 2.

32. HTC, 8, and NYPL, 3.

33. HTC, 8.

34. J. Z. Laurence, "A Short Account of the Bearded and Hairy Female," *The Lancet* 2 (11 July 1857): 48.

35. George M. Gould and Walter L. Pyle, *Anomalies and Curiosities of Medicine* (Philadelphia: W. B. Saunders, 1897), 229.

36. J. Sokolov, "Julia Pastrana and her Child," *The Lancet* 1 (3 May 1862): 467–69, quotation at 468.

37. Ibid., 468.

38. Francis T. Buckland, *Curiosities of Natural History*, vol. 4 (London: Richard Bentley and Son, 1888), 40–43, quotations at 41.

39. Laurence, "Short Account," 48.

40. Ibid.

41. Late-twentieth-century medical accounts of Pastrana's body do not invoke gender to produce pathology. Rather, they focus on the terminology of her abnormality. For example, a 1993 article in the *American Journal of Medical Genetics* argues that Pastrana was an example of "congenital, generalized hypertrichosis terminalis with gingival hyperplasia," rather than one of "hypertrichosis languinosa." See Jan Bondeson and A. E. W. Miles, "Julia Pastrana, the Nondescript: An Example of Congenital, Generalized Hypertrichosis Terminalis with Gingival Hyperplasia," *American Journal of Medical Genetics* 47(1993): 198–212, quotation at 198.

42. Gould and Pyle, *Anomalies*, 229.

43. Otto W. Hermann, *Fahrend Volk* (Leipzig: J. J. Weber, 1895), 123; my translation.

44. Buckland, *Curiosities*, 42.

45. HTC, 9.

46. Ibid., 9–10.

47. Thomas, *Man and the Natural World*; Halttunen, *Confidence Men and Painted Women*; and Yi-Fu Tuan, *Dominance and Affection: The Making of Pets* (New Haven, Conn.: Yale University Press, 1984).

48. Gamaliel Bradford, *Damaged Souls* (Port Washington, N.Y.: Kennikat Press, 1923), 216.

49. Rosemarie Garland Thomson, "Crippled Girls and Lame Old Women: Sentimental Spectacles of Sympathy in Nineteenth-Century American Women's Writing," in *Nineteenth-Century American Women Writers: A Critical Reader*, ed. Karen L. Kilcup (Cambridge, Mass., and Oxford, U.K.: Blackwell, 1998), 128–145.

50. HTC, 12.

51. Hermann, *Fahrend Volk*, 125.

52. Ibid., 123–24.

53. HTC, 12.

Part II   Exploring Cultural Self-Transformation

"One Hundred Percent American": How a Slave, a Janitor, and a Former Klansman Escaped Racial Categories by Becoming Indians

Chapter 5

LAURA BROWDER

Aᴌᴛʜᴏᴜɢʜ ᴍᴜᴄʜ ʜᴀs ʙᴇᴇɴ ᴡʀɪᴛᴛᴇɴ about "passing" as a way for those defined as African American to escape into whiteness, there is another kind of ethnic imposture that has, for the past 150 years, offered Americans an escape from the black/white binaries in which so many have found themselves trapped. This chapter will discuss the phenomenon of the impostor, or voluntary, Indian.[1]

For nearly as long as the United States has been in existence, there have been fake Indians. Perhaps the first Indian impostor, in life or in print, was William Augustus Bowles, an American Tory dressed up as an Indian, who managed to pass in the upper crust of London society in 1791 as "commander-in-chief of the Creek and Cherokee nations." Since Bowles, there has been a veritable cavalcade of fake Indians and impostor autobiographies, whose messages have changed with the years; as the stereotypes of Indianness have changed. Thus, in the mid-nineteenth century, James Beckwourth, the fake "savage," emerged. By the 1920s the celebrity Chief Buffalo Child Long Lance appeared, presenting himself as the tragic representative of a doomed race who was, however, on his "Trail Upward," gamely adapting to "civilization." The 1930s produced a Nazi Indian, Big Chief White Horse Eagle, whose autobiography was elicited and edited by one of Hitler's race theorists; White Horse's value lay in serving as an exemplar of a pure but doomed race. In a decade that saw renewed interest in environmental issues, it seems only fitting that the 1930s also heralded the appearance of the first environmental fake Indian— Grey Owl, alias Archie Belaney, an Englishman who was acutely aware of the value of his "native" persona to the conservation cause he promoted.[2]

The late sixties and seventies, a time when many Americans became interested in exploring alternative religious practices, brought an efflorescence
of spiritually attuned Native Americans, many of them European Americans
who had, through a process of elective affinity, become Indian. This group
includes, at least according to many scholars, such figures as Hyemyohsts
Storm, author of the influential spiritual work *Seven Arrows*, as well as Jamake
Highwater, author of the best-selling *The Primal Mind* (which became a made-
for-TV movie), who has claimed to be Cherokee and also Blackfoot and has
denied being a Greek American film maker from Toledo named Gregory J.
Markopoulos.[3] The dawning of the New Age has cast light on a number of
voluntary Indians, like Lynn Andrews, author of *Jaguar Woman* (1985), *Crys-
tal Woman* (1987), and other accounts of her spiritual adventures. Finally,
Forrest Carter, author of the best-selling Cherokee memoir *The Education of
Little Tree* (1976), turned out to have been a member of the original Ku Klux
Klan of the Confederacy and a speechwriter for George Wallace.

First as embodiments of threat and then as living legacies of conquest,
Indians have always provided a focal point for a range of cultural anxieties.
The successful Native impostor offers perhaps the purest expression of American fantasies about those whose near extermination provided the basis for our
nation's existence, a Rorschach blot that, if read properly, offers the key to
understanding the barely articulated, often nearly unconscious, needs and desires of our culture. Created to fulfill the needs both of impostor and culture,
the success of the ersatz Indian rests on his or her ability to embody the cultural fantasies of his or her time. The book sales, cinematic appearances, published interviews, and other hallmarks of impostor success are the tangible
evidence of the love affair between invented Indian and audience. Just as in-
fatuated lovers may be blind to the flaws of their beloved, so audiences will
ignore the most glaring evidence that an Indian spokesperson may not be quite
what he or she appears. Thus readers of the 1920s failed to remark that Chief
Buffalo Child Long Lance's account of his youth included roaming the plains
with his Blackfoot tribe and participating in the great buffalo hunts—during
a time, the mid-1890s, when the buffalo had long been reduced to heaps of
bleached bones and the Blackfoot had for fifteen years been settled onto reservations. Lovers may turn a blind eye to evidence of duplicity. Thus the publication of a 1976 article exposing the imposture of Forrest Carter went
generally unremarked: fifteen years and six hundred thousand copies later, the
news came as a fresh shock to the public. And just as a love affair may, in
retrospect, take on an entirely new meaning, so an impostor, reviled at one
time for deception, may be embraced by a subsequent generation for reasons
that would seem baffling to him or her.

Although there are many impostors on whose lives it would be tempting to dwell, I've chosen to focus on three—Forrest Carter, James P. Beckwourth, and Chief Buffalo Child Long Lance—whose stories seem as emblematic of the complex dance of successful imposture as they themselves once seemed emblematic of an "authentic" Native voice. James P. Beckwourth, whose autobiography was published in the 1850s, provides an ironic exemplar of how one generation's imposture may be seen as another's multiculturalism. Long Lance offers us a look at the first imposture to take place in the age of mass media. And finally, Forrest Carter, the most famous impostor Indian of our time, demonstrates the way Indian identity can offer a way out of a life spent exploiting, rather than being exploited by, racist categories.

Carter, in fact, must provide the pivot for this discussion for the simple reason that his exposure in 1991 was the most widely publicized of the three. Long Lance was only fully exposed as an impostor in 1982, some fifty years after his death, with the publication of Donald B. Smith's comprehensive biography *Long Lance: The True Story of an Impostor,* and James Beckwourth's ethnic identity, although debated, was never considered a truly shocking revelation, but the exposure of Forrest Carter as an inauthentic Indian became a touchstone for discussions about the meaning of ethnic identity. As Dan T. Carter, in the *New York Times* op-ed piece he wrote exposing Forrest Carter as a fake, asked, "What does it tell us that we are so easily deceived?" The question was echoed by newspaper and magazine articles around the country.

It could be, however, that Dan T. Carter's question was the wrong one to ask; perhaps the real question was why the notion of authenticity carried so much freight with him and others—and what Indian identity meant to those who assumed it, as well as to "real" Indians. After all, Asa Carter and other "imposters" were using voluntary concepts of identity not taken from the obvious black/white tradition. They were active agents, rather than passive inheritors of genetic coding. In an era of rigidly defined group identities, these individuals successfully insisted on their power of choice in their racial or ethnic self-identifications. Together, these three texts demonstrate the many ways in which American autobiographers have employed an Indian identity as a way to negotiate or escape black/white binaries. Most of all, they show the ways in which this third identity—Indianness—must be constructed to fit into the prevailing racist stereotypes of its time in order for these impersonators to succeed.

A Double Passage: The Curious Case of James P. Beckwourth

The autobiography of James P. Beckwourth was published by Harper & Brothers in 1856, when Beckwourth was fifty-six, or perhaps fifty-eight. Dictated by Beckwourth to T. D. Bonner, a con man, temperance advocate, and drunk,

The Life and Adventures of James P. Beckwourth, Mountaineer, Scout and Pioneer, and Chief of the Crow Nation of Indians fulfills all the expectations its title suggests. Beckwourth's life of western adventure began with his first stint as a fur trapper, work he took on after getting into a fight with the St. Louis blacksmith to whom he was apprenticed as a teenager. Beckwourth's colleagues at the trapping company included William Sublette, who would discover the geysers at Yellowstone; Jim Bridger, the future discoverer of the Great Salt Lake; and Jedediah Smith, supposed by many to be the greatest mountain man of all time. Most of Beckwourth's narrative is centered on the thirteen years he spent as a war chief with the Crow Indians, but his book also includes accounts of his dozen or so marriages, his later work with trapping companies, his employment as a soldier on the government side of the Seminole wars of 1837, the restless wanderings that took him through Taos and Denver, to California where he discovered the Beckwourth Trail, which became the most commonly used route for pioneers coming from the Great Basin of Nevada to California, and his retirement as an innkeeper at Beckwourth Ranch, along the trail. The autobiography, with its tales of exotic adventure and bloody heroism, was an immediate bestseller, and an immediate source of controversy: typical of the complaints that Beckwourth was no more than a "gaudy liar" was the note Francis Parkman scribbled in his copy of the autobiography, denouncing Beckwourth as "a fellow of bad character—a compound of black and white blood, though he represents otherwise."[4] Parkman, in *The Oregon Trail*, went on to describe him as "a mongrel of French, American and Negro blood . . . a ruffian of the worst stamp."[5] In fact, although early historians often acknowledged Beckwourth's status as one of the greatest of frontiersman, they generally linked his veracity (or lack thereof) to his color: Charles Christy, who headed a chapter in his 1908 frontier memoirs "Nigger Jim Beckwith," after noting that "Jim was born in that section of the United States where they spell Afro-American with a double g," went on to call Beckwourth "the biggest liar that ever lived."[6] These historians seemed able only to see Beckwourth in terms of black or white; his autobiography demonstrates both the slipperiness of racial and ethnic identity and the way that Beckwourth himself remained rhetorically imprisoned by the identity trap that he in his life seemed to escape.

To understand the significance of Beckwourth's choice, it is necessary to view his autobiography in the context of the anthropological debates of his time. By the second half of the nineteenth century, American anthropology was beginning to emerge as a discipline. The great scientific war of the period concerned whether the races were polygenetic in origin, or monogenetic— that is, whether different races were actually different species or if they belonged to the same human family. When Beckwourth published his memoir in 1856, the polygeneticists were clearly winning this war of ideas: in 1854 two leading racial scientists, Josiah Clark Nott and George Robin Gliddon, had published their eight-hundred- page study, *Types of Man*, which disseminated the idea of separate species of man to a broad audience and included chapters by such prominent scientists as Harvard's Louis Agassiz. Even at the high price of seven and a half dollars, the first printing sold out immediately, and by the end of the century the book had gone through at least nine editions.[7] Although by end of the 1850s the spread of Darwin's ideas had effectively discredited polygeneticist theories in scientific circles, it merely shifted the focus of race theory: the "scientific" study of race now had an evolutionary model, which held that Africans and Indians were simply less evolved stages of humanity.

In fact, Beckwourth was not, as he represented himself in his memoir, white, but was born a slave, the son of his master. Although he speaks of his childhood relocation to St. Louis, to which "my father removed . . . taking with him all his family and twenty-two negroes," he was not among the "family" that he described.[8] Thus, the autobiography entails what might be called a double passage, for in it Beckwourth, a man defined by his culture as black, passes as a white man, who is himself passing as Indian.[9]

Even early defenders of the autobiography often centered their discussions around the issue of his race: for instance, the editor of the 1892 British edition of the work (a previous British edition had come out in 1856), while defending Beckwourth's veracity, cites an "authority" as saying that "Beckwourth was the offspring, not of a *negress*, but of a *quadroon* and a planter."[10] A contemporary eyewitness describes an elderly gentleman with a "complexion like a Mexican, and eyes like an Indian. It is James P. Beckwourth, the half-breed, so long a chief among the Crow tribe, and the most famous Indian fighter of his generation."[11] Even as Beckwourth described his escape from the strictures of identity in his memoir, the reception of that work depended on what reviewers saw as the irreducible fact of his race.

What one might call this race-based reception of Beckwourth and his work continued for over a century, even as the grounds for it changed. Beckwourth's heritage seemed to change with the passing decades. In the 1951 Universal Studios Western *Tomahawk*, Beckwourth is played by white actor Jackie Oakie. As William Loren Katz writes in his 1986 study, *Black Indians: A Hidden Heritage*, "Generations of young people never learned that this tough pioneer fur trapper was a black man."[12] Indeed, Beckwourth's racial identity grows more distinct over the years. The publisher's blurb for Leigh Brackett's 1963 *Follow the Free Wind* describes Beckwourth as "A half-breed rebel in search of his identity," whereas by 1966 Harold W. Felton published *Jim Beckwourth: Negro Mountain Man*.[13] By 1969 the autobiography itself was reprinted in Arno

Press's series *The American Negro: His History and Literature*. Perhaps the greatest sign of Beckwourth's rehabilitation as African-American hero was the 1992 biography for young readers, which appeared, complete with an introduction by Coretta Scott King, as part of Chelsea House Publishers' *Black Americans of Achievement* series, which also includes biographies of such figures as Hank Aaron, Paul Robeson, and Sojourner Truth, civil rights leaders James Farmer, Rosa Parks, and Ralph Abernathy. Thus, the story would seem to be complete—and the use of the binary is restored. As the publisher's blurb describes Lawrence Cortesi's 1971 biography *Jim Beckwourth: Explorer-Patriot of the Rockies*, "Captured by Indians who adopted him as a long-lost brave whose skin had been burned dark by the desert sun, Jim learned to respect and love his tribe." What we would have in the story of Beckwourth, who escaped the restrictions of life as a black man in St. Louis, would seem to be a story we have heard before, one of a suppressed history recently unearthed, of oppressed peoples banding together against a common enemy. And yet the truth is much more complicated than that.

Far from being a tale of the solidarity of people of color in the face of the crushing powers of the government, Beckwourth's autobiography is an apologia for white racism. Rather than feeling any great unity with the Crow among whom he lived for so long, Beckwourth describes them as "savages" and as "wily Indians." His chosen stance is as interpreter to white America of Crow and other Indian culture, "a subject which at the present day is but imperfectly understood by the general reader"(26). His autobiography points up both the fluidity of racial and ethnic identity in the nineteenth century, and the dangers of trying to simplify the narrative of race and ethnicity.

After all, Beckwourth's book appeared just a year before the 1857 Oregon state constitution, which mandated the exclusion from the state of free blacks. This provision was popular among voters: as Oregon's delegate to Congress explained in 1850, the issue of admitting free blacks to the state

> is a question of life and death to us in Oregon. . . . The negroes
> associate with the Indians and intermarry, and, if their free ingress is
> encouraged or allowed, there would a relationship spring up between
> them and the different tribes, and a mixed race would ensure inimical
> to the whites; and the Indians being led on by the negro who is better
> acquainted with the customs, language, and manners of the whites,
> than the Indians, these savages would become much more formidable
> than they otherwise would, and long and bloody wars would be the
> fruits of the commingling of the races.[14]

Within the context of this legally encoded fear of racial alliances, Beckwourth's positioning of himself as a white writer makes sense: mid-nineteenth-century literacy rates among Indians and blacks insure that he is, after all, addressing a primarily white audience. However, the ambivalence of such a strategy shines through on the page in his comparison of his presumably white self to a slave and in his pride at the success of his racial imposture. Adding another layer of complexity to the story is the fact that Beckwourth, as a black man, had an advantage in trading with Indians, who were more inclined to trust him than his white counterparts. As Colonel James Stevenson, of the Bureau of American Ethnology, who had spent thirty years working with and studying Native Americans, wrote in 1888, "The old fur trappers always got a Negro if possible to negotiate for them with the Indians, because of their 'pacifying effect.' They could manage them better than the white men, and with less friction."[15] With his dark skin a commodity whose value was heavily situational, Beckwourth was able to use, deny, and change his racial identity as he saw fit.

While taking care to distinguish his own work from that of other travelers, whose "tales that were related as actual experience now mislead the speaker and the audience," Beckwourth relates in detail the way he himself has created a life out of such stories: his life as a Crow Indian begins when one of his fellow trappers "invented a fiction, which greatly amused me for its ingenuity" (51, 140). This fiction that Beckwourth was a small Crow child kidnapped by the Cheyenne during the course of warfare and sold to the whites, is accepted by the Crow. Taking the slavery metaphor further, Beckwourth, who has become a restored, favorite son, one redeemed from captivity, finds himself captured by Crow, who, anxious to verify Beckwourth's false biography, form an examining committee. "I believe," Beckwourth writes, "never was mortal gazed at with such intense and sustained interest as I was on that occasion." In a scene highly reminiscent of that at a slave market, "Arms and legs were critically scrutinized. My face next passed the ordeal; then my neck, back, breast, and all parts of my body, even down to my feet" (146).

However, this is a story in which the black man whose body is being so minutely examined ends up triumphant. When one of the old women discovers a resemblance in him to her lost son, Beckwourth accepts her interpretation without commentary, other than to marvel that "it is but nature, either in the savage breast or civilized, that hails such a return with overwhelming joy" (146).

His imposture is successful not only with the Crow, but also with the white settlers: Beckwourth soon accompanies the Indians to Fort Clarke to trade pelts, and goes unremarked upon by the white trappers: "Speaking nothing but Crow language, dressed like a Crow, my hair long as a Crow's, and myself black as a crow," Beckwourth tells us, "no one at the post doubted my being a Crow" (177).

However proud he might be of his ability to "pass" as a Crow, or as a man as black as a crow, Beckwourth is anxious to reassure white readers of where his primary loyalties lie. He lives as a Crow, taking eight Indian wives, and most pages of his narrative are replete with accounts of the warfare he engages in and the enemy scalps he takes, leading Bernard De Voto to claim that Beckwourth "gave our literature our goriest lies", and that in no other book are as many Indians killed.[16] Yet Beckwourth is careful to distance himself from the violence he describes at such loving length. After describing, in graphic detail, a battle in which he killed eleven men, in which "it was . . . a work of great difficulty to keep one's feet, as the mingled gore and brains were scattered every where round this fatal place," he extends a caveat:

> I trust that the reader does not suppose that I walked through these
> scenes of carnage and desolation without some serious reflections on
> the matter. Disgusted at the repeated acts of cruelty I witnessed, I
> often resolved to leave these wild children of the forest and return to
> civilized life; but before I could act upon my decision, another scene
> of strife would occur, and the Enemy of Horses was always the first
> sought for by the tribe.

His tribe needed him, so the justification goes, and as the Crows' best warrior, he could not let them down. And yet, in another logical flip-flop, Beckwourth claims that he is acting for the best interests of white Americans:

> But, in justification, it may be urged that the Crows had never shed
> the blood of the white man during my stay in their camp, and I did
> not intend they ever should, if I could raise a voice to prevent it.
> They were constantly at war with tribes who coveted the scalps of the
> white man, but the Crows were uniformly faithful in their obligations
> to my race, and would rather serve than injure their white brethren
> without any consideration of profit. (198)

And so it goes: Beckwourth describes the "natural ferocity of the savage, who thirsts for the blood of the white man for no other purpose than to gratify the vindictive spirit that animates him. . . . Such is Indian nature." Yet he will follow this up by noting, "When I fought with the Crow nation, I fought in their behalf against the most relentless enemies of the white man. If I chose to become an Indian while living among them, it concerned no person but myself; and by doing so, I saved more life and property for the white man than a whole regiment of United States regulars could have done in the same time" (233). Beckwourth's use of "white man" rather than "American" is hardly accidental: he is constantly drawing racial and ethnic distinctions in which others come out unfavorably, as when he notes that "quelling the Indian problem" will be impossible, "as long as our government continues to enlist the offscouring of European cities into our army." On the other hand, "with five hundred men of my selection I could exterminate any tribe in North America in a very few months." He not only compares himself to European offscourings, but to blacks: upon hearing that a mulatto has joined with a number of "my Indians" (249) and a group of white men, in robbing a trader, he confronts the man, to whom he assigns primary responsibility for the crime, asking him "What are you doing here, you black velvet-headed scoundrel? . . . I will have your scalp torn off, you consummate villain!" (250) On another occasion, he compares an escaping Indian to "a negro with an alligator at his heels" (339).

Yet, even as Beckwourth takes care to align himself with white men, to the point of seeing European features as the touchstone of beauty in the Crow women he marries, he remains insistent on his own apparent Indianness: he cites many examples of his going unrecognized by white traders, of trappers telling him that "I should certainly not have distinguished you from any other Indian" (299). However, his thirteen years among the Crow do not prevent him from offering advice to his readers on how to exterminate the Indians most effectively—sell them liquor—nor from taking his own counsel, and eventually going to work for a trading company that does just that. Characteristically, he takes as much pride in his ability to sell huge amounts of liquor to Indians as he once did in scalping the enemies of the tribe.

If Beckwourth was a hero, he was one singularly unsuited to the needs of contemporary schoolchildren and the biographers who write the inspirational narratives designed for them. Rather, he is a hero from a much older mold: a shape-changer, a slaughterer of thousands, a survivor. Beckwourth may have escaped the racial strictures of antebellum America, perhaps even triumphed over them through sheer force of will. It is difficult to extract a neat moral from his life, however.

James Beckwourth passed away in 1866 from an undiagnosed illness, while visiting the Crow. Yet a persistent rumor would have it that the Crow, delighted to have Beckwourth back among them, asked him to be their chief again, an honor that he graciously refused, on the grounds that he was too old. At the feast to celebrate Beckwourth's return, this story goes, he was fed poisoned dog, because even in death he would be "good medicine." The annals of nineteenth-century disease and medicine being what they are, it is impossible to say what finally killed James Beckwourth. However, it seems only fitting that his death is as ambiguous as was his life.

As the West was won, and as Native Americans were pushed farther west and herded onto steadily shrinking reservations, popular and official attitudes toward the Indians began to change. As the century waned, the "savages" Beckwourth had joined were no longer the threat they had once been. By the time the frontier officially closed in 1890, Native American refusal to be quietly relocated to reservations had resulted in a series of Indian Wars that swept the prairies and mountains, leaving the tribes devastated and nearly powerless. And after the Civil War, Christian concern for the defeated Indians gained momentum, and a group of people who called themselves "the friends of the Indian" began to dominate the debate over the direction government policy should take. This direction was one of "Americanization" and Christianization. As reformer Carl Schurz rhetorically asked, in calling for the establishment of Indian boarding schools like Carlisle, "Can Indians be civilized?" His answer was a resounding "yes."[17] And as he and other reformers, now in charge of many Indian agencies, diligently worked for the passage of an Indian Citizenship Act, for the assimilation into white America of the defeated tribes, a new kind of Indian autobiography began to emerge. Perhaps the most noteworthy of these early-twentieth- century autobiographies was that of Long Lance, whose life is an exemplar of the cult of personality that began to emerge in the 1920s, and whose work stressed both his American success and his connection to a tragically vanished past.

Chief Buffalo Child Long Lance: Romantic Racialism and Native American Autobiography

In his foreword to *Long Lance*, the 1928 autobiography of Chief Buffalo Child Long Lance, humorist Irvin S. Cobb wrote admiringly of his friend's many accomplishments, not included in this childhood memoir: his mastery of half a dozen tribal languages besides his own, his presidential award of appointment to West Point, his bravery in World War I, from which he came out "as a captain of infantry, his body covered with wounds and his breast glittering with medals bestowed for high conduct and gallantry," his distinction as a writer for magazines.

Indeed, by the time Long Lance's autobiography appeared, he was well on his way to becoming a celebrity. The international press showered praise on his autobiography. *The Silent Enemy*, an ethnographic film about Indian life in northern Canada in which Long Lance starred the following year, was dubbed by Paramount into German, Swedish, Dutch, Polish, French, Spanish, Italian, and Portuguese. Authenticated at the time by Madison Grant, one of America's leading naturalists, it is a movie still acclaimed by film historians. Long Lance became a cultural icon: he appeared in comic strips, attended glittering cocktail parties with movie stars and aristocrats, and lived in New York at the famed Explorers Club, whose members included Fritjof Nansen, Theodore Roosevelt, and Ernest Thomas Seton. He authored a bestselling book on Indian sign language and even had his own line of B. F. Goodrich running shoes, endorsed by none other than the great athlete Jim Thorpe.

Long Lance was a self-invented Indian, however. Born in North Carolina in 1890 as Sylvester Long, the son of former slaves who claimed white and Indian, rather than black, forebears, Long Lance was classified according to the racial laws of Winston-Salem as being colored. A binary definition of race allowed him little latitude. His family was part of the black community in Winston-Salem, where Sylvester Long, as he was then known, worked as a janitor, one of the few jobs open to him.

In the world of American mythmaking, it is appropriate that Sylvester Long first learned how to be an Indian at the circus and Wild West show he ran away and joined as a youth of fourteen, traveling throughout the South and then again, when he was eighteen, with Robinson's Circus and Wild West Show (see note 22). Although there may have been no room on the prairies and in the forests for Indians, they were popular attractions at the Wild West shows. The shows depended for their success on their "authenticity," and "Everything Genuine" was a staple of their promotional literature. By the 1880s, Wild West shows had become popular events where actual Indians and cowboys reenacted frontier history. At times, these performances threatened to change the future, as well as to offer a version of the recent past for public consumption: in 1890, when White Horse, an Indian who traveled with Buffalo Bill Cody's Wild West Show, left the show in Europe and returned to tell a *New York Herald* reporter that "all the Indians in Buffalo Bill's show are discontented, ill-treated, and anxious to come home," the charges caused a public outcry, not least because of fears that the report would further inflame reservation Indians caught up in the Ghost Dance movement.[18] Bill Cody quickly replied in another *Herald* article: the damage control was important, since he needed government permission to recruit Indians for the show each season. The relationship between the Wild West shows and the government was complex. Government officials considered participation in the shows a good way of keeping potential troublemakers off the reservations and safely involved in performance: what they performed on stage they could not, thus, enact in real life. In fact, about thirty Indians captured at Wounded Knee were forced by the army to tour with Buffalo Bill in lieu of prison sentences.[19]

Although the government may have valued the Wild West shows for custodial reasons, Indian Bureau officals engaged in "civilizing" Indians through the boarding school system also recognized the power of the shows to shape public perceptions of Native Americans. The same year that the Wounded Knee massacre occurred, Commissioner of Indian Affairs Thomas J. Morgan issued a report to the secretary of the Interior in which he decried Indian participation in these shows: "The schools elevate, the shows degrade."[20] The struggle over whose version of the Indian the public would see was played out most dramatically at the Columbian Exposition of 1893, at which the Indian

Bureau opened a model school at which Indian youths were expected to sew, study, recite lessons, and cook meals for the entertainment and edification of Exposition visitors. The school was among the least popular of the Exposition's attractions; the ethnographic exhibit representing "the ancient people of the New World" was mobbed, and outside the fairgrounds, Buffalo Bill's show, banned from participation in the Exposition's official activities, was besieged by visitors.[21] Above all, the Wild West show was the embodiment of ethnicity as performance; with its stress on both authenticity and theatricality, it was the perfect proving ground for Long Lance's self-fashioning. In his travels through the segregated South with the circus, it would not be hard for Sylvester Long to see how the "exoticism" of his Indian role could enable him to escape the black/white banaries of the world in which he had grown up.

Sylvester Long's first act of self-fashioning occurred when he lied about his ancestry on his application to the Carlisle Indian Residential School: he was too white to qualify under the regulations. At Carlisle, he was shunned by the other students, who suspected him of being black. As his Indian classmates shed their pasts as part of the assimilationist policies mandated by the school, Sylvester Long took on their stories as his own. By the time he left the school, he had become Sylvester Long Lance, half-white and half-Cherokee. In 1913, as Sylvester Long Lance continued his education at St. John's, a prestigious military school, President Wilson was pushing for increased formal and official segregation. While Long Lance was enlisting in the Canadian army and working his way up as a journalist, Wilson was arranging for the segregation of and systematic firing of black federal employees. As D. W. Griffith's *Birth of a Nation* (1915) reframed the nation's racial history to audiences of millions, spurring the rebirth of the Ku Klux Klan and its incredible growth during the 1920s, Long Lance moved further and further away from the binary racial definitions of the period: as a Native American, Long Lance was able to do all kinds of things prohibited him as a black man. Ten years later, realizing that Cherokees were not sufficiently iconographically Indian to the general public, Sylvester Long Lance, who by this time was working as a journalist in Alberta, had evolved into Chief Buffalo Child Long Lance, a Blackfoot Indian.[22] From his experiences in the Wild West show, he understood that Plains Indians were most easily recognizable to Americans; the most famous Wild West Show, Buffalo Bill's Wild West, employed primarily Sioux.[23]

The story of Long Lance offers useful lessons about the slippery nature of racial and ethnic identity in America. By taking on an Indian identity, Sylvester Long managed to escape the limitations of his "colored" status. As an articulate, handsome international spokesman for the Native American, he proved appealing to Europeans and Americans alike, furnishing them with a focus for their primitivist fantasies. Long Lance took characteristics that could have been disabilities, like dark skin, and used them to transform himself into a consumable icon, becoming in Europe the symbol of Native Americanness. He took on an identity from the past and racially cross-dressed, making his color performative. Having a racial identity that was indeterminate, and at the time tragic, he inserted himself into one that, fifty years previously, would have been immensely problematic. Because the battles were long over, it became nostalgic rather than fraught. Classified as colored, he took his color and packaged it. His politics, likewise, seem slippery. Although he began by criticizing the Bureau of Indian Affairs, he ended by consorting with aristocratic Nazi sympathizers in Europe. Thus, a study of Long Lance points up the provisional nature not only of race and class, but of nationality and the very self.

Irvin S. Cobb's foreword to Long Lance's autobiography served as an endorsement, not only of the book's literary quality, but of its authenticity: "I claim there is authentic history in these pages and verity and most of all a power to describe in English words the thoughts, the instincts, the events which originally were framed in a native language."[24] These words are clearly similar to those of the abolitionists who authenticated slave narratives: no slave narrative would appear without an endorsement by a white sponsor. However, while most of the authenticators of slave narratives pledged themselves committed to racial justice, or, at the very least, the end of slavery, Irvin S. Cobb, the son of a Confederate army veteran, was a humorist whose living depended on his vast store of "darkie" jokes. Madison Grant, the naturalist who authenticated *The Silent Enemy*, was the author of *The Passing of the Great Race* (1916), in which he alerted Americans to the danger of its superior races, the Nordics, being submerged by inferior immigrants. In his 1933 work, *The Conquest of a Continent*, he warned of the dangers of racial miscegenation, advocating not only laws banning intermarriage but also the constant vigilance that Nordics must maintain to unmask mulattos passing for white.

It was no accident that both Long Lance's autobiography and his film were authenticated by men dedicated to racist theories, for by the turn of the century Native American autobiography held a special place in an American culture that was concerned both with mourning a people who could never return and with using Indian narratives to maintain racial theories of the time. Indeed, a prominent Native American autobiography published in 1931, *We Indians: The Passing of a Great Race*, the autobiography of White Horse Eagle, an Osage, was elicited and edited by Edgar von Schmidt-Pauli, a German academic whose chief scholarly interest lay in demonstrating the inevitability of the rise of the German race in general, and of Adolf Hitler in particular.

We Indians is among the more bizarre "Indian" autobiographies of its era: White Horse Eagle, its narrator, claimed to be 107 years old, and to have been acquainted with every United States president since Lincoln. He is capable of a number of remarkable feats, among them the ability to sense the presence of gold, silver or water in the earth beneath his feet, and the ability to read Egyptian hieroglyphics. His most salient trait, however, is his exemplification of racial purity. According to Schmidt-Pauli, White Horse Eagle is a "thorough gentleman"; the only time he becomes enraged is when sorely provoked, as Schmidt-Pauli's example illustrates: "I once remember a tipsy and uneducated man shouting out that all colored races, Indians, Hindoos, and niggers were equal. All at once this bowed and aged man seemed to assume gigantic proportions, his countenance became distorted with fury as though he was on the warpath and about to scalp his adversary." White Horse Eagle himself rarely misses an opportunity to proselytize on racial matters: the Osage culture was effective, he tells us, because it "was founded upon a severe disciplinary system which preserved us from thinking that everyone was equal. That is nonsense, as the Great Manitoo has differentiated everything in nature." [25] As H. David Brumble points out, to Schmidt-Pauli, "White Horse Eagle and the Indians in general [were] living—or rather dying—evidence of inborn racial characteristics."[26] For Schmidt-Pauli, White Horse Eagle's amanuensis, the Indians faced such a grim future because "they began to succumb to the seductions of civilization. They began to be attracted to white women. Cross-breeding ruined the ancient stock." According to some reports, "White Horse Eagle found it profitable to travel Europe in the 1920s and 1930s, adopting unsuspecting museum directors and chairmen of anthropology departments into his tribe. Photographs show him sporting a feather bonnet, Navajo silver jewelry, and a button reading *Lions Club Pasadena*. A Viennese museum director found him particularly convincing, because the Big Chief had made it a matter of principle not to shake hands with Jews."[27]

Long Lance's autobiography occupied a curious place within this nexus of social Darwinist or romantic racialist thought. It appeared just three years after the Indian Citizenship Act of 1925, which made every Native American an American citizen, and fifteen years after the publication of Joseph K. Dixon's 1913 volume of photographs and text, *The Vanishing Race*, a book that had come out of what might be termed the Bureau of Indian Affairs' official farewell to the disappearing Indians.[28] With Dixon as prime mover, the Bureau had arranged the Last Council, a meeting of chiefs and aging warriors from several of the western tribes. The achievement of Long Lance was to negotiate the territory between the tragic nostalgia emblematized by Dixon's work and the assimilationist claims of the Citizenship Act. Long Lance became the ultimate American: a Horatio Alger hero whose story resonated with the mythology of the frontier, a natural man who was able to adapt to industrial America while preserving his "authenticity."

Long Lance, in his autobiography, was able both to present a vanished way of life—he even included a chapter on hunting the buffalo, which in any event had vanished long before his childhood—and to present himself as an example of one who, as witnessed by the title of his 1926 *Cosmopolitan* article, "My Trail Upward," had managed to effect a Booker T. Washington-style transformation. Writing that "I'm proud to be as much like a white man as I am—and I'm proud, too, of every drop of Indian blood that runs through my veins," he built a reassuring bridge between the white and Indian worlds. As he concluded,

> I have reached no dizzying heights of material success, but I have succeeded in pulling myself up by my boot straps from a primitive and backward life into this great new world of white civilization.
> Anyone with determination and will can do as much.[29]

Long Lance both maintained an affectionate distance from his "roots" and from the reservation he claimed to visit a few times a year and asserted the superiority of a white way of life. Most important, he offered a reassuring message to those who might have qualms about the laws, dating back to the Indian Removal Bill of 1830, that had effectively destroyed the possibility of Native Americans living their traditional lives. It was all right, Long Lance, seemed to be saying. Although the end of this way of life may be sad, it was not tragic, since any Indian with determination could succeed in the white world—and, as Irvin Cobb writes of Long Lance in his preface, not only survive but conspicuously flourish. In fact, he dedicated his autobiography to "The two White Men who have guided and encouraged me most since I have taken a place in civilization." While acknowledging that his grandfather's dire predictions of the end of the traditional Indian way of life have come true, Long Lance ends his autobiography by claiming that these changes are, in fact, not only inevitable but ordained by the deity: "But the new day is here: it is here to stay. And now we must leave it for our old people to sit stolidly and dream of the glories of our past. Our job is to try to fit ourselves into the new scheme of life which the Great Spirit has decreed for North America."[30]

Long Lance, whose autobiography is full of stirring scenes of warfare, fit for an audience that craved boys' adventure stories, thus perfectly fulfilled the needs of an audience perhaps not fully comfortable with the conditions that had made Indian autobiography possible. Indian autobiography is a postcontact literary form and one that has been predicated on defeat and disappearance: Native American memoirs did not exist before the passage of the Indian Removal Act of 1830, which mandated the forced migration of the eastern tribes to locations west of the Mississippi. The first Indian autobiography, the *Life of Ma-Ka-tai-me-she-kia-kiak or Black Hawk* by the Sauk leader, appeared in

1833, after his defeat by Federal troops in the campaign known as the Black Hawk War. Native American autobiography has always been a solicited form, traditionally elicited and edited by a white although narrated by its subject, for, as Arnold Krupat points out, "the production of an Indian's own statement of his inevitable disappearance required that the Indian be represented as speaking in his own voice."[31] While nineteenth-century Native American autobiographies were the stories of defeated leaders, of heroes in the mold of Kit Carson or Sam Houston, twentieth-century Indian autobiographies began to represent the process of Americanization. Many of these works, like Long Lance's, stress not only the assimilation but the Americanness of their teller. The life history of the Crow Chief Plenty-Coups, for example, was published in 1930 under the title *American: the Life Story of a Great Indian*. The title of Charles Eastman's 1916 memoir emphasized the same kind of progress as did Long Lance's: *From the Deep Woods to Civilization*. Long Lance's self-fashioning to fit the needs of his audience was particularly successful, as evidenced by a 1930 *Herald Tribune* article about him, entitled "One Hundred Percent American," which begins with the claim, "There is romance always in the man who can play the game and live the life of another race." Rather than questioning Long Lance's identity, though, Beverly Smith, the article's author, attributes the American success of Long Lance, "a splendid specimen of the American Indian," to his Indian background. It is his very foreignness, his exotic qualities, that make his heroism in the service of the nation possible. For instance, his acts of bravery in World War I, for which he claimed to have been decorated by three governments, came about because "there was war in Europe, and it called to the warrior blood in Long Lance."[32]

The publicity material released by Paramount to promote his movie, *The Silent Enemy*, reflected this preoccupation with authenticity, as did the movie's reviews. The marquee of the Criterion, a theater in New York, advertised the picture as "A drama of wild life, wild people, wild beasts." *Exhibitors Herald World*, a trade publication, noted that "The characters are all real Indians, who act in a manner in keeping with the tone of authenticity sustained throughout the entire production."[33]

Although in his other published writings Long Lance emphasized individual accomplishment, his constructed autobiography, ironically enough, exemplified many of the traditions of Indian autobiography enumerated by Hertha Wong: "Lack of rigid chronology, incorporation of multiple voices that emphasize tribal identity."[34] Long Lance's chronology, including such iconographic yet historically impossible scenes as hunting buffalo, can hardly be called rigid. And, since Long Lance incorporated into his narrative stories from his Blackfoot friends like Mike Eagle Speaker, as well as those that he had heard from his classmates at the Carlisle Indian School, he was in a sense creating a new tribal identity: it just wasn't his own.[35] The fact that his autobiography had been elicited and edited by Ray Long, the editor in chief of Cosmopolitan, simply placed him in a long tradition of other Native speakers.

If, as Arnold Krupat writes, "victory is the ennobling condition of western autobiography, [but] defeat is the ennobling condition of Indian autobiography," Long Lance managed to have his cake and eat it too, by recording both the tribal defeat and his individual triumph.[36] Thus, Long Lance was drawing from two distinct traditions of American autobiography: that of ethnic autobiography, understood by both teller and audience to be the story of a group as much as of an individual, and that of self-construction, the triumphant individual struggle upward of Benjamin Franklin or Booker T. Washington.

As a skilled journalist with nearly a decade of newspaper and magazine experience under his belt by the time he wrote his autobiography, Long Lance had the professional writer's ease with forms. And as someone who had negotiated his way between a number of ethnic and racial identities, Long Lance was well aware of his audience's expectations. One of the best eyewitness accounts of Long Lance's performative skill comes from Norwegian journalist Theodor Findahl, who in his travelogue *Manhattan Babylon: En Bok om New York Idag* [*A Book About New York Today*], described an evening he spent with Long Lance, whom he characterized as "a full-blooded redskin and a genuine aristocrat," at the Park Avenue home of Irvin S. Cobb. To Findahl's evident surprise, Long Lance

> was by no means on the warpath, wore no paint, nor a feather
> headdress, but was dressed in a fashionable New York tuxedo, patent
> leather shoes, and a white waistcoat . . . the rouged ladies, glittering
> with pearls, are thrilled. "Isn't it wonderful," one of them whispers to
> me, "that colored people can seem so distinguished? All the Indians
> I've seen before this have seemed just like gypsies, and this one is a
> gentleman. So confident in his manner, so effortlessly superior. I could
> almost imagine addressing him as 'your highness,' like him," and she
> glanced over at the desk, where Mussolini's portrait, with a long
> handwritten inscription, a souvenir from Irvin Cobb's last visit to
> Rome, glared menacingly back at us. "And listen to what perfect
> English he speaks, and what interesting things he talks about."

Among the interesting things Long Lance was talking about was Indian sign language:

> Though the fifty-eight languages spoken by North American tribes
> were as different as Turkish and English, Indians had nonetheless
> developed a sign language so wonderfully colorful and poetic as to be
> understood by every redskin, so witty and gracious that the sign

language white civilization has created for the deaf is clumsy and helpless by comparison.

He gave a demonstration:

> Just by gesturing with his hands and arms, Long Lance conjured visions before our eyes. . . . *Spring*, his hands fluttered as though to indicate rain, and suddenly he thrust a hand upwards to indicate the spring's regenerative powers. . . . *Winter*—snowflakes which dance in the air, masterful portrayal with his fingers.

Long Lance speculated on why even the Anglo-Saxons with the strongest racial instincts, the ones most fearful of miscegenation, were still proud to claim even a drop of Indian blood: "Could it be a subconscious acknowledgment of the fact that the country's true heirs and owners are Indians, is it in sympathy with the Indians' tragic destiny, or is it just that Indians are no longer dangerous at all?" As he continued to discourse on such topics as his tribe's marriage customs, and prophesied the eventual return of the "only true Americans,"

> "Irvin," said an elderly woman in a stage whisper, "You must help me get the chief to lecture to lecture to my women's club. He'd be a sensation. You must, you hear?"[37]

This performance of Long Lance's thus entailed not only an act of literary imposture but one that encompassed his every waking moment: his life was a stage he could never leave, whether inventing Indian sign language at a cocktail party or politely listening to Irvin Cobb's seemingly endless, and oft-repeated, store of "darkie" jokes. However, his comments about "true Americans" also reveal how well he understood his audience's expectations. It is no wonder that Long Lance was immensely successful in his disguise, when he so fully understood the ramifications of the role he was playing. However, no matter how skillfully he was able to escape the trap of binary racial definitions, he of necessity found himself on the outside looking in. His imposture meant that he could never go home to see his parents or siblings, who were firmly ensconced in the black community of Winston-Salem. Although his stories, which became increasingly grandiose, were generally believed, there were dangerous moments, questions put to him that forced him to improvise a past quickly. Interestingly enough, one man who had his suspicions about Long Lance and might have been expected to voice them remained silent: Chauncey Yellow Robe, the great-nephew of Sitting Bull and Long Lance's co-star in *The Silent Enemy*. Yellow Robe was made suspicious by Long Lance's demeanor on the set—his punctuality, his boisterousness, his small talk with strangers. This was behavior which, though it may have fulfilled white expectations, certainly did not meet those of Yellow Robe, who made discreet inquiries while in New York on a lecture tour following the production of the movie. Although he eventually had his suspicions confirmed by the Bureau of Indian Affairs, and went so far as to contact the movie's legal counsel, he eventually came to Long Lance's defense. Although Yellow Robe never explained why he shifted his stance, it is probable that he chose to embrace a more inclusive definition of what it meant to be an Indian. James P. Beckwourth was, after all, readily adopted by the Crow Indians; the Seminoles he fought on behalf of the U.S. government had admitted many African-Americans to their tribe.[38] Interestingly enough, Yellow Robe had, in a 1914 address to the Fourth Annual Conference of the Society of American Indians, spoken out against government support of "wild-west shows, moving-picture concerns, and fair associations for commercializing the Indian"—the very venues by which Long Lance had achieved his fame. Given his call for "equal opportunities, equal responsibilities, equal education" for the American Indian, and in criticizing depictions of "savage" Indians, it is also possible that Yellow Robe was reluctant to unmask an Indian spokesman who had achieved so much.[39]

Long Lance's was at best an ambiguous accomplishment. Although in the early years of his journalistic career he had rethought the assimilationist goals of the Carlisle Indian School, and was using his position to forcefully criticize positions taken by the Canadian Department of Indian Affairs, such as the government decree to ban potlatch ceremonies, he eventually retreated from this confrontational stance. When members of the Blood Indian tribe expressed dismay that Long Lance was using his ceremonial adoption by them for his own ends, he grew resentful that they were not sufficiently grateful. One sign of his movement away from activism was the dedication of his autobiography to Duncan Campbell Scott, the Deputy Superintendent of Indian Affairs in Ottawa, a powerful government official who had questioned the sense of expending money and social services on a "dying people" and had lobbied for Indians to conform to what he called "that worldwide tendency towards universal standardization which would appear to be the essential underlying purport of all modern social evolution."[40]

Unfortunately, Long Lance was finally unable to inhabit the narrative he had written for himself. He committed suicide in 1932, at the age of forty-two, in the home of Anita Baldwin, one of his wealthy patrons. He left no note, so one can only guess that the strain of living a lie for over twenty years had finally become unbearable. Back in Winston-Salem, where Long Lance had not visited in twenty years, his brother, Abe Long, whom Long Lance had written to request that "If there is anything in the papers, Abe, you will be careful about names, won't you," spent the thirties and forties directing the flow of traffic up the steps to the colored gallery of the Carolina

Theater.[41] In a diary he kept all his life, he commented on progress in civil rights. He opened one such entry by writing "We the better thinking negroes."[42]

Long Lance's autobiography continued to be reprinted for decades.

The Education of Little Tree Reconsidered

In 1973, little more than fifty years after Long Lance's death, Forrest Carter, or Little Tree, was born, with the publication of his first novel, *The Rebel Outlaw, Josey Wales* (1973), which became the source for the Clint Eastwood vehicle *The Outlaw Josey Wales*.[43] *The Education of Little Tree* followed three years later. Although the book did reasonably well at the time of its first publication, it was not until its reprinting in 1986 that it slowly began to gain the immense popularity that would make it a publishing sensation.

In October 1991, *The Education of Little Tree*, Forrest Carter's memoir of his Cherokee boyhood, was the book of the moment. It had sold more than half a million copies since its first publication in 1976 and was then number one on the *New York Times* best-seller list. *Little Tree*, treated in the industry as a publishing phenomenon, was a true word-of-mouth success.[44] The director of marketing for the University of New Mexico Press, Peter Moulson, recalls purchasers buying a dozen copies at a time to distribute to friends. Groups of school children had formed Little Tree fan clubs, and there was talk that Hollywood was planning to bring Carter's gentle, New Age-tinged message of multiculturalism and environmentalism to the big screen. For thousands of *New York Times* readers, then, 4 October 1991 must have brought an unpleasant surprise.

According to an op ed piece written by Dan T. Carter, a history professor at Emory University, the critically acclaimed Cherokee memoir was a fake. Not only was its author, Forrest Carter, also known as Asa Carter, not the Native American he claimed to be, but, as Dan T. Carter wrote, "Between 1946 and 1973, the Alabama native carved out a violent career in Southern politics as a Ku Klux Klan terrorist, right-wing radio announcer, home-grown American fascist and anti-Semite, rabble-rousing demagogue and secret author of the famous 1963 speech by Gov. George Wallace of Alabama: 'Segregation now . . . Segregation tomorrow . . . Segregation forever.'" Even his new first name, Dan Carter revealed, had been taken from Nathan Bedford Forrest, who founded the original Ku Klux Klan in 1866. Articles about the hoax appeared in *Newsweek*, in *Time*, in *Publishers Weekly*. For editorialists across the country, the exposure of Forrest Carter was an occasion for soul-searching. "What does it tell us that we are so easily deceived?" Dan T. Carter had asked, a question echoed not only by pundits but by the studio heads who had been, until that point, involved in a bidding war over movie rights. Readers swamped Dan Carter's office with heartbroken calls. Equally taken aback were Forrest's friends of his later, Texas years, for whom he would, after a couple of drinks, perform Indian war dances and chant in what he said was the Cherokee language. Carter told Eleanor Friede, his agent, that he could only write when he retreated to fast, meditate and commune with nature, and she defended his authenticity to the end.[45] Nobody seemed able to come up with an explanation for Carter's ethnic imposture: the story seemed so bizarre as to be anomalous.

In fact, Dan Carter's article was not the first exposure of Forrest Carter as an impostor Indian. Some Alabamans, acquainted with the Klansman they had known as Asa Carter, recognized him in Forrest Carter's 1974 interview with Barbara Walters on the *Today* show. One, journalist Wayne Greenhaw, went so far as to publicize the fact in a brief New York Times article in August 1976, but news of the imposture seemed not to have registered in the public consciousness.[46] Yet when the news hit for the second time, it did so with a cataclysmic impact.

What was it about the book that seemed to resonate so with readers? *Little Tree* sold much better than any other Native American autobiography published at the same time. It found adherents in the Washington State court system, where it was used to rehabilitate youthful offenders, and among the cast of the Broadway musical *The Will Rogers Follies*, who received gift copies from their director, Tommy Tune.[47] In fact, as Rennard Strickland, director of the Center for Indian Law and Policy at the University of Oklahoma, himself a Cherokee, noted in his foreword to the University of New Mexico Press edition, the book was sold in tribal souvenir shops on Indian reservations; according to Strickland, "Students of Native American life found the book to be as accurate as it was mystical and romantic."[48] Asa Carter's past, grinding out impassioned speeches in a basement office of George Wallace's statehouse, seems to have served him well in writing *The Education of Little Tree*. The book is, in fact, a hack's dream, a slender volume of 216 pages in which every rhetorical trick known to the speechwriter is used to full advantage. Carter manages to appeal effectively to a number of different constituencies in telling the story of Little Tree's life with the grandparents who adopted him after the death of his parents.

Environmentally oriented audiences can warm to Little Tree's descriptions of "Mon-o-lah, the earth mother, [who] came to me through my moccasins. I could feel her push and swell here, and sway and give there . . . and the roots that veined her body and the life of the water-blood, deep inside her. She was warm and springy and bounced me on her breast, as Granma said she would."[49] Nature is not only a mother, but one whose creatures, especially the hunting

dogs belonging to Little Tree and his grandparents, seem incessantly to perform cute, Disneyfied antics. Living in harmony with Mother Earth is a theme
endlessly repeated throughout the text: as the narrator notes, "Granpa lived
with the game, not *at* it."[50]

Little Tree may only be the latest iteration of what the English impostor
Archie Belaney, who became Grey Owl, an Apache half-breed, expressed when
he declared, "The Indians were always conservationists. Indians are in tune
with their surroundings."[51] Grey Owl's authority as a "Native" spokesperson
enabled him to so lecture effectively throughout North America and Britain
on the subject of conservation, to broadcast his appeals, and to publish a number of books on the subject of conservation, specifically on beavers, which he
referred to as "little Indians." Whatever his other motivations, Grey Owl used
his identity to present his environmental message in the most dramatic way
he knew; by the time of his death in 1938 he had used his position as "care-
taker of animals" for the Canadian Park Service as a platform to advance his
environmental cause across the world. Advising his publicity agent that he
wished to be packaged as a "modern Hiawatha," Grey Owl posed in his version of full native dress when on tour (during his first British tour, in 1935,
he addressed more than fifty thousand people); he gave a Royal Performance
in 1937 for the king and queen of England and starred in the movies produced by the Canadian Park Service. Although Grey Owl may have anthro-
pomorphized the beavers whose preservation he advocated, he seems to have
used his native persona primarily for political purposes. His version of
Indianness involved a somewhat romantic, but relatively uncomplicated vision of nature.[52] For Little Tree, nature is a much more directive force.

Knowledge of Mother Earth, is, of course, integral to understanding The
Way, for in *The Education of Little Tree* nature is not just a mother who must
be respected but also a guide to wisdom. Little Tree's grandparents teach him
the secret of living in harmony with nature, so that "I knew now why we only
used the logs that the spirit had left for our fireplace." Interestingly, Granpa
also preaches a kind of social Darwinism of the forest, telling Little Tree not
to be distressed at the sight of a hawk eating a quail, for "It is The Way. Tal-
con caught the slow and so the slow will raise no children who are also slow."
In one of the poems that stud the text, Little Tree advises readers to "Learn
the wisdom of Mon-o-lah," his (invented) term for the earth, in order to "know
The Way of all the Cherokee."[53]

In this mystical amalgam, spiritual knowledge is tied to the Cherokee Way,
which is itself tied to a knowledge of nature. The idea that Native Americans have a primordial wisdom is one to which many Americans have responded, especially since the 1960s. *Little Tree* goes this notion one better,
and mixes in such New Age concerns as reincarnation into the spiritual stew.

"Granma said your spirit mind could get so big and powerful that you would eventually know all about your past body lives and would get to where you could come out with no body death atall."[54]

Little Tree plays into the idea that "authenticity" is to be found through a return to cultural primitivism and, not incidentally, anti-intellectualism. Thus, Little Tree tells us that "Granma began to hum a tune behind me and I knew it was Indian, and needed no words for its meaning to be clear." And Granpa, who is by turns mystically attuned to the earth and homespun, tells Little Tree that "the meddlesome son of a bitch that invented the dictionary ought to be taken out and shot." The primal wisdom of the Native Americans occurs in a universe outside of time, outside politics. Thus, when Granpa hears news of the ravages of the Depression, "fellers was jumping out of winders in New York and shootin' themselves in the head about it," he explains to Little Tree that "New York was crowded all up with people who didn't have enough land to live on, and likely half of them was run crazy from living that-a-way, which accounted for the shootin's and the winder jumping." It is not economic hardship but cultural impoverishment that leads people to despair during the Great Depression. A post-Watergate readership, disillusioned with the political process, would seem a natural constituency for a narrative in which politicians appear suspect.[55]

The Education of Little Tree is not only a fantasy about Native American primal spirituality, it is also a fantasy perfectly attuned to an American public well-versed in the rhetoric of self-actualization and, more specifically, the recovery movement. If previous impostors have given us Indians as noble savages, romantic racialists, people specially attuned to the environment, spiritual guides, Little Tree presents us with a new vision of Native American identity for the seventies and beyond: what I call the inner child Indian. We look to Indians for what we think we have lost. If Long Lance and Grey Owl presented themselves, in the twenties and thirties, as Indians whose virility was unquestioned, and whose masculinity in fact rested on their Native identities, Little Tree offers us a world where sex is not even an issue, an idealized world of childhood.[56] In the era of AIDS, this world seemed appealing to many readers.

In a time of rising divorce rates and fractured families, Little Tree provides a vision of an idyllic family unit.[57] In a period when pop psychology writers like Jon Bradshaw have brought discussions of the inner child, of toxic families, to talk shows like Oprah Winfrey's and Phil Donahue's, seen by millions, and when such works as M. Scott Peck's *The Road Less Traveled* remained firmly ensconced on the *New York Times* best-seller list, Little Tree offered readers a vision of a family that healed rather than inflicting pain.[58] And, in his portrait of his grandparents, especially his grandfather, whose father had survived the Trail of Tears, Little Tree offered a model of successful recovery from trauma. While Dee Brown's best-selling *Bury My Heart at Wounded Knee* (1973) presented a history of unrelieved horror, Little Tree's narrative offered a way out of history.

When we first meet Little Tree, it is on the occasion of his mother's death, when he is five, a year after the loss of his father. The bond between the child and his newly discovered grandfather is instantaneous and instinctive: while a crowd of relatives "thrashed it out proper as to where I was to go, while they divided up the painted bedstead and the chairs," Granpa stays aloof from the fray, uninterested both in material possessions and in treating the child as a thing to be disposed of. He is every child's fantasy, the chosen parent: Little Tree literally picks him from the crowd, holds on to his leg, and won't let go— and so the matter is decided. Granma lulls the boy to sleep with an Indian song in which the forest, wind, and various animals welcome him, promising that "Little Tree will never be alone," and "I knew I was Little Tree, and I was happy that they loved me and wanted me. And so I slept, and did not cry."[59]

Little Tree grows up in a near-Rousseauvian idyll: Granpa and Granma do not restrain him. No matter how dirty or wet he gets while playing, his grandmother doesn't mind, for "Cherokees never scolded their children for having anything to do with the woods." They encourage every aspect of his growth: "Granpa bragged on me a lot to Granma at the supper table and Granma agreed that it looked like I was coming on to being a man."[60] Not once in the book does Little Tree feel anger at either grandparent, nor does either grandparent behave, at any point, in a less than loving way. The world of the family is safe, free from conflict, a nurturing cocoon.

Tellingly, family happiness is dependent on isolation from the mainstream of American life, in which dysfunction is rampant. Little Tree must venture into the wider world to find brutality (a sharecropper whipping his daughter), dishonesty and sanctimony (he is sold a dying mule by a man claiming to be Christian), exploitation (big city bootleggers trying to muscle their way into Granpa's bootlegging business), and racism. Whereas James P. Beckwourth claims to have become an Indian only in order to aid the American government, and while Long Lance prides himself on his "trail upward" from the enclosed world of his tribe and his family into American "civilization," Little Tree can only attain maturity within the sheltered context of his family: exposure to the outside world is scarring, both literally and figuratively. And whereas citizenship and its responsibility are eagerly embraced by Beckwourth and Long Lance, only the folly of government intervention can endanger Little Tree's idyll.

Government intervention takes many forms, such as Granpa's imprisonment for bootlegging, but it reaches its worst level when the state takes Little

Tree from his grandparents and places him in an orphanage of Dickensian horrors. Within the orphanage can be found childhood in its most dysfunctional form, civilization at its most discontented: the minister—the Reverend—who runs the orphanage brands Little Tree a bastard and tells him that as such he cannot be saved. According to the Reverend, "Granpa was not fittin' to raise a young'un, and . . . I more than likely had not ever had any discipline." This, to Little Tree and his readers, is the beauty of the arrangement. Discipline, in the Reverend's terms, includes a beating so severe that he breaks a stout stick across Little Tree's back and fills his shoes with blood. The reason for this punishment is the boy's innocent reference, in class, to mating deer, which causes his teacher to "holler, 'I should have *known*—we *all* should have known . . . filth . . . filth . . . would come out of you . . . you . . . little *bastard!*'" The orphanage is a world in which the disabled, as represented by Little Tree's club-footed roommate and only friend, are humiliated. It is a world of disconnection from nature, of sexual repression, of Christian pieties and manufactured sentiment: "The white-headed lady said Christmas was might near on us. She said everybody was to be happy and sing." Politicians visit at Christmas, as do drunken country club members, who distribute broken gifts to the children; to mark the occasion, "a male pine . . . died slow, there in the hall." It is only by talking to an oak tree and communicating with his grandparents by watching the Dog Star at night, so that his grandparents can "sen[d] me remembrance," that Little Tree can survive and can finally tell them that he wants to return home. As conditions in the orphanage worsen, Little Tree relies more and more heavily on Indian ways to survive—whether he is letting his "body mind" sleep, in order to endure the pain of the reverend's physical abuse, or listening to the oak tree: "She was supposed to be asleep, but she said she wasn't, on account of me. She talked slow—and low."[61]

Little Tree has no doubts that his grandparents will rescue him, and indeed, Granpa shows up on Christmas to reclaim Little Tree and return him to the world of the mountain, where he can live happily, listening to his grandparents' message of harmony with nature, freedom from government intervention, distrust of language, love and respect of one another, and condemnation of racial and ethnic prejudice.

As Granpa tells Little Tree, "foreigners is people that happens to be someplace where they wasn't born." He also discusses Jews, as personified by the kind old peddler, Mr. Wine. When Little Tree asks, in response to overhearing a slur, "Granpa, what is a damn Jew?": "Granpa stopped and didn't look back at me. His voice sounded tired too. 'I don't know; something is said about 'em in the Bible, somewhere's or other; must go back a long ways.' Granpa turned around. 'Like the Indian . . . I hear tell they ain't got no nation, neither.'"[62] Granma and Granpa preach tolerance, and remain dignified in the face of prejudice. Little Tree is full of touching stories of people reaching out across seemingly insurmountable cultural and ideological chasms to help one another—a fragile peace that is, likely as not, shattered by government intervention. Former Union soldiers help former Confederates (and their still-loyal former slave); Grandpa and Mr. Wine find common cause; brotherhood seems not only possible but the only real choice, if one is to follow The Way.

In 1955, having been hired as a spokesman by the anti-integration American States Rights Association, Asa Carter was fired for his on-air diatribes against National Brotherhood Week, sponsored by the National Conference of Christians and Jews. Caught up in the movement to halt civil rights progress, he ran into trouble with other Alabama Citizens Council leaders because he would not allow Jews into his white supremacist organization: "We believe that this is basically a battle between Christianity and atheistic communism," he told a reporter. As late as 1978, in his guise as Forrest Carter, he delivered a drunken speech to the Wellesley College Club in Dallas, in which he talked, à la Little Tree, about the need of people to love one another. As reporter Dana Rubin writes, "In an expansive moment, Carter pointed across the podium at his fellow speaker, historian Barbara Tuchman. 'Now, she's a good ol' Jew girl,' Carter said. Then he swung his arm toward Stanley Marcus, who was in the audience. 'Now, Stanley,' he went on, 'there's a good ol' Jew boy.'"[63]

As far as is known, however, Carter confined his anti-Semitism to verbal abuse. This was not true of his feelings toward African Americans. In the mid-fifties, he was among the men who incorporated a shadowy paramilitary group called the Original Ku Klux Klan of the Confederacy, six alleged members of which, on Labor Day 1957, kidnapped a black handyman, sliced off his scrotum, and poured turpentine on his wounds. In speeches, Asa Carter vowed to put his "blood on the ground" to halt integration. By the time George Wallace hired him as a speechwriter in 1958, after having been trounced by a Klan-backed candidate in his quest for the lieutenant governorship, Carter's reputation as an extremist was such that Wallace's men, nervous about having him linked to their candidate, paid him through back channels and, after Wallace's victory, gave him a rear office in the state capitol. Over time, he became disillusioned with Wallace, whom he saw as caving in to integrationist forces. He came in fifth in a field of five in his protest bid against Wallace in the 1970 governor's race. The statewide paramilitary force he set up in 1971 failed, as had his venture the previous year to set up a string of all-white private schools. The following year Carter was arrested three times on alcohol-related charges. The year after that, he and his wife sold their home, bought their sons a home in Abilene, Texas, and moved to Florida. That year, Forrest Carter, who sold his first book, a Confederate adventure novel, *The Rebel Outlaw, Josey Wales*, was born.

When he visited his sons in Texas, Forrest called them his nephews. He made new friends, for whom he invented an Indian past. He began to speak ungrammatically, to wear jeans and a black cowboy hat, to talk about his people, the Cherokee, with whom he claimed to live for part of the year. Apparently, Asa's new identity was a fantasy in which even his wife, India, participated, in her own way. After Wayne Greenhaw exposed Carter for the first time in his August 1976 article for the *New York Times*, India wrote to him to clear matters up. Forrest was, according to her, not Asa at all, but was instead Asa's sensitive, artistic nephew, with whom she had fallen in love during his visit to her and Asa, for whom she had left her racist husband, and to whom she was now married.[64] Ironically, while James P. Beckwourth and Sylvester Long escaped the historical trap of their racial identity by becoming Indian, Asa Carter took on a Native self as, among other things, a way of leaving his racist reputation behind him.

Little Tree was very much an Indian for the nineties. As the waif look became popular in fashion in the late eighties, as lifestyle pages reported that "cocooning" had become a new trend, as Earth Day was resurrected in 1990 and New Age and spiritual volumes filled the shelves of bookstores, Asa Carter stepped forward to give Americans the Native American they wanted, in the process shedding, not quite effortlessly, his racist past. As a white supremacist, Asa Carter's day had passed. By the early 1970s, his following had evaporated; his name surfaced in the newspapers only to report his arrests for drunken driving. His re-creation of himself as a Native American offered Carter a second chance, a way out of the black-white binary in which, ironically, he had trapped himself through his white supremacist politics. While Long Lance and Beckwourth certainly did not choose to be trapped by their "blackness" the way that Carter, in his first life, chose to capitalize on his whiteness, he, like them, found himself trapped by racial categories, and escaped racial binaries through assuming an Indian identity. However, like Long Lance and James Beckwourth before him, Carter succeeded in his impersonation by trading on his deep knowledge of racial and ethnic stereotypes, a knowledge honed during his years as a professional racist. Sylvester Long's choice of escaping his colored identity by becoming Indian seems fairly understandable: it is easy to see that being a film star and Indian chief would offer more possibilities than being a janitor. Asa Carter was never forced into a life as a white supremacist, however. After a career spent capitalizing on his whiteness, he simply chose to manipulate stereotypes of race and ethnicity in another way. Just as James Beckwourth was challenged by critics who saw his ethnicity at birth as being an impediment to his ability to tell the truth, and Long Lance built his career as an Indian through collaboration with white supremacist race theorists, so Asa Carter skillfully employed his knowledge of racialist thinking to create an Indian self who could appeal to the masses.

Notes

1. Although I use the term "ethnic impostor" throughout this essay it is not without wincing. Imposture implies that there is an "authentic" identity that can be impersonated. I thought, for a while, of employing the term "voluntary ethnicity," but rejected it because it seems to downplay the cultural leap taken by these impostors, or volunteers. While I am arguing against authenticity, I am also aware that, much as we may like to think that race and ethnicity are not essential qualities, they are certainly treated as such in our culture. For a Klansman to speak as a Cherokee orphan, for a "colored" janitor to speak as an Indian chief, is certainly not seen, in late twentieth-century America, as a "natural" state of affairs. In a culture where such categories exist, we need to take their transgression as a serious issue, one worthy of examination—for what it tells us not only about the individuals whose stories are related in this work, but also about American culture as a whole.

2. Belaney was only the first in a long tradition of fake environmental Indians and fake Native American speeches: witness, for example, Chief Seattle's speech, in its original form a late nineteenth-century product of American manifest destiny thinking. In 1969–70 a new speech was written by, though never attributed to, University of Texas English professor Ted Perry; it is this speech, moving in its connection to the earth and its sensitivity to nature, that has been endlessly reprinted by the World Wildlife Fund and others and can, in poster form, be seen on the walls of countless elementary school classrooms.

3. Alice B. Kehoe, "Primal Gaia: Primitivists and Plastic Medicine Men," *The Invented Indian*, ed. James A. Clifton (New Brunswick, N.J.: Transaction Publishers, 1990), 193–209.

4. Cited by Bernard De Voto, introduction to *The Life and Adventures of James P. Beckwourth* (New York: Knopf, 1931), xix.

5. Francis Parkman, *The Oregon Trail* (1877; reprint, New York: Library of America, 1991), 119.

6. Charles Christy, "The Personal Memoirs of Capt. Charles Christy," *The Trail* 1 (October, 1908:16–18.

7. See Thomas F. Gossett, *Race: The History of an Idea in America* (New York: Schocken Books, 1963), p. 65. For a fuller discussion of the reception of the work, see William Stanton, *The Leopard's Spots: Scientific Attitudes Toward Race in America, 1815–1859* (Chicago: University of Chicago Press, 1966), 161–173. See also Stephen Jay Gould, *The Mismeasure of Man* (New York: W.W. Norton, 1981), chap. 2.

8. T. D. Bonner, *The Life and Adventures of James P. Beckwourth* (1856; reprint, Lincoln: University of Nebraska Press, 1972), 14. Unless otherwise noted, all page numbers refer to this edition.

9. It was not just the nature of Beckwourth's racial identity that was challenged by his contemporaries. Even the ownership of Beckwourth's memories of his Crow life was thrown into question: upon his autobiography's publication Beckwourth was angrily denounced by a fellow trapper from Kentucky, Robert Meldrum. Meldrum attacked him for the usual racial reasons, on the grounds that his mother had been a Negress and that he was therefore a mulatto. More than a desire to debunk, however, was a competitor's jealousy. According to the journals of Lieutenant James H. Bradley, Meldrum, "upon quitting his service, enamoured of the savage life he had tasted for three years, remained upon the plains making his home among the Crow Indians. Adopting their dress, gluing long hair to his own to make it conform to the savage fashion, having his squaw and lodge, and living in all respects the life of an Indian, he was quickly enabled by a superior intelligence and courage to acquire great influence with his savage associates. . . . He was a man

of many adventures, and was accustomed to complain bitterly that Beckwourth, in the autobiography published by Harper Brothers, had arrogated to himself many of his own experiences." Quoted in Elinor Wilson, *Jim Beckwourth: Black Mountain Man and War Chief of the Crows* (Norman: University of Oklahoma Press, 1972). Meldrum, however, refused to be mollified by Harper Brothers' offer to publish his authentic memories: as Bradley recalls, "he proudly rejected all overtures."

10. T. D. Bonner, *The Life and Adventures of James P. Beckwourth,* edited, with preface, by Charles G. Leland (London: T. Fisher Unwin, 1892), 9. Emphasis in original.

11. A. D. Richardson, *Beyond the Mississippi* (Hartford, Conn.: American Publishing Company, 1867), 299.

12. William Loren Katz, *Black Indians: A Hidden Heritage* (New York: Atheneum, 1986), 121.

13. Leigh Brackett, *Follow the Free Wind* (Garden City, N.Y.: Doubleday, 1963). Other juvenile biographies of Beckwourth include Olive Burt, *Jim Beckwourth: Crow Chief* (New York: Julian Messner, 1957); Harold W. Felton, *Jim Beckwourth: Negro Mountain Man* (New York: Dodd, Mead, 1966); Lawrence Cortesi, *Jim Beckwourth: Explorer-Patriot of the Rockies* (New York: Criterion Books, 1971); and Sean Nolan, *James Beckwourth* (New York: Chelsea House Publishers), 1992.

14. Elizabeth McGlagan, *A Peculiar Paradise: A History of Blacks in Oregon, 1788–1940* (Portland, Oreg.: Gregorian Press, 1980); Samuel Thurston quoted on 30–31.

15. Quoted in Katz, *Black Indians,* 115.

16. Bernard De Voto, *The Year of Decision, 1846* (Boston: Houghton Mifflin, 1943), 63.

17. For a discussion of the "Friends of the Indian," see Francis Paul Prucha, ed., *Americanizing the American Indians: Writings by the "Friends of the Indian" 1880–1900* (Lincoln: University of Nebraska Press, 1973).

18. *World Columbian Exposition Illustrated* (Chicago: 1893), 262. For a fuller discussion of the battle over the Indian image, see L. G. Moses, "Wild West Shows, Reformers, and the Image of the American Indian, 1887–1914," *South Dakota History* 14, no. 3 (1984): 193–221; Moses, "Indians on the Midway: Wild West Shows and the Indian Bureau at the World's Fairs, 1893–1904," *South Dakota History* 21, no. 3 (1991):205–229; Moses, *Wild West shows and the Images of American Indians, 1883–1933* (Albuquerque: University of New Mexico Press, 1996); and Robert A. Trennert, Jr., "Selling Indian Education at World's Fairs and Expositions, 1893–1904," *American Indian Quarterly* 11, no. 3 (1987): 203–220.

19. Sarah J. Blackstone, *Buckskins, Bullets, and Business: A History of Buffalo Bill's Wild West* (Westport, Conn.: Greenwood Press, 1986), 86.

20. Quoted in Prucha, ed., *Americanizing the Indians,* 311.

21. *New York Herald* 19 November 1890; quoted in Blackstone, *Buckskins, Bullets, and Business,* 25.

22. See Donald B. Smith, *Long Lance: The True Story of an Impostor* (Lincoln: University of Nebraska Press, 1982).

23. Other Wild West shows that employed Indians from other tribes often required them to dress as Sioux and enact Sioux rituals. For instance an encampment of Cree Indians who visited Cincinnati in 1895 "wore pseudo-Plains clothing in untraditional ways and decorated themselves with feathers that fell from some of the birds at the zoo." Susan Labry Meyn, "Mutual Infatuation: Rosebud Sioux and Cincinnatians," *Queen City Heritage* 52, no.1–2 (1994):30–48.

24. Long Lance, Chief Buffalo Child, *Long Lance* (New York: Cosmopolitan Book Corporation, 1928).

25. White Horse Eagle, *We Indians: The Passing of a Great Race* (New York: E. P. Dutton, 1931), 26, 84.

26. H. David Brumble III. *American Indian Autobiography* Berkeley: University of California Press, 1988, 152.
27. Christian F. Feest, "Europe's Indians," in *The Invented Indian: Cultural Fictions and Government Policies*, ed. James Clifton (New Brunswick, N.J.: Transaction Publishers, 1990), 313–332.
28. This nostalgia extended to Buffalo Bill's Wild West Show, whose bandmaster, Karl H. King, dedicated an intermezzo, *Passing of the Red Man*, in the 1914 and 1915 shows. See Don Russell, *The Wild West: A History of the Wild West Shows* (Fort Worth, Tex: Amon Carter Museum of Western Art, 1970), 88.
29. Chief Buffalo Child Long Lance, "My Trail Upward," *Cosmopolitan*, June 1926, 72, 73, 138.
30. Long Lance, *Long Lance*, 278.
31. Arnold Krupat, *For Those Who Come After: A Study of Native American Autobiography* (Berkeley: University of California Press, 1985), 34.
32. Beverly Smith, "One Hundred Percent American," *New York Herald Tribune*, 19 January 1930.
33. Harry Tugend, "*The Silent Enemy*: The Indian's Unhappy Hunting Grounds," *Exhibitors Herald-World* 24 May 1930, 36.
34. Hertha Wong, *Sending My Heart Back Across the Years: Tradition and Innovation in Native American Autobiography* (New York: Oxford University Press, 1992), 142.
35. In a slightly different context, see Paul Gilroy's *Black Atlantic* for a useful discussion of the ways in which persons caught between racial categories—for instance, black Europeans—undermine binary definitions of race.
36. Krupat, *For Those Who Come After*, 48.
37. Theodor Findahl, *Manhattan Babylon: En Bok om New York Idag* [A Book About New York Today] (Oslo: Gyldendal Norsk Forlag, 1928), 45–48. My translation.
38. Although it is important to make the point that Indian tribes were often elastic, rather than essentialist, in their definition of who might be considered a member of the tribe, this is clearly an area too vast for discussion here. For more extensive discussion of this and related issues, see R. Halliburton, Jr., *Red Over Black: Black Slavery Among the Cherokee Indians* (Westport, Conn.: Greenwood Press, 1977); Daniel Littlefield, *The Cherokee Freedmen: From Emancipation to American Citizenship* (Westport, Conn.: Greenwood Press, 1978); Katja May, *African Americans and Native Americans in the Creek and Cherokee Nations, 1830s to 1920s* (New York: Garland Publishing, 1996), and William Loren Katz, *Black Indians: A Hidden Heritage* (New York: Atheneum, 1986).
39. Chauncey Yellow Robe, "The Menace of the Wild West Show," *The Quarterly Journal of the Society of American Indians* (July-September 1914): 224–225.
40. D. Smith, *Long Lance*, 95.
41. Ibid., 210.
42. For biographical information about Long Lance, I have relied extensively on D. Smith's *Long Lance*, a work invaluable for its thoroughness.
43. Eastwood, who became a close friend of Carter's, wrote a letter to the *New York Times* after Asa Carter was exposed for the second time, defending his friend's capacity for—and right to—change: "If Forrest Carter was a racist and a hatemonger who later converted to being a sensitive, understanding human being, that would be most admirable." Quoted in the *Montgomery (Alabama) Advertiser*, 26 October 1991.
44. "Big Sales for New Mexico's 'Little Tree,'" *Publishers Weekly*, 10 May 1989: 49.
45. See Eleanor Friede, memo to readers of *The Education of Little Tree*, 31 October 1991.
46. Nor in the consciousness, according to Greenhaw, of Dan Carter, who wrote the

1991 *Times* story without once acknowledging Greenhaw's earlier exposé. See Greenhaw's letter in *Publisher's Weekly*, November 15, 1991, 8.

47. Diane McWhorter, "Little Tree, Big Lies," *People*, 28 October 1991, 119–21.
48. Forrest Carter, *The Education of Little Tree*, 15th ed. (Albuquerque: University of New Mexico Press, 1993), vi. Although Strickland continued to defend Carter after his unmasking, other Cherokee historians were less charitable: Geneva Jackson, a member of the Cherokee Eastern Band in North Carolina, called the book "the closest thing to a farce that has been published in the Cherokee name. The position of 'storyteller-in-council to the Cherokee Nation,' as Carter was described in promotional copy, does not exist. And there was no evidence, according to tribal officials, that Carter ever made any of the donations to the tribe from his book royalties, as he had claimed." McWhorter, "Little Tree."
49. Carter, *Little Tree*, 7. As Sam Gill notes, Mother Earth, although of great importance among pantribal groups today, is a concept of relatively recent origin: Gill dates the introduction of the Mother Earth story as an essential ingredient of Native American mythography by European writers in 1885. "Examination of the history of this figure," Gill writes, "shows that she arose in the process of the formation of a pantribal identity among native Americans who, in this century, have increasingly forged a common identity in the face of a common experience of oppression and loss. As the Indian peoples lost the land base on which their various group identities depended, the Mother Earth figure grew in importance among them." "Mother Earth: An American Story," in Clinton, ed., *The Invented Indian*, 129–143.
50. Carter, *Little Tree*, 23.
51. John Hayman, "Grey Owl's Wild Goose Chase," *History Today*, January 1994, 42–48.
52. Indians have not consistently been seen by Euro-Americans as having such mystical ties to the earth. In a 1905 speech to the Chicago Literary Club, for example, George E. Adams, a trustee of Chicago's Newberry Library and Field Columbian Museum, informed his audience that the beauty of the New Hampshire mountains dated from the arrival of European settlers and explorers; before then "there was no eye to see it, no soul to feel it. True, the Indians were there . . . but the red Indian, being a primitive man, did not have that delicate sense of beauty, of form and color, which has been developed in the modern man, the heir of centuries of civilization." Quoted in Lawrence Levine, *Highbrow/Lowbrow* (Cambridge, Mass.: Harvard University Press, 1988), 145–146.
53. Carter, *Little Tree*, 62, 9, 12.
54. Ibid., 60.
55. Ibid., 4, 90, 91.
56. The name that Sylvester Long chose for his new identity seems hardly random. In fact, while Long Lance was living at the Explorers Club, the Scottish chieftain who lived in the room next door had a standard reply for the scores of women who called for his neighbor at all hours of the day and night: "No, this is not Long Lance . . . I am chief Longer Lance." See Smith, *Long Lance*, 189.
57. By contrast, Long Lance opens his autobiography with the memory of his mother cutting off one of her fingers in mourning for a brother who had been slain in war; Long Lance's account of his upbringing stresses such matters as the custom of whipping children to toughen them, enforced daily plunges into icy water, and severe punishments for dishonesty. Long Lance's was a childhood designed for a more strenuous age: unsurprisingly, many of the practices he described did not occur in Blackfoot culture but were borrowed by him from other tribes or invented entirely.

58. At the time of Little Tree's 1991 unmasking, *The Road Less Traveled* had spent 413 weeks on the Times best-seller list.
59. Carter, *Little Tree*, 1, 5.
60. Ibid., 57, 50.
61. Ibid., 184, 193, 194, 189, 193.
62. Ibid., 37, 177.
63. Dana Rubin, "The Real Education of Little Tree," *Texas Monthly*, February 1992, 79–81, 92, 94–96.
64. Douglas Newman, interview with Wayne Greenhaw, Alabama, March 1994.

"From This Moment Forth, We are Black Lesbians": Querying Feminism and Transgressing Whiteness in Consolidated's Business of Punishment

Chapter 6

SHARON P. HOLLAND

If something doesn't fit the story, it just gets left out. Until it
sneaks back one day, suddenly appears amid the other
memories, and the simple narrative line is wrecked, the neat
explanation no longer works. If there is a truth at all in this
world of overlapping subjectivities, it sometimes seems too
complicated to hold in my head.

—Marion Winik, *First Comes Love*

"A black lesbian with a nose ring studying literature by the
disabled—that would get you a job."

—Disgruntled white male job seeker, quoted in
Chronicle of Higher Education

MUCH OF HARD-CORE popular industrial thrash and rap music conforms to an impressive list of "isms" too frightening to list.[1] When a friend first introduced me to Consolidated, she explained that they were an eclectic thrash band—"white boys" who mixed it all up, creating a pastiche of rap, rhythm and blues, and industrial music.[2] Add lyrics denouncing all forms of fascism, homophobia, jingoism, and vivisection to the driving beat and you've got a sure sell for committed radical lefties all across the country. I later learned that the San Francisco–based band consists of three members, Adam Sherburne (singer), Philip Steir (drummer), and Mark Pistel (bassist). Getting their start on the local park concert scene in 1978 and releasing their first album, *The Myth of the Rock*, in 1990, the group headlines the politics of the radical left, especially those pertaining to women's political, economic, and reproductive rights.[3]

I went out and bought their then popular third CD, mostly because I couldn't believe that such a band actually existed, and secretly, because I wanted to prove my friend wrong. I would (inevitably, as with most thrash and industrial music) find something that she missed and punish her for it, as we on the left are known to do to one another. I listened to the CD, waiting

to be insulted. But it didn't happen and I anxiously awaited their next release. When *Business of Punishment* arrived, I bought it, and played it nice and
loud. I especially liked track nine with its signature driving beat, audience commentary, and the refrain "if you don't want a nazi in your house don't let one
don't know a fundamentalist 'til you've met one if you've memorized your civil
rights don't forget one if you don't want an abortion don't get one." When
I got to the last one—a sampling of open mike responses during their live
performances—I was stunned when in response to the question, "Why aren't
there any women in your band," one of the members responded, "From this
moment forth, we are black lesbians."

They had stepped beyond the boundaries of good taste and personal politics. Didn't they know that I, the *black lesbian* listening to their music, was
the truly authentic, speaking subject? Isn't subjectivity earned rather than
stated, lived over a period of time, as opposed to attained in an instant? As a
participant in their moment of self-revelation, I had to ask myself, is the
speaker *really speaking for me* when he shouts, "From this moment forth we
are black lesbians"? Is this an act of solidarity or pernicious co-optation? Does
radical politics happen only when solidarity and co-optation occur in a kind
of voluptuous simultaneity? And is this space of desire and pleasure, co-
optation and solidarity always constitutive of death for one subject and life
for another?

Shocked into my own personal theoretical conundrum, I was forced to
rethink my understanding of "identity," "subjectivity," and for that matter,
feminism. I began to contemplate the preternatural relationship between the
three and the cultural moment that allows for a blurring of the boundaries
between them. For the purposes of this discussion, I'd like to keep to a general definition of subjectivity. Regenia Gagnier has produced an extremely cogent explanation of the subject writing itself in her book, *Subjectivities*. In the
introduction, she observes that "[g]ranting the subject's social embeddedness,
an embeddedness most pronounced when one begins to write, one must also
grant—at least this study has taught me to grant—the subject's mediation (i.e.,
transformation) of structures and systems, including systems as large as language or the state."[4] Gagnier's caution not only extends to the subject speaking for itself, but also to the "embeddedness" of the author reinventing the
person or persons under the pen.[5] This reinvention is always an act of appropriation, no matter how politically correct our motivations. Moreover,
Gagnier's parenthetical use of "transformation" in regard to the interaction
between speaking subjects and existing structures, resonates with the premise
of this article. A premise that begins with three white male subjects *subjecting*
themselves to constant erasure—until ultimately, they reach the "end" of the
black/white (if black can be seen as an end point, and white can be seen as a

beginning) binary itself; they pronounce themselves black, lesbian subjects. Subjectivity is used here not to transform existing social structures but to perform a dramatic remaking, or killing of the self. Staging a variety of queer acts, Consolidated's music presupposes that identity equals subjectivity—to say that you are someone else is to become that person. With each new identity—from sex worker to HIV teenager to black lesbian—band members die a little, tinkering with the desire in us all to manifest being in mere utterances. However, if whiteness *is* social structure or at least how it is *read*, then Consolidated's final act of self-erasure can constitute both a change of self and a change in existing structures.

While whiteness has the leisure of reinventing itself as "other" (in blackface, for example) in the popular imagination, blackness is truly embedded—it is indeed a mark upon the body and the mind, like no other—surpassing sex and sexuality. Or, depending on your theoretical perspective, embodying and therefore consuming both. For example, a woman identified as a "black lesbian" might choose to change her sex *and* her sexuality, but s/he will always be a black subject *making* those alterations. And such transformations, of desire and organs, will be interpreted as having been arrived at under the static regime of blackness.[6] Perhaps this is why the black lesbian is so important as the primary, but invisible, subject of feminism. She is the last resort, the end point, if you will, of feminism's attempt to assert itself in the public arena. Noticing the enabling presence of black lesbians to feminist discourse, Evelynn Hammonds issues the following challenge: "White feminists must refigure (white) female sexuality so that they are not theoretically dependent upon an absent yet-ever-present pathologized black female sexuality."[7] I will have more on the end point of black lesbian subjectivity and its relationship to feminism, in particular, toward the end of this article.

Listening to Consolidated's music requires the attending critic to adjust the distances between centered and marginal subjects. Group members consistently take on the identities of the people they sing about in their lyrics—ultimately claiming to transcend their whiteness and maleness as they become women in the sex industry, people who are HIV positive, and finally black lesbians. In their attempt to deal with prevalent social issues and government responses to them, they explore the feminist concept of the personal-is-political as well as attempt to divest themselves of their own white privilege. Consolidated fans represent a "diverse" assembly of postmodern youths, many of whom are sampled on the album, thereby conflating the static distance between performer(s) and audience(s). Why haven't we created a theoretical paradigm appropriate to the multiple crossings performed in Consolidated's "text," let alone a comparable model for the transformation of existing ways of speaking about personal politics, feminism, or whiteness?

It is not my intention to let Consolidated off the hook here. I understand the long and tired history of white performers "borrowing" black style and, sometimes, black rage, for their own profit.[8] However, there are more immediate concerns I'd like to focus upon. Consolidated's presence in a marginal subgenre of the music industry is simultaneous with a nexus of academic work and popular political reform focusing upon and restructuring marginal identities and subjectivities. And it is this simultaneity that I'd like to tease out in the following pages. Consolidated does not appear in a vacuum, and this inquiry is most concerned with the cultural and critical moment that *produces* Consolidated, rather than the cultural and theoretical material that they reproduce.

It is paramount to keep in mind that one of the chief critical moments that informs Consolidated's manifestation is the shift in intellectual scrutiny from black subjects to white subjects.[9] Consolidated puts whiteness under the spotlight by forcing us to ask if whiteness can be transcended, if whiteness in the popular imagination takes on the same kind of embeddedness as blackness. Or, to amend the question, can whiteness and maleness be transcended in the face of an overwhelming oppositional subjectivity—blackness and lesbianness? And if so, *what* are the politics of, or at least *how* can we theorize about, this activity? Of the many subjects that Consolidated raves about, I'd like to focus specifically on three: feminists (a stand-in for white women), white men, and black wommin.

While attempting to answer these questions, I want also to keep in mind aspects of pleasure/desire that constitute the *experience* of listening to Consolidated's music, as well as function to keep the three subjects in play with one another. This same relationship of desire and pleasure is outlined in George Cunningham's examination of black male images and "Body Politics." He writes, "Triangles of desire chart the contours, textures, and structures that unite race and gender as an embodied and subjective experience. . . . I am interested in examining the ways in which this paradigm of triangulation structures the often contradictory possibilities of resistance and complicity in racial and gender hierarchies. I argue that the subject positions available to black men are intimately entwined with those available to white men, black women and white women."[10] Cunningham's articulation of the enmeshed relationship between all three subjects emphasizes the incredible codependency of subjectivity. Such codependency not only enlarges the field of subjects at play (and at pleasure) but also cautions the critic against the usefulness of a dysfunctional oppositional paradigm. While several (post) modernist theorists have attempted to cut across various social narratives and the subjects they produce, popular music places such queries in full view—challenging the limits of critical intervention. For example, at least for the compact-disk consumer, Consolidated's physical ventriloquism—their becoming black lesbians—can be achieved. For the listener, there is no body boundary to move past, there is just the knowledge that the people speaking might not *look or sound* like black lesbians, but there is no guarantee that they cannot *be* black lesbians, at least politically. If "being" a black lesbian is always already a political state of existence, does "being" only tell us who we are as social subjects, sans the narrative that creates the gerund in the first place?

It is precisely this last query that highlights the importance of the place of feminism in Consolidated's transformation. Having already established themselves as "good" even "radical" feminists by their attention to abortion, reproduction, pornography, and corporate greed with songs like "Butyric Acid," "Born of a Woman," "No Answer for a Dancer," and "Worthy Victim," respectively, Consolidated's feminism is seemingly above reproach. In defense of themselves as such, they resort to "being" black lesbians as the ultimate cover for their lack of diverse membership. On the album, they *are* every (feminist) woman, and their invocation of the black lesbian as a knee-jerk defense of feminist privilege wonderfully demonstrates the continued disinheriting of blackness within feminist discourses, as well as the ironic (powerful?) place that it holds as feminism's last resort.[11] Specifically, Consolidated's ownership of feminist discourse demonstrates the need to historicize popular interpretations of feminism. To illustrate this need, we'd have to go back to feminist beginnings—to the struggles of the early Second Wave to encompass the subject positions of women of color or lesbians in their revolutionary tracts before the rise of academic feminism.[12]

Second Wave Feminism: The Lesbian Divorce

As a daughter of feminism, I cut my teeth on the work of the early Second Wave, under the brilliant eye of Lila Karp, a member of one of the first feminist groups in New York in 1968.[13] In literature denouncing contemporary feminist practice, critics often reduce the history of feminism to one moment, rather than treating its rise to popularity as a series of events, all worthy of our attention. We forget that our quarrel with Second Wave feminism is not with what it was but with what it became. We especially forget that early feminist groups such as Cell 16 and the New York Radical Feminists had black women like Florence Kennedy, Cellestine Ware, Margo Jefferson, and Patricia Robinson either in their ranks or writing some of feminisms' most powerful ideology.[14] Black women contributed both to the early radical ideology of the feminist movement, short-lived though it was, and to its publications.[15] As the radical, "no more fun and games" feminism of 1969 quickly gave way to the "a woman's place is in the house *and* in the senate" campaign of liberal feminism, it lost some of its early strident critiques of capital, state-sanctioned racism, and institutions such as marriage.[16] Some feminists, dismayed by the mainstream voice of liberal feminists, began to focus upon "women's culture," and from this emphasis, cultural feminism was born. It is this later brand of Second Wave feminism that nourishes the very problematic feminism of New Age America. What the "new" feminisms left behind was not only radical politics but also black subjects whose situation in America could best be addressed through that lens. In light of this premise, some attention to the rift between radical and cultural feminism might be appropriate here.

As left politics began to embrace and encourage the essentialism coming out of groups like the Black Panthers and US (Ron Karenga), women became a distraction to the central goal of masculinist revolution.[17] As women defected from the Left, they also took with them the destructive politics of vanguardism, so that each group, from Cell 16 to NYRF (New York Radical Feminists) to The Feminists to WITCH (Women's International Conspiracy from Hell), had to put forth the most radical posture, had to prove that it was the vanguard of the new movement. In fact, in one of the founding pieces of cultural feminism, ex-politico cum feminist Jane Alpert signaled a radical re-reading of Firestone's influential *The Dialectic of Sex*. In her 1973 piece, "Mother Right: A New Feminist Theory," published in *Ms.* magazine, she writes, "The unique consciousness or sensibility of women, the particular attributes that set feminist art apart, and a compelling line of research now being pursued by feminist anthropologists all point to the idea that *female biology is the basis of women's powers*. Biology is hence the source and not the enemy of feminist revolution."[18]

According to Alpert, Firestone's work misfired in two directions: its reliance upon technology to free women from biology and its insistence upon biology—as defined by men—as a determinant of social roles. Alpert's insistence upon biology as aiding female agency contributed to the growth and popularity of cultural feminism. However, to rely upon biology, one also has to rely upon machinations that sustain such an organic system—one of which is procreation. In essence, Alpert's pronouncement signaled not a turning away from maleness as biologically determined and therefore disruptive to essential female identity, but actually a gradual embrace of "maleness" as the countering principle, albeit in absentia, to the female principle. How can one herald "biology" as providing the parameters of women's space and expression without simultaneously naming the heterosexual liaison it entails as necessary to ensure the survival of the species?

Other feminists were coming to similar conclusions, even before Alpert's landmark 1973 letter to *Ms.* magazine. In her 1971 "The Fourth World Manifesto," Barbara Burris proclaimed somewhat cautiously that "the split between the male and the female will only be bridged and a fully human identity developed . . . when the female principle and culture is no longer suppressed and male domination is ended forever."[19] For this group of feminists, the desired end point to feminist intervention would be a recognition of male and female cultures, in place of the hierarchy in which the male principle and culture dominated.

Gone from the agenda is any attention to focusing feminist activism and ideology against a dominant culture; absolutely present is a commitment to look inward to the self for sources of feminist resistance and cultural resilience. Alpert fingers consciousness raising as one of the key factors in women's individuation. She explains that "we began to be able to define ourselves as individuals and as women. . . . What we discovered in each other was the pulse of a culture and a consciousness. . . . gaining confidence in our thoughts, feelings, resentments, desires, and intuitions as attributes that we shared as a people and which were therefore valid—became the basis of beginning to trust ourselves as individuals." This process of individuation is directly linked to a recognition of what Alpert calls a "female" culture. Moreover, to adhere to this new direction, and therefore, this "new age" that Alpert heralds, seekers must "raise the issue of the interconnection between female biology and religious and secular power."[20] She ascertains that the "power" attributed to matriarchal culture might be parallel to the kind of power lodged in the "soul" of feminist art, and the "power" that women begin to feel in the process of defining themselves as separate from men.

This redefining proved to be the straw that broke the camel's back, as a rising cultural feminism had to deal with the specter of vanguardism that haunted the male Left. Cultural feminists had to ask themselves who in this "new age" model would be more able to lead the movement: women who were still tied to men sexually or women who were more liberated and chose sexual relations with other women. This rather new development coincides with other kinds of separatism voiced in the black power movement. Constituent to the transition from radical to cultural feminism is the specter of black power—and its attendant masculinist perspective—that informs the move to a female- centered female culture, made up of mostly white lesbian bodies. Each band, whether lesbian separatist or black nationalist, holds as sacred some biological principle; whether this sacredness is identified as male or female, its biology makes it a prime candidate for both an elevation to the status of religion—and therefore an ideology not to be questioned—and for reconciliation of male and female in the act of procreative desire.

The move from radical to cultural feminism forced this "new age" of feminism to relate to blackness in ways similar to the dominant culture. Cultural (lesbian) feminists mimed their desire for black subjectivity as they played out their own vanguardism through heralding lesbianism as the quintessential element of being feminist. In a wonderful harangue that becomes almost self-satirizing, lesbian feminist Jill Johnston proclaims

> And biology is definitely destiny. The woman in relation to man
> historically has always been defeated. Every woman who remains in
> sexual relation to man is defeated every time she does it with the man
> because each single experience for every woman is a reenactment of
> the primal one in which she was invaded and separated and fashioned
> into a receptacle for the passage of the invader and that's why every
> woman is a reluctant and a fearful bride.[21]

What better way to keep women's liberation at the vanguard of radical politics than, at the precise time that "black liberation" was being declared as the quintessential (à la the Weathermen) center of left politics, to declare from within the women's movement a cadre of folk oppressed within the larger push for female or feminist liberation? Early feminist critiques of the male left found a palimpsest in the rhetoric of the black left, as "The Fourth World Manifesto" made clear in its deconstruction of the anti-imperialist discourse of Franz Fanon.

Alpert's philosophy found its most solid stronghold in emerging lesbian separatism. An example from the 1975 anthology *The Lesbian Reader* parallels Alpert's original findings and fulfills her predictions:

> We have lived by our wits, as an oppressed and helpless people, for
> centuries. But we have not, despite massive and brutal conditioning,
> forsaken our Mother Nature; and she has not forsaken us. It took four
> hundred years to wipe out the last large concentration of evolved
> women (the witches, the wise women) but some of them survived the
> Burning Time and their genes have traveled through time to us. And
> we feel it; we know it. We are beginning to see into the past and into
> the future, to heal and create again, to be aware of our own strange
> abilities.[22]

The embrace of this new feminist principle paved the way for cultural feminists to leave behind a more outspoken politics for the safe harbor of what Andrew Ross observes as "offering a weak vocabulary of social responsibility somewhat removed from the politics of class, race, gender and sexual preference waged by the post-sixties left."[23]

What I find here, however, is that cultural feminism and the lesbian separatism it engendered moved more toward the politics of reconciliation between the sexes than its philosophy would suggest. Under the mother's right, in this "new age" of feminism, practitioners had to come to grips with the fact that men would want to partake of the new fruits of the evolving movement and that the "spiritual" or "new age" dimensions of their cultural feminism left women no option but to open the "circle" to include men who recognized the power in Mother Nature. The "new age" provided the perfect palimpsest upon which to repair the damaged relationship between white men and white women. Feminist politics were rerouted to accomplish this repair over the bodies of the many radical women who would have abhorred any such transition. The move toward reconciliation, simultaneous with an abandoning of radical politics, also left the space open for men to form their own "political" groups. In the last decade we have witnessed such a possibility in the Million Man March (a day of atonement), the Iron John movement, and the Christian Right's Promise Keepers.

If anything, we as (radical) feminists must take a hard look at representations of the "new age," because in them we can find evidence about what really went wrong in 1973. Two relatively recent books—*Daring To Be Bad* by Alice Echols and *Fundamental Feminism* by Judith Grant—both have as their subplots a subconscious reluctance to name the politics of early lesbian feminism as the most likely contributor to what we now know as the New Age.[24] No matter in which direction feminists ran—whether to the sweat lodge or to the ivory tower—their anxieties about biology and destiny consumed them. For example, we would not have a Judith Butler worrying about the fixity of "sex," "gender" and the subject of feminism if it weren't for those tiresome, New Agey, biology-is-destiny, proud-to-proclaim-themselves-as-feminists" feminists in the community holding sacred circles and looking to what's behind their navels for inspiration. More appropriate to this evaluation, we would not have Consolidated mimicking the competitive vanguardism displayed during the reconstruction of early feminism. Consolidated continues to mime the dance of reconciliation between feminism and its feared opponent and sometime friend—masculinist discourse, masculinist posturing. If they have appropriated feminism and become its subject(s), then this act is not an anomaly. Read through the historical trajectory outlined in this chapter, the band's appropriation falls neatly into the popular terrain that feminism mapped for itself in the early moments of its reincarnation. What Consolidated performs for us is not a new and extremely fluid postmodern subjectivity. Instead, they mimic a feminist vanguardism that sees black subjects as fodder for the machinery that sustains relationship between white male and female counterparts. Women of color have been particularly frustrated with the ghosting of whiteness in feminist criticism. What I have tried to argue here is that ghosting is not only a result of feminist preoccupation with white bodies but also a complex rendering of the heterosexual relations buried in the discourse feminism created in its second evolution.

Judith Butler, Kobena Mercer, and the Slippery Subject of (Radical) Feminism

Many practicing feminist theorists wouldn't describe their work as a product of the historical tensions outlined here. I would argue, however, that much of the attempt to inject more theoretical "rigor" into the canon of feminist inquiry stems precisely from the popular belief that the feminist movement has been rerouted by New Age spiritualism and somehow gone soft on its examination of feminist categories of sex, gender, sexuality, and experience. Consolidated seems aligned with the call for a return to "rigor" as they mix in the jargon of postmodernist theory on cuts like "Woman Shoots John." In the midst of recounting this story of female vigilantism, they drone "the extreme form of power is all against one the extreme form of violence is one against all," and "does power grow out of the barrel of a gun or is it that power and violence are opposites where one rules absolutely the other is absent?"[25] Consolidated's claim to rigor in their feminist politics allows them a free reign with the identities and subjects they play on stage.

A return to the "continued disinheriting of blackness" in the territories of critical theory might be helpful as a backdrop for understanding what produces Consolidated's reproductions of feminist sound bites. Therefore, I'd like to turn for a moment to a similar slip in subject(s) that occurs in theory as well; a moment where a tension between the implied and the stated subject belies a kind of perpetual fault line in the practice of feminist theoretical inquiry.

In the first chapter of her now widely read *Gender Trouble: Feminism and the Subversion of Identity*, Judith Butler observes that

> [w]ithin feminist political practice, a radical rethinking of the
> ontological constructions of identity appears to be necessary in order
> to formulate a representational politics that might revive feminism on
> other grounds. On the other hand, it may be time to entertain a
> radical critique that seeks to free feminist theory from the necessity of
> having to construct a single or abiding ground which is invariably
> contested by those identity positions or anti-identity positions that it
> invariably excludes.[26]

I find this to be one of the most powerful statements about the direction of feminist inquiry in the late twentieth century. In the last sentence, Butler mentions her own attempt to "entertain a radical critique," "free[ing] feminist theory" from a "single . . . ground," already "contested by those . . . it invariably excludes." She appropriates radical politics as if feminism, in its various incarnations, hasn't contemplated any such notion, and places radical politics in service to theory, rather than practice. What this maneuver accomplishes is profound, as Butler is able to circumvent naming the multiple voices in feminism. She is able to destabilize "women" as the subject constituent of feminist identity, without having to examine when and where this destabilization occurs. There is absolutely no politicized point of entry here—no causal relationship; feminism is assaulted from all sides by invisible antagonists.

Kobena Mercer offers a more precise articulation of what happens when "radical critiques" meet what Butler calls a "single" or "abiding" field of inquiry:

> Just now everybody wants to talk about identity. As a keyword in contemporary politics it has taken on so many different connotations that sometimes it is obvious that people are not even talking about the same thing. One thing at least is clear—identity only becomes an issue when it is in crisis, when something assumed to be fixed, coherent and stable is displaced by the experience of doubt and uncertainty.[27]

For Mercer, identity is only destabilized when its fixity is somehow queried. I am interested here in the apparent *proof* of Mercer's observation in Consolidated's response to an audience question. Their identity as a profeminist band is momentarily threatened, and the answer to such a crisis is to call in the heavy artillery—to take on and therefore embody the ghost of feminist discourse—the vanguardism embedded in black lesbian subjectivity. I am also interested in Butler's reluctance to *name* the forces that act upon feminist theory so that it (is forced to) become(s) a discipline that "excludes."

In all fairness, it is true that Butler and Mercer have different theoretical agendas, but I would not say that they have different politics. As Butler reminds us, "[in the course of this effort to question 'women' as the subject of feminism, the unproblematic invocation of that category may prove to preclude the possibility of feminism as a representational politics. . . . What relations of domination and exclusion are inadvertently sustained when representation becomes the sole focus of politics?"[28] Although it is absolutely appropriate and theoretically astute to declare that representation need not be the "sole focus of feminist politics," it is somewhat more complicated and therefore dangerous to suggest that in the ensuing complex of competing identities there is *no* subject of feminism that can be held accountable for what appears to be its simultaneous demise and slow reconstruction. In this political matrix, those who rage against the original machine go unnamed and those who maintain a central place in that machine have identities that are so fluid that they become nonsubjects when the formal inquiries and accusations begin. A perfect parallel is Consolidated's shift from white males to black lesbians. Although "representation" ought not to be the "sole focus of politics," it is difficult to *have* politics without some discussion of what is actually being represented.

Mercer differs from Butler in naming a politically charged identity for those individuals who cause a crisis in leftist thinking. Mercer's political agenda is circumscribed by the following statement,

> The ambiguity of "identity" serves . . . as a way of acknowledging the presence of new social actors and new political subjects—women, black people, lesbian and gay communities, youth—whose aspirations do not neatly fit into the traditional Left/Right dichotomy. However, I am not sure that "identity" is what these movements share in common: on the contrary, within and between the various new movements that have arisen in postwar, Western, capitalist democracies, what is asserted is an emphasis on "difference."[29]

Ambiguous identities work in an entirely different way for Mercer; his paradigm seeks to center Marxist/socialist discourse, proving that identity and difference converge in the most contested spaces. For Butler's inquiry to work, the multifarious subjects of feminism would also be its representatives; they would have to be, at various times, the ancestors *and* authors of feminism's current dilemma. We know from experience that this is not true—for example, a black lesbian subject, in the popular or academic mind, has never held the coveted position of being *author* of the feminist discourse that Butler now finds imperiled.

A possibility in language does not make for a possibility in practice, especially if that avenue forecloses the very discussion necessary for such a change to be universally accepted. But contemporary feminist theory so relies upon this potentiality and obfuscation that followers in both academia and the lay population—that even a group like Consolidated—can grasp the paradigm, thus absolving themselves of their (white male) identities and claiming a new set of clothes in each creative endeavor. However, their killing of the self, or miming of marginal experience, ultimately proves that radical politics cannot take place without attention to the experiential life of those subjects who are necessary to a revolutionary rethinking of archetypes and identities.

Consolidated: White Anger, White Angst

Claiming both a feminist *and* a radical stance, Consolidated performs the complicated politics of maneuvering between identities. I'd like to switch gears again and read the necessity for Consolidated's trespass in the context of other national events. Because of Consolidated's roots in the Bay area, it might be wise to use recent California politics as a palimpsest for understanding the simultaneous *rage* and *appropriation* that the band utilizes for their radical politics. Historicizing this claim more fully, I turn to the work of Tom·s Almaguer. In his epilogue to *Racial Fault Lines: The Historical Origins of White Supremacy in California*, Almaguer observes:

> What stands out most clearly from this comparative history is that European Americans at every class level sought to create, maintain, or extend their privileged access to racial entitlements in California. *California was, in the final analysis, initially envisioned as a white masculinist preserve.* It bears recalling that the European American editors of one of the territory's first English-language newspapers, the *Californian*, proclaimed in 1848, "We desire only a white population in California."
>
> While this study has explored these issues in historical terms, only the most politically naive would deny that we continue to live this history in very fundamental ways. . . . *California remains a contested racial frontier* and the site of continued political struggle over the extension of this society's most cherished civil rights and equal opportunities to all cultural groups.[30]

The passage of propositions 184, 187, and 209 in California indicates the deep racial divide in the state.[31] It is difficult to grow up and create music in California and not be deeply affected by its climate of what Almaguer calls "racializing discourses." More importantly, as magazine reporter Peter Schrag reminds his readers, "Where California goes, the nation is usually not far behind."[32]

It is no mystery that this nation has seen a plethora of political movements led by white men since the mid-1980s.[33] It is also noteworthy that these movements emerged simultaneously with the critical dismantling of the monolith of whiteness that began earlier in the decade. Interesting also is that just when affirmative action and decades of civil rights work began to bear fruit, suddenly there is a national outcry that the interests of the minority culture have somehow overshadowed those of the majority.[34]

ACT-UP activism is the perfect example of the pallet upon which a white masculinist and heterosexist preserve gets remixed and redefined.[35] During the 1980s, white gay males active in the fight against HIV/AIDS felt the particular painful conundrum of being "white" in America but at the same time subject to a hatred and fear reserved for more marginal "subjects" of the state. This difference did not keep some men from maintaining their white privilege. As Leo Bersani recalls, men active in early HIV/AIDS activism "had no problem being gay slumlords during the day, and in San Francisco for example, evicting from the Western Addition black families unable to pay the rents necessary to gentrify that neighborhood."[36] Bersani's statement demonstrates that in the midst of radical politics, there is still business as usual. Again we seem to have another moment where popular discourse feels the pressure from academic/theoretical discourse—where the *political* acts of white male subjects reassert their dominance in the public realm as if to stave off an impending divestiture in a whiteness that enables them to purchase land, become land-lords, and thus benefit from a booming market economy.

The political fallout from HIV/AIDS is that gay white men who saw them-selves as oppressed within the larger white culture had to think about align-ing with folks whose lot they considered themselves immune to. The "crisis" of white male subjectivity began when white men who thought they had di-vested themselves of their own supremacy found themselves unwilling to let go of that particular ideology in the face of *becoming like* their colored coun-terparts. Perhaps the "crisis" was just as much the dis-ease within their own group, as it was the dis-ease with which they approached coalition building with other marginalized peoples. The white male anger expressed in anti-HIV/AIDS protest and telecast via satellite to major cities all over the world trig-gered an avalanche of public response, one of which was the return to "fam-ily values." This return can also be read as a reinscription of white male heterosexuality as the more legitimate force in a growing display of white male rage.[37]

As if in answer to the request "Will the real representative white man please stand up," a surging mass of conservative and sometimes Christian white men advanced to denounce homosexuality altogether, while at the same time asking the government for many of the same things demanded by "minori-ties" and "gays" (at least theoretically): governmental accountability, prefer-ential treatment in light of the crisis (declining family values or HIV/AIDS, for example) and increased representation from political constituencies.[38] From this middle group—the various Christian-based coalitions—has grown an even more radicalized contingent—militia groups—bent on achieving all three ends by any means necessary.[39] The parallels are frightening and chilling, but if we are to move against and beyond dichotomies, we have to at least be willing to entertain not only the possibility of a parallel, at least theoretically, but also the potential for meaning in any relationship between these divergent displays of white male angst.

More than anything else, the media attention to white male anger not only reopened the popular discussion of white subjectivity but also fundamen-tally changed the nature and definition of white masculinity. The question I want to consider is that in the shadow of a resurgence of mostly extremist, sometimes brutal white masculinity, how does any white man move to speak against a subject position designed for him by the media? The media portrayal of white male anger has made it difficult for white men to substantiate their own forms of protest distinct from already established avenues of public *and* political expression. Consolidated might be the perfect "pill" for the crisis of white male subjectivity, but the group members' inability to voice their own rage and therefore their own subjectivity, in response to what they believe is a neofascist movement underfoot these days, demonstrates their continued silence under the shadow of other expressions of white male anger. Why is it that they continually cross-dress to get their point across? Is it because white male protest has been so delegitimated that in order to launch their own protest they have to wear someone else's clothes? Perhaps their own rage against the machine here is not a matter of what has been done to us (black lesbians), but what has been done to the collective image of white masculinity.[40] Ultimately arguing that white male rage is impossible without an act of appropriation to legitimate its presence, and following in the footsteps of Eric Lott's theorizing of white male desire and black bodies, I'd like to end with the assertion that white male rage is always an act of desire for the "other," and in Consolidated's case, for blackness specifically.[41]

Black Lesbians: The Perfect Answer to the Problem of Feminism

In the midst of this national reexamination of white masculinity and expression of white rage, there is Consolidated stating that "from this moment forth, we are black lesbians." In a 1994 *Rolling Stone* interview announcing the debut of Consolidated's fourth release, *Business of Punishment*, Adam Sherburne comments, "In the past we made calculated decisions to go with concrete ideas because these ideas have been obliterated in post-modern, post-subjective culture."[42] Sherburne's words run parallel to his actions. If indeed, we are in a "post-subjective" culture, what better way to demonstrate this phenomenon than to state that what you see is not always what you get.

What is remarkable about Sherburne's definitive statement "From this moment forth, we are black lesbians" at the end of *Business* is its total collapse of the categories of subjectivity and identity. If, in Butler's cosmology, the subject of feminism is endangered by the various struggles between the identities that it chooses to embrace and/or reject, then Consolidated's music would provide the perfect example of such intense conflict. Consolidated obviously performs the postmodern crisis of feminist subjectivity by explicitly engaging several marginal identities.

During the course of the album, band members never sing about what it might be like to *be* a black lesbian. This experience is ghosted much like the provocateurs that destabilize feminism(s) in Butler's chronicle of feminist posturing. On the album, every other marginal identity gets represented, but black lesbian female identity is simply stated, transgressed into so easily because of its accessibility on the menu of politically correct mantras. Furthermore, band members support this conclusion by producing the declaration "From this moment forth, we are black lesbians" as an end point. The crowd's loud affirmation of their pronouncement demonstrates that this change in subject positions is enough of an answer to the accusation of sexism—"Why are there no women in your band"—brought by a member of the audience.

This work began with a series of questions about Consolidated's unorthodox closure to *Business*, and many of the potential answers take us in equal and opposite directions. On the one hand, the band's statement can be seen as another co-optation, another successful expedition to the terrain of the marginalized; on the other, it can be quite revolutionary for three white men in an age where white male anger is soaring, and continually legitimized, to relinquish, if even for a moment, their own subjectivity. If subjectivity is based upon an individual's experience of the world, then Consolidated's band members have only the experience of (an)other to constitute theirs.

I'd like to focus on the possibilities that the latter statement opens. Consolidated's resistance to self-representation is evident in another place on their album, and it is to that space that I now move. While the story of "being" a black lesbian is never articulated in Consolidated's most recent work, her rage is appropriated for use in yet another moment. In a diatribe against William F. Buckley, Ted Nugent and Rush Limbaugh written by band members and comedian Greg Proops, the audience receives detailed descriptions of the appropriate ways in which each of these figures can be killed. During the song, "Consolidated Buries the Mammoth," they reserve a particular punishment for Clarence Thomas:

> One of the most appropriate ways for Clarence Thomas to expire
> would be, he goes to a conference called, "The Black Women for
> Power League," and he's gonna speak there and he thinks that he's
> gonna get a lot of chicks. But when he gets there it's all black lesbians
> [and] they lock the doors and fuckin' kill him with cocktail forks.[43]

Again, the particular power of black lesbian presence is enlisted to provide an end point—to produce a deadly end, in this case.

What intrigues me about Consolidated's choice of assassins is how it remarks upon black feminist politics surrounding the Thomas/Hill hearings, which took place in October 1991. Dismayed by both the result and the spectacle of the hearings, black women from across the country contributed to a campaign called "Black Women in Defense of Ourselves." Spearheaded by Elsa Barkley Brown (of the University of Michigan) and others, the campaign focused on the publication of a full-page advertisement in the *New York Times* with the names of black female contributors superimposed upon an Africanist silhouette of a black woman's head. A symbolic gesture at best, the campaign served to unite black women in an effort to comment on the invisibility and subsequent denigration of black women in the culture at large. For many people, the advertisement was just a small step, and not nearly enough needed to generate the long-overdue discussion about black women and race in this nation. Consolidated must also have seen this demonstration as ineffectual in the grand scheme of things.

I read their killing of Thomas as the *perception* of a failure in black feminist politics. If black lesbians hold the masculine position of (angry) escort to feminism, then the anger of straight black feminists is not enough. The retaliation for such a public disgrace of black feminist politics needs to be much more severe, and for this work you need the appropriate (angry) subject of feminism—the black lesbian—and black female heterosexual anger is certainly not sufficient. In fact, the proof of this is in the demeanor of Anita Hill during the October proceedings. As Karla Holloway insists,

> My grandmother was right, nice girls did not wear red, I thought—
> and Professor Hill had clearly been raised as a nice girl. She was
> properly mannered, neatly attired, softly spoken, and in every
> dimension certainly a "credit to the race." Professor Hill was clearly
> what my grandmother had in mind when she encouraged me and my
> sisters to carry ourselves well, to speak with precision and care, and
> to bring honor to our families. However, although all of the same
> behavioral codes from my private, family-centered education were
> being remarkably emulated in Professor Hill's polite demeanor, the
> occasion was nonetheless a serious challenge to the weightier
> directives I had been urged to follow in public situations. For all the
> frank talk about sexual harassment, pubic hair, and pornography,
> Professor Hill may as well have worn red.[44]

Regardless of how black women carry themselves or ask to be addressed, certain "codes of conduct," Holloway suggests, are employed so that black female subjects appear as always already wearing red, as always already unruly subjects.[45] If straight black women were to unleash even legitimate anger, it would divest them of their ability to inhabit the category of women. But black lesbians are never portrayed as afraid of such a loss, for they have stood in for the male in feminist discourse for so long that they embody him; they have never been considered as decidedly female in the first place. In a sense, Consolidated's ritual killing of Thomas with cocktail forks alludes to the false "femininity" that black lesbians possess—the weapon they use here is sheer absurdity in the face of the murderous rage being released.

We have to ask ourselves difficult questions here—why is Consolidated's reading of *this* particular subject of feminism so accurate? Why is the perfect escort of contemporary feminism, and queer studies for that matter, the (enraged) black lesbian? I'd like to suggest an even earlier point of departure for our ruminations on the place of the "black" in feminist, and subsequently lesbian (queer) studies.

In "Black Bodies, White Bodies: Toward an Iconography of Female Sexuality in Late Nineteenth Century Art, Medicine and Literature," Sander Gilman traces the place of the black female body in relationship to the study of female reproduction and in the service of the burgeoning eugenics movement.[46] His scholarship reveals the absolute connection between racist nineteenth-century scientific thought and the construction of "deviant" sexualities through lesbianism and prostitution. It appears that the words "lesbian" and "black" are forged in blood, in physiognomy, and ultimately in racist science. The link between lesbianism and the black body cannot be obfuscated, yet within queer studies, not much has been made of this connection. Such a deep psychic connection provides ample territory for a discussion of the racialized lesbian body. Can we think of a lesbian without thinking about her origins? Is a lesbian, therefore, always inscribed, written, identified as black *first*, and then she becomes white through a series of transgressions, through the theorists' pen?

These questions are important because they help to realize a relocation of a politics of the lesbian and feminist subject, as well as to provide an explanation for the scandalous paucity of written work on the black lesbian as the (angry) subject of feminist discourse.[47] Obviously, this construction of the black lesbian is so prevalent that even casual readers of radical feminism—Consolidated—can see the appropriate place of the black lesbian feminist in the paradigms of feminist discourse. Black lesbian subjects and their women-of-color allies have always haunted feminism's attempt to articulate itself—putting themselves in the position of challenging the racial inclusiveness of feminist theory and practice, while at the same time pushing a developing lesbian/gay studies to describe the face of its constituency. The place of the black lesbian within queer studies has been defined by decades of use-value as the heavy hand of feminism, as Judith Roof so cogently argues: "In 1985's proliferation of feminist literary critical anthologies, the myriad differences among women are often reduced to the formula 'black and lesbian.'" She also later surmises, "This is just another version of the power analogy; feminist critics battle male theory and have again enlisted diversity on their side."[48] It was a good thing that poststructuralist postmodernism came along, or the claims of racism in both feminism and lesbian/gay studies would have begun to appear well founded.[49] But now that the "subject" and/or authors of feminism have no names, no faces (or at least interchangeable ones), we cannot hold either discipline accountable for the actions of a de-faced host(ess), even though the actions of people of color began the political unrest that made each field of inquiry possible.

The killing of Clarence Thomas in *Business* suggests that there is something extraordinarily menacing about a black man who, because of his relative wealth and social/political connections, escapes the usual wrath of a system specifically designed to enmesh him. Such a man is dangerous, and in the example of both Clarence Thomas and most recently, O. J. Simpson, the miscarriage of "justice" can only be rectified through the assassination/murder of the escapee from the penal colony. In my conversations after the hearings and trial, respectively, I heard many people call for the death of either as a quick solution to such brilliant escapes. What is most powerful about a similar call to arms in Consolidated's work is the utilization and/or threat of black lesbian bodies as the ultimate defense against an accusation of sexism. Flaccid feminism is no match for the phallic power of the quintessential black lesbian.

If anything, Consolidated's reading of black lesbianism should provide, however obscure, a wake-up call for academic feminism—for its complete failure in addressing and therefore dismantling the myths about female sexuality and lesbianism. Such a failure requires a new approach to feminist discourse— one that names the people, places, and events that continue to gnaw at a concept of centered feminism. It is time for queer studies and its feminist allies to address the culpability of its major figures in the "battle" against a winning patriarchy. For, if the ultimate goal of feminism is truly, in the words of the Second Wave, to "obliterate the patriarchy," then more of our attention should be focused upon how that patriarchy has managed to escape our attention, to mask itself and to survive.

Saying that there is no unified subject of feminism, or any other discursive field, will not stop the police from singling out black subjects at the corner of University Avenue and Bay Road in East Palo Alto, California; nor will it prevent a university advisory committee from dismissing the importance of black feminist scholarship. Such acts merely demonstrate that there are some subjects who always appear as targets of a triumphant patriarchy. I am not advocating the discontinuance of stimulating intellectual discourses on the subject of the body and fluctuating identities, but what I would like to see is a suspension of the pretense of "politics" in the course of this discussion. As one woman pronounces during the open mike session at the end of Consolidated's CD: "The politics stop, man, when the sexism stops, when the fucking bullshit that women deal with every day of their lives—when *that* fucking stops man, then the politics can stop."

Performance Problems

Evaluating black female sexuality, Evelynn Hammonds remarks, "Nor are black queer female sexualities simply identities. Rather, they represent discursive and material terrains where there exists the possibility for the active production of speech, desire and agency."[50] Much of this energy, in the popular and theoretical terrain, has yet to be released. I have tried to demonstrate here that removing black queer female voices to the space of silence, to such an inarticulate space, might not be solely a result of our own racism. Rather, such inattention can stem from a variety of paradigms so entrenched that they go unrecognized even to the trained critical eye. When the critical eye fails to see, it is sometimes popular culture that places a magnifying glass over the missed area, performing for all to see, a piece of the problem.

Introducing a collection of theoretical essays on performativity and performance, Andrew Parker and Eve Kosofsky Sedgwick conclude:

> These essays strikingly refrain from looking at performativity/
> performance for a demonstration for whether or not there are
> essential truths or identities, and how we could, or why we couldn't,
> know them, as *a certain stress has been lifted momentarily from the issues
> that surround* being something, an excitingly charged and specious
> stage seems to open up for explorations of that even older, *even newer
> question of how saying something can be doing something.*[51]

Parker and Sedgwick's opening remarks cast a deep and parallel shadow over the kind of exploration of identity and performance I have been conducting here. When we do switch from *being* to *saying* something, and therefore *doing* it, a new avenue of critical work opens. If we aren't carefully attuned to and responsible for the kind of "specious stage" we've stumbled onto, however, we most likely begin to perpetuate the very behaviors we are trying to eradicate. This project doesn't pretend to have all the answers, but asking the right kind of questions can take us in a myriad of directions. We are always in the position of *being* something to or for somebody, and the present challenge is not to eclipse the distance between saying and doing, but to qualify the ways in which "being" enacts itself in the (post)modern terrain.

Notes

1. In particular, I am thinking about "oi" music, which extols the virtues of white nationalism and supremacy, as well as some forms of "gangsta rap," which has made such terms as "bitch," "ho," and "niggah" current among America's youth.
2. I am grateful to my friend Carrie Perdue for introducing me to some of industrial music's alternative politics.
3. In a 1991 press release I. R. S. Records notes that Consolidated's "unconditional support for women's equality . . . set it far apart from those in all music genres who

have long upheld an overwhelmingly sexist tradition in entertainment." From *Consolidated 1991 Biography.*

4. Regenia Gagnier, *Subjectivities* (New York: Oxford University Press, 1988), 10.

5. Gagnier refers to subjects as social creatures who read themselves through identification or nonidentification with different structures. Her use of "embeddedness" refers not to a model of autonomous subjectivity but to a subjectivity negotiating various terrains, seeking to arrive at some agency in the midst of institutions and ideas.

6. I am also reminded here of Marjorie Garber's findings in "Spare Parts: The Surgical Construction of Gender." She notes that surgeons who perform transsexual operations and their patients share "the conviction that masculine identity, male subjectivity is determined and signified by the penis." *differences* 1, no. 3 (1989): 142. No other figure in popular culture is proof of the static nature of "blackness" than Michael Jackson and his several attempts at unracing himself. For an excellent evaluation of critical approaches to Jackson's racial dilemma see Michael Awkward, *Negotiating Difference: Race, Gender and the Politics of Positionality* (Chicago: University of Chicago Press, 1995), 175–92.

7. Evelynn Hammonds, "Black (W)holes and Geometry of Black Female Sexuality," *differences* 6, no. 2 & 3 (1994): 131.

8. See Dick Hebdige, *Subculture: The Meaning of Style*, (London: Routledge, 1988), and George Lipsitz, "Land of a Thousand Dances: Youth, Minorities, and the Rise of Rock and Roll," in *Recasting America: Culture and Politics in the Age of Cold War*, ed. Larry May (Chicago: University of Chicago Press, 1989).

9. I am thinking here of Toni Morrison's groundbreaking, *Playing in the Dark: Whiteness and the Literary Imagination* (Cambridge, Mass.: Harvard University Press, 1992), and of David Roediger's *Towards the Abolition of Whiteness* (New York: Verso, 1994).

10. George P. Cunningham, "Body Politics: Race, Gender and the Captive Body," in *Representing Black Men*, ed. Marcellus Blount and George P. Cunningham (New York: Routledge, 1996), 135–36.

11. I drop the word "lesbian" momentarily because it is obvious from the popularity of works by lesbian feminists that lesbians are no longer the stepchildren of feminism, but rather its most recent inheritors.

12. For readings on the Second Wave of feminism see Anne Koedt, Ellen Levine, and Anita Rapone, *Radical Feminism* (New York: Quadrangle, 1973); Judith Hole and Ellen Levin, *Rebirth of Feminism* (New York: Quadrangle, 1971); Redstockings, *Feminist Revolution* (New York: Random House, 1978); Leslie B. Tanner, *Voices from Women's Liberation* (New York: New American Library, 1971); (Jo Freeman), *The Voice of the Women's Liberation Movement*, newsletter, March 1968–69; *Notes from the Second Year*, 1968; *Notes from the Third Year*, 1970; *Notes on Women's Liberation*, (Detroit: News & Letters, 1970); Ti-Grace Atkinson, *Amazon Odyssey: The First Collection of Writings by the Political Pioneer of the Women's Movement* (New York: Links Books, 1974); Shulamith Firestone, *The Dialectic of Sex: The Case for Feminist Revolution* (New York: Morrow, 1970); and Kate Millett, *Sexual Politics* (New York: Simon and Schuster, 1969).

13. Lila Karp was an original member of The Feminists in New York. She is also the author of *The Queen Is in the Garbage* (New York: Vanguard Press, 1969). She was director of the Princeton University Women's Center, when I was an undergraduate there, 1982–1987.

14. See Cellestine Ware, *Woman Power: The Movement for Women's Liberation* (New York: Tower Publications, 1970); Florence Kennedy, *Born in Flames*, video recording, 1983; and Patricia Robinson, "A Historical and Critical Essay for Black Women of the Cities," *No More Fun and Games*, no. 3 (November 1969).

15. The publications of the Second Wave are legion. Many were either published in pamphlet form or by individuals and groups. Here are a few: *Free Space: A Perspective on the Small Group in Women's Liberation*, Pam Allen (January 1970); *The Hidden History of the Female: The Early Feminist Movement in the United States*, Martha Atkins; *Tooth and Nail*, Bay Area Women's Liberation vol. 1, no. 4 (January 1970); *The Political Economy of Women's Liberation*, Margaret Benston (September 1969); *Amazon Expedition: A Lesbianfeminist Anthology*, Phyllis Birkby, Bertha Harris, Jill Johnston, Esther Newton, and Jane O'Wyatt (1973); *The Demands of Women's Liberation*, Boston Women United (9 October 1970); *No More Fun and Games*, Cell 16, vol. 1–4 (October 1968, November 1969, April 1970); *The Fight for Women's Freedom*, Clara Colon (March 1969); *Rape, Racism and the White Women's Movement: An Answer to Susan Brownmiller*, Alison Edwards; *Socialism, Anarchism, & Feminism*, Carol Ehrlich (January 1977); *The Tyranny of Structurelessness*, Jo Freeman (1970) reprinted, British; *Which Way for the Women's Movement?*, Cindy Jaquith and Willie Mae Reid, (April 1977); *The Lesbian Tide*, The Tide Collective, vol. 1, no. 9 (April 1972); *Liberation of Women: Sexual Repression and the Family*, Laurel Limpus; *Working Women and Their Organizations: 150 Years of Struggle*, Joyce Maupin (1974); *Women: The Longest Revolution*, Juliet Mitchell (reprinted from *New Left Review*, November-December 1966); *What Is the Revolutionary Potential of Women's Liberation?* Kathy Mcaffe and Myrna Wood (originally titled "Bread & Roses," reprinted from June 1969 issue of *Leviathan*); *How Harvard Rules Women*, New University Conference (1970); *Notes from the Third Year: Women's Liberation* (June 1970); *Abortion and the Catholic Church: Two Feminists Defend Women's Rights*, Evelyn Reed and Claire Moriarty (March 1973); *Women's Liberation & the New Politics*, Sheila Rowbotham, Women's, No. 17 (October 1971, British); "Sex and The State: Or Let's Kill Ozzie and Harriet: A Lesbian Perspective," Shim and Cedar (paper delivered April 1976); *Sisterhood Is Powerful*, Betsey Stone (March 1972); *Woman and Her Mind: The Story of Daily Life*, Meredith Tax (Bread and Roses,1970); *The Politics of Women's Liberation Today*, Mary-Alice Waters (June 1970); The Woman's Center, Northampton, Mass., *The Woman's Journal*, vol. 1, no. 3 (December 1971); and *Dick and Jane As Victims: Sex Stereotyping in Children's Readers*, Women on Words & Images (1975 expanded edition). All of the preceding pamphlets are from my private collection.
16. For a critique of Second Wave feminism, see Alice Echols, *Daring to Be Bad: Radical Feminism in America 1967–1975* (Minneapolis: University of Minnesota Press, 1989).
17. For a discussion of women in the midst of the new left movement see Jane Alpert, *Growing Up Underground* (New York: Morrow, 1981); Paul Jacobs and Saul Landau, *The New Radicals: A Report with Documents* (New York: Random House, 1966); and Sara Evans, *Personal Politics: The Roots of Women's Liberation in the Civil Rights Movement and the New Left* (New York: Knopf, 1979).
18. Jane Alpert, "Mother Right: A New Feminist Theory," *Ms.* (August 1973): 91.
19. Barbara Burris, "The Fourth World Manifesto," *Notes from the Third Year: Women's Liberation*, June 1970, 118.
20. Ibid., 90, 94, 92.
21. Jill Johnston, *Lesbian Nation: The Feminist Solution* (New York: Simon and Schuster, 1973), 174.
22. Gina Covina and Laurel Galana, *The Lesbian Reader: An Amazon Quarterly Anthology* (Oakland, Calif.: Amazon Press, 1975), 105.
23. Andrew Ross, "New Age Technoculture," in *Cultural Studies*, ed. Lawrence Grossberg, Cary Nelson, and Paula Treichler (New York: Routledge, 1992), 545.
24. Alice Echols, *Daring to Be Bad* (Minneapolis: University of Minnesota Press, 1989), and Judith Grant, *Fundamental Feminism: Contesting the Core Concepts of Feminist*

Theory (New York: Routledge, 1993). There have been extremely cogent critiques of Echols's *Daring*, two of which are found in *Radically Speaking: Feminism Reclaimed*, ed. Diane Bell and Renate Klein (Melbourne, Australia: Spinifex Press, 1996). Diane Richardson, "Misguided, Dangerous and Wrong: On the Maligning of Radical Feminism," and Tania Lienert, "Who is Calling Radical Feminists 'Cultural Feminists' and Other Historical Sleights of Hand," both take Echols to task for taking the position that radical feminism gave way to cultural feminism. I think the difference between scholars here is one of place, not purpose; I feel that radical feminism is alive and well *outside* the academy, but that its relationship to a broader intellectual project has been sorely marginalized by the popularity of cultural feminist concerns. I am grateful to London-based Clare Hemmings for her critique of this portion of the project and for her suggestion of the Spinifex volume.

25. *Business of Punishment*, 1994.
26. Judith Butler, *Gender Trouble: Feminism and the Subversion of Identity* (New York: Routledge, 1990), 5.
27. Kobena Mercer, *Welcome to the Jungle: New Positions in Black Cultural Studies* (New York: Routledge, 1994), 259.
28. Butler, *Gender Trouble*, 5–6.
29. Mercer, *Welcome*, 260.
30. Tomás Almaguer, *Racial Fault Lines: The Historical Origins of White Supremacy in California* (Berkeley: University of California Press, 1994), 210–11; emphasis added.
31. Proposition 184 was passed by public referendum autumn 1994 and called for a "three strikes, you're out" policy toward repeat offenders. Proposition 187, known as the "anti-immigrant" referendum, passed in the same year and mandated the denial of health care and schooling to undocumented people. In autumn 1996, Proposition 209, erroneously named the "California Civil Rights Initiative," demanded the immediate suspension of existing affirmative action policies and programs in the public sphere.
32. Peter Schrag, "Son of 187: Anti-Affirmative Action Propositions," *New Republic*, 30 January 1995, 16–18.
33. I would argue that there are three movements in this country that demonstrate both legitimate and illegitimate forms white male anger. They are: early HIV/AIDS activism, Christian coalition politics, and paramilitary militia activity. These groups are similar because they demonstrate cognate beginnings—that the initial call to political action rested on the sense that white men were not getting all that they were entitled to receive at the hands of government.
34. See the early work of Denesh D'Souza, and Jesse Helms's early campaign against the National Endowment for the Arts (NEA) and later against National Public Radio (NPR).
35. Several collections of essays place early struggles against HIV/ AIDS in practical and theoretical perspective: Douglas Crimp, ed., *AIDS: Cultural Analysis and Cultural Activism* (Cambridge: The MIT Press, 1988); Judith Pastore, ed., *Confronting AIDS Through Literature: The Responsibilities of Representation* (Urbana: University of Illinois Press, 1993); Timothy F. Murphy and Suzanne Poirier, eds., *Writing AIDS: Gay Literature, Language and Analysis* (New York: Columbia University Press, 1993); and Simon Watney, *Practices of Freedom: Selected Writings on HIV/AIDS* (Durham, N.C.: Duke University Press, 1994).
36. Leo Bersani, "Is the Rectum a Grave?" in *AIDS: Cultural Analysis and Cultural Activism*, ed. Crimp, 206.
37. For a discussion of white male rage, see Ann Hulbert, "Angels in the Outfield," *New Republic*, 18 November 1996, 46; Schrag, "Son of 187," 16–18; and Mary B. Harris, "Sex and Ethnic Differences in Past Aggressive Behaviors," *Journal of Family Violence* 7, no. 2 (1992): 85–103.

38. For an understanding of the outgrowth of various Christian coalition politics, see Joe Conason, Alfred Ross, and Lee Cokorinos, "The Promise Keepers Are Coming: The Third Wave of the Religious Right," *The Nation*, 7 October 1996, 11–19.

39. I am referring to the FBI siege of the compound in Waco, Texas, and the Oklahoma City bombing and the subsequent FBI crackdown on paramilitary groups in the nation. Many of the nation's extremist paramilitary groups have as their ideological foundation, some of the tenets expressed in Andrew Macdonald's novel, *The Turner Diaries* (Hillsboro, W. Va.: National Vanguard Books, 1995).

40. For example, in the acknowledgments to their 1992 release, *Play More Music*, band members rail against vestiges of white supremacy with "No thanks and a big FUCK YOU to the NRA, Ted Nugent, Operation Rescue, Patriarchy, Procter and Gamble, The Sky God, and all the slamdancers."

41. See Eric Lott, *Love and Theft: Blackface Minstrelsy and the American Working Class* (New York: Oxford University Press, 1993).

42. Ann Powers, "The Left Stuff: Consolidated Mix Politics with Humor," *Rolling Stone*, 13 December 1994, 33.

43. Consolidated, Business, track 11.

44. Karla F. C. Holloway, *Codes of Conduct: Race, Ethics, and the Color of Our Character* (New Brunswick, N.J.: Rutgers University Press, 1995), 15.

45. Ann duCille has remarked, "The most important questions, I have begun to suspect, may not be about the essentialism and territoriality, the biology, sociology or even the ideology about which we hear so much but, rather, about professionalism and disciplinarity; about cultural literacy and intellectual competence; about taking ourselves seriously and insisting that we be taken seriously not as objectified subjects in someone else's histories—as native informants—but as critics and as scholars reading and writing our own literature and history." From "The Occult of True Black Womanhood: Critical Demeanor and Black Feminist Studies," *Signs* 19, no. 3 (1994): 603.

46. After the 1985 publication of Gilman's piece in *'Race', Writing and Difference*, critics took issue with Gilman's decision to reprint the devastating pictures of Sarah Bartmann's genitalia, crafted by George Cuvier. See also Anne Fausto-Sterling, "Gender, Race and Nation: The Comparative Anatomy of 'Hottentot' Women in Europe, 1815–1817," in *Deviant Bodies: Critical Perspectives on Difference in Science and Popular Culture*, ed. Jennifer Terry and Jacqueline Urla (Bloomington: Indiana University Press, 1995), 19–48.

47. Anita Cornwell, *The Black Lesbian in White America* (Tallahassee, Fla.: The Naiad Press, 1983), and Audre Lorde, *Zami: A New Spelling of My Name* (Freedom, Calif.: The Crossing Press, 1982), are probably the only in-depth studies of their kind. See also Barbara Smith, *Home Girls: A Black Feminist Anthology* (New York: Kitchen Table Press, 1983).

48. Judith Roof, *A Lure of Knowledge: Lesbian Sexuality and Theory* (New York: Columbia University Press, 1991), 217, 229.

49. I have commented more extensively on the subject of black bodies and queer studies in my essay: Sharon P. Holland, "(White) Lesbian Studies," in *New Lesbian Studies: Into the Twenty-First Century*, ed. Bonnie Zimmerman and Toni A. H. McNaron (New York: The Feminist Press, 1996), 247–55.

50. Evelynn Hammonds, "Black (W)holes and the Geometry of Black Female Sexuality," *differences*, 141.

51. Andrew Parker and Eve Kosofsky Sedgwick, eds., *Performativity and Performance* (New York: Routledge, 1995), 16; emphasis added.

Part III

Mapping New Theoretical Territory

The Accent of "Loss": Cultural Crossings as Context in Julia Alvarez's *How the Garcia Girls Lost Their Accents*

Chapter 7

DAVID T. MITCHELL

*It would be years before I took the courses that would
change my mind in schools paid for by sugar from fields
around us, years before I could begin to comprehend how
one does not see the maids when they pass by.*

Julia Alvarez, Homecoming

For POSTCOLONIAL NOVELISTS, the enunciative position of the exile, émigré, or expatriate serves as an apt metaphor for the paradoxical desire of their fictions to capture the ambivalence of immigrant lives. The "loss" of an ability to depict an absent homeland empirically becomes a key characteristic of postcolonial writing; the central tension is informed by a desire to look back on what has been "lost" in order to restore or regain one's place of origin. The impossibility of such a repossession, imaginative or otherwise, produces profound uncertainties about cultural belongingness and the artistic pursuit of "authentic expression."

This defining ambivalence characteristic of postcolonial writing inscribes the idea of "loss" in terms of a negativity that forever places the postcolonial writer in a subordinate position to those who retain "unhindered" access to the desired artistic object of the homeland. The critique of culturally produced binaries that separate enunciative positions such as home/exile, patriot/expatriate, and citizen/alien serves as the guiding impetus of the postcolonial writer's narrative explorations and calls into question those divisions as flawed and unnatural categories of contemporary cultures and identities that are always already hybrid cultural products.

Crucial to understanding the contemporary postcolonial writer's definitive sense of "homelessness" is the analysis of the ways in which he or she seeks to go beyond the stale binaries of state-imposed identities in narrative. Often this objective is accomplished by demonstrating that each character possesses only some of the pieces that make up an absent or inaccessible whole. Postcolonial writers privilege the culturally mixed heritages and influences of their protagonists in order to de-essentialize nationalist polemics that seek to define the characteristics of the true geographical native. By challenging authorial and authoritative claims to geographic and cultural binaries that falsely legislate what counts as the official experience of a community or place, postcolonial writers strategically foreground and celebrate either the limitations of the first-person perspective or proffer multiple narrators who decenter readerly identifications with a singular or omnisciently controlling narrative perspective.

Such a project informs *How the Garcia Girls Lost Their Accents*, the first novel by postcolonial writer Julia Alvarez. The careful positioning of the verb "lost" at the heart of the novel's title promises a document that will ferret out the moment or moments of cultural extinction/assimilation for the title characters—four sisters who grow up in an upper-class family in the Dominican Republic and are later forced into exile in the United States. Parallel to other postcolonial writers, such as Salman Rushdie, Michelle Cliff, and Bharati Mukhergee, Alvarez attempts to destabilize the binary of the postcolonial writer's "absence" from, or "presence" in, a geographical homeland. Alvarez's first novel seeks to delineate the complex interplay of colliding ideological and political systems that inform the experiences of her culturally hybrid subjects of the Dominican Republic and the United States. By pluralizing the lost accents of the title, Alvarez presents a novelistic strategy that fragments and multiplies the story of immigrant experience into competing accounts and thus rejects the impulse to reduce the interplay of individual and cultural influences to a static binary of dominated and dominant.

How the Garcia Girls Lost Their Accents, which won the Pen/Faulkner award in the ethnic fiction category, marks Alvarez's debut as a novelist who contemplates the complex intersections of class, nationality and race for her Dominican American characters.[1] Since Alvarez's family was part of a wave of middle-class immigrants who came to settle in New York City during the second half of the twentieth century, her work privileges the cultural limbo of migratory groups as an important site of fictional investigation.[2] The geographical and imaginative terrain of *How the Garcia Girls Lost Their Accents* is consistently saturated with the economic and political influence of an exported U.S. capitalism that has resulted from years of military and market control. As Alvarez explains in an autobiographical essay, "An American Childhood in the Dominican Republic," the two cultures are inextricably bound together:

> [My mother] enrolled her daughters in Carol Morgan's school where
> we began each day by pledging allegiance to the flag of the United
> States, which I much preferred to the Dominican one, for it had the
> lovely red-and-white stripes of the awning at the ice-cream parlor. . . .

We also sang the marine song, "From the halls of Montezuma to the shores of Tripoli," marching in place to the rallying beat. The marines had occupied the country often, most recently when they had installed Trujillo as head of state two and a half decades before, and their song as well as the light-skinned, light-eyed children with American names in the barrios were some of the traces that they had been there.[3]

Such entwined racial and national histories openly inform the narrative trajectory of *Garcia Girls* as well as the novel's oscillation between assimilating into the life-styles promulgated by middle-class consumer culture in the United States and longing for a lost Dominican origin. The oscillation of her characters between the "promise" and "tragedy" that each cultural experience affords establishes the binary nationalist affinities that compete for authority in the midst of her characters' migratory movements between two countries.

The argument that this essay pursues is located in an analysis of the significance of this nationalist ambivalence in postcolonial narratives. For Alvarez, the infiltration of U.S. culture, military, and governments into the Dominican Republic has produced neither a sense of colonial resentment nor an open ideological embrace of capitalist infiltration. Instead, the writer explores the class and racial dimensions of such a relationship in ways that complicate an understanding of cultural privilege in the colonial commerce of nations:

> What kept my father from being rounded up with the others [political dissidents of the Trujillo Regime] each time there was a purge . . . was his connection with my mother's powerful family. It was not just their money that gave them power, for wealth was sometimes an incentive to persecute a family and appropriate its fortune. It was their strong ties with Americans and the United States. As I mentioned, most of my aunts and uncles had graduated from American schools and colleges, and they corresponded regularly with their classmates and alumni associations. . . . The family subscribed to American magazines, received mail-order catalogues, and joined American clubs and honorary societies. This obsession with American things was no longer merely enchantment with the States, but a strategy for survival.[4]

It is this particular history of cultural appropriations and incestuous political crossings that structures the postcolonial backdrop of Alvarez's novel. As members of a privileged class in the Dominican Republic, the Garcia family has the capacity to negotiate the fraught binaries that exist between nationalist loyalties and political tyranny. Rather than cast the colonialist heritage of the Dominican Republic as a choice between colonial servitude and naive ideological indoctrination, Alvarez's family consciously embraces their Dominicanized version of an exported American culture in order to maintain and bolster their economic and social advantage. By surrounding the family with the accoutrements of a U.S. export economy, they temporarily secure their safety despite their opposition to the United States–backed Trujillo regime. In attending to this aspect of Alvarez's interests, this essay goes on to explicate the ways in which class privilege interrupts and complicates strict nationalist binaries by promoting the alternative values of postcolonial multiplicity.

How the Garcia Girls Lost Their Accents charts the reactions and responses of familial and cultural relations among four sisters: Carla, Sandra, Yolanda, and Sofia. Sociological studies have often endeavored to use sibling groups as a means of charting the ways in which environment and/or genetic inheritance affect the development of children who are brought up in the same environment. Alvarez employs a similar strategy by maintaining a simultaneous focus upon a cast of characters who develop within a shared social and familial milieu. In situating her characters together as a discursive "family," Alvarez seeks to explore the means by which her characters appropriate and recognize their narrative stories as shared and/or separate from a unitary body of gendered familial identities. Throughout the novel, numerous commentators remark on the poor fortune of a family that consists entirely of girls—"what, four girls and no boys?"—while each daughter struggles to free herself from the limitations of a communal designation that strips them of their uniqueness and individuality. Because the label "Garcia Girls" stands in for the plural identities submerged beneath the faceless anonymity of daughters (who, unlike their male counterparts, do not need to be individuated as distinct human beings), Alvarez remains ambiguous about the prospects for her four narrators throughout the novel.

Since multiple narrators (or what I will term multiperspectivity from this point on) afford novelists the opportunity to simulate access to a variety of first- and third-person narrators within the same text, How the Garcia Girls Lost Their Accents exploits such a tactic by oscillating between diverging narrative lines that upend and dynamically revise each other. Multiperspectivity succeeds in breaking the binary between narrator and narrated and paves the way for the interruptive force of hybrid postcolonial forms. Rather than explicating one specific response to the dislocating sensations of cultural transition, the novel situates the notion of "loss" in terms of each characters' responses to the intersection and clash of U.S. and Dominican cultures. Alvarez's use of multiple first-person narratives formally mirrors her understanding of the shifting and multiple nature of postcolonial identity itself.

The poster image of the Palmolive woman near the Garcia daughters' home in the Dominican Republic establishes the influence of American postcapitalist forms long before any member of the family ever sets foot in the land of "concrete cities and snow." Because the novel moves backward in time from 1989 to 1956, rather than forward to chart the movement (in some progressive chronological sense) of the Dominican family's transition from the island to the States, readers are set up to anticipate that the novel will present a vision of the Dominican homeland prior to U.S. cultural infiltration and military intervention. Yet the reader's arrival at the multiple first-person narratives of the title characters does not coincide with this notion of a "pure" cultural setting. Despite the narrative's interest in explicating the alienating cultural terrain to which the daughters are exposed in the United States, Alvarez's analysis becomes increasingly geared toward plotting the ways in which such a sense of estrangement seems present from the outset. In doing so, Alvarez attempts to imagine the contradictions inherent in any return to a geographic space once occupied and then relinquished.

Although the *Garcia Girls* charts numerous reactions on the part of its characters to the move from the Dominican Republic to the United States, the most significant aspect of negotiating such "returns" entails the ability or inability of each daughter to understand her specific relation to the family servants. Unlike the more prototypical plot lines of the immigration novel, *Garcia Girls* details the experiences of characters who operate within the upper echelons of economic status and political power in their homeland. Their cultural positioning is interesting because they literally move from a position of dominance to a racially marginal position in the United States. Alvarez's story contemplates the exploitive social conditions of each culture and refuses to privilege the country of origins over the newly adopted nation—each exists in a dialectical tension within the minds of her narrators in such a way that the binary of national identity gradually falls away to be replaced by the more indeterminate identity of a multinationed clan.

Thus, the move from the Dominican Republic to the United States involves a "fall" from influence for the family. After discovering that they will be forced to leave the family compound because of a failed CIA-backed governmental coup, the family's visionary mother, Mami, explains that the relocation means an abdication of material wealth and relative security:

> So, Laura thinks. So the papers have cleared and we are leaving. Now
> everything she sees sharpens as if through the lens of loss—the
> orchids in their hanging straw baskets, the row of apothecary jars
> Carlos has found for her in old druggists' throughout the countryside,
> the rich light shafts swarming with a golden pollen. She will miss this
> glorious light warming the inside of her skin and jeweling the trees,
> the grass, the lily pond beyond the hedge.[5]

The "lens of loss" that Alvarez uses to underscore Mami's instantaneous sense of desire for the home and countryside she has come to cherish epitomizes the way the novel situates nostalgia for the homeland. In the wake of the class privileges that have been stripped from the island family once they are forced to seek exile to escape Papi's impending imprisonment and the random searches of the government *guardias*, each family members' narrative investigates how their experiences on the island of the Dominican Republic condition their responses throughout their lives. The household accoutrements that Mami longs to retain even before she has stepped outside the compound for the last time indicate the history of acquisitions and purchases that represent the multinational life of consumption she has created for herself and her family.

Such longing for the life that has been lost reverberates throughout the novel, and like Yolanda's craving for guavas, the native fruit she ate as a young girl, all the characters in this fiction attempt to reclaim the present in terms of the past—their experiences in the United States compared and contrasted to their lives before the family's exile. The imaged or imagined homeland that haunts each narrator serves as a barometer to gauge the "success" or "trauma" of the years that follow. The "lens of loss" inevitably alters, however, and as each child relates her story to the reader, individual notions of "loss" shift and collide. When Yolanda, for instance, arrives on the island after a five-year hiatus in the United States, her memory of the land she left is rekindled and reinvested with the startling beauty of the country and the warmth her relatives provide:

> All around her are the foothills, a dark enormous green, the sky more
> a brightness than a color. A breeze blows through the palms below,
> rustling their branches, so they whisper like voices. Here and there a
> braid of smoke rises up from a hillside—a campesino and his family
> living out their solitary life. This is what she has been missing all
> these years without really knowing that she has been missing it.
> Standing here in the quiet, she believes she has never felt at home in
> the States, never. (12)

Yet, despite the apparent parallels between Mami's earlier sense of loss for the island atmosphere and her third daughter's nostalgia for "palms . . . [that] whisper like voices [, . . . and the] solitary life" of the hillside *campesinos*, Yolanda's return is tempered by her growing awareness of the servant classes who make the family's life of relative luxury possible. Rather than smoothly assimilate back into her prior existence as the pampered daughter of a wealthy political official, Yolanda's experiences in the United States provide her with a politicized context of class consciousness that troubles the family's once naturalized Dominican lifestyle. Rather than circulate on the periphery of the family, the maids immediately erupt into Yolanda's description of the scene. The "invisible" labor force that populates and "invisibly" maintains the family estate forms a separate enclave that is openly excluded from the closeness the rest of the family enjoys: "She [Yolanda] pictures the maids in their mysterious cluster at the end of the patio" (11).

Because "home" has taken on differing significances for Yolanda now that she has, like the narrator of the epigraph with which I began, taken "the [college] courses which would change [her] mind," the homecoming that establishes the narrative tone and mood of *Garcia Girls* is one of tension and profound ambivalence. The mature narrative perspective that begins this novel cannot simply recapture the girlhood geography of her previous recollections. Alvarez invests her imaginative reunion with images that disrupt and revise her protagonist's relationship to the familial and cultural beliefs that she fails to recognize at an earlier age. The benefits she and her immediate family have reaped at the expense of the servant classes they employ and exploit lose their luxurious gloss. Armed with a repertoire of political theories from her college classes and her own racial experiences in the United States, which irreparably change her vision of home, Alvarez points to the ways in which her characters respond to the context of upper-class privilege in the Dominican Republic that once went unarticulated in their day-to-day lives. The racial binary of U.S. culture (dark/light) provides a new context from which to collapse a previously unchallenged binary of self/darker-skinned other that the class system of the Dominican Republic perpetuates.

This exposed "absence" of the novel's working classes does not, nonetheless, allow Alvarez's fictional servants a space from which they may speak their own lives. Although the eldest maid, Chucha, briefly narrates her own response to the family's departure later in the novel, *Garcia Girls* attempts to theorize the significance of the racialized dimensions of class overtly. While the novel engages in the significant political act of articulating the experiences of Dominican Americans who have remained largely invisible in U.S. discourses, her own concerns also focus upon the "others" she cannot quite reach in the Dominican Republic. While the novel offers developed subject positions to its upper-class Dominican characters, it simultaneously acknowledges that granting "voices" to some falls short of "speaking" for other marginalized perspectives.

In fact, the lost accents of the title alludes to the difficulties inherent in the Garcia family's ability to "read" or "represent" the experiences of servants who prove absolutely essential to maintaining the familial fabric. In the wake of becoming political exiles living in the United States, they struggle to understand the changes that assault them once they land on foreign soil—"There

have been so many stops on the road of the last twenty-nine years since her
family left this island behind. She and her sisters have led such turbulent
lives—so many husbands, homes, jobs, wrong turns among them" (11)—but
such a volatile transition has not necessarily enabled them to make anything
more than a nod in the direction of the "inscrutable" nature that the maids
seem to harbor: "In the fading light of the patio, Yolanda cannot make out
the expression on the dark face [of the maid ironically named, Illuminada]"
(10). For Alvarez and Third World theorists such as Trinh and Spivak, the
subject speaking position of these subaltern characters already presupposes
the impossibility of capturing the "lost accents" of difference that the title
contemplates.[6]

Despite Yolanda's attempts to analyze the meaning of the family's willingness to use its class position at the expense of other island denizens, the
sisters' narratives, which conclude Alvarez's novel, completely overlook the
hierarchical class system from which their family has benefited. This fact is
perhaps most evident in the oldest sister, Carla's, chapter, "An American Surprise." While the adult Yolanda's chapter moves back and forth between her
sense of security in the island homestead and her growing dis-ease with the
now ever present servant class who fulfill the needs of the Garcia clan, Carla's
narrative demonstrates that even her own experience of racial denigration
in the United States cannot bring her to an awareness of the Dominican
situation.

Because Carla is the oldest of the four sisters, her relationship to the
family's live-in maids is the most established of the four sisters. As in Mami's
"lens of loss," Carla's chapter begins most forthrightly with a contemplation
of her own private sense of loss in the wake of the family's relocation. Unlike
the "welcome back" cake that Yolanda is offered as a sign of appreciation from
her island relatives, the celebration dinner in "An American Surprise" marks
the day the Garcias turn "one American year old." After Carla listens to her
father make a speech that misquotes the poem on the Statue of Liberty, she
wonders exactly what such a celebration means to her own experience in her
newly adopted country: "What do you wish for on the first celebration of the
day you lost everything?" (150). The homesickness she feels manifests itself
most specifically in terms of her unfamiliarity with English slang and colloquial-
isms that elude her comprehension. As soon as she asks God to let the family
return home and helps blow out the celebration candles that line the cake,
she recalls a scene that vividly reminds her of her exclusion from the culture
she now circulates within:

> Down the block the neighborhood dead-ended in abandoned
> farmland that Mami read in the local paper the developers were
> negotiating to buy. Grasses and real trees and real bushes still grew

beyond the barbed-wire fence posted with a big sign: PRIVATE, NO TRESPASSING. The sign had surprised Carla since "forgive us our trespasses" was the only other context in which she had heard the word. She pointed the sign out to Mami on one of their first walks to the bus stop. "Isn't it funny, Mami? A sign that you have to be good." Her mother did not understand at first until Carla explained about the Lord's Prayer. Mami laughed. Words sometimes meant two things in English too. This trespass meant that no one must go inside the property because it was not public like a park, but private. Carla nodded, disappointed. She would never get the hang of this new country. (151)

Because language represents one of the most significant barriers to the characters' ability to discover a space from which to speak and be understood, Carla's frustration serves to highlight the fact that accents are not just lost but also get in the way. Her inability to comprehend the alternative context for the trespassing sign (that is, her lack of knowledge about the rules of private property) is highlighted by her "only other context," the Lord's Prayer, which she has memorized as a young girl and carried with her from the Dominican Republic. To the oldest daughter the alien notion of "no trespassing" serves a dual function: to highlight the narrator's inability to contemplate the "meanings" of an Other culture that deviates from the linguistic rules to which she has grown accustomed, and to signal a metaphorical exclusion as well. Not only does Carla sense her loss of cultural privilege in the transition from a social context she understands to one she does not, but Alvarez also wants to foreshadow the impending hostility that will greet the transplanted family in the "new world." The Garcias' relocation to a different culture upends their sense of class privilege and simultaneously challenges the American myth of a classless society. This cultural transition not only thrusts the family into a new national context but also revises the daughter's previously uninterrogated class identity in the Dominican Republic. "No trespassing" represents the loss of access to the institutions of authority and meaning making that matter in an American context.

Parallel to the immigrant-novel tradition from which it hails, *How the Garcia Girls Lost Their Accents* explicitly engages in a critique of the inhospitable promised land that remains indifferent and even violent toward its newly arrived inhabitants. Unlike other versions of the genre, such as *The Rise and Fall of David Levinsky*, *The Breadgivers*, *China Men*, *The Borderlands*, and *Jasmine*, Alvarez's novel emphasizes the time before the relocation of her characters.[7] Instead of positing a moment when her characters were fully "at home" on their native soil (that is, a time when the characters believed in their thorough comprehension of cultural codes, customs, and social contracts), Alvarez's

attention to the daughters' experiences in their childhood prior to expatria-
tion demonstrates that their collective sense of security is founded upon their
familial myths of class and social privilege. The cultural codes that Carla finds
obscure and difficult to interpret in the United States may just as easily be
located on the island. While Carla moves in and out of the servant circles at
her parents' house, the naturalized social hierarchy cannot be unmoored or
questioned. The children's acculturation in the naturalized Dominican binaries of racial and class differences proves a necessary ideological component
to their participation in their family's privileged status.

Carla's lack of access to Mami's point of view underscores the novel's re-
current theme of impassable cultural boundaries. As Gladys, one of the
household's recent arrivals to the servant's quarters, prepares the table for dinner, she sings a popular ditty that Carla listens to from the corridor:

> Yo tiro la cuchara,
> Yo tiro el tenedor
> Yo tiro to' lo' plato'
> Y me voy pa' Nueva Yor'.

> I loved to hear Gladys' high, sweet voice imitating her favorite singers
> on the radio. Someday she was going to be a famous actress, Gladys
> said. But my mother said Gladys was only a country girl who didn't
> know any better than to sing popular tunes in the house and wear her
> kinky hair in rollers all week long, then comb it out for Sunday mass
> in hairdos copied from American magazines my mother had thrown
> out. (258)

The young narrator can report but not comment upon the divergent interpretations of Gladys's behavior. Despite Mami's diminutive tone toward
Gladys's desire to westernize her appearance, the lines of cultural influence
and each character's relationship to them remain tangled. Since the American magazines belong to Mami to begin with, Gladys's appropriation of them
seems to be more than a case of her uncomprehending capitulation to American standards of beauty. In fact, the song Carla listens to but fails to analyze
would suggest that Gladys thinks of the United States as a place away from
the exploitive world of the Dominican caste system. Her desire to free herself
from the utensils that signify the tools of her class oppression, implies a refusal
to surrender to the order of maids and masters to which the Garcias subscribe.

Despite moments when the household servants communicate their concern and attachment to various family members, the cultural constraints of
racial and class identifications prevent empathy or understanding from taking place:

Chucha held each of our heads in her hands and wailed a prayer over us. We were used to some of this strange stuff from daily contact with her, but maybe it was because today we could feel an ending in the air, anyhow, we all started to cry as if Chucha had finally released her own tears in each of us. (221)

In this instance, the unitary "we" pronoun that the second-oldest sister, Sandra, uses to represent her own as well as her sisters' shared perspectives about Chucha's "strange stuff" indicates their inability as a group to accept the maid's sorrow and forge a connection to her. The narrator's own sense of sadness evolves not out of a shared understanding with the "tears" the maid releases "in each of us" but as a result of the "feel [of] an ending in the air." Not only will they leave behind the familiar Dominican world, they also will surrender their lives as social insiders who benefit from sedimented economic stratifications deeply embedded in Dominican society.

Yet, to begin to counter the mystique that surrounds the lower classes of *Garcia Girls*, Alvarez interrupts the textual space separating the first three "I" narratives and the final "I" of the artist figure Yolanda with Chucha's own account of the day her employers vacate the family compound. With her proliferation of multiple first-person accounts, Alvarez seeks to transcend the limitations of the class binaries that separate the Garcias from the servants. The narrative device of multiperspectivity enables the novel to resist closure and more singular readerly identifications by moving from one story to the next, in effect denying the reader's desire to follow through more thoroughly on any single story. Left behind in the wake of the family's sudden exit, Chucha wanders through the empty house imagining what life will hold for the Garcias as they head off to encounter the "pale Americans" who make up "a nation of zombies" (221):

They have left—and only silence remains, the deep and empty silence in which I can hear the voices of my *santos* settling into the rooms, of my *loa* telling me stories of what is to come . . . I am to close up the house, and help over at Dona Carmen's until they go too, and then at Don Arturo's, who also is to go. Mostly, I am to tend to this house. Dust, give the rooms an airing. The others except for Chino have been dismissed, and I have been entrusted with the keys. (222)

The "voices" and "stories" that Chucha anticipates hearing positions her as the future curator of the family's multiple histories and identifies her role with that of the novel, which can house so many differentiated stories and accounts. Chucha's social and metaphorical charge to "tend to this house" becomes indicative of Alvarez's own reclamation project where she preserves the neglected stories of the "Dominican" life of the family before exile, which is rapidly fading from view. The deployment of multiperspectivity as an artistic form is an attempt to simulate a reader's access to the personal and personalized narrative lines of individual perceptions, which are in danger of being "lost" forever if they are not reconstituted in writing or some other analogous activity.[8]

Perhaps Chucha describes the dangers and potentialities of such a process most accurately as she imagines the difficulties the daughters will face once they arrive in New York:

> In the girls' room I remember each one as a certain heaviness, now in my heart, now in my shoulders, now in my head or feet; I feel their *losses* pile up like dirt thrown on a box after it has been lowered into the earth. I see their future, the troublesome life ahead. They will be haunted by what they do and don't remember. But they have spirit in them. They will invent what they need to survive. (223)

The prophetic voice that resonates in Chucha's claim that the girls will "invent what they need to survive" suggests the novelistic weight that Alvarez wants to give to the interruption of the maid's narrative. The prediction she makes serves to underscore that the Garcias transport from one geographic locale to another will not mean the catastrophic "loss" of cultural upbringing, but rather an altered constellation of experiences. Instead of surrendering access to a life that can never be reclaimed, the Dominican past will continue to reverberate in the United States for each family member. For Alvarez, identity is understood not in terms of the binary of being Dominican or American, but as a hybrid invention that mirrors the multiple perspectives that make up her postcolonial narrative. The cultural bricolage that such an adjustment inevitably entails will prove difficult—"They will be haunted by what they do and don't remember"—but the "spirit" that Chucha bequeaths to all of them will allow each Garcia to "invent" what is necessary to her survival. The "losses" that "pile up like dirt thrown on a box after it has been lowered into the earth" metamorphose into the stories that populate Alvarez's fiction, for what is not remembered (or what is too painful to remember) moves underground while continuing to wield influence.

The core of familial identity in this novel ultimately proves difficult to specify for Alvarez and her characters, because unlike Chucha, they all fail to develop a successful critical framework within which to understand their lives. Unlike the narrative voice of the opening epigraph, the "homecoming" in *Garcia Girls* does not prove to hold any particular resonance for any of the daughters. Although each narrator's version of events collides with and contradicts those that precede and follow, Alvarez remains skeptical about the ability of her characters to assess their present in terms of the past. Ultimately, the novel seeks to fill in the absence of such a process by committing to textual "memory" the child and adult experiences she believes had a significant impact upon her fictional family (the past they do and don't remember). The utilization of multiperspectivity provides an example of what Homi Bhabha terms "living perplexity," the evolution of a minoritized narrative form that is neither "the transcendental . . . idea of History nor the institution of the State, but a strange temporality" where the story oscillates between past and present in a contest to a controlling master narrative.[9]

This reverberation of the past in the narrative present becomes most overtly foregrounded in the final chapter, "The Drum." Since Yolanda's narrative "I" begins and ends the novel, Alvarez's artistic stand-in can be read in terms of the tensions and gulfs that exist for her own immigrant status as an artist in the United States. The story uses the gift of a drum from Yolanda's grandmother as the narrative vehicle for exploring questions of voice. Because we receive more information about Yolanda's experiences in the United States than any other character (the novel devotes six chapters out of fifteen solely to her impressions), the difficulties of negotiating the relocation are largely documented through her particular observations and concerns. Because Yolanda's character evolves into the figure of the writer, the narrative privileging of her memories situates the issue of locating a "voice" or reclaiming "lost accents" as a central preoccupation. How can the experiences of an upper-class Dominican family who move to the United States be recounted and represented effectively? How does the surrender of class privileges figure as a legitimate and understandable narrative concern without embracing a model that justifies exploitation and inequality? Can the Garcias come to comprehend the exploitation of their pasts while simultaneously coping with their marginalized condition in the United States?

Because Yolanda's story line most overtly addresses such concerns, I want to begin by charting the ways in which her perspective acts as a frame for the novel's focus. When we meet Yolanda for first time in the opening chapter she approaches her childhood home with anxiety and a tinge of guilt about the responses her appearance will produce in her island relatives. She immediately anticipates that her experience in the United States will result in disapproval, that her aunts will see her "shabby in a black cotton skirt, . . . her wild black hair held back with a hairband" (3). The internalized gaze that she will turn upon herself in a self-conscious critique of her status as a cultural emissary of a world she "never felt comfortable in" results in a moment of cultural tension that will be maintained throughout the novel. Her ability to create the stories that her relatives will tell themselves about her "fall" in the States—despite their apparent embrace of her return—sets up Yolanda as

a product of her childhood environment that comes replete with myths of the
fallen western woman who lets herself "go so as to do dubious good in the
world" (4). These competing nationalist versions of the cultural other—
represented sometimes as the Dominican Republic and sometimes as the
United States—are negotiated both at the level of plot and within Yolanda's
psyche as the evidence of a subjectivity in transition.

This negotiation of internal conflicts becomes most poignant near the
end of the opening chapter when the young writer finds herself alone on a
deserted back road with a flat tire. Like her sisters, who are incapable of imagining the perspectives of the family servants who populate their island homestead, Yolanda's concern about the "dark men" who approach her while she
waits for help to arrive from nearby results in her own inability to construct
counternarratives of Dominican masculinity. Her first impulse is to run as they
suddenly appear out of the woods, and once she rejects the idea because she
sees that they are "strong and quite capable of catching her" her legs freeze
and feel as if they are "hammered into the ground beneath her" (19). Once
the men kindly agree to change the flat for her so she can get on her way
before she is trapped out in the country on dark back roads, Alvarez leaves
the reader to mull over the reasons behind her protagonist's response. Because
Yolanda has been subjected to the terror and threat of violation in the patriarchal cultures of the United States and the Dominican Republic, her initial
suspicion of the approaching men leaves the racial implications of her response
ambiguous.

The complexity of negotiating the dual structure of racism and gendered
violence resonates throughout the remainder of the novel. Yolanda's immediate response of fear and flight is highlighted as an understandable reaction;
not only has she recently been warned about the unfeasibility of taking a
"*camioeta* full of *campesinos*" by her island aunts, she has also been exposed to
her older sister's near abduction and traumatic encounter with male sexuality
in the United States. In addition, the Dominican daughters struggle throughout the novel for a sense of self-worth in spite of the limited options available to women in both cultures. By placing readers in present time, we are
drawn into the confusing interplay of gendered fears and racial assumptions
in Yolanda's mind while also being asked to assess the competing cultural origins of such expectations.

Yolanda goes on to encounter discriminatory attitudes about her Dominican background in the United States, demonstrating that racial and gendered
attitudes are equally conflictual in both contexts. In one scene Yolanda's
boyfriend's parents comment on the pride her parents must feel about the
achievement of "her 'accentless' English." This particular inflection upon the
loss or repression of an accent as evidence of the nearly seamless "achieve-

ment" of acculturated speech further multiplies the valences of "loss" in the title. The parent's centrist statement explains the cultural mire of the immigrant experience, in which one is congratulated for assimilating at the expense and devaluation of the culture one has left behind. Conversely, Yolanda also finds herself retreating into her "native tongue" in order to avoid answering difficult questions about her personal desires put to her by her later lover, John. In this scenario the narrator is able to use her mixed cultural heritage as an escape hatch into a self-willed loss of comprehension. Such a textual conflation of cultural obstacles situates a matrix of meanings behind Alvarez's pivotal notion of "loss" for her characters.

The "American Drum" that Yolanda proudly beats in her yard after being reprimanded for beating it too loudly in the house provides her with the impetus for making herself heard around the family compound. As she struts up and down "saluting the bougainvillea and drumm[ing] until the hummingbirds were ready to fly off to the United States of America in the middle of December," she contemplates the unfortunate condition of her banishment to the "outside" at the behest of her mother:

> That was just like my mother to let me have a drum and then forbid
> me to drum it, ba-bam, ba-bam, in any significantly inspired way. And
> how could I judge the significance in a drum unless at least one
> grownup clapped her hands over her ears? And how could I judge
> inspiration unless there was noise in it, drumming from my ten flexed
> toes, from my skinny legs that would someday improve themselves,
> drumming from the hips I swayed when I was womanish, and up, up
> the rib cage, where the heart sat like a crimson drum itself among
> ivory drumsticks. (277)

The narrator's despondency over her ability to provoke a discernible response from her audience—"how could I judge the significance in a drum unless at least one grownup clapped her hands over her ears?"—functions as an artistic question of voice that Alvarez herself desires to allegorize in nearly all of the personal anecdotes that constitute her novel. Since Yolanda represents the artistic conscience of the family, the one whose impulse it is to organize this family tree of stories, the question of a drum's ability to elicit some sign of artistic impact foregrounds the novel's concern with the feasibility of attaining a "voice," or many voices, that can create a stir in her readership. If writing is equated with the desire to drum with authority, then Yolanda's chapter, which ends the collection, sits strategically poised as the novel's central preoccupation with a minority woman's ability to evolve a viable artistic voice.

The close parallels that Yolanda draws between her drumming and her physical development into a "womanish" adult make this goal of attaining a mature artistic "voice" explicit. Because the drum comes from, in her grandmother's words, the "magic store" back in the United States (F. A. O. Schwartz), pure lines of artistic and cultural lineage are blurred even at the furthest chronological narrative moment recorded in the novel. While Yolanda locates her own maturity as a function of growing into a "responsible drumm[er]," the novel posits the nature of such "maturity" as ambiguous and conflicted (277). The imported drum comes to symbolize the business of cultural imports and exports in a novel that refuses to reduce the complexities of individual or social heredity to a matter of one "pure" lineage versus another. Alvarez adopts the imported drum as a crucial piece in the puzzle of familial and cultural identity and influence. The impossibility of locating a truly original version of a homeland culture prior to its infiltration by the United States underscores the novel's interest in exploring the ramifications of accents that are altered but never entirely lost.

Such an ambiguity is further emblematized when Yolanda confesses that she quickly misplaces the original drumsticks (one is mysteriously lost and the other is irreparably broken when her "crazy aunt, Tia Isa," accidentally sits on it) that accompany her grandmother's gift. Despite some valiant attempts on the part of her mother and grandmother to substitute "pencils or the handles of wooden spoons used for making cake batter," Yolanda sadly explains that "the sound was not the same, and the joy went out of drumming" (278). Yolanda's loss of interest in drumming suggests that there is no substitute for the original instruments of a once authentic "voice." Yet this longing for a nonartificial mode of expression proves inevitably flawed. The narratives in *Garcia Girls* can only take shape as a product of the "artificial" and mediating forces of memory, time, and narrative retrospection. The drumsticks are not valuable because they make the drum sound authoritative and drumlike; rather, Yolanda associates the original drumming sound with authenticity and therefore cannot revise her ideas about what a drum should sound like. Thus, Yolanda's story of the drum acts as an allegory for the situation of the hybrid cultural subject who would privilege her "Dominican" experience only at the expense of sacrificing her Dominican American identity.

Of course, this question of returning to a homeland that represents a life uncomplicated or complicitous in impure discourses of cultural influence is possible for Alvarez in part because she moves her characters from a position of power and authority in the Dominican Republic to one of marginality and relative invisibility in the United States. Unlike, for instance, Toni Morrison's *Beloved*, which posits the possibility of an "other (liveable) place"—that is, Africa prior to the western military invasions and cultural appropriations— Alvarez's task is to unveil the illusion of a romanticized homeland unfettered by the bonds of caste, gender, and racial violence.[10] For Yolanda, the "wailing" that signals "some violation that lies at the center of my art" implies a connection between the "lost accents" of the title and the "void" that sits at the heart of artistic representation. While the impossibility of contemplating the "dark other" seems to place Alvarez as a firm believer in, and documentor of, the logistics of cultural "loss," I want to argue in the remainder of this essay that the text transforms the discursive category of "loss" into a metaphor for the multiple combinations that occur in cross-cultural appropriations and exchanges.

When Yolanda accidentally stumbles upon a kitten in the tool shed that sits tucked away on the back lawn of the family compound, she decides, despite her mother's explicit orders to the contrary, to enter and remove the kitten from the new litter. As she moves away from the scene of the theft she quickly tucks her new pet into the hollow of the drum that she no longer plays but rather wears "riding [her] hips like a desperado's revolver" (278). After dodging the kitten's mother and sneaking through the house to her bedroom, the narrator spends her time trying to quiet the kitten's meowing from the inside of the drum. Her efforts prove futile, and instead of returning her hostage, she lifts the screen and throws "the meowing ball out the window" (288). In the process the small kitten is injured and the narrator returns periodically to the window in order to watch the wounded kitten make "its broken progress across the lawn" toward the shed. The period of time that follows places the howling mother cat at her bedside "wailing until dawn," and the narrator continues to be haunted by her apparition until the family finally vacates the island to the United States. As the novel winds down and the final narrative voice moves toward its conclusion, Alvarez explains the impulse that resides behind her storytelling desires:

> Then we moved away to the United States. The cat disappeared altogether. I saw snow. I solved the riddle of an outdoors made mostly of concrete in New York. My grandmother grew so old she could not remember who she was. I went away to school. I read books. You understand I am collapsing all time now so that it fits in what's left in the hollow of my story? I began to write, the story of Pila, the story of my grandmother. I never saw Schwarz [the kitten] again . . . I grew up, a curious woman, a woman of story ghosts and story devils, a woman prone to bad dreams and bad insomnia. (289–290)

For "a woman of story ghosts and story devils," such a denouement seems glaringly inadequate. The haunting nature of the "loss" that she cannot fill—the narrative "hollow of my story"—solidifies around her sense of guilt about the theft and injury of the kitten she "illegally" abducts from its family. Her attempt to "collaps[e] all time" so that its fills in the emptiness she feels now that she has left her island homeland and taken up residence in the United States becomes the impetus for writing. In the hope of recapturing what's been lost or left behind, she begins the process of recording the "story of Pila, the story of my grandmother": all of the stories that have come to make up the very novel we have before us. In leaving the homeland she also leaves behind the fears and anxieties that haunted her as a child, but the adult narrator must reconstruct those repressed sentiments in order to produce a narrative that revives the experience of the lost homeland.

Such a process—the inevitable sense of inadequacy that accompanies any attempt to reinvent a past in the hopes of regaining a whole self, culture, experience, and so on—is the core component of Alvarez's novel. "Lost Accents" become the discursive site of what's found; a narrative production that exploits a sense of loss in order to locate a family/community of voices once invisible (or unvocalized), and now found (or reconstructed). The competing cultural influences in the Dominican Republic and the United States that would propose to usurp or cancel each other out must be seen not as a "loss" but as a productive tension that allows a myriad of influences to coexist. Alvarez seeks to go beyond the binary of a cultural either/or by creating a novel that defines the immigrant subject as an uneasy hybrid product of conflicting social positions such as class, gender, race, and nation.

While Yolanda mourns her inability to capture her artistic object adequately on canvas, Alvarez's novel self-consciously exposes the absence of perspectives that it cannot adequately represent. The stories that each of the Garcia Girls relate in the finale of "I" narratives that bring this novel to a close all situate their inability to imagine various racialized and class perspectives; consequently, the text foregrounds the myriad ways in which all their stories are bound together in a shared project rather than distinctly separate and "lost." The lack of overt narrative commentary on the part of the narrators gestures toward a hybrid narrative space that reflects the multiplicities of Dominican American identity.

For Alvarez, the notion of multiple versions of "loss" situates her attempt to use the very concept of loss as the terrain upon which she can locate the uniqueness of her narrative vision. In a parallel to Gloria Anzaldúa's arguments, finding oneself living between the illusion of monolithic cultural identities must be articulated in and of itself as a speaking position that undermines the very idea of cultural purity. As a Mestiza American woman, she attempts to specify the numerous colliding and contradictory influences she must negotiate each day. Her valorization of the notion of "borderlands" takes shape as the need and desire to vocalize the myriad ways in which cultural subjects find themselves on the cusps of numerous discursive communities:

I am a border woman. I grew up between two cultures, the Mexican (with a heavy Indian influence) and the Anglo (as a member of a colonized people in our own territory). I have been straddling the *tejas*-Mexican border, and others, all my life. It's not a comfortable territory to live in, this place of contradictions . . . Living on borders and in margins, keeping intact one's shifting and multiple identity and integrity, is like trying to swim in a new element, an "alien" element. . . . Strange, huh? . . . No, not comfortable, but home.[11]

In order to maintain and participate in such a community of "border residents," Alvarez utilizes the narrative strategy of multiperspectivity to suspend and illustrate this notion of "shifting and multiple identity" both thematically and formally. Such a suspension allows Alvarez to write across the boundaries of dueling nationalities in order to present immigrant or border subjectivities as a dynamic hybrid prototype of the postcolonial novel. The narrative tool of multiperspectivity allows Alvarez's text to straddle the divide(s) of personal, political, and cultural interpretive systems, in order to capture the kaleidoscopic arrangements of individual and communal perception.

Notes

1. The Pen/Faulkner award had never been awarded to a first novel before *How the Garcia Girls Lost Their Accents* won in 1991.
2. Immigration data and trends for the Dominican Republic have been compiled by several different studies, but this figure was taken from Peter Winn, *Americas: The Changing Faces of Latin America and the Caribbean* (New York: Pantheon Books, 1992). Winn's portrait of Dominican immigration parallels the trajectory of Alvarez's novel closely: "Unlike the Puerto Rican migrants, the new Dominican community in New York is largely composed of middle-class people whose educational and financial resources are greater than those of most of their compatriots. Many are children of small landowners from the countryside who were seeking ways to supplement their family incomes or to save money with which to expand or modernize their family farm. Others had owned businesses in Santo Domingo and looked to set up their own enterprises in New York, or else to accumulate the capital to establish a business back home. Most were forced to accept work that was beneath their occupational status in the Dominican Republic, jobs they left as soon as they had accumulated the capital to open their own businesses" (586–87).
3. Julia Alvarez, "An American Childhood in the Dominican Republic," *The American Scholar* 1 (winter 1988): 77–78.
4. Ibid., 80.
5. Alvarez, *How the Garcia Girls Lost Their Accents* (Chapel Hill, N.C.: Algonquin Books of Chapel Hill, 1991), 212. All future references to the novel are made parenthetically in the text.
6. Trinh T. Minh-ha, *Woman, Native, Other: Writing Postcoloniality and Feminism* (Bloomington: Indiana University Press, 1989); Gayatri Spivak, "Can the Subal-

tern Speak?", in *Marxism and the Interpretation of Culture*, ed. Cary Nelson and Larry Grossberg (Urbana: University of Illinois Press, 1988).

7. Traditionally, the key common denominator of immigrant novels has been the conflict of the underclasses coming to the United States in pursuit of a more economically viable lifestyle. In each of the examples listed here, the United States exists as a prosperous Mecca that lures the immigrant toward its mythic promise of class mobility. The saturation of the Third World with U.S. exports (for example, product lines, films, and corporations) ensnares those cultures that have been subject to U.S. military and cultural occupation while simultaneously obliterating the historical lines of this intervention. Alvarez's novel revises this plot line by demonstrating her characters' manipulation of U.S. dependency rather than making them simply consumers of the mythic vision itself.

8. Part of the failure of Alvarez's novel to imagine the perspectives of her lower-class figures is that Chucha's chapter, which is the only one allotted to any of the servants in the novel, articulates the now largely clichéd role of the loyal domestic slave. Although a great deal of the novelistic weight is offered to Chucha's charge as household retainer, she nonetheless is left to mourn her kind keepers and worry over their turbulent departure from home. Such an impulse has been espoused fairly often in American letters (Faulkner's Dilsey most immediately comes to mind); thus, this mode of characterization seems to mar Alvarez's project despite her apparent cognizance of the "gaps" in her own narrative path.

9. Homi K. Bhabha, *The Location of Culture* (New York: Routledge, 1994), 157.

10. Toni Morrison, *Beloved* (New York: Alfred A. Knopf, 1997), 198.

11. Gloria Anzaldúa, *Borderlands/La Frontera: The New Mestiza* (San Francisco: Spinsters/Aunt Lute Book Company, 1987), i.

Chapter 8

Historical Multiculturalism: Cultural Complexity in the First Native American Novel

TIMOTHY B. POWELL

THE FIRST NATIVE AMERICAN NOVEL, *The Life and Adventures of Joaquin Murieta, Celebrated California Bandit*, was written in 1854 by John Rollin Ridge, a Cherokee Indian and a survivor of the Trail of Tears. *Joaquin Murieta* is the story of a young Mexican who comes to California during the 1849 gold rush seeking the American Dream only to discover the American Nightmare— after successfully striking gold he is run off his land by "lawless and desperate" white miners who "looked upon [all Mexicans] as no better than conquered subjects of the United States, having no rights which could stand before a haughtier and superior race."[1] After a series of atrocities, Murieta vows revenge and assembles a revolutionary army that declares war on the white "American race." Because Ridge's novel is the earliest Native American novel to have thus far been recovered and because it offers such a radically different cultural perspective of the imperial conquest of the continent that whites referred to as "Manifest Destiny," *Joaquin Murieta* is an extremely important literary and historical document. Yet, surprisingly, Ridge's novel remains virtually unknown to most scholars of American literature and history.[2]

One reason, I believe, that *The Life and Adventures of Joaquin Murieta* has not received more critical attention is because the novel's sheer multicultural complexity raises a number of perplexing critical questions that make the text difficult to interpret. As the first known Native American novel, *Joaquin Murieta* bears the heavy (and perhaps unfair) critical burden of being asked to speak for those Native Americans and Mexican Americans who were brutally repressed in the first half of the nineteenth century and whose voices have, for the most part, been lost to historians and literary critics of American culture. In a well-intentioned endeavor to recover those voices, the critical tendency in interpreting Ridge's novel is to collapse the Mexican American character of Joaquin Murieta into its Cherokee author and to view the text as a powerful expression of "minority" rage at the "dominant" white culture. To approach the first Native American novel with a rigid set of ideological expectations, however, is to miss the cultural complexity of Ridge's own life and his intricate literary representation of the historically tangled ethnic origins of "American" identity. Because of this multicultural complexity, *Joaquin Murieta* does not fit easily into the binary critical framework of center/margin, colonized/colonizer, oppressor/oppressed, that for the last two decades has been used as a critical tool for recovering the voice of the "Other" in American history and literature.

Originally conceptualized by Caribbean and French scholars, such as Frantz Fanon and Jean Paul Sartre, this binary model came to be institutionalized in the United States with the publication of Edward Said's *Orientalism* (1978) and has since become a theoretical paradigm used in virtually every form of cultural criticism.[3] This binary form of analysis can be said to have reached its zenith with David Lloyd and Abdul JanMohamed's collection of essays, *The Nature and Context of Minority Discourse* (1990). My point in singling out Lloyd and JanMohamed's collection of essays is not to say that this is the definitive or even the most effective example of binary criticism. Rather, I believe that this collection constitutes something like the high-water mark of binary analysis—the point at which the idea of collapsing Asian American, African American, Native American, and Mexican American culture into the singular category of "minority discourse" not only attained its most wide-reaching expression but, more to the point, began to appear critically problematic. I will, therefore, use Lloyd and JanMohamed's conception of "minority discourse" as a theoretical reference point to mark the binary that this essay attempts to move beyond.[4]

Because Ridge's novel was "discovered" in 1955 when a copy of the text was found in the collection of Thomas W. Streeter and published by the University of Oklahoma Press, criticism of the novel has been largely limited to this binary type of analysis.[5] Constrained by a dualistic critical vision that bifurcates Ridge's multicultural novel into the overly simplistic theoretical categories of oppressor and oppressed, critics have sought to explain the explosive racial rage that permeates the novel by linking Ridge's history as a Cherokee survivor of the Trail of Tears to the history of Mexican Americans in California. Joseph Henry Jackson, for example, writes in the introduction to *Joaquin Murieta* that Ridge's experience of being removed from Georgia along with sixteen thousand other Cherokees caused him to be "conditioned by violence and sudden death in his boyhood." Jackson concludes, therefore, that Ridge chose to write about Joaquin Murieta's self-declared war on white society because of "thoughts of revenge buzzing in his head" that he then "transfer[red] . . . to his subject [Murieta]," thereby "perhaps . . . gaining some measure of psychological relief."[6] Likewise, Ridge's biographer, James W. Parins, collapses the cultural and historical distinctions between Native Americans and Mexican Americans by describing *Joaquin Murieta* as being "the story of the plight of 'foreigners' in the goldfields of the early 1850s [and] of their unfair treatment by the 'Americans.'"[7] Louis Owens, whose treatment of Ridge as a mixed-blood Indian in *Other Destinies* is much more nuanced, nonetheless also invokes the oppressor/oppressed binary to explain why the first Native American novelist would choose to write about a Mexican American bandito—"in his only novel, Ridge transforms himself and his bitterness against the oppression and displacement of Indians, becoming a haunted shapeshifter writing between the lines."[8]

There is a good deal of compelling historical, biographical, and textual evidence that gives credence, in part, to this oppressor/oppressed model of interpretation. I will argue, however, that this binary analysis ultimately obscures, more than it clarifies, the intricate cultural complexities of "American" identity that Ridge presents in his novel. In the first part of the essay I will examine carefully the critical strengths and weaknesses of the argument that Ridge "transforms" his own rage at the "dominant" white society into the revolutionary character of Joaquin Murieta, and I will explain why this type of binary analysis is critically problematic. In the second section of the essay I will attempt to move beyond the binary by focusing on the way in which Ridge's own cultural identity and his embattled position within the Cherokee nation not only complicates the idea of a singular "minority discourse" but also opens the way for mapping a more theoretically nuanced and historically accurate form of multicultural criticism. Finally, in the third section, I will endeavor to apply this new multicultural analysis by giving a close reading of the contentious interaction of Native American, Mexican American, Chinese, and white cultures in John Rollin Ridge's *The Life and Adventures of Joaquin Murieta*.

Into the Binary

The most pressing pedagogical issue, especially when teaching *Joaquin Murieta* in a course on Native American literature, is to explain why the first Native American novel does not take as its subject an Indian protagonist but focuses instead on the life of a Mexican American bandit. The critical allure of a binary analysis of Ridge's novel is, therefore, that it offers a quick and easy explanation of the relationship between Ridge's own firsthand experience with the horrors of Indian Removal during the Jacksonian period and the atrocities inflicted on his Mexicano protagonist just after the conclusion of the Mexican-

American War in the state of California. The theoretical foundation for this type of analysis is, as David Lloyd and Abdul JanMohamed write in the introduction to *The Nature and Context of Minority Discourse*, the assumption that "cultures designated as minorities have certain shared experiences by virtue of their similar, antagonistic relationship to the dominant culture, which seeks to marginalize them all." "All of [these minority discourses]," Lloyd and JanMohamed continue, "occupy the same oppressed and 'inferior' cultural, political, economic, and material subject-position in relation to the Western hegemony."[9]

Undoubtedly, these "shared experiences" of political, economic, and spiritual oppression at the hands of the "dominant" white society can at times come together to create a powerful bond between what Lloyd and JanMohamed call "minority cultures." Certainly the Los Angeles riots provide a powerful historical example of the shared rage of the Mexican American and African American communities at the "dominant" white society's racist legal practices. Analogously, in the case of Native and Mexican Americans living in the United States in the 1850s, it is possible to critically reconstruct compelling reasons for why Ridge might have looked sympathetically upon the plight of Mexican Americans in California.

Like many Mexican American *haciendados*, Ridge's family and the Cherokee nation had been systematically and unfairly dispossessed of their ancestral lands. Ridge's father and grandfather, for example, were important members of the Cherokee contingent that took its case against the state of Georgia all the way to the U.S. Supreme Court, where Chief Justice John Marshall ruled in its favor by arguing that the Cherokee were the "undisputed possessors of the soil from time immemorial." To the horror of Ridge's family, who were deeply invested in the legal struggle, President Andrew Jackson refused to uphold the Supreme Court's ruling and stood silently by as white squatters in Georgia razed and burned Cherokee houses and raffled off Cherokee land, often with the Cherokee still on it.[10] John Ross, for example, one of the most important chiefs in the Cherokee nation, returned home from Washington, D.C., to find whites occupying his house and was brazenly ordered to turn over the horse on which he was sitting.[11] In 1838, the Cherokee were removed from their ancestral homelands in an episode that would become known as the Trail of Tears. Rounded up into detention camps where dysentery, diarrhea, and cholera raged, the Cherokee were forced to march to Indian Territory in what is now the state of Oklahoma. On the journey—which averaged 116 days although the government had provided provisions for only 80 days— epidemics of measles, whooping cough, pleurisy, and bilious fever broke out. A traveler from Maine who encountered the Cherokee in the southern part of Kentucky wrote that "on the road where the Indians passed . . . they buried fourteen or fifteen at every stopping place, and they make a journey of ten miles per day on average."[12] In all, historians estimate that more than four thousand Cherokee died.[13]

Mexican Americans living in California in the 1850s suffered through a similarly brutal and unjust process of being dispossessed of their lands. The Treaty of Guadalupe Hidalgo, which ended the Mexican-American War in 1848, stipulated that "property of every kind, now belonging to Mexicans . . . shall be inviolably respected . . . guarantees equally ample as if the same belonged to citizens of the United States."[14] Furthermore, according to the terms of the treaty, all Mexicans who chose to remain in the United States after the war would automatically become American citizens. Despite these guarantees, however, Mexican Americans were forced to pay a *Foreign* Miners Tax that was so exorbitant that it effectively barred them from participating in the gold rush.[15] Lynchings became so common in the California hills that Mexicans there called Anglo-American democracy "Linchoracacia."[16] Moreover, in 1851 the state legislature passed the California Land Act, which effectively called into question every Mexican land claim. The average time for settlement of a case was seventeen years, thus allowing white squatters to stake claims on contested California *haciendados'* property. By 1853, the year before Ridge published his novel, squatters had settled onto every *rancho* around San Francisco.[17]

When viewed through the critical lens of the center/margin binary, it thus appears to be theoretically accurate to state that both Native and Mexican Americans were similarly marginalized and excluded from the rights of "American" citizenship as defined by the "dominant" white society. In 1854, for example, Manuel Dominguez, a signer of the California Constitution of 1849, was not permitted to testify in court because of his Indian blood—a telling example of how, from the point of view of the white center, Indians and Mexicans were legally blurred together into an excluded "Other."[18] Indeed, the political rhetoric of the time is replete with such references. John C. Calhoun, for example, in a speech before the U.S. Senate on 4 January 1848 debating whether the territories of Mexico should become part of the United States, argued, "It is without example or precedent, either to hold Mexico as a province, or to incorporate her into our Union. . . . We have conquered many of the neighboring tribes of Indians, but we never thought of . . . incorporating them into our Union. . . . Ours, sir, is the Government of a white race."[19]

There is, furthermore, compelling biographical evidence that might connect Ridge's own sense of rage to Murieta's personal war of vengeance. In the novel, Joaquin Murieta initially enjoys success in the mines and is able to buy property and build himself a house in the hills. This image of the American dream is shattered, however, by a mob of white nativists who drive him from his lands, rape his mistress, and hang his half-brother "without judge or jury" (12). It is then, Ridge writes, that "the character of Joaquin changed, suddenly and irrevocably . . . he contracted a hatred to the whole American race, and was determined to shed their blood, whenever and wherever an opportunity occurred" (14). Just as Murieta's "native honesty" was transformed by "wanton cruelty and the tyranny of prejudice," so too was Ridge's life irrevocably altered by an act of horrific brutality. After having been removed from Georgia to Indian Territory near Arkansas, Ridge's father and grandfather were both assassinated on the same day by Cherokee nationalists for having signed the removal treaty of New Echota.[20] Ridge, then only twelve years old, watched in horror as his father was stabbed to death before his eyes. As Ridge himself described the incident, "Two men held him by the arms and others by the body, while another stabbed him with a dirk twenty-nine times. . . . It has darkened my mind with an eternal shadow."[21] Ridge later avenged his father's death by killing a member of the assassination party, a crime that subsequently caused him to flee to California, where he wrote *Joaquin Murieta*.[22]

In the opening pages of the novel it initially appears that there is indeed a kind of "minority" alliance between the novel's Cherokee author and its Mexican American protagonist. As Murieta assembles his revolutionary army to avenge the white conquest, Ridge notes that Joaquin "induced the Indians to aid them in [the] *laudable* purpose" (26) of stealing horses to supply the bandits. Moreover, it appears that Ridge himself is supportive of Murieta's guerilla war. After being "bound to a tree, and publicly disgraced with the lash" (12), Murieta embarks on a killing spree during which he "*wiped out* most of those prominently engaged in whipping him" (13)—to which Ridge adds the authorial comment, "Thus far, who can blame him?" (14). Indeed, Murieta is described in the first half of the novel as a "*hero* who has revenged his country's wrongs and washed out her disgrace in the blood of her enemies" (80).

At the end of the novel, however, this "minority" alliance between Ridge and Murieta is profoundly complicated by the appearance of "two Cherokee half-breeds" who fight on the side of the white rangers pursuing Murieta and his men. Ridge writes that a member of Murieta's band falls into the hands of the Cherokee, who perform the "necessary ceremony" of hanging the Mexican American bandit (124). Later, Captain Ellas, the leader of the posse assembled to claim the ten-thousand-dollar bounty on Murieta's head, captures another of Murieta's men and turns him over to the "Cherokee half-breeds." The Cherokee, in turn, "give a 'good account' of the Mexican" by hanging him from "a tree by the side of the road" (128). The Cherokee in Ridge's novel are thus clearly allied ideologically with the "dominant" white society against the revolutionary forces of Murieta and his men.

This binary analysis leaves a number of important critical questions unanswered, however. The oppressor/oppressed model, for example, glosses over the fact that, on the biographical level, the "thoughts of revenge" that Jackson believes were "buzzing in [Ridge's] head" were not, like Murieta's, directed at the "dominant" white society but were instead trained on the Cherokee nationalists who murdered his father and grandfather for having signed the treaty that subsequently led to the Trail of Tears. Because members of the Cherokee treaty party and members of the Cherokee nationalist faction are, according to a binary analysis, equally "marginalized" in relation to centralized white power, there is no real room in this theoretical framework to explore historical tensions between groups that have been simplistically categorized as "Other." A related problem is that the "minority discourse" theory articulated by Lloyd and JanMohamed makes an a priori assumption that "all" of these "minority" groups "occupy the same oppressed and 'inferior' cultural, political, economic, and material subject position" and that they therefore share a common "antagonistic relationship to the dominant culture."[23] This rigid ideological construct, however, makes it virtually impossible to explain why it is that the Cherokee Indians in Ridge's novel fight on the side of the whites against Murieta and his men.

This is not to say that binary analysis or the work of Lloyd and JanMohamed should be completely dismissed. A fairer appraisal would be to see their work on "minority discourse" within a historical framework—as a necessary phase that Cultural Studies had to pass through to move beyond the binary to a new reconstructive form of cultural analysis that is better able to understand the fluidity, contradictions, and hybridity of cultural identity. Lloyd and JanMohamed's *Nature and Context of Minority Discourse* was effective in the sense that it attacked entrenched forms of oppression and brought together scholars working in different fields of Cultural Studies. But while this binary form of analysis may have been politically effective in creating ideological alliances between scholars, there are distinct analytical problems with the overly simplistic oppressor/oppressed binary that need to be further addressed. More specifically, the problem with this kind of binary analysis is that it implicitly assumes an ideological link between Native and Mexican Americans because they occupy the "same oppressed . . . subject position." A new theoretical paradigm, respectful, yet suspicious, of Lloyd and JanMohamed's work, is needed to bring together a multiplicity of cultural perspectives and to provide greater analytical complexity than a binary analysis allows.

Beyond the Binary

In recent years critics have begun to move beyond such binary forms of cultural analysis to more theoretically complicated interpretive models. In *The*

Black Atlantic, for example, Paul Gilroy sharply criticizes what he calls the "pernicious effects of the dualistic, binary thinking in which one partner in the cognitive couple is always dominated by its repressed and subjugated other half—male/female, rational/irrational, nature/culture, light/dark."[24] As a way around this "manichean" way of looking at the world, Gilroy begins with the assumption that "it ought to be obvious and self-evident" that the "cultures and consciousness of the European settlers and those of the Africans they enslaved, the 'Indians' they slaughtered, and the Asians they indentured were not, even in situations of the most extreme brutality, sealed off hermetically from each other" but instead produced an "unashamedly hybrid character."[25] Whereas Gilroy's *Black Atlantic* works to break down this simplistic binary form of criticism by focusing on the "syncretic interdependency of black and white thinkers," I want to expand this analysis to take into consideration a *multiplicity* of cultural influences that come together to shape Ridge's literary construction of the imagined community of "America."[26]

As Gilroy points out, "To purge cultural studies of its doggedly ethnocentric focus" requires "the work of reinterpretation, reconstruction, reinscription and relocation." The reconstruction of a truly multicultural sense of "American" identity must be careful, Gilroy continues, not to fall into the trap of either "nationalist essentialism" or "skeptical, saturnalian pluralism." More specifically, what Gilroy is alluding to is that in the wake of the deconstruction of Eurocentrism there has emerged a new critical tendency to either, on the one hand, re-inscribe the old centrist way of thinking by searching for "authentic" or "essentialist" definitions of "Black," "Indian," or "Chicano" identity or, on the other hand, to slip into an equally simplistic and historically inaccurate form of pluralism in which cultural identity is seen as so completely de-centered that it is no longer possible to conceptualize racial or ethnic identity as being, in Gilroy's words, "lived as a coherent (if not always stable) experiential sense of self."[27]

In the analysis that follows I will attempt to delineate a new critical paradigm that I am calling "historical multiculturalism," specifically designed to avoid the problems of essentialism and pluralism. Unlike other forms of political multiculturalism, which tend to be ideologically prescriptive, "historical multiculturalism" is first and foremost descriptive. Rather than imposing an ideological agenda onto the material (for example, the assumption that Ridge and Murieta "occupy the same oppressed and 'inferior' cultural, political, economic, and material subject position"), this paradigm explicitly engages a multiplicity of cultures without making any a priori political assumptions. The ideological contradictions that emerge from this historically grounded exegesis do not confound but rather enrich the analysis. I will begin this historical multicultural study by illustrating in this section how Ridge's own exceedingly complex cultural identity breaks down any essentialist notion of either "minority" or "Indian" or even "Cherokee" identity. In the concluding section, I will demonstrate how this new type of multicultural analysis can avoid the simplistic pluralism that Gilroy cautions against by working to reveal the complicated cultural hybridity of "American" identity that is forged in the midst of the contentious and racist forces of cultural exclusion in nineteenth-century California.

Because there are no other contemporary nineteenth-century Native American novels to compare and contrast to Ridge's work, it is particularly important to be alert to the critical tendency to read *Joaquin Murieta* as representative of the "Indian" perspective and to allow Ridge's rage to speak on behalf of the Pequots, the Navaho, the Sioux, and all the other Native American tribes that were unjustly dispossessed of their ancestral homelands. The culturally distinct identity of each Native American nation and the historical tensions that existed between Indian tribes can in fact be seen throughout Ridge's novel. In describing "the old chief, Sepatarra" of the "Tejon Nation," for example, Ridge writes caustically that "caution . . . is a quality that particularly distinguishes the Californian Indians, amounting to so extreme a degree that it might safely be called cowardice" (37). Later in the novel Ridge describes the so-called "Digger Indians" who were used by whites to mine for gold and to carry letters, as "having a superstitious dread of that mysterious power which makes *a paper talk without a mouth*" (130). As a member of the Cherokee Nation, which had invented its own alphabet and published the first Native American newspaper, Ridge's depiction of Californian Indians as cowardly and superstitious clearly reveals the cultural distinctions and biases within the theoretical construct of "Indian" identity.

As Gilroy points out, it is important not to push this deconstruction of an essentialist view of "Indian" identity to the point where tribal cultures become so sharply differentiated that one loses sight of the historically real alliances that existed between Native Americans. In a letter that Ridge wrote to the *New Orleans True Delta* in 1851, for example, he condemns what he calls the "civilized ignorance" of whites and in particular their brutal treatment of the Digger Indians in California who were slaughtered with the justification that "it was nothing but a d—d Digger, and what was the difference."[28] In his many newspaper articles, Ridge frequently defended the cause of the Californian Indians, yet Ridge's pan-Indian sensibility was often undercut by his own prejudices as a member of one of the "Civilized Tribes." As he writes, in the same letter in which he protests white violence against the Diggers, "Were these Indians like the genuine North American red man, in the times of the bloody frontier wars of the United States, brave, subtle, and terrible in their destruction, it would be a different matter. But they are a poor, humble, degraded, and cowardly race."[29] What is therefore necessary, from a theoretical point of view, is to construct a multicultural analytical model that recognizes cultural distinctions and historical prejudices between (and within) the various Native American nations and yet does not lose sight of the very real political alliances that existed between Indian tribes in the face of California Governor Peter Burnett's vow that "a war of extermination will continue between the two races until the Indian race becomes extinct."[30]

Before a critical reconstruction of Ridge's complex sense of cultural identity can be undertaken, it is necessary to take this deconstruction of "Indian" identity one step further and try to better understand the historical intricacies of "Cherokee" identity in the years just before and after the Trail of Tears. Although Ridge would assume the essentialist subject position of a "genuine North American red man" in his newspaper writing, the Cherokee were in fact historically unique among Native American tribes in terms of their cultural interaction with whites and their willingness to adopt what whites called "the ways of civilization." As William Wirt argued before the U.S. Supreme Court in *Cherokee Nation v. Georgia* (1830), in which the Cherokee attempted to sue the state of Georgia in order to retain possession of their ancestral lands, "We asked them to become civilized, and they became so. They assumed our dress, copied our names, pursued our course of education, adopted our form of government, embraced our religion, and have been proud to imitate us in every thing in their power. . . . They have even adopted our resentments; and in our war with the Seminole tribes, they voluntarily joined our arms, and gave effectual aid in driving back those barbarians from the very state that now oppresses them."[31]

As early as 1802 the Cherokee accepted missionaries into the tribe. As an act of compromise they even legalized slavery in order to appear more "civilized" to their white neighbors in Georgia. Perhaps the most telling document detailing the degree of cultural exchange between white and Cherokee people, however, is the Cherokee Constitution, which begins "We, the People of the Cherokee Nation."[32]

Ridge himself was a living testimony to the multicultural hybridity that characterizes "Cherokee" as well as "American" identity. His father had married a white woman named Sarah Bird whom he had met at the new American Board of Commissioners for *Foreign* [emphasis mine] Missions school in Cornwall, Connecticut. (It is revealing of the deeply contentious nature of the multicultural hybridity of "American" identity that Ridge's father and mother were denounced by local newspapers, castigated by preachers, and forced to flee when rioting broke out in the town; apparently it was acceptable to the people of Cornwall to educate the Indians so long as they remained "Foreign" and did not attempt to marry any of the town's daughters).[33] Like his father, Ridge was educated at white schools—studying for two years at the Great Barrington Academy in Great Barrington, Massachusetts—and was himself married to a white woman.[34] It is theoretically important, therefore, to critically reconstruct the multicultural complexities of Ridge's life and not become caught up in his self-conscious attempt to depict himself as a "genuine . . . red man."

There is perhaps no clearer example of the problems inherent in trying to appropriate an authentic "Cherokee" or "Indian" identity than the tragedy that befell the Ridge family. By 1835 John Rollin's grandfather and father, Major Ridge and John Ridge, had grown frustrated and distrustful of Andrew Jackson after his refusal to uphold the Supreme Court's ruling that the Cherokee had legal right to their lands. Certain that the Cherokee would never be allowed to remain on their ancestral lands and desperate to get some form of reasonable compensation for the tribe, John and Major Ridge signed the Treaty of New Echota in 1835 agreeing that the Cherokee would remove to Indian Territory in exchange for five million dollars and seven million acres of land west of the Mississippi.[35] The legality of the treaty was immediately contested. More than sixteen thousand Cherokee signed a petition protesting the treaty, which, after a prolonged battle in Congress, was ratified by the margin of a single vote.[36] Major Ridge is reported to have said, "I have signed my death warrant" as he made his mark upon the treaty.[37]

A historical multicultural critique needs to be cautious, at this point, to avoid what Gilroy calls the dangers of "nationalist essentialism"—in other words, the assumption that the Ridge family's role in the removal of the Cherokee can be explained in terms that equate John Ridge's marriage to a white woman with his "betrayal" of the Cherokee people. Once again the Cherokee provide a vivid example of how history is far more complicated than the simplistic theoretical paradigms that are too often used to explain cultural identity. It is instructive here, for example, to note that the leader of the Cherokee nationalist party was John Ross, who was seven-eighths white (he was called Cooweescoowee, or "Mysterious White Bird") and spoke Cherokee so haltingly that he had to use a "linkster" to translate his speeches. Major Ridge, John Rollin's grandfather and the leader of the treaty party, on the other hand was a full-blooded Cherokee who spoke no English.[38] The point is that it is theoretically and historically inaccurate to try to equate racial ideology with racial purity.

Having complicated the notion of "Indian" and "Cherokee" identity, it is now possible to return to Ridge's novel to try to answer more fully the apparent contradiction between his Mexican American protagonist's rage at the "dominant" white society and the complicit role that the "Cherokee half-breeds" play in the dismantling of Murieta's revolution. Many students, their

views shaped by overly simplistic debates about political correctness, will want
to know whether Ridge's own views are encoded in his Mexican American
protagonist's rage at white America or his Cherokee characters' collusion with
white law enforcement agents at the end of the novel. To frame the question
in these terms, however, is to revert back to a binary-based analysis that would
critically collapse this contradiction by labeling Ridge as *either* an Uncle Tom
or a radical separatist merely for the sake of interpretive clarity or ideological
consistency.

Further research of Ridge's work reveals that these conflicting feelings of
a deep-seated racial rage at white society and an equally powerful desire to be
included into "America" coexist uneasily although inseparably throughout
Ridge's literary and journalist writings. In "The Cherokee. Their History—
Present Condition and Future Prospects," an article written for the Clarksville
(Texas) *Northern Standard* in 1849, Ridge notes that the violence and turmoil
within the Cherokee Nation was created by Andrew Jackson's Indian Removal
policies: "It was owing to the oppressions, practiced upon them by the State
of Georgia [and the United States government] . . . that parties arose amongst
[the Cherokee], producing confusion and bloodshed, whose effects are yet fear-
fully apparent." This rage at the "oppressions" inflicted on the Cherokee by
whites is counterbalanced in the same essay by a desire to see "the Cherokee
nation [made] an integral part of the United States, having Senators and Representatives in Congress, and possessing all the attributes, first of a territorial
government, and then of a sovereign State."[39]

Just as it is theoretically necessary to be careful of making essentialist assumptions about "minority" or "Indian" or "Cherokee" identity, so too is it
critically important to beware of oversimplifying the "dominant white culture"
in Ridge's multicultural conception of "American" identity. For the "United
States" of which Ridge dreams of being an "integral" part is deeply influenced
as much by Ridge's southern culture as by his Cherokee heritage. During the
Civil War, for example, when he lived in Grass Valley, California, Ridge edited the *National*, a Copperhead newspaper noted for its political support of
the South and its vehement attacks on Lincoln and abolitionism.[40] Ridge's
cousin, Stand Watie, served the Confederacy in the Civil War and was the
last Confederate general to surrender his sword.[41] Another cousin, Elias Cor-
nelius Boudinot, was elected as the Cherokee delegate to the Confederate
Congress in Richmond.[42] Ridge's Confederate sympathies can be seen in the
text of *Joaquin Murieta* in his description of Captain Ellas, who leads the white
rangers against Murieta, as "a chivalrous son of the South" and a "natural . . .
leader" (111) and the fact that the "Cherokee half-breeds" side with Ellas
against Joaquin Murieta. It thus becomes clear that any theoretical conception of "minority cultures" or even of "the dominant culture" needs to be care-

fully formulated in order to bring to light the historically important complexities that can be hidden behind the language of binary analysis.

Having explored the cultural nuances that shape Ridge's conception of both "Cherokee" and "American" identity, it is now possible to make sense of his divided sympathies in the novel between Joaquin Murieta's war of revenge on his white oppressors and the "Cherokee half-breed's" willingness to fight on behalf of Captain Ellas. This contradiction clearly reflects Ridge's rage at the federal government for removing the Cherokee from their ancestral homelands in the South and his deeply felt desire to see the Cherokee included as "an integral part" of the Union. Rather than being interpreted as an ideological inconsistency, however, this contradiction needs to be seen as providing a critical point of entry into a more historically accurate and theoretically sophisticated paradigm for understanding the multicultural complexities that are constitutive of "American" identity.

The Multicultural Hybridity of "American" Identity

One of the most important struggles for Cultural Studies is to overcome the all too simplistic kind of pluralism that is too often invoked in the name of "multiculturalism" and to establish a rigorous theoretical framework that will allow for nuanced understandings of the contentious history of the nation's historically complex cultural diversity.[43] As Wahneema Lubiano observes, "the work of . . . radical multiculturalism is to keep it from being reduced to slogans, to meaning things like 'Different strokes for different folks' . . . or 'All we need is peace, love, and understanding,'" or what she calls "empty noncritical pluralism." To do so, Lubiano continues, it is necessary to recognize that "contestation is the driving force" of a rigorous and thoughtful multicultural analysis. Following Lubiano's caveat, a historical multicultural analysis must work to move beyond simplistic pluralism to a carefully nuanced study of the kind of intricate cultural complexity embodied by both Ridge's life and his novel.[44]

What makes Ridge's novel valuable to the critical project of historical multiculturalism is that *Joaquin Murieta* demonstrates how the multicultural hybridity of the nation is forged in the midst of the violent contestation of a multiplicity of cultures that collide, conflict, yet nevertheless come together. In the opening pages of the novel Ridge provides a radical critique of the myth of the "American Dream," or the kind of "empty pluralism" that Lubiano condemns. Joaquin Murieta comes to the United States from Mexico, for example, "tired of the uncertain state of affairs in his own country, the usurpations and revolutions which were of such common occurrence" and "fired with enthusiastic admiration of the American character" (8). After "amassing a fortune from his rich mining claim," however, Murieta is driven from his lands by a white, nativist mob for whom the prejudice of color . . . afforded . . . a convenient excuse for their unmanly cruelty and oppression." Murieta is beaten and his lover raped "before his eyes." Fleeing to the mountains Murieta is once again driven from his "fertile tract of land . . . with no other excuse than that he was 'an infernal Mexican intruder!'" (10). Finally, after Murieta is "publicly disgraced with the lash" and his half-brother is "hung without judge or jury", Ridge writes that Murieta vowed "that he would live henceforth for revenge and that his path should be marked with blood" (12, 13).

Ridge thus makes it clear that although the economic allure of the "American Dream" is a very real thing—it is, after all, the Gold Rush that brings Murieta and Ridge himself to California—there also exists another darker, racist dimension to the myth of the "American Dream," what Malcolm X called "the American Nightmare."[45] What *Joaquín Murieta* demonstrates is that multiculturalism in the United States is not simply a matter of consent, nor can it be reduced to being merely a cultural by-product of democratic freedom and economic opportunity. To the contrary, the multicultural character of the nation is an inherently violent and radically unstable historical phenomenon in which forces of democratic inclusion clash openly with forces of racist exclusion, the will to imperial expansion collides head on with the will to monocultural unity, and the capitalist need for new markets and cheap labor is sharply undercut by a nativist backlash that seeks to define the cultural boundaries of "American" citizenship along strict racial lines.

An example of the contentious nexus of historical forces that work to keep the nation multicultural in spite of its deep-seated fear of miscegenation and its cherished belief in cultural unity is the case of the Mexican Americans in California after 1848. As I noted earlier, Mexicanos had been granted citizenship by the Treaty of Guadalupe Hidalgo, which ended the Mexican-American War. Because Mexicanos were more experienced working in the gold mines, and therefore more successful, there was a sharp nativist backlash in 1850 that led to the passage of the Foreign Miners Tax, specifically directed at Mexican Americans; it effectively drove them out of the gold mines. The Foreign Miners Tax was repealed, however, by Sacramento several years later when white merchants throughout the state complained because of the loss of cheap labor and the buying power that the Mexican Americans had provided to the local economy.[46] Economic forces of cultural inclusion and racist forces of cultural exclusion, in this case, created a highly tense and inherently unstable nexus of conflicting historical forces that aptly characterizes the tenuous and violent nature of multiculturalism in America.

Ridge's novel thematizes this deeply conflicted quality of America's historic multicultural identity in terms of the tension that exists between *Joaquín*

Murieta's narrative of the destructive powers of racial rage and the cultural hybridity of the novel's form. On the narrative level, Ridge details the intracultural violence that continually tears at the fabric of the country's national identity. The brief alliance between Mexican and Native Americans at the beginning of the novel, for example, is fractured because "the ignorant Indians suffered for many a deed that had been perpetuated by civilized [Mexican American] hands" (27). Turning against the Mexicano revolutionaries, the Tejon chief Sepatarra captures Murieta and attempts to turn him over to white law enforcement agents. A judge in Los Angeles dismisses Sapatarra's offer because he believes "that the capture was the result of a little feud between some 'greasers' and the Tejons" (39). Sapatarra then orders Murieta and his men to be "stripped entirely naked . . . and whipped." Declaring the "ends of justice satisfied," Sapatarra sends Murieta and his gang "forth into the wilderness as naked as on the day that they were born and stricken with a blanker poverty than the veriest beggar upon the streets of London or New York" (40).

Ridge's narrative of cultural rage thus demonstrates how the violence born of racist exclusion is not historically focused solely on white nativists but instead comes to be refracted until nearly every segment of American society is drawn into fray. Murieta, for example, after being released by Sepatarra, moves throughout the state "robbing a few peddling Jews, two or three Frenchmen, and a Chinamen" (50). Ridge notes wryly that "the miserable Chinamen were mostly the sufferers, and they lay along the highways like so many sheep with their throats cut by the wolves," adding that "it was a *politic* stroke [for Murieta and his men] to kill Chinamen in preference to Americans, for no one cared for so alien a class, and they were left to shift for themselves" (97, emphasis added). Ridge's narrative of intracultural violence culminates when Captain Harry Love, the leader of a company of Mounted Rangers, shoots Murieta three times and then cuts off his head, which is exhibited throughout the state of California in a pickle jar "to prove, to the satisfaction of the public, that the famous and bloody bandit was actually killed" (155).

The unrelenting contestation of cultures in the first Native American novel reveals a "politics" of racial violence in which the rage born of endemic racism fissures outward along multicultural fault lines that destabilize any coherent or unified sense of "American" identity. Yet to say that Ridge's narrative of racial rage ends in a nightmarish vision of what Arthur Schlesinger calls the "disuniting of America," is far too simplistic an analysis of *Joaquin Murieta*'s multicultural complexity.[47] In the midst of this intense cultural violence there is a coming together of the different and antagonistic cultures to form the multicultural hybridity of "American" identity. In Ridge's novel this hybridity is embodied by the form of the novel itself and the way in which

Ridge adopts elements of Mexican American, Cherokee, and white cultures to construct his multicultural tale of racial rage.

A literary archaeology of Ridge's novel reveals, for example, that the narrative development of *Joaquin Murieta* can be traced back to Mexican American *corridos*. In *"With His Pistol In His Hand": A Border Ballad and Its Hero*, Americo Paredes writes that the *corrido* has its origins in the Spanish romances sung by the conquistadors but that it crystallized in its modern form following the Mexican-American War in 1848. For Paredes, the *corrido* is defined as much by its poetic structure of octosyllabic quatrains as by its content— the clash of Mexican and Anglo cultures in the borderlands. As Paredes writes, the hero of the *corrido* "is always the peaceful man, finally goaded into violence by the *rinches* and rising in his wrath to kill great numbers of his enemy. His defeat is assured; at the best he can escape across the border, and often is killed or captured. But whatever his fate, he has stood up for his right."[48] Like the hero of the *corrido*, Murieta is described by Ridge as being distinguished by the "native honesty of his soul" (11), whose "character is changed suddenly and irrevocably" (12) by the racist violence inflicted upon him by the *gringos*. And, most importantly for Paredes' definition of the *corrido's* hero, Murieta dies, finally, "with his pistol in his hand," fighting to the very end "for his right."

Whereas the narrative development of *Joaquin Murieta* is derived from the Mexican American *corrido*, the historical romance form of the novel that Ridge adopts can be traced back to Anglo-American culture. The historical romance was extremely popular during Ridge's lifetime. White Americans like James Fenimore Cooper, in search of a distinctly "American"literature that would help define the cultural identity of the new nation, borrowed the historical romance from British writers like Sir Walter Scott and infused it with themes from the New World.[49] In the South, where Ridge spent his youth, the historical romance form was popularized by William Gilmore Simms, who described his novel *The Yemassee* as "an *American* romance . . . so styled as much of the material could have been furnished by no other country."[50] Ironically, the historical romance was used by many white writers, like Cooper and Simms, to imaginatively justify Andrew Jackson's removal of Native American tribes. In *The Yemassee* (1835), for example, published five years after the Indian Removal Act and two years before the Trail of Tears, Simms sets his novel recounting the Yemassee Indians' extinction a hundred years earlier in order to historically justify the "disappearance" of Native American tribes from the South during the Jacksonian era. Simms writes, for example, that "it is utterly impossible that the whites and Indians should ever live together. . . . The nature of things is against it, and the very difference between the two, that of colour . . . must always constitute them an inferior caste in our minds."[51]

Ridge, however, well aware of the imaginative powers of the historical romance to define the cultural boundaries of the imagined community of "America," ironically reverses Simms's discursive erasure of Native Americans from "history." In the preface to *Joaquin Murieta*, for example, Ridge states that the purpose of writing his novel is "to contribute my mite to those materials out which the early history of California shall one day be composed"(7). Ridge, to borrow a phrase from Henry Louis Gates, thus literally sets out to write Native Americans and Mexican Americans into historical existence using the very form which had popularized the myth of the Vanishing American.[52]

Intertwined with *Joaquin Murieta*'s use of Mexican American narrative structure and Anglo-American form, Ridge also employs thematic traces of Cherokee myth. His most explicit use of Cherokee myth is in a passage where he writes that Murieta's "extraordinary success . . . would almost lead us to adopt the old Cherokee superstition that there were some men who bear charmed lives and whom nothing can kill but a silver bullet" (139). A more subtle, although more prevalent, trace of Cherokee myth can be found in Ridge's use of the trickster image. I am thinking here of the character Untsaiyi, who is described in Cherokee mythology as a gambler who "knew how to take on different shapes, so that he always got away."[53] In what is perhaps a subtle link to the gambler Untsaiyi, Ridge notes in the novel that Murieta works for a time dealing monte. Like Untsaiyi, who transforms himself into an old woman making pottery and then into an old man carving a pipe, Murieta also has an uncanny ability to change shape and assume disguises.

In the course of the narrative, Murieta disguises himself as a Mexican señorita to escape white Rangers(35), he "passes" as a white merchant named Samuel Harrington to rescue members of his gang who have been captured (95), and he disappears into the crowd as a Mexican beggar wrapped in a se-rape (51). Playing upon the inability of white law enforcement agents to distinguish one Mexican from another, Ridge notes wryly that Murieta "was actually disguised the most when he showed his real features" and that he "frequently stood very unconcernedly in a crowd . . . and laughed in his sleeve at the many conjectures which were made as to his whereabouts and intentions"(31). Just as Untsaiyi is caught at the end of the myth, so too is Murieta finally captured at the end of Ridge's narrative. Despite his capture, however, the figure of Murieta as a trickster who makes fools of the whites who pursue him radically reverses the power relation that Simms, for example, attempts to inscribe in *The Yemassee* when he writes of the "obvious superiority" of whites and the "inferiority" of Native American culture, which dooms it to "sink into slavery and destitution."[54] Ridge, in this sense, uses the trickster figure from Cherokee mythology to simultaneously undermine the racist stereotypes of white culture and inscribe Native and Mexican Americans into

U.S. "history." As Gerald Vizenor writes in *The Trickster of Liberty*, the narrative function of the Native American trickster is "to elude historicism, racial
representations, and remain historical."[55]

It is this interweaving of elements of Mexican American, Cherokee, and
white culture that constitutes what I am calling the historical multicultural
hybridity of Ridge's novel. What *Joaquin Murieta* reveals is that even in the
midst of the violent historical forces of white racism and the ensuing racial
rage that threatens to shatter any unified sense of national identity, there is a
critically important and perhaps even ultimately affirmative moment of exchange that takes place as these historically different and socially antagonistic cultures come together to create the multicultural hybridity of "American"
identity.

Notes

*Special thanks to Diane Price Herndl and David Schoenbrun for their careful reading of
the manuscript and to David Payne for his help with the Cherokee mythology.*

1. John Rollin Ridge, *The Life and Adventures of Joaquin Murieta, Celebrated California Bandit* (Norman: University of Oklahoma Press, 1955), 9. Hereafter cited in
   text parenthetically with page numbers only.
2. It is indicative of just how little known Ridge's novel is that Gerald Vizenor writes,
   "*Wynema* [1891] by Sophia Alice Callahan [was] the first novel attributed to a
   native author." *Native American Literature*, ed. Gerald Vizenor (Berkeley: University of California Press, 1995), 14. For confirmation that Ridge is indeed the first
   known Native American novelist see Louis Owens, *Other Destinies* (Norman: University of Oklahoma Press, 1992).
3. See Frantz Fanon, *Black Skin, White Masks* (New York: Grove Press, 1967); Jean
   Paul Sartre's introduction to Léopold Senghor, *Anthologie de la nouvelle poésie nègre
   et malgache de langue française* (Paris: Presses universitaires de France, 1972); Edward Said, *Orientalism* (New York: Pantheon Books, 1978).
4. Abdul JanMohamed and David Lloyd, "Introduction: Toward a Theory of Minority Discourse: What Is To Be Done?", in *The Nature and Context of Minority Discourse*, ed. Abdul JanMohamed and David Lloyd (New York: Oxford University
   Press, 1990).
5. For a fuller explanation of the publication history of *Joaquin Murieta*, see Joseph
   Henry Jackson, "Introduction," *The Life and Adventures of Joaquin Murieta* (Norman:
   University of Oklahoma Press, 1955).
6. Ibid., xlix.
7. James W. Parins, *John Rollin Ridge: His Life and Works* (Lincoln: University of Nebraska Press, 1991), 96.
8. Owens, *Other Destinies*, 32.
9. JanMohamed and Lloyd, *The Nature and Context of Minority Discourse*, 1,10.
10. Thurman Wilkins, *Cherokee Tragedy: The Story of the Ridge Family and of the Deci-
    mation of a People* (New York: Macmillan, 1970), 237.
11. Ibid., 242.
12. Ibid., 314.
13. Four thousand deaths is a conservative estimate; Russell Thornton, for example,
    has estimated that as many as eight thousand Cherokee died on the Trail of Tears.

See Russell Thornton, "Cherokee Population Losses During the 'Trail of Tears': A New Perspective and a New Estimate," *Ethnohistory* 31 (November 1984): 289–300. For more on Cherokee Removal see Grant Foreman, *Indian Removal* (Norman: University of Oklahoma Press, 1989); Brian W. Dippie, *The Vanishing American: White Attitudes and U.S. Indian Policy* (Middletown, Conn.: Wesleyan University Press, 1982); Ronald Satz, *American Indian Policy in the Jacksonian Era* (Lincoln: University of Nebraska Press, 1975).

14. David Weber, ed., *Foreigners in Their Native Land* (Albuquerque: University of New Mexico Press, 1973), 164.
15. Rodolfo Acuna, *Occupied America: A History of the Chicanos* (New York: Harper and Row, 1981), 101.
16. Ibid., 106.
17. Ibid., 102.
18. Weber, *Foreigners*, 152.
19. Ibid., 135.
20. Wilkins, *Cherokee Tragedy*, 322.
21. Parins, *John Rollin Ridge*, 30.
22. Ibid., 60.
23. Lloyd and JanMohamed, *The Nature and Context of Minority Discourse*, 10, 1.
24. Paul Gilroy, *The Black Atlantic: Modernity and Double Consciousness* (Cambridge, Mass.: Harvard University Press, 1993), 52.
25. Ibid., 2, 99.
26. Ibid., 31.
27. Ibid., 11; 100.
28. John Rollin Ridge, "A True Sketch of 'Si Bolla,' A Digger Indian," in *A Trumpet of Our Own: Yellow Bird's Essays on the North American Indian*, ed. David Farmer and Rennard Stickland (San Francisco: Book Club of San Francisco, 1981), 63.
29. Ibid., 62.
30. Reginald Horsman, *Race and Manifest Destiny* (Cambridge, Mass.: Harvard University Press, 1981) 279.
31. Wilkins, *Cherokee Tragedy*, 215.
32. Dale Van Every, *Disinherited: The Lost Birthright of the American Indian* (New York: William Morrow, 1966), 65–72.
33. Parins, *John Rollin Ridge*, 11.
34. Ibid., 36.
35. "Treaty with the Cherokee, 1835," *Indian Affairs: Laws and Treaties*, vol. 2 (Washington, D.C.: Government Printing Office, 1903), 825.
36. Satz, *American Indian Policy in the Jacksonian Era*, 100.
37. Wilkins, *Cherokee Tragedy*, 278.
38. Ibid., 199.
39. Ridge, "The Cherokees. Their History—Present Condition and Future Prospects," in *A Trumpet of Our Own*, ed. Farmer and Stickland, 52.
40. Parrins, *John Rollin Ridge*, 196.
41. Wilfred Knight, *Red Fox: Stand Watie and the Confederate Indian Nations During the Civil War Years in Indian Territory* (Glendale, Calif.: Arthur H. Clark, 1988), 16.
42. Parins, *John Rollin Ridge*, 211.
43. For an overview of different forms of multicultural analysis see David Theo Goldberg, "Introduction: Multicultural Conditions," in *Multiculturalism: A Critical Reader*, ed. David Theo Goldberg (Cambridge, Mass.: Basil Blackwell, 1994); Christopher Newfield and Avery F. Gordon, "Multiculturalism's Unfinished Business," in *Mapping Multiculturalism*, ed. Avery F. Gordon and Christopher Newfield (Minneapolis: University of Minnesota Press, 1996).

44. Wahneema Lubiano, "Like Being Mugged By A Metaphor: Multiculturalism and State Narratives," in *Mapping Multiculturalism*, 67, 69.
45. Malcolm X, "The Ballot or the Bullet," *Malcolm X Speaks*, ed. George Breitman (New York: Grove Press, 1965).
46. Weber, *Foreigners*, 151.
47. Arthur Schlesinger, Jr., *The Disuniting of America: Reflections of a Multicultural Society* (New York: W. W. Norton, 1992).
48. Americo Paredes, *"With His Pistol In His Hand": A Border Ballad and Its Hero* (Austin: University of Texas Press, 1958), 149.
49. See Richard Slotkin, *The Fatal Environment: The Myth of the Frontier in the Age of Industrialization, 1800–1890* (Middletown, Conn.: Wesleyan University Press, 1985), chap. 5.
50. William Gilmore Simms, *The Yemassee: A Romance of Carolina* (New Haven, Conn.: College & University Press, 1964), 24.
51. Ibid., 301–302.
52. Henry Louis Gates, Jr., "Writing 'Race' and the Difference It Makes," in *"Race," Writing, and Difference*, ed. Henry Louis Gates, Jr. (Chicago: University of Chicago Press, 1985).
53. James Mooney, "Untsaiyi, The Gambler," *Myths of the Cherokee* (Nashville, Tenn.: Charles Elder Bookseller, 1972), 311.
54. Simms, *The Yemassee*, 303.
55. Gerald Vizenor, *The Trickster of Liberty: Tribal Heirs to a Wild Baronage* (Minneapolis: University of Minnesota Press, 1988), xi.

Newsprint Masks: The Comic Columns of Finley Peter Dunne, Alexander Posey, and Langston Hughes

Chapter 9

JOHN LOWE

CROSS-CULTURAL STUDIES of humor could easily start by recognizing that this very endeavor is frequently the raw material for popular jokes. Consider the following classic example from the European Community:

> *Question:* What constitutes ethnic heaven?
> *Answer:* Heaven is where the French are the cooks, the Italians are the lovers, the English are the policemen, the Germans are auto mechanics, and everything is organized in clockwork fashion by the Swiss.
> *Second question:* What constitutes ethnic hell?
> *Answer:* In Hell, the English are the cooks, the Swiss are the lovers, the Germans are the policemen, the French are the auto mechanics, and everything is organized by the Italians!

What's funny about this joke? In the first part, we laugh in recognition at the easy ethnic stereotypes that we partly believe—and they're all relatively harmless. In the second part of the joke, we laugh in surprise at the unexpected juxtapositions, which explode our expectations by crossing boundaries. The result? The liberating but artificial anarchy of comic chaos. Not surprisingly, cartoons and comic columns to this very day draw on the images, positive and negative, found in this joke.

We have jokes like this in America, too. Unfortunately, many of them veer off into ugly stereotypes, racism, and sexism, when they're created by people outside the groups in question. Fortunately, ethnic Americans of all categories have vital comic traditions of their own and are quite capable of defending themselves; what has not been so noticed, however, is the long tradition of cultural influence and borrowing that has continually enriched American humor. Although this process could be illustrated with many different combinations from the ethnic kaleidoscope, this essay will focus in particular on Irish-Americans, African Americans, and Native Americans, who have created their own systems and rituals for dealing with ethnic slurs, a strategy that has often been seen to best advantage in ethnic newspaper columns. It will also, I hope, point to the usefulness of going beyond the usual binary approach to American diversity, to a consideration of the multiple ways in which ethnic cultures have influenced each other as they have engaged in the dynamic process of aesthetic, ideological, and social exchange. Partly because of its universal popularity and ubiquity in all areas of human contact, humor provides an ideal center and starting point for this endeavor.

The genre of ethnic newspaper columns developed in the nineteenth century with mock letters to the editor, which in turn evolved into regular columns. The original core structure appears to be dyadic, between the writer and the editor, but is actually triadic, in that the true audience is not the editor but the reader. Moreover, in humorous columns of this type, the structure frequently evolved further into a continuing dialogue between the speaker—always in some way a man of the people—and a rather passive "straight man" (who replaced the editor), thereby floating a dyadic structure atop a deep triadic one.

I can hardly overemphasize the importance of this peculiar genre, as it supports, and is in return subverted by, the humorous contortions of these ethnic "editors," all of whom keenly understood what Mary Douglas has formulated:

> A joke is a play upon form. It brings into relation disparate elements
> in such a way that one accepted pattern is challenged by the appear-
> ance of another which in some way was hidden in the first . . . any
> recognizable joke falls into this joke pattern which needs two
> elements, the juxtaposition of a control against that which is being
> controlled, this juxtaposition of being such that the latter tri-
> umphs . . . a successful subversion of one form by another completes
> or ends the joke for it changes the balance of power.[1]

The Irish American Finley Peter Dunne and Creek Indian Alexander Posey actually *were* editors, while Langston Hughes, better known as a great African American poet, had long-standing associations with many newspapers, so all three thoroughly understood the form, the audience for it, and the popularity of already existing parodies, which frequently appeared side by side with the real item. I would therefore like to take the implications of Douglas's statement further, as well. Stereotyping of the minority group by the dominant culture constitutes, on a far greater scale than is usually the case, a socially significant and shared "joke." A stereotype, whether we care to admit it or not, frequently builds upon what is recognized to be a truth about a people, as in the joke that began this discussion. Widely held stereotypical attitudes would seem to be variations on the "form," that is, on the general (frequently negative) image that the ethnic group is assigned by the dominant culture. We may theorize that ethnic humorists within the group in question begin with the stereotype, and "deconstruct" it to reveal the deep core of truth that is embedded in it. This essay will validate this statement through an examination of key texts by these important writers, whose works respectively represent three very different ethnic traditions.

Ethnic newspapers grew up during the age of immigration, alongside of preexisting American papers that were beginning to feature stories about these "strange" new arrivals. As Werner Sollors has noted, newspapers of both types provided orientation, "'nationalized' and 'ethnicized' readers, created national unity as well as ethnic divisions, and promised revelations across ethnic boundaries, yet also affirmed the existence of 'veils' around ethnic groupings."[2] By the turn of the century, there were hundreds of foreign-language papers in the United States, along with other ethnic papers published in English. Among these were those circulating on Indian reservations; more than 320 Indian papers appeared between 1900 and 1910 alone, and there were more than 150 African American presses.[3]

The great paradigm for this genre is Finley Peter Dunne's talkative immigrant Irishman, Mr. Dooley, who doled out drinks and wisdom in equal measure to his rather dense and dumb (as in mute) sidekick, Mr. Hennessy. Originally intended at least in part to counter anti-Irish sentiment, which Dunne had felt himself, Dooley accepted the stereotype imposed on him and inverted it. The comic bartender first appeared in the *Chicago Journal;* after his musings were picked up all over the country, they were collected and published as books. Other ethnic writers across the nation took heart from this ploy and imitated it in comic creations of their own. Out in Oklahoma, Alexander Posey was reading ethnic jokes in local Indian newspapers, as well as Mr. Dooley's columns, during the early years of this century, and a decade or so later, Langston Hughes was laughing at Mr. Dooley too, in Harlem. Like Dunne, who was writing at the same time, Posey hoped to shepherd his people through a difficult period of transition, to preside over the end of the Creek nation and the transformation of the people into Oklahomans. As the first Indian to own and edit a daily newspaper, he was able to create his "Fus Fixico letters," which, like Dunne's Mr. Dooley columns, featured a local man-of-the-people, Fus, who spoke in native dialect about matters before the public. The seventy-two letters were written between 1902 and Posey's tragically early death in 1908 and represent one of the signal achievements of early-twentieth-century Native American literature.

What exactly did Posey like about Mr. Dooley and/or his avatars in the reservation newspapers? The comic Irishman is well known, but a brief description of his charms is in order here. Finley Peter Dunne had a great success with his fictional Irish saloonkeeper who filled Dunne's Chicago newspaper columns with Irish wit and wisdom, in the form of conversations with the slow Mr. Hennessy. Posey, employing a technique akin to the one later used by Hughes, uses Fus Fixico (the name means "Heartless Bird" in Creek) himself as a kind of reporter on the conversations he has heard and participated in in the local Creek community. Fus at first is the dominant voice, but soon other characters take over, especially the volatile and salty Hotgun, who serves as a less refined version of Fus. It seems important to note that all three writers began to alter their style, their humor, and their characters once the columns began to gather momentum. As with any soap opera today, a series generates its own history, which in turn shapes and dictates the course of events in a strange manner, one that mimics the course and structure of actual history. This same pattern appears in Hughes's "Simple" tales as they unfold over the years. Moreover, Hughes, first in columns, and then in the five "Simple" books he published between 1950 and 1965, inverted the formula used by Dunne; Simple, the folk-philosopher, gets questioned in Harlem bars and streets by Boyd, a college-educated "straight-man" whose congruence with Hennessy comes not from ignorance but from his lack of a firm folk base. As such, Simple is his teacher in a reeducation process.[4] Moreover, Boyd is the narrator, whereas the Mr. Dooley sketches are related by an omniscient narrator.

Before we examine these writers' structures in detail let me point out why such a procedure might be valuable. Humor intersects all human boundaries and enters into virtually every aspect of life; it has functioned in a particularly important way in the difficult and complex process of "Americanization" that every national "family" has experienced. In many cases, that task is never really finished, especially now that we have entered, for better or worse, the age of cultural pluralism, now popularly dubbed "the ethnic mosaic." One of the more unfortunate results of the breakdown of American Studies into ethnic enclaves has been the increasing trend toward ethnic specialization in various branches of the humanities and social sciences, and the growing tendency to assume that only so-called ethnic insiders can effectively analyze and comment on the history/literature/psychology, and so on, of the group in question.

In literature, this trend has resulted in quite a few texts like the recent anthology of essays, *Ethnic Theatre in the United States*, which commendably tries to provide an analysis of some of the more interesting texts of our national drama.[5] Unfortunately, each ethnic group is studied individually, most often by an "ethnic insider," and little attempt is made to relate the plays, the authors, or the groups in question to simultaneous developments in other ethnic theatres, or for that matter, to examine the cross-cultural manifestations that so often figure prominently in the plays actually under consideration. Humor studies have similarly been fragmented and are often limited to joke collections or literary anthologies.

American literature scholars devoted relatively little attention to ethnic literature until quite recently, and so far most studies have been confined to one "strain" or family of ethnicity and its writers—for example, "The Jewish Writer" or "The Black Tradition in Fiction." Still another problem has been the refusal of literary scholars to recognize the important connections between literature and folklore. The latter still continues to be regarded as suspiciously "unscientific," of low cultural value, and, most importantly, to exist separately from print culture. Critical theorists might be wise to look precisely at folklore's contribution to American literary texts, for as Alan Dundes has observed, folklore, "consisting as it does of native documents or autobiographical ethnography, is prime data for investigations of cognitive patterning," surely a subject that has much to do with the analysis of literature as well.[6] Zora Neale Hurston, Mark Twain, William Faulkner, and Philip Roth, to name but a few examples, can profitably be reexamined from this perspective, but the work of Dunne, Posey, and Hughes would be impossible without this key material. At the heart of folklore, one finds the engine of humor, a word that has been defined any number of ways; these three writers, however, would seem to structure their literary pieces with a number of attitudes toward humor in mind.

First, ethnic humor, frequently a weapon of oppression wielded by the group in power, can, through inversion, become a weapon of liberation. At times it can be used aggressively to serve the purposes of revolution, but it can also serve as a mode of communication and conciliation. Langston Hughes understood this quite well; as he said, "Humor is a weapon, too, of no mean value against one's foes. . . . Think what colored people in the United States could do with a magazine devoted to satire and fun"—especially, he notes, one aimed at the racists of society. "Since we have not been able to moralize them out of existence with indignant editorials, maybe we could laugh them to death with well-aimed ridicule. . . . I would like to see writers of both races write about our problems with black tongue in white cheek or vice versa. Sometimes I try. Simple helps me."[7]

Second, humor, which so often is created by yoking opposite ideas, events, or people in incongruous conjunction, may also be used to bring people closer together in a human community, through laughter that focuses on the human condition rather than merely the ethnic condition. It can also understand history better through the lens of humor, and Dunne, Posey, and Hughes were all speaking at critical historic moments in American culture. As Mikhail Bakhtin has noted, "We cannot understand cultural and literary life and the struggle of mankind's historic past if we ignore that peculiar folk humor that always existed and was never merged with the official culture of the ruling classes. . . . We do not hear the voice of the people . . . all the acts of the drama of world history were performed before a chorus of the laughing people. Without hearing this chorus we cannot understand the drama as a whole."[8]

Third, humor, with its frequent base in anarchic disregard for order, rules, and systems, may also be regarded as the fountain of artistic creativity, for in creating the vortex it fosters the possibility of new combinations, new energies, and new structures. The bricks for these new structures are of course words, and they are to be the words of the people in the case of all three of our writers.

Fourth, there is a pride in the dialect used by all three writers, stemming from their joint awareness that dialect is rich, humorous, laden with metaphor, and therefore tactile and appealing. Since dialect, at least to the oppressor, is part and parcel of the negative stereotype, pride in dialect constitutes inversion. Dialect therefore becomes transformed from an oppressive signifier of otherness into a pride-inspiring prism, one that may be reversed for the critical inspection of "the other," white Protestant America. At the same time, dialect writing is a kind of protective cloak that a critic can wear; the rustic satirist is less inclined to draw the immediate ire of the urbane reader.

Dunne himself spoke about the advantages of dialect: "While I was writing editorials for the *Post*, we became engaged in a bitter fight with the crooks in the city council. . . . It occurred to me that while it might be dangerous to call an alderman a thief in English no one could sue if a comic Irishman denounced the stateman as a thief."[9] All three of these artists use this ploy to great advantage, mounting savage attacks on the central government and the excesses of mainstream capitalist society in a curiously disarming manner.

The technique involved, while purely American in detail, is actually classical in concept, for Dooley, Simple, and Fus are all modern avatars of Silenus, a rather homely, hair-covered old man who had a beautiful soul. Ancient Greek culture used him as a trope for mystical inversion: crude and simple without, but complex and finely wrought within. There is a hedonistic strain to Silenus too, for he was the teacher of Bacchus. This pose suited Socrates and Rabelais as well; closer to home, the Yankee peddler figure Brother Jonathan, Uncle Sam, the frontier humorist, and the cracker-barrel philosophers who populate the pages of "traditional" American literary humor all share this stance. Our three comic figures, however, all belong to oppressed ethnic groups who perforce must have a doubled pose and consciousness as participants in American society, who are nevertheless not perceived as or treated as full citizens. As such, they need to do what James Weldon Johnson said members of the Harlem Renaissance should do: "The colored poet in the United States needs to do . . . something like what Synge did for the Irish; he needs to find a form that will express the racial spirit by symbols from within rather than by symbols from without . . . a form . . . which will still hold the racial flavor; a form expressing the imagery, the idioms, the peculiar turns of thought, and the distinctive humor and pathos, too . . . which will also be capable of voicing the deepest and highest emotions and aspirations, and allow of the widest range of subjects and the widest scope of treatment."[10] Johnson's eloquent call had actually found an answer already in Dunne and Posey's Irish and Indian communities, and it would soon find a response in Johnson's intended audience, in the work of Hughes. Clearly, all three groups need this special kind of approach not only as a way out of oppression by the majority but also as a way toward cultural authenticity and creativity, which would answer the spurious charges of racial and ethnic bias.

If anyone needs proof of the shared exclusionism and ridicule these three groups suffered, I refer them to James Dorman's recent articles on popular cartoons and songs of the period, which document the cruel racial caricatures, frequently combined in a kind of sideshow gallery, that found favor with many ordinary patrons of popular culture.[11] *Judge* and *Puck* were two of the most popular magazines of this type. Posey subscribed to them, and Dooley and Hughes surely knew them too.

Another aspect of this doubled nature of the consciousness of the oppressed is that it is peculiarly suited to handle the doubled nature of humor, which so frequently results from incongruously doubled meanings. Moreover, as Leo Strauss has demonstrated in "Persecution and the Art of Writing," oppressed artists often are forced to find a way to "write between the lines," to embed a message beneath the surface of the text. Thus, the exoteric book, as he calls it, "contains two teachings: a popular teaching of an edifying character, which is in the foreground; and a philosophic teaching concerning the most important subject, which is indicated only between the lines." When writers are more daring, they take the course of having an apparently disreputable character utter these teachings; hence the presence in great literature of so many "interesting devils, madmen, beggars, sophists, drunkards, epicureans and buffoons."[12] Strauss neglects, however, to link his important formulations to the devices of the comic writer, or to the exoteric-esoteric labels of ethnic/nonethnic distinctions.

Fifth, the comic newspaper column frequently used humor as a come-on and a mask, for under the pose was a preacher, and under the jokes was a

jeremiad. Over and over, these three folk-philosophers, under the guise of making fun of rampant greed and corruption, manage to simultaneously present,
frequently without overt moral commentary, the terrible conditions of the
people they describe and the factors that led to those conditions.

Finally, an important structural device of a rather abstract kind is built
into all three comedies; in social conditions conducive to humor, the atmosphere is relaxed, and participants don't feel constrained by the formality of
the occasion. The psychological effect of imagining yourself in an intimate
bar with Simple or Mr. Dooley, or relaxing around the fire over a pitcher of
white mule with Fus, provides a familiar setting for unwinding, for telling jokes
and stories.

Mr. Dooley really is true, moreover to the traditional role the saloonkeeper
had always played in Ireland, where he was often a politician as well. In New
York, too, the saloon was the political center of the community in more ways
than one. Ethnic drama frequently unfolds in a barroom, and most of the
Simple sketches take place in bars, where Simple meets Boyd over a beer. Fus
Fixico's conversations with Hotgun and his cronies often develop over cups
as well. The liquor, stimulating and communally shared, becomes a metaphor
for both the conversation and the warming humor. It stimulates the requisite
creative juices of the comic imagination and thus becomes an essential ingredient in ritualistic comic performances and contests. The colloquial speech
of all three writers is in keeping with this common setting and creates the
right background for verbal and comedic improvisation, which so frequently
disregards the structural norms of language in a reach for liberation.

Perhaps most importantly, ethnic humor always raises the issue of the eso-
teric/exoteric factor that governs many of our responses to so-called ethnic
jokes. If the joke is told about our group by a member of our group to our
group, then it's permissible to laugh; if the joke is told by a member of
our group about our group to another group, it may or may not be acceptable
to laugh. (Here one thinks in particular about the varied reactions black
Americans have had to the comedic routines of both Richard Pryor and Eddie
Murphy.) If a nonmember of our group tells a joke about our group to us, it's
not acceptable, and if he tells it to other groups when we aren't there, it's
outrageous.

Now we need to examine exactly how each of our writers adapted these
comedic structures to the contours and needs of the culture in question. I won't
consider the ethnic-specific factors (such as marking, signifying, the dozens
in Hughes's stories) unless they have direct parallels in the other two cultures.
Also, because much has already been written about Mr. Dooley and Simple,
I'll be spending more time with Posey's Indian characters, but I also hope to
show the fascinating connections one finds between the humorous structures

of all three writers. We'll be looking at the purely ethnic qualities of the writing—the coloration of each bit of the ethnic mosaic, if you will—but we'll also try to ascertain how the pieces interact to create new patterns and colors as the ethnic kaleidoscope (a much more accurate metaphor than mosaic) turns.

Dunne, writing about immigrant culture, offers a key example of the process, usually called Americanization, that every immigrant has to endure. Because the Irish were one of the first groups to arrive in massive numbers in American ports and cities, they were relatively ill equipped to deal with this process, mainly because indigenous Americans had little experience in dealing with sudden influxes of a particular group in massive numbers; moreover, because most of those who came as a result of the potato famines were impoverished and unskilled, they suffered a great deal of abuse. Fortunately, the rich tradition of Irish wit, molded as it had been for centuries in the crucible of Anglo oppression, rose to the occasion and soon began to influence both the group's self-image and its reflection in the larger society; this process was vastly facilitated because the Irish (though some die-hard Anglos might deny it) spoke English. Mr. Dooley opines in 1906: "I was afraid I wasn't goin' to assimilate with th' airlyer pilgrim fathers an' th' instichoochions iv th' counthry, but I soon found that a long swing iv th' pick made me as good as another man an' it didn't require a gr-reat intellect, or sometimes anny at all, to vote th' dimmycrat ticket, an' befure I was here a month, I felt enough like a native born American to burn a witch."[13]

Unified and comically deepened by references to the original immigrants, the Pilgrims, the essay's final point is that all of us are immigrants. Although it isn't readily apparent, this essay on immigration is also a caustic attack on those "lace-curtain" Irish—the first ones over who now have "made it"—who now want to keep other Irish out of the country. Moreover, as with Hughes and Posey, Dooley criticizes American processes and practices as well. As Mr. Dooley tells Hennessy, "They'se wan sure way to keep thim out. . . . Teach thim all about our instichoochions befure they come."[14]

That's Mr. Dooley's idea of Americanization. Pretty simple, right? And indeed, as Philip Gleason reminds us in his work on American identity and Americanization, to be or become an American was, for a long while, quite simple. One merely committed himself to the political ideology centered on the abstract ideals of liberty, equality, and republicanism. Period. As Crèvecoeur put it in 1782, "Here individuals are melted into a new race of men, whose labours and posterity will one day cause great changes in the world."[15] Hence the melting pot. But the catch was that one was expected to melt into an Anglo-Saxon identity; the enduring question for the nation has thus remained, What does it mean to be an American? The debate over this question has often been a tragic brawl or even a war, but many aspects of it have been hilarious as well. Dooley, Hughes, and Posey saw both aspects and wrapped the serious in the humorous.

Andrew Greeley suggests a number of steps that ethnic groups (especially the Irish) have undergone in the process of assimilation. First, obviously, there is culture shock, followed by organization and emergent self-consciousness. Then the elite get accepted by the larger society, thereby embittering those left behind, who turn militant. This stage is quickly followed by self-hatred and antimilitancy, and finally by emerging adjustment.[16]

Things are similar yet different for Native Americans and blacks. The former group was here to begin with, and the latter hardly came to America freely. Nevertheless, they too have been and still are pressured to conform to the normalcy standards of white America, which lost the Anglo tag long ago with the acceptance of white immigrants into the fold.

In terms of the Americanization process, a writer gets the readers hooked with the humor, and then "educates" them, defusing their possible hostility through a number of facts. First, consider the stance of all three; Dooley stands, impassive, behind a bar, a businessman talking to his customer, a situation that demands courteous speech. A sixty-year-old, clean-living, little-drinking bachelor to boot, he is wise, but seemingly harmless. Like many male outsider figures in our popular culture (Uncle Remus, Tonto, Charlie Chan, Gary Coleman—the list is long), he is a sexual neuter in his public stance. The outsider, by social convention, never gets the girl—at least not the *white* girl. Although he himself married a white woman, Posey's Fus is similarly sexless, and, indeed, women rarely appear in the Fixico letters. Simple is an exception to this, of course, as the title of the third book in the Simple Pentateuch shows (*Simple Takes a Wife*). But even though Simple has a never-seen, ultimately-to-be-divorced wife in Baltimore, a "good girl" girlfriend he eventually marries, and a "bad girl" companion, Zarita, he himself is no dreamboat, avoids fights, and hardly represents a sexual threat, certainly not to white women. Thus his connection to the Silenus-like Uncle Remus—"the very hipped, race-conscious, fighting-back, city-bred great-grandson"—that Arna Bontemps notes in a letter to Hughes makes sense, although his militancy, especially in *Simple's Uncle Sam*, is at odds with the Remus passivity.[17]

Both Dunne and Hughes had stage stereotypes to work with and improve upon as they designed Dooley and Simple. The stage Irishman, a British stage convention, had been around for eons. He was generally Pat, Paddy, or Teague, spoke in a brogue, made constant jokes, flubbed the King's English outrageously (especially with malapropisms), and punctuated his utterances with wild screeches and oaths. He had the gift of blarney, loved to con one and all, was lazy and prone to drinking, fighting, and sentimental religion. Usually he had red hair and smoked a pipe.

This character came in for radical revision after famine victims began their exodus to the states at mid-century. Irishmen after this period were generally portrayed in crueler, cruder stereotypes. L. Perry Curtis has linked this role reversal with the darker aspects of social Darwinism: "The gradual but unmistakable transformation of Paddy, the stereotypical Irish Celt of the mid-nineteenth century, from a drunken and relatively harmless peasant into the dangerous ape-man or simianized agitator, reflected a significant shift in the attitudes of some Victorians about the differences between not only Englishmen and Irishmen, but also between human beings and apes."[18] James Dorman's work on depictions of Indians, blacks, and Irishmen in the popular press, especially in cartoons, during the late nineteenth century demonstrates that this attitude of contemptuous humor toward so-called undeveloped races (eerily foreshadowing our current put-down, "underdeveloped countries") was not confined to any particular ghetto. Moreover, the stage Negro, most ubiquitous in the minstrel show format, frequently shared many of these characteristics with the stage-Irishman, and at times so did the stage-Indian, although more frequently he appeared as a noble savage or a melancholy member of a vanishing race, à la Cooper.[19] The Irish, however, gradually began to improve their lot through the traditional routes of hard work, standard English, education, and white skin. Their image in popular culture began to change again, and Mr. Dooley had something to do with it. The same wasn't true for Indian and black Americans until quite recently, and many stereotypical depictions survive even today.

We might profitably examine a key factor here: the Irish took to writing themselves, and turned the apparent vices into virtues in the grand old tradition of Brother Jonathan, who defiantly sounded his barbaric but philosophical yawp over the rooftops of the world, drowning out the acid observations of British observers like Mrs. Trollope. If we look at each new ethnic group as an emerging nation much like the young United States, we see the structure of ethnic humor emerge along similar lines. Each group used it to invert stereotypes, to create strength out of apparent weakness, to forge group identity and solidarity, and to press on to Americanization and Horatio Alger–inspired success. Dunne, Hughes, and Posey quite consciously took on the mantle of media shaman for these purposes, presiding over the ritualistic acquisition of acceptance and dignity in the mainstream culture. Obviously, Finley Peter Dunne chose this role as an adjunct to his existing position of newspaper editor during his early days in Chicago, constantly seeking to educate both his newly arrived fellow Irish and the general population, who needed to be

disabused of their hostility to both Irish and Catholics, modernizing and eth-
nicizing simultaneously.

We should note that immigrant writers like Dunne, Abraham Cahan (the
great writer and editor of New York's Jewish *Daily Forward*), and other ethnic
"shamans" all had an asset—namely, membership in the particular ethnic group
in question—that declined in worth as the process of Americanization pro-
ceeded. As members "melted" into mainstream society, ethnic markers increasingly disappeared, partly because they were deemed embarrassing reminders
of an impoverished past, even if the markers were part of a rich native folk
culture. This was especially true in Cahan's case. As editor of a Yiddish-language
newspaper, his exhortations to go out and learn English inevitably meant the
shrinkage of his pool of readers, while his overarching Americanization message diluted group solidarity as well.

If we accept Greeley's definition of the stages of acculturation, we can
see why the Irish, the blacks, and the Creek Indians initially accepted these
comic everymen as their own. By communally laughing at their foibles and
sentimentally weeping over their virtues and the lost "auld sod," familial values from "down home," or legendary, paradisiacal days back in the Georgia
hunting grounds respectively, they achieved a much needed sense of ethnic
identity and solidarity.

Conversely, as William Jansen points out, the larger and more self-
confident the group, the weaker the esoteric element in its folklore.[20] Since
Dunne offered up a relatively unchanging image of the Irishman (while he,
ironically, was moving closer and closer to the position of the rich, landed
WASP gentry) he as writer was eventually viewed as out of step with the mainstream, archaic, outdated. In short, Dunne's comic vision of the Irish finally
came to be seen by many of the Irish themselves as exoteric and false. One
suspects that many black and American Indian readers today would be of similar minds about Simple and Fus.

Alexander Posey had to deal with stereotypes of Indians that were, for
the most part, anything but funny. For much of our history, that stern, un-
yielding profile of the Indian that used to grace our nickels has dominated in
the popular imagination; Indians, it was believed, never laughed, despite the
early testimony of none other than Washington Irving to the contrary. Writing about his 1832 trip to the Prairies, he declared, "They are by no means
the stoics that they are represented. . . . When the Indians are among themselves . . . there cannot be greater gossips. . . . They are great mimics and buffoons,
also, and entertain themselves excessively at the expense of the whites . . .
reserving all comments until they are alone. Then it is that they give full scope
to criticism, satire, mimicry, and mirth."[21] Vine DeLoria, in a superb essay on
Indian humor, finds it remarkable that whites have yet to understand how hu-

mor permeates virtually every area of Indian life; indeed, he asserts, "Humor has come to occupy such a prominent place in national Indian affairs that any kind of movement is impossible without it." Interestingly, he feels that humor doesn't necessarily pacify: "Often people are awakened and brought to a militant edge through funny remarks. I often counseled people to run for the Bureau of Indian Affairs in case of an earthquake because nothing could shake the BIA [Bureau of Indian Affairs]. And I would watch as younger Indians set their jaws . . . determined that they would shake."[22]

Paradoxically, as was the case for years with white studies of black culture, it was assumed that the tragic business of being a member of a tragic (here, "vanishing") race precluded the existence of a comic tradition.[23] Posey proved them wrong. He created a rich cast of Indians and corrupt politicians that rivals Mark Twain's uproarious crew in *The Gilded Age*. The "book" constituted by Posey's letters actually more resembles Johnson Jones Hooper's Simon Suggs stories, where "it is good to be shifty in a new country." Instead of the Gilded Age's Orpheus Seeker, we have real figures like Senator Owen, dubbed "Col. Robert L. Owes-em."

Alexander Lawrence Posey is hardly a household name; let's examine the revealing first page of the memoir William Elsey Connelley wrote to precede Posey's collected poems in 1910: "Alexander Lawrence Posey was a Creek Indian. He was a poet of the first order, a humorist, a philosopher, a man of affairs. He achieved fame as an English-Indian dialect writer and journalist. He was the leading man of the Creeks and the one great man produced by the Confederacy known as the Five Civilized Tribes. Posey was born in what is now McIntosh County, Oklahoma, eight miles west of Eufaula, August 3, 1873. He was accidentally drowned in the North Canadian river, near Eufaula, May 27, 1908."[24] Connelley's flowery tribute to Posey has to be read critically—he's always telling us what Indians are supposedly like, inserting opinions such as "He belonged to a people but two or three generations removed from barbarism."[25] Posey's father was Scotch-Irish, but spoke Creek fluently and was proud of his full-blooded-Creek wife's warrior family, the powerful Harjos of the strongest Creek family, the Wind Clan.

Fus Fixico, like Simple and Mr. Dooley, speaks nonstandard English, mixing tenses and negatives freely, as in "I didn't had not time to write." All three writers clearly employ dialect because it provides a comic mask, yes, but also because they delighted in its pungent, folk-drenched metaphors, its ability to create delightfully unexpected expressions out of quotidian realities. Posey was fortunate in that there was a long tradition of comic dialect writers in Native American culture in Oklahoma, that he knew well through newspaper exchanges.[26] Whites who had married Indians, Indians with African ancestors, and writers from all the five "civilized tribes" contributed to this genre in local papers. Posey, who had also read and admired white dialect writers such as Dunne, George Ade, Joel Chandler Harris, and John Whitcomb Riley among others was able to combine the two traditions and take dialect writing to new heights during the run of his columns. He was also blessed in that his own family was famous for storytelling. His father was a notorious prankster and raconteur; his mother, who survived her son, was an unsurpassed storyteller who passed on to her children all the Creek legends and histories, including creation myths and ghost and fairy stories. Indeed, she told the story of Posey's life to Connelley. Her memories, however, were understandably partial, in both senses of the word. Dan Littlefield's authoritative biography has now filled in the gaps, and we know much more about this Creek sage.[27]

Posey began to tell stories himself as a distinguished student at the Indian University, a Baptist school he attended from the age of seventeen to the age of twenty-two. He set type for the Baptist Indian University *Instructor* and wrote both poetry and prose for it, much of which retold ancient Indian myths, including "Fixico Yahola's Revenge," the story of a warrior who took the form of a bear. Soon after graduation, Posey in quick succession was elected to the Creek legislature, became superintendent of the Creek Orphan Asylum at Okmulgee, and married. With his white wife, who was from Arkansas, he moved to his family home and began farming. Most of his poems date from the happy first two years of his marriage. He spent some time most days talking to "droll characters" and other members of his tribe. He was called back to administrative work at the National High School at Eufaula, and there he began writing poems and sketches for Eufaula's *Indian Journal*. Eventually, he became editor of the *Journal*, just when the Dawes Commission was closing the business affairs of the Five Tribes and forcing Indians to accept specific parcels of land, thereby giving up tribal claims to larger tracts. Indians were being bilked and duped by both lawyers and the federal government agents themselves. Posey, in his satirical "Fus Fixico" letters, tried to expose these outrages, first in the Eufaula paper, briefly in the *Fort Smith Times*, the *Muskogee Phoenix*, and more extensively in the *Muskogee Times*, all in Oklahoma. Other letters would follow in other Indian newspapers.

Throughout these years (1902–1908), however, there is a deep ambivalence to Posey's actual role as social commentator; the most critical event in modern Creek history occurred in 1906, during Posey's heyday, when the national government of the Creek Tribe was dissolved under pressure from the federal government. Posey, as an agent of the United Indian Agency, actually worked for this goal. Why? He knew that if any Indian didn't take his allotment, the tribal land would be taken anyway. Accepting one's allotment at least insured receiving some land, rather than none. In principle, Crazy Snake, the great chieftain who led opposition to the Dawes Commission, was surely right; from a practical standpoint, however, one can argue that Posey's stance made sense.

Posey tried to present both sides of this and other arguments, but his sympathies really lie with the various parties within the Creek nation, especially the Crazy Snake partisans, rather than with any white faction, although as noted, he actually supported some federal government goals, both in his public life and in his fictive letters.

Significantly, early in his career, Posey used a pen name for his poetry, that of Chinnubbie Harjo, who in Muskogee mythology was a trickster who could change character; Posey wrote at least four stories about him.[28] This name bears some similarity to that of Chitto Harjo, or Crazy Snake, Posey's opponent in the battle to get Creeks to agree to the abolishment of their tribal rights. Posey certainly must have been ambivalent about this stubborn warrior, who wanted a return to the old ways, and who appears here as a magnificent anachronism. It is tempting to speculate that Posey saw himself as a literary and comic trickster who in some ways could vindicate the struggles of his spiritual double, Chitto Harjo.

Nevertheless, in the first letter in the series, Fus Fixico quotes his friend Hagee, who has just come back from a Creek council meeting in Okmulgee. "He says it ain't do nothing but run in debt. He say it will be good thing when we get deeds so we can shut up that old council house if we can't rent it to some mens like the Dawes commission that's got lots a time and money in Washington."[29]

Unlike Simple and Mr. Dooley, however, Fus Fixico's comic wisdom is rendered from a rural rather than urban perspective, and crop reports, observations on the all-important weather, and so forth frequently precede his vignettes of life on the reservation and Indian—United States government relations. We should also note the strong connection all three writers make between their comic diatribes and local settings, very much in the tradition of the local-color movement. Dunne's first Dooley book, *Mr. Dooley in Peace and War*, significantly begins by describing the setting: "Archey Road stretches back for many miles from the heart of an ugly city to the cabbage gardens that gave the maker of the seal his opportunity to call the city 'urbs in horto.' Somewhere between the two—that is to say, forninst th' gas-house and beyant Healey's slough and not far from the polis station—lives Martin Dooley, doctor of philosophy. . . . 'There's no bether place to see what' goin' on thin the Ar-rchey Road,' says Mr. Dooley. 'Whin th' ilicthric cars is hummin' down th' sthreet an' th' blast goin' sthrong at th' mills, th' noise is that gr-reat ye can't think.'"[30] Descriptions such as these, rendered with local-color brushstrokes, frequently precede widely ranging political observations, wrapped of course in the humorous banter and dialect of the barkeep and his customer.

Similarly, Posey may begin by painting a poetic and detailed scene: "Well, so, the wind was from the south and Hotgun and Tookpafka Micco and Wolf Warrior and Kono Hargjo they was light they pipes and get in the shade a the catapa tree, and talk on politics, while the women folks was go out and pick up some dead wood and start a fire under the sofky pot and make the smoke bile out a the chimney like it was put near dinner time. The old squirrel dog he was come out a the fence corner and get in the way 'round the kitchen door and keep order 'mong the chickens and choates." How easy then to segue into a diatribe against the federal government: "Well, maybe so . . . the boll weevil was ruin the cotton and the chintz bug was get in his work on the corn and the Big Man at Washington was put a few more kinks in the red tape a the Loyal Creek payment, but all the same the Japs was still doing a Rushing [Russian] business and they was lots a good prospects in the Flowery kingdom."[31]

It comes as no surprise that Hughes, ordinarily a poet, is best of the three at this business: "Pavement hot as a frying pan on Ma Fraizer's griddle. Heat devils dancing in the air. Men in windows with no undershirts on—which is one thing ladies can't get by with if they lean out windows. Sunset. Stoops running over with people, curbs running over with kids. August in Harlem too hot to be August in Hell." This seemingly casual description sets the stage, however, for a comic rendition of the saga of Carlyle, whose bare-bones narrative actually exemplifies a recurring tragedy of the community. "Midsummer madness [sexual temptation] brings winter sadness, so curb your badness. If you can't be good, be careful."[32] Carlyle impregnated a girl the preceding summer, subsequently married her, and then left her when he couldn't support the family. Now he can't come back or she'll lose the welfare she lives on. A grim story, but one told humorously, and punctuated by Simple's mixed-metaphor catcalls to the scantily clad women who pass as he tells it: "Man, look at that chick going yonder, stacked up like the Queen Mary! . . . Wheee-ee-ooo! Baby, if you must walk away, walk straight—and don't shake your tail-gate."[33] Underlying the surface comedy of this and other Simple stories lurks the overpowering presence of the other culture—that of a bureaucratic white society.

This alternation between local setting and free-ranging, even international, political comedy, seems integral to the overall structure of ethnic humor of this genre and fits well with the general graph that ethnic humor follows. As we have seen, ethnic writers frequently begin with the stereotype, which Walter Lippman tells us is a distortion of reality. Beginning with these realistic "slice of life" vignettes both counters the stereotypes and tempers one's reaction to the freewheeling comic invention that follows. To illustrate with a graphic model, imagine "line" and "distortion" as actual ethnic life and fictional ethnic life, respectively. Fiction, of course, may be truthful in some respects. Now imagine the imposition of an exoteric/racist stereotype as distortion; the local color vignette as correction into "line"; the comic wrap as esoteric "distortion" (and therefore favorable); and the resolution/return to order at the end of the anecdote/sketch as both "line" and traditional comedic closure: distortion (exoteric) > line > distortion (esoteric) > line. The same general pattern and technique is especially visible in Posey's tales (as with Simple's remarks on welfare), when white legalities intrude. The Fixico letters, in fact, have running through them a Dickensian leitmotiv of legal tragicomedy (as in *Bleak House*), for Fus and his friends are obsessed with land titles. As Fus ironically says, after his friend Porter gives up trying to settle Creek land deeds, "I think the Creek counsil ought to get some white man to fix up them deeds for us anyhow. It's too much work for one Injin." The deed, involving multiple letters and the post office, becomes surrounded with bureaucratic metaphors and symbols: "Please you must tell postmaster I was not want my deed go back to Porter or dead letter office." This latter destination becomes synonymous with the futility of land transactions. Fus at one point decides that he'd better shut up about it, "tight like terrapins." His friend Hotgun tells him that all he has to do to get the deed is "drink lots sofky [corn whiskey] and wait till it was come."[34] The clear parallel in the Simple stories is the endless maneuvering over Simple's divorce from Isabel.

Fus, like Simple and Mr. Dooley, would no doubt love the recent T-shirt slogan first coined by Shakespeare: "First, we kill all the lawyers." This comic but partly serious sentiment has a long and honorable comic tradition, especially among the poor, and was especially appropriate during Posey's day, when corrupt lawyers and officials had a field day with Indian rights and properties.

Legal matters are particularly ripe for comic treatment because of the obvious gap between legal aspiration and corrupt bureaucratic realities. Fus, even more than Dooley or Simple, enjoys putting contraries like this together, even when another kind of law—in this case, biblical myth—is involved. His imaginative retelling of the Noah myth recalls Zora Neale Hurston's book-long recreation in black dialect of *Moses, Man of the Mountain*; this time, however, the dialect is "Injin": "Well, I think was have to make big ark like old Noah and put my families in it if it was keep on raining the way all time. . . . But I was want no animal in that ark except lots a hog meat and 'bout wagon load of sofky corn, and also 'bout hundrd bundles a divil shoestrings to pizen fish with maybe." Old Hotgun, the Indian carpenter who is going to show Fus how to make a better ark than old Noah had, is suspected of ulterior motives: "Maybe so Hotgun thinks he could get in and go to Mexico easy this way, but he was had to look out himself like me."[35]

Washington, the frequent destination of Indian negotiators, becomes the repeated object of Fus's ridicule. "Well, reckon so them Injin delegates was all in Washington looking at lots a things to talk 'bout and was drink lots good whiskey instead old sour sofky like at home. One Snake Injin says he was stay at Washington put near six months maybe and had good times. He say Washington was like Saturday in Eufaula all time, but he say he was see not cotton and renters like in Eufaula. He says them big white mens was ride in wagons that didn't had no horses hitched to it neighter and run like down hill all time." This reductio ad adsurdum gets practiced on Indian politicians too: "Creek politics was getting warm like hot tamale and candidates for chief was thick like fleas under a pole cabin in the summer time, or maybe so bed bugs in a dollar day hotel when you blow the light out."[36]

All three writers mention other ethnic groups, frequently with derision, but sometimes with admiration. Fus, asked why he doesn't speak good English, tells a sympathetic yet comic story about two Irishmen who are scorned for their English. Later, a joke about hopelessness uses the metaphor of a hand car with some Irishman pumping it up grade against the wind. Conversely, when Hotgun is talking about the "Democrat stomp dance down to Durant" as tame doings, he says the Republicans wondered why there wasn't a "quick witted Irishman present, like Mike Conlan, with sticks a dynamite for firecrackers to make it more interesting." Accused of talking in parables, he describes the preceding winter's Republican "cat fight" where this Conlan, "the bloody Irishman, was had a mob agin another mob from Coalgate, and tried to stir up harmony in the old Elephant party with a bundle a dynamite. He teched it off and throwed a string a box cars off a the right a way and pied all the roasts set up and ready for press in the print shop a Sister Smiser."[37] Clearly, the Irish are recognized as both hopeless and revolutionary, a central insight from the sage of Archey road. One begins to understand why Mr. Dooley spoke so deeply to the issues that mattered for Posey and Hughes.

Posey also frequently mentions blacks, often negatively; commenting on the crush of blacks in Muskogee, Fus notes: "Niggers was thick like black birds behind a plow. Can't see no white mens hardly, and can't find no Injins neither." Histories of the Creek nation reveal that many blacks had married into the tribe but the full-blooded Creeks considered the resultant progeny black. Blacks presumably get so much scorn from Posey because of their gullibility to carpetbaggers who prey on them for support for various schemes. The Grab-a-gun Opera House hosts a meeting of the Lilly Whites and the Damn Blacks who conspire to rob Indians of their rights under the proposed statehood schemes. "These mugwumps was looked like missionaries up hear the head a the Nile in Africa . . . the manager . . . had to turn on more electric lights so the scribe from Uganda could see how to write the minutes."[38]

We should also note in passing that Mr. Dooley's tales are full of seemingly negative references to blacks and other ethnic groups as well, although Brom Weber has argued that such slurs are superficial and mask an underlying sympathy for, and identiciation with, these groups.

Much of the same feeling emerges in Hughes's Simple stories, although Jess takes comic but telling offense at the relative privileges enjoyed by nonblack immigrants. His folk-inspired poem shows this:

> I wonder how it can be
> That Greeks, Germans, Jews,
> Italians, Mexicans,
> And everybody but me
> Down South can ride in the trains,
> Streetcars and busses
> Without any fusses.
> But when I come along-
> Pure American-They got a sign up
> For me to ride behind:
> COLORED . . .
> Dixie, you ought to get wise
> And be civilized![39]

"Simple on Indian Blood" uses ethnic stereotyping to comic and didactic effect without overt castigation of Indians. Claiming to be part Indian—"My uncle's cousin's great-grandma were a Cherokee. I only shows mine when I lose my temper—then my Indian blood boils . . . when I get mad, I am the toughest Negro God's got. It's my Indian blood . . . I am a colored Indian . . . A Black Foot Indian, daddy-o, not a red one." On the other hand, although Simple obviously approves of his woman acting like a squaw, "She better not look like no squaw . . . I want a woman to look sharp when she goes out with me. No moccasins. I wants high-heel shoes and nylons, cute legs—and short dresses. But I also do not want her to talk back to me. As I said, I am the man . . . I just do not like no old loud back-talking chick. That's the Indian in me." Simple's ethnic cross-dressing, in these remarks and elsewhere, is thus selective, sexist, and self-serving, and the supposed didactic portion of this set piece comes not from him, but from Boyd, his intellectual alter ego, who declares, "Everybody should take each other as they are, white, black, Indians, Creole. Then there would be no prejudice." Simple draws the line, however, when the overly philosophic Boyd asserts that race relations aren't personal, and thereby floats the real message of the piece on a stereotypical phrase: "That's how it is if you're part Indian—everything is personal. *Heap much personal*[emphasis in original]."[40]

We saw previously how Hughes felt that many readers would miss the ironic implications of Simple and his stories. Posey, like Hughes, often used rather subtle irony that many readers probably missed. In a pre-Christmas letter, Fus says he is going to hang up his socks for a Creek deed. The next day he reports, "I was had bad luck Christmas times. I was fly out of bed soon about daylight and look in my socks, but I was see nothing in there but big holes. Maybe so, my deed was fall out in the fire or mabeso, Old Santa Claus think I was not want any deed, like Chitto Harjo and Hotgun."[41] Obviously, the real Santa referred to here is the government.

Similarly, humor is used to underline the impoverished conditions of the Indians. "Hotgun he say it was get so cold last Sunday night he was had notion to change his name. I ask him what he call himself then and he say Blowgun was have more truth to it than Hotgun Sunday night when the wind was keepon blowing the rags out the cracks in his cabin." Other times, more direct means are used. Indian Thanksgiving day celebrations are oxymorons to Crazy Snake: "If they was any Injin here that was thankful, let 'im hold up his hand, so the light horse could take him out and give 'im fifty lashes next to the skin for lying like a dog."[42]

Posey has a keen eye for political ambition and the nuances of faction. Assessing the possible candidates for chief, he notes, "Porter was not say nothing yet, but I think he was had his eye on it like buzzard on dead cow in winter time. . . . But I was druther had somebody else for chief. Porter was stay too much in Muskogee and St Louis and Washington. . . . Injins was not like that." Fus, like Silenus and Simple, remembers the points of lessons but not the details. Talking about the overly optimistic talk of Creek progress and development omnipresent in boosterish newspapers, he says, "Hotgun he say he think he was had to put beeswax in his ears like Few Leases [Ulysses] in olden time."[43] The classical comparison is altered, both to create a linguistic joke (and we note that the point of Ulysses' example is not misunderstood, only his name) and to further explode the lies in the paper by letting the mistaken name stand for the truth: there has, in fact, been little progress because of few leases.

The great debate that extends over many "Fus" letters concerns the question whether Oklahoma will be admitted to the Union as one state, or as two, Indian Territory and Oklahoma. At an Indian powwow, Chief Make Certain shrewdly remarks, "Oklahoma was had its mind made up to file on us for a pasture and I think it was time to raise a big kick like a mule that don't want to pull the load up the hill all by itself." On the other hand, Hotgun, when finding there might not be saloons in double statehood, decides "he was druther be tacked onto Oklahoma so he wouldn't had to drink busthead [Indian beer] and get put in the calaboose for being sick on the street."[44]

As with Simple and Mr. Dooley, Fus is fond of using animal imagery in yet another variety of reductio. Graft takers like Plenty So Far, Jay Gouge

Right, and Tom Needs It are described as being chased out of the Indians' corn patch and up a tree by inspector Brosius, and these "old coons" are accompanied by "young coons" like little Charley Divide Some and little Cry For the Cobb and little Jimmy Eats Huckleberries. They're huddled together so close to the top of the tree that "you couldn't see nothing but the rings roun they tails . . . maybe so he was put em in the zoo so everybody could take a look at 'em."[45]

Class distinction comes in for some comic digs as well. Hotgun and Wolf Warrior, discussing Crazy Snake's recent visit to Washington, approvingly note that he and his cronies for once didn't have to rely on busthead and white mule to wet their whistles; they could go in a bar, "so they was had Bourbon and Monogahela older than the Dawes Commission; and booze like that was put a man in congress instead a the calaboose."[46]

Langston Hughes, like Posey and Dunne, set most of his scenes around the metaphor of liquor. Simple meets his intellectual friend Boyd in Harlem bars or on the street. Simple's pronouncements, like Hotgun's or Dooley's, are brief and to the point, but occasionally expand into story when Hughes feels he has a good thing going. This was increasingly the case as the Simple stories became more politicized and as Simple's story gained the momentum of its own history. But how did that history develop?

Langston Hughes had a great interest in the possibilities of African American humor, and he especially admired the way southern blacks had used it. As a freshman in high school he was fascinated by the southerners who came into the refreshment parlor where he worked: "I never tired of hearing them talk, listening to the thunderclaps of their laughter, to their troubles . . . their complaints. . . . They seemed to me like the gayest and the bravest people possible—these Negroes from the Southern ghettos—facing tremendous odds, working and laughing and trying to get somewhere in the world."[47] As a college student at Columbia, Hughes skipped a final exam to go to the great black comedian Bert Williams's funeral, and he spent night after night in the gallery watching the record-breaking black musical comedy, *Shuffle Along*.[48]

One might even say that the writer's greatest literary contribution grew out of his fascination with African American comedy. Moreover, Hughes surely felt, as the folklorists Prange and Vitols once expressed it, that "the fact of being Negro is the most frequent concern in Negro humor."[49] Over and over, Boyd accuses Simple of being obsessed with race, and many of the jokes in Simple's stories do indeed have a racial base. Hughes never had a son, so Simple, who was born 13 February 1943 in the pages of the *Chicago Defender*, can be considered one. The name, Jesse B. Semple, reverberates with meaning. Most notably, it of course leads to the nickname "Simple" and a link to Simple Simon and that variety of wise fool. The name "Jess Simple," as in "just simple," although actually an ironic commentary, superficially confirms white concepts of naive, childlike blacks who are happily unaware of their ignorance. The kicker comes with the insertion of the initial B.: the name thereby becomes a prescription, Just Be Simple, and indeed, that turns out to be both Simple's and Hughes's philosophy for happiness, so akin to that of figures such as Thoreau, Gandhi, and Mies van der Rohe. Moreover, we have it from Simple himself that he inserted the B, and that it has no meaning: "I just put it here myself since they didn't give me no initial when I was born."[50] Yet more: the biblical Jesse is the father of David, slayer of Goliath. Similarly, there is a real sense here of Semple's progeny—that is, his humorous creations, the only children he has in the tales, paralleling the same circumstance in Hughes's own life—going out to slay the giant of racism. Hughes stated shortly after Simple's birth, "The character of My Simple-Minded Friend is really very simple . . . It is just myself talking to me . . . I have developed this inner discussion into two characters: the *this* being me, and the *that* being Simple, or vice versa [emphasis in original]. We are both colored, American and Harlemized." Hughes did admit, however, being inspired by meeting a fellow like Simple once "who worked in a war plant."[51] Arna Bontemps spoke for most when he said, "Here was a Harlem peasant, Lenox Avenue ne'er-do-well, spouting the folklore of the city streets. It was all so familiar, so true to the character, that it was recognizable immediately for its authenticity." He praised Simple's wit and drawl, and went on to say, in a letter to Hughes, " . . . he is funny, man, downright funny. . . . *Simple* is the kind of funny man who will not make Negroes ashamed. He is the very hipped, race-conscious, fighting-back, city-bred great-grandson of Uncle Remus."[52] Despite Bontemps' assurance, Hughes *was* criticized for being "vulgar" in the Simple stories and in poems like "Red Silk Stockings" by genteel readers who objected to statements like: "Put on yo' red silk stockings, Black Gal./Go out and let the white boys/ Look at yo' legs."[53] Critics, who, as Hughes felt, missed the "ironic" dimension of poems like this and anecdotes like Simple's, labeled him "The poet lowrate of Harlem":

> Others called the book a disgrace to the race, a return to the dialect
> tradition, and a parading of all our racial defects before the public. . . .
> There was a reason for it, of course. They had seen their race laughed
> at and caricatured so often in stories like those by Octavus Roy
> Cohen, maligned and abused so often in books like Thomas Dixon's,
> made a servant or a clown always in the movies, and forever defeated
> on the Broadway stage. . . . Jessie Fauset's novels they loved, because
> they were always about the educated Negro—but my poems, or
> Claude McKay's *Home to Harlem* they did not like, sincere though we
> might be. . . . I sympathized . . . but . . . the masses of our people had

as much in their lives to put into books as did those more fortunate ones who had been born with some means. . . . Anyway, I didn't know the upper class Negroes well enough to write much about them.[54]

These remarks indicate Hughes's profound awareness of the doubled visage his humor would always wear for his black audience and his long-lasting belief in its ultimate effectiveness. By the mid-sixties, however, disturbed by the violence of the racial situation, Hughes had decided that Simple had outlived his usefulness, telling friends "the racial climate has gotten so complicated and bitter that cheerful and ironic humor is less understandable to many people"; his remarks were probably partly caused by letters like the one he received from a Harlem reader: "Why do you continue to perpetuate the stupid, ignorant offensive character you call Jess Semple? I say he is dead and died with all the other Uncle Toms like him."[55] Hughes still felt, however, that he had exploded the stereotype through Simple's wit and underlying dignity.

Along these lines, one of the things that unites Fus and Simple is their belief in the power and dignity of one's name. Fus's fury knows no bounds when he hears that the "Big Man at Washington" "he say . . . the Injin was had to change his name just like if thae marshal was had a write for him. So, if the Injin's name is Wolf Warrior he was had to call himself John Smith or maybe so Bill Jones, so nobody else could get his mail out of the postoffice. Big Man say Injin name like Sitting Bull or Tecumseh was to hard to remember and don't sound civilized like General Cussed Her or old Grand Pa Harry's Son." This recurring obsession with names and the humor associated with names occurs in the works of all three of the writers that concern us here, and for good reason, but most powerfully in Posey:

> Well, so Big Man at Washington was made another rule like that one
> about making the Injin cut his hair off short like a prize fighter or
> saloon keeper. Big Man he was say this time the Injin was had to
> change his name just like if the marshal was had a writ for him. So, if
> the Injin's name is Wolf Warrior he was had to call himself John
> Smith or maybe so Bill Jones, so nobody else could get his mail out of
> the postoffice. Big Man say Injin name like Sitting Bull or Tecumseh
> was to hard to remember and don't sound civilized like General
> Cussed Her or old Grand Pa Harry's Son . . . Crazy Snake he say he
> was hear white man say all time you could take everything away from
> a him but you couldn't steal his good name. Guess so that was all right
> 'cause they was nothing to a name nohow if you can't borrow some
> money on it at the bank.[56]

Adorno speaks of the primordial fear of losing one's own name, and the return to elemental chaos it implies—one truly becomes the ultimate version of Ellison's invisible man.[57] The desperation of this sentiment becomes masked in the casual ironies Posey employs, especially in the devastating play with the ubiquitous, nondistinctive name "John Smith," even though the original of the name of course pairs ironically with Pocahontas in legend.

Another joke here works on two levels. First, the opposition of Sitting Bull and Tecumseh to Custer and Harrison is a devastating reminder of Indian massacres, and of the nobility of Indian chieftains. Second, the phonetic rendering of the white officers' names into silly nonsense exposes the idiocy of the government's policy. Ironically, Posey does just that throughout his parodies of Indian-government relations. We have already seen Roosevelt become Rooster Feather; Secretary Hitchcock was "Secretary Its-cocked," Pliny Soper was "Plenty-so-far," and Senator Owen was "Col. Robert L. Owes-em." Some names lend dignity, however. Simple frequently stops his girlfriend Joyce from throwing up white role models to him by saying "and I AM JESSE B. SIMPLE." The loss of one's native culture is in fact identical in many ways to losing one's name, particularly when that culture has provided that name. How nice to invert the principle by bestowing comical variations on Anglo-Saxons, thereby also illustrating Adorno's further insight that names can sometimes be frozen curses.

This last example offers clear evidence of how the most serious issues may effectively use humor as their vehicle. It would seem that our current interest in black humor, magical realism, and the theater of the absurd would attract us to a re-examination of these three writers, who work in similar ways. Why then, has interest faded in these three comic philosophers? The easy answer is that readers simply won't wade through dialect any longer, or that dated material that requires endless explanatory footnotes turns off a tuned-out TV generation. The sociologist Christie Davies has another explanation. Humorous anecdotes are stories that sometimes claim to be true, which tell about the comic adventures of a named person or the encounters of this person and his friends and acquaintances. The point of the story is never just the ending, but also the embellishment, the local detail, and the proper unfolding of events. By contrast, today's urban fast-steppers want to go for the punch line right away. Urban jokes are much more compact in nature, don't require memorization of copious detail, and allow one if pressed to reconstruct the beginning and the middle, if they logically lead up to the punch line. In some ways this means comic narrative is no longer in favor, and some of the dreadful comedies on TV and in movie houses today confirm the fact that most contemporary comedies are a series of one-liners loosely strung together. Mr. Dooley, Simple, and Fus are all masters of one-liners, to be sure, but they always provide a context and a continuing folk structure.

We might also examine one of the more unfortunate aspects of the ethnic revival, namely the whitewashing of many ethnic references from popular comedy. The disdain many "polite" readers felt for Hughes's "vulgar creations" hasn't gone away. All too often, genteel readers or viewers demand that anything smacking of the ethnic be jettisoned, even if the offending character, image, or scene actually represents folk culture in a benign way. Some of this resistance might be overcome if teachers and scholars could do more to emphasize the pleasures of these particular texts that are relatively unique. Although the physical act of reading dialect is difficult at first, readers quickly acquire their own breakthroughs into the "code"; once at that point, the reader can move on to a new level of appreciation, since authors like Dunne and Posey wrote with a lot of "eye-dialect" comedy built in, that is, words misspelled in order to represent both substandard speech and dialect, bizarre punctuation, long strings of multiple consonants, and so on, which create comic print images on the physical page.

On yet another level, Mr. Dooley, Simple, and Fus are less threatening to the readers whose mastery of English is poor. Actually, of course, a closer analysis of the language used in all three cases reveals a masterful and shrewd command of language, verbal tricks, and fireworks. In all three humorous narratives, language is richly inventive, tactile, and metaphorical. These writers are masters of comic exaggeration, invective, verbal dueling, mimicry, mockery, and punning. This dazzling arsenal appears to be undercut, but in actuality is enhanced, by the apparent commission of malapropisms, spoonerisms, improper syntax, and so on. Dunne, Posey, and Hughes thus employ the same technique with language that we observed earlier to be operative with ethnic humor in general, using the terms line and distortion. In all three texts there is at least one voice that provides a "norm" of standard English that can then be "distorted" by the creative ethnic comedian; the intriguing moment comes when the reader discovers the "truth" of the text embedded in the humorous "distortion" of the Remus/Silenus figure. On a subconscious level, our three writers are thus implicitly waging a battle against the acceptance of "polite" speech and writing as the undoubted receptacle/vehicle of social truth, urging what Melville called an investigation of the "little lower level."

There are a number of limitations to the comedic structures employed by Dooley that Hughes and Posey avoid. By investing so heavily in Mr. Dooley's brogue and by keeping him behind the bar, Dunne eliminated a comic mainstay of other ethnic writers, code-switching. In Abraham Cahan's fiction, for instance, a Polish Jew will frequently use ritual Yiddish curses, American slang, with body language thrown in for lagniappe, in one exhilarating sentence. Fus similarly will freely mix white slang, Indian customs, dialect, and a chorus of approving grunts from his listening "chorus" of tribal elders. Simple's sidekick Boyd is always there to help mix things up linguistically too, although Simple himself is quite capable of mimicking the speech patterns of others. One of the mainstays of the ethnic stage was a bubbling Babel of conflicting and contrasting tongues. The cross-cultural conflicts in Dunne are rather pallid by comparison. On the other hand, Mr. Dooley gains stature and presence by his continuity, even an ex-cathedra quality for his pronouncements. At the same time, his humor is more appealing because of its intimacy, which could only grow over the years as he became more and more familiar to American readers. Simple obviously profited from the same effect; Fus wasn't around long enough for this to happen. Even so, Posey's objective of getting attention for the Creek's problems was met before his death; the letters were copied all over the United States in the nation's presses and surely achieved Posey's aims in this regard.

Why were these three comic heroes so attractive to mainstream American readers? Partly because all three had so many obviously American traits. In his first collection of Dooley's monologues, Mr. *Dooley in Peace and War*, Dunne provided the following synopsis of his hero's talents and abilities: Traveller, archeologist, historian, social observer, saloon-keeper, economist, and philosopher. . . . He reads the newspapers with solemn care, heartily hates them, and accepts all they print for the sake of drowning Hennessy's rising protests. . . . His impressions are transferred to the desensitized plate of Mr. Hennessy's mind. . . . He is opulent in good advice, as becomes a man of his stastion (who) oiwns his own house and furniture, and is only slightly behind on his license."[58]

Besides, as Mr. Dooley "hisself" reports "what an incyclopeeja a man gets to be in this profissyon. Ivry man that comes in here an' has three pans iv nicissry evil tells me, with tears, th' secrets iv his thrade an' offers to fight me if I don't look inthrested. I know injyneerin', pammistry, plumbin', Christyan Science, midicine, horse-shoein' asthronomy, th' care iv th' hari, an' th' laws iv exchange, an' th' knowledge I have iv how to subjoo th' affictions iv th' ladies wu'd cause manny a pang. I tell ye we ar-re a fine body iv men."[59] Posey (and his alter ego, Fus Fixico), while not quite as accomplished as this paragon, was, as the biographical sketch I read indicated, similarly Protean. Simple, who stands on the street corner, reads the papers, listens to the radio, and talks to numberless people in bars, is also, in many ways, well educated and well rounded. In this way all three fit Ralph Waldo Emerson's formula for the ideal American, except that only Posey can claim a rural background: "A sturdy lad . . . who in turn tries all the professions, who *teams it, farms it, peddles*, keeps a school, preaches, edits a newspaper, goes to Congress, buys a township, and so forth, in successive years, and always, like a cat, falls on his feet is worth a hundred of these city dolls."[60] Moreover, Emerson's dictum that American art must be authentic finds comic replication in all three writers under discussion; he would no doubt applaud Mr. Dooley's wry and withering reaction to the aesthetic influence of the 1893 World's Fair in Chicago: "They tell me th' wan we had give an impetus, whativer that is, to archytecture that it hasn't raycovered fr'm yet. Afther th' fair, ivrybody that was annybody had to go to live in a Greek temple with an Eyetalian roof an' bay-windows. But thim that wasn't annybody has f'rgot all about [it] . . . whin ye say annything to thim about th' fair, they say: 'D'ye raymimber th' night I see ye on th' Midway? Oh, my!'"[61]

It seems useful to compare three writers from three different pieces of the ethnic kaleidoscope, for these three sets of texts have more in common with each other than they do with other texts written in their particular group; Simple and Dooley resemble each other much more than Dooley resembles Studs Lonigan, for example. I would also like to stress that these writers are all writing from their own ethnic context, but all three are really writing on the boundary that separates ethnic from American, a boundary, as Fredrik Barth has shown us, that is the real definition of the group, more so than the culture that it encloses. As such, the boundary is constantly shifting, constantly being redefined.[62] In that sense, I would like to posit that these three writers, trained by agents of the opposing culture in Western traditions, writing for both ethnic and non-ethnic audiences, were in one sense walking a high wire aesthetically, subject to falling into disfavor with their ethnic group on the one side, and with dominant white culture on the other. With Barth's formulation in mind, however, we would do better to see Dunne, Posey, and Hughes as artistic surfers on the waves of ethnicity, seeking the longest and most daring ride on the biggest wave, which of course penetrates the shore farther than the other waves before retreating back to the sea. These three daring writers, seeking to further communications between cultures and to obviate ethnic differences, used both humor and humorous jeremiads (themselves instruments traditionally used in America to obviate difference) to create these boundary-pushing waves. To use a more classic metaphor, Freud claims that jokes function in the human consciousness much as dreams do, in that "joke-work" and "dream-work" help us work out subconscious conflicts. It seems equally valid that joke-work in a social context helps redefine the boundaries that divide ethnic groups, bringing opposed elements into a temporary, and sometimes permanent, harmony.

One of the most important differences between the humor of Hughes and Dunne and that of Posey is that in the first two writers one can definitely see a transformation in both comic stance and mode as Simple and Dooley age and develop alongside the very real happenings of American racial history. Dooley, after the Irish seem to be on their way to white-bread homogenization, becomes much more global in his interests and remarks. As such, his dialect becomes much more of a liability and an embarrassment, and, in fact, Mr. Dooley fell out of favor with the American public. Simple and his creator, however, got a new lease on life with the powerful developments in the civil rights movement in the late fifties and early sixties. Hughes allows Simple much more militant, albeit humorous views, and there is a marked change in Hughes's habitual misogyny as well. Indeed, Rita Dandridge has written persuasively about the "Black Woman as a Freedom Fighter in Langston Hughes' *Simple's Uncle Sam*." Simple's cousin Minnie, for example, an object of ridicule and scorn for the most part in the earlier works, emerges as a militant freedom fighter akin to Malcolm X.[63] This transformation of artistic concepts and uses of humor over the years surely has much to do with Barth's formulations of shifting ethnic boundaries.

The jokes in these three cultures also arise because of the injustice of the existing order. Humor, in its archaic, liberating mode, subverts the order and creates an absurd or ideal order, albeit a temporary one, and creates a momentary group solidarity in the face of the common enemy. It may well be, in fact, that threatened groups are more inclined to humor than others; certainly the richest comic traditions in contemporary America would seem to belong to the Jews and the blacks, who for so long had to fight a revolutionary battle against oppression.

Along these lines, Hughes titled another work *Laughing to Keep from Crying*; this common attitude overlooks, however, one of the reasons why humor has traditionally been scorned (albeit for the wrong reasons) by zealous revolutionaries. Not for nothing was the headline "Garbo Laughs" written in connection with her role as a stern priestess of the Russian Revolution. Revolutionaries want people to believe in the seriousness of their struggle; the early comparative humorlessness of the women's movement is another example, now thankfully washed away by torrents of feminist humor epitomized by the cartoons of Nicole Hollander, the routines of Lily Tomlin, and so on. Rose Coser's study of humor in a hospital setting, however, pinpoints the validity of some revolutionaries' prejudices against humor, for instance, Richard Wright's distaste for Zora Neale Hurston's 1930s comic novels. Coser found that patients often banded together to make all kinds of jokes about the hospital, doctors, nurses, the food, everything. She also notes that laughter must be shared; he who laughs alone is considered asocial. The liberating effect of humor is noted, but so is the fact that the humor drains away the pent-up resentment, and the patients as a result seldom rise up in rebellion together against hospital tyranny.[64] Dunne, Hughes, and Posey had to face this possibility as well, for all three were interested in using humor to affect social change; they built in protective devices to deal with any and all situations. The risk was well worth it, for all three authors understood that the desire for middle-class respectability, be it in Irish, black, or Native Americans, was leading to the banishment and/or effacement of ethnic humor, which represented one of the great aesthetic achievements of the group in question, and one of its most effective weapons against racism and cultural imperialism to boot. They knew how to exploit stereotype for larger purposes than merely representing their cultures to outsiders. Their struggles to resurrect folk wisdom and ethnic values in the face of massive pressure to Americanize is made more poignant when one realizes that all three of these artists had been trained away from their respective traditions via the old variety of the Western aesthetic/ intellectual tradition. Mr. Dooley, who understood that humor is the salt of the earth, used a culinary metaphor to make a recommendation for ethnic humor's usefulness in creating understanding among America's peoples in his essay on immigration: "May be if we'd season th' immigrants a little . . . they'd go down better."[65]

Clearly, Posey and Hughes "cooked" this way too. Using humor to make their cultures more palatable, these writers also knew, of course, that this was only an opening gambit, one that would ideally lead to a full exploration of the glories of their traditions, which had so much to give to *all* Americans. As Hughes so movingly put it, "There is so much richness in Negro humor, so much beauty in black dreams, so much dignity in our struggle, and so much universality in our problems, in us—in each living human being of color— that I do not understand the tendency today that some Negro artists have of seeking to run away from themselves, of running away from us, of being afraid to sing our songs, paint our own pictures, write about ourselves." Simple, of course, said it more cogently: "Jazz, jive, and jam would be better for race relations than all this high-flown gab, baff, and gas the orators put out."[66]

Notes

1. Mary Douglas, "The Social Control of Cognition: Some Factors in Joke Perception," *Man* 3 (1968), 395.
2. Werner Sollors, "Immigrants and Other Americans," in *Columbia Literary History of the United States*, ed. Emory Elliott (New York: Columbia University Press, 1988), 568.
3. Ibid., 580.
4. For the best treatment of the Simple stories, consult Donna Akiba Sullivan Harper, *Not So Simple: The "Simple" Stories by Langston Hughes* (Columbia, Mo.: University of Missouri Press, 1995).
5. Maxine Schwartz Seller, ed., *Ethnic Theatre in the United States* (Westport, Conn.: Greenwood Press, 1983).
6. Alan Dundes, *Interpreting Folklore* (Bloomington: Indiana University Press, 1980), 137.
7. Langston Hughes, *Simple Stakes a Claim* (New York: Rinehart, 1957), 12.
8. Mikhail Bakhtin, *Rabelais and His World*, trans. Helene Iswolsky (Bloomington: Indiana University Press, 1984), 474.

9. Cited in James DeMuth, *Small Town Chicago: The Comic Perspective of Finley Peter Dunne, George Ade, Ring Lardner* (Port Washington, N.Y.: Kennikat Press, 1980), 30.

10. James Weldon Johnson, ed., *The Book of American Negro Poetry*, rev. ed. (1931; New York: Harcourt Brace, 1969), 41–42.

11. James Dorman, "Ethnic Stereotyping in American Popular Culture: The Depiction of American Ethnics in the Cartoon Periodicals of the Gilded Age," *Amerikastudien/American Studies* 30 (1986): 489–507.

12. Leo Strauss, *Persecution and the Art of Writing* (1952; reprint, Westport, Conn.: Greenwood Press, 1975), 36.

13. Finley Peter Dunne, *Observations by Mr. Dooley* (New York: R. H. Russell, 1902), 51.

14. Ibid., 54.

15. J. Hector St. John de Crèvecoeur, *Letters from an American Farmer* (1782; reprint, New York: Dutton, 1957), 39.

16. Andrew Greeley, *Ethnicity in the United States: A Preliminary Reconnaissance* (New York: John Wiley, 1974).

17. Cited in Charles H. Nichols, "Comic Modes in Black America (A Ramble through Afro-American Humor," in *Comic Relief: Humor in Contemporary American Literature*, ed. Sarah Blacher Cohen (Urbana: University of Illinois Press, 1978), 270.

18. L. Perry Curtis, *Apes and Angels: The Irishman in Victorian Caricature* (Washington, D.C.: Smithsonian Institution Press, 1971.

19. Werner Sollors, *Beyond Ethnicity: Consent and Descent in American Culture* (New York: Oxford University Press, 1986), 102–130.

20. William Hugh Jansen, "The Esoteric-Exoteric Factor in Folklore," *Fabula: Journal of Folktales Studies* 2 (1959): 205–11.

21. Cited in Keith Basso, *Portraits of "the Whiteman": Linguistic Play and Cultural Symbols Among the Western Apache* (Cambridge: Cambridge University Press, 1979), x.

22. Vine DeLoria, "Indian Humor," in *Custer Died for Your Sins* (New York: Macmillan, 1969), 153.

23. For a book-length study of Native American humor, consult Kenneth Lincoln, *Indi'n Humor: Bicultural Play in Native America* (New York: Oxford, 1993); unfortunately, Lincoln omits Posey from his study. See also John Lowe, "Coyote's Jokebook: Humor in Native American Literature and Culture," in *Dictionary of Native American Literature*, ed. Andrew Wiget (New York: Garland, 1994): 193–205.

24. William E. Connelley, "Introduction," *The Poems of Alexander Posey*, ed. William E. Connelley (Topeka, Kans.: Crane, 1910), 5.

25. Ibid., 63.

26. Daniel L. Littlefield, Jr., "Introduction," in Alexander Posey, *The Fus Fixico Letters by Alexander Posey*, ed. Daniel F. Littlefield, Jr. (Lincoln: University of Nebraska Press, 1993), 22–31.

27. Daniel L. Littlefield, Jr., *Alex Posey: Creek Poet, Journalist, and Humorist* (Lincoln: University of Nebraska Press, 1992).

28. Connelly, *Poems*, 57.

29. Alexander Posey, *The Fus Fixico Letters*, ed. Daniel F. Littlefield, Jr., and Carol A. Petty Hunter (Lincoln: University of Nebraska Press, 1993), 52. Subsequent quotations are noted parenthetically in the text.

30. Finley Peter Dunne, *Mr. Dooley in Peace and War* (Boston: Small, Maynard, 1898), ix–xi.

31. Posey, *Letters*, 187.

32. Langston Hughes, *Simple Takes a Wife* (New York: Simon and Schuster, 1953).

33. Ibid., 101.
34. Posey, *Letters*, 56.
35. Ibid., 59–60. This story has a terribly ironic side to it, for Posey was drowned during a flood, when he tried to cross a flooded river by walking over a washed-out railroad trestle.
36. Ibid., 60, 103.
37. Ibid., 91, 132, 182.
38. Ibid., 62, 158.
39. Langston Hughes, *The Best of Simple* (New York: Hill and Wang, 1961), 30.
40. Ibid., 18–20.
41. Posey, *Letters*, 63.
42. Ibid., 69, 42.
43. Ibid., 70, 88.
44. Ibid., 99.
45. Ibid., 129–30.
46. Ibid., 154.
47. Langston Hughes, *The Big Sea* (1940; reprint, New York: Hill and Wang, 1963), 54–55.
48. Ibid., 85.
49. Arthur Prange, Jr., and M. M. Vitols, "Jokes among Southern Negroes: The Revelation of Conflict," in *Mother Wit from the Laughing Barrel: Readings in the Interpretation of Afro-American Folklore*, ed. Alan Dundes (Englewood Cliffs, N.J.: Prentice-Hall, 1973), 634.
50. Hughes, *The Best of Simple*, 18.
51. Quoted in Faith Berry, *Langston Hughes: Before and Beyond Harlem* (Westport, Conn.: L. Hill, 1983), 309–10.
52. Quoted in Nichols, "Comic Modes," 269–70.
53. Langston Hughes, "Red Silk Stockings," in *Fine Clothes to the Jew* (New York: Knopf, 1927), 73.
54. Hughes, *The Big Sea*, 267–68.
55. Quoted in Berry, *Langston Hughes*, 325–26.
56. Posey, *Letters*, 87.
57. Theodor W. Adorno and Max Horkheimer, *The Dialectic of Enlightenment*, trans. John Cumming (New York: Herder and Herder, 1972), 31.
58. Dunne, *Mr. Dooley in Peace and War*, xxii.
59. Finley Peter Dunne, *Dissertations by Mr. Dooley* (New York: Harper and Brothers, 1906), 311.
60. Ralph Waldo Emerson, "Self-Reliance," in *Selected Writings of Ralph Waldo Emerson*, ed. William H. Gilman (New York: New American Library, 1965), 273.
61. Finley Peter Dunne, *Mr. Dooley's Opinions* (New York: Harper and Brothers, 1901), 140–141.
62. Fredrik Barth, *Ethnic Groups and Boundaries: The Social Organization of Culture Difference* (Boston: Little, Brown, 1969).
63. Rita Dandridge, "The Black Woman as a Freedom Fighter in Langston Hughes' Simple's Uncle Sam," *College Language Association Journal* 18, no. 2 (1974): 273–83.
64. Rose Laub Coser, "Some Social Functions of Humor: A Study of Humor in a Hospital Setting," *Human Relations* 12, no. 2 (1959): 171–82.
65. Finley Peter Dunne, *Observations*, 52.
66. Hughes, *The Best of Simple*, 242–243.

Genealogy, Genre, Gender: Sui Sin Far's "Leaves from the Mental Portfolio of an Eurasian"

Chapter 10

NICOLE TONKOVICH

Sᴜɪ Sɪɴ Fᴀʀ ᴄᴏɴᴄʟᴜᴅᴇs her autobiographical essay, "Leaves from the Mental Portfolio of an Eurasian" (1909), with this assertion: "I have no nationality and am not anxious to claim any. Individuality is more than nationality. . . . I give my right hand to the Occidentals and my left to the Orientals, hoping that between them they will not utterly destroy the insignificant 'connecting link.'"[1] Born of British and Chinese parents in England, Sui Sin Far (Edith Maude Eaton) had also lived in Canada, Jamaica, and the United States. While her siblings assumed ethnic identities consistent with the preconceptions of the dominant societies in which they lived, passing as Spanish/Mexican, Japanese, or white, Sui Sin Far chose to emphasize her Chinese lineage and called herself "Eurasian." In her autobiographical essay, as well as in her self-construction as a racial subject, she challenges a common nineteenth-century pattern of binary thinking that assumed Occidental to be superior to Oriental and that ignored complex racial genealogies and national identifications that had resulted from more than a century of Anglo colonial domination.

The opposition of Occidental to Oriental is apparently overcome in the contemporary classification of "Asian American." Yet to organize literary production by national identity maintains a pattern of binary thinking about literary traditions based in genealogical tropes. Sui Sin Far has been claimed as the first Chinese American woman writer and as one of two first Asian American writers of fiction.[2] Although these categories recognize some of the complexity of her ethnic identity, they assign status to "first" over "subsequent"; imply that writing by women can and should be distinguished from writing by men; and value imaginative writing over nonfiction, biography, and journalism.[3]

236

Although such patterns of thinking yield useful classifications, they result in negative understandings when applied to the work of Sui Sin Far. Scholars anxious to establish a genealogical Asian American literary tradition claim her as a foremother. For others, however, her writings have set a difficult, even negative, precedent for subsequent writers. The editors of an early anthology of Asian American literature, for example, place her at the beginning of a Chinese-American literary tradition overwhelmed by feminine sensibilities.[4] Other literary historians have classified the genres in which Sui Sin Far wrote as feminized, evaluating her vignettes, sketches, and short fictions in the local color tradition as less rigorous than epic or lyric poetry, philosophical essays, or even novels.[5] S. E. Solberg attributes Sui Sin Far's choice of these genres to her position as a first writer. He suggests that the lack of an authorizing national literary tradition hindered her ability to treat subjects "in depth or at length" and declares that Sui Sin Far did not produce an original form of writing, one capable of expressing authentic Amerasian identity. Thus she is "not a great writer."[6]

The intertwined issues of genealogy, genre, and gender—words that share a common etymology—structure Sui Sin Far's autobiographical essay, "Leaves from the Mental Portfolio of an Eurasian." The imprecision of national, generic, and gendered classifications are demonstrated in the essay's implicit argument that literary understandings do not depend on stabilizing a text's (or body's) meaning through binary logic. "Leaves" suggests, rather, that literary histories will be immeasurably enriched by discarding such categorical thinking in favor of seeking to understand the textual production of writers whose experiences fall outside the deceptively simple categories of national tradition and gendered notions of literary value.

Genealogy

During the years in which Sui Sin Far pursued her writing career, Canada and the United States were gripped by a nationalist fervor that assumed the white "race" to be superior to any other. Canadian sentiment reached a peak in 1867 with the nation's independence from England and the completion of the Canadian transcontinental railroad. Similar events in the United States fed a jingoistic fervor in the last decades of the nineteenth century. The transcontinental railroad tangibly linked the coasts. At the same time, an escalating rhetoric of national unity attempted to heal the divisiveness caused by the Civil War. Both nations were particularly sinophobic, assuming that Chinese were "subhuman," quaint, exotic, unassimilable, heathen, and inferior to all other races.[7] In both nations, political parties endorsed anti-Chinese platforms, passed exclusion laws in an attempt to ban the members of a race that only decades before had been welcomed as a source of cheap labor, and enacted zoning laws that confined Chinese to restricted urban neighborhoods.[8]

Governmental policy was echoed in cultural politics. Canadian nationalism included overt efforts to develop a characteristically national literature, led, in part, by *Dominion Illustrated*, a periodical whose editorial policy declared, "We are for building up a homogeneous, united, patriotic nation, and for ignoring all prejudice of race and sect."[9] This seemingly liberal and inclusive sentiment carries ironic overtones for the contemporary reader, for subsequent histories demonstrate that the much vaunted homogeneity was achieved through racial exclusions, while racial difference, prejudice, and discrimination were left unmitigated. A similar campaign of literary nationalism occurred in the United States. Houghton Mifflin issued standard collections of the works of classic authors in its Riverside Editions, promoting them as school texts especially effective at producing an "American ethos" in students.[10] As a result of such efforts, "American" literature came to signify texts written by white male New Englanders.

In the United States, preoccupation with pure blood and national identity entered the domestic arena in the guise of patriotic societies whose membership was genealogically determined and whose agendas were publicized in the same magazines for which Sui Sin Far wrote.[11] Donald K. Pickens has identified seventy such societies in the United States by 1900, including the Society of Mayflower Descendants, the Sons of the American Revolution, the Daughters of the American Revolution, and the Colonial Dames of America. Thirty-five such organizations were established in the last decade of the century. Most of them required would-be members to prove their lineal descent not from nobility or royalty, but from white American patriots.[12] In California, where Sui Sin Far spent several years in her later career, the Native Sons of the Golden West (NSGW) limited membership to "white males born in California on or after July 7, 1846"; membership later expanded to include "Native Daughters."[13] Such societies were not the exclusive purview of whites, however. In 1895, American-born Chinese in San Francisco, excluded from the NSGW by racial bias, established a parallel organization, the United Parlor of the Native Sons of the Golden State, in 1915 renamed the Chinese-American Citizens Alliance. This group actively pursued assimilation, at the same time seeking the respect of foreign-born Chinese of "pure" blood.[14]

Such nationalist fervor overlooked the fact that centuries of colonial domination and transnational migration had produced ambiguous racial identities in citizenries presumed to be racially "pure," as details of the Eaton family genealogy make clear. Sui Sin Far's father, Edward Eaton, was British, and her paternal grandmother Irish. Her Asian heritage was ambiguous, as well. Her mother, Grace A. (Lotus Blossom) Trefusis, may have been the child of parents of different races (her mother's name is recorded as Ah Cheun and her father's as A. Trefusis—not a Chinese name).[15] Abducted from her Chinese home, Lotus Blossom was eventually adopted by British missionaries and taken to England, where she learned "English ways and manner of dress" ("Leaves," 126). She later returned to China as a missionary. There she met and married Edward Eaton, whose father had "set him up in business" at the Port of Shanghai.[16]

The fourteen Eaton children could claim no national citizenship; rather, they exploited the ambiguity of their physical appearance to carve out identities within a dominant society that believed that bodily appearance guaranteed racial identity. Although they had been raised and socialized as "white," spoke English—not Chinese—at home, and had been educated in British and Canadian schools, they were accepted neither by the majority white cultures in which they lived nor by the smaller, marginalized Chinese community. In an aggressively sinophobic climate, they assumed racial identities other than Chinese. Sui Sin Far's eldest brother, Edward, embraced his Anglo identity and married a white woman; a sister, May Darling, who lived in California, claimed to be Spanish or Mexican. Another sister, Lillie Winnifred, assumed at least two ethnic identities as a writer. Under the Japanese-sounding pseudonym of Onoto Watanna, she penned a number of best-selling novels about Japanese topics.[17] She fabricated an autobiography to match, informing *Who's Who* that she had been born in Nagasaki in 1879, when, in fact, she had been born in Montreal in 1875. Later she embellished that fiction in the *New York Times* obituary she wrote for her sister, claiming that their mother had been "a Japanese noblewoman."[18] In 1907, Winnifred wrote another novel, *The Diary of Delia, Being a Veracious Chronicle of the Kitchen with Some Side-lights on the Parlour*, in Irish-American dialect under the name Winnifred Mooney. Her publishers, however, insisted that the book be published under her more recognizable pseudonym, Onoto Watanna.[19]

While Winnifred's Japanese identity seems to have been primarily a means of marketing books, Sui Sin Far chose to identify as Chinese as a means of exposing, discussing, and attempting to mitigate issues stemming from racial hierarchy and domination.[20] The only one of the fourteen Eaton children to identify herself as Chinese, she discovered that most Chinese of "pure" blood accepted her reluctantly, if at all. Her writings seek to explain Chinese immigrant cultures to the dominant white communities in which they lived and to demonstrate how irrational sinophobia adversely affected children of mixed racial heritage. She is critical of both white and Chinese prejudices, and although she apparently supports an agenda of assimilation, she argues equally eloquently that Chinese immigrants be allowed to maintain their unique cultural practices. This ambiguous stance—critical of both cultures, yet seeking an accord between them—may have contributed to the difficulties Sui Sin Far encountered in establishing herself as a professional writer. Her sketches and stories were frequently presented as oddities, curiosities, or bits of local color, as was their author. For example, she was featured by Charles Lummis in his *Land of Sunshine* column, "In Western Letters," as "our little 'Chinese Contributor'"—this despite an accompanying photographic portrait of the writer that could easily be read as Anglo.[21] Such characterizations virtually ensured her exclusion from a literary historical narrative emplotted around nationalist agendas.

Lummis's classification of Sui Sin Far as Chinese has recently been replaced by more precise terminologies, such as Amy Ling and Annette White-Parks's category of "Asian North American." The "origins" of this specific ethnic literary tradition, they claim, may be found in the work of the Eaton sisters. Yet even this precise ethnic category is confounded by the self-fashioning of Onoto Watanna and Sui Sin Far. According to Ling, Sui Sin Far stands at the beginning of Chinese American fiction, but because Lillie Winnifred wrote under a Japanese pseudonym, she does not hold a similar position for Japanese American literature. Indeed, if ethnicity becomes an important criterion, according to Ling, "we would have to say that *Miss Nume of Japan* was the first Chinese American novel and that the twelve other 'Japanese' novels of Onoto Watanna should be classified, despite their themes and settings, as Chinese American fiction."[22]

Such literary preoccupations with national identity, as well as the domestic and political issues of pure blood and genealogical entitlement, are confronted in "Leaves from the Mental Portfolio of an Eurasian." The essay challenges the ideas of national origin and language as determinants of racial identity by detailing the complex genealogies of members of the Eaton family. It further undermines the hierarchical evolutionary thinking of racial prejudice by demonstrating that genetic fitness is not confined to those of pure blood. Although "Leaves" acknowledges cultural preoccupations with eugenics and genealogy in its attention to lineage, racial identity, physiognomic inheritance, health, and fitness for reproduction and for labor, it also presents an indelible image of a family whose members confound the prejudicial assumption that Chinese Americans—indeed, any peoples of mixed racial heritage—are unfit physical specimens. For example, although Sui Sin Far details her "mother's screams of agony when a baby is born," she also makes it clear that Lotus Blossom Eaton survived six births in seven years while still in her twenties ("Leaves," 127). Eight more children followed—a significant support for her daughter's assertion that "some day a great part of the world will be Eurasian" ("Leaves," 129).[23]

Throughout the sketch Sui Sin Far emphasizes the state of her own health, as well, admitting, "I am not as strong as my sisters, which makes me feel somewhat ashamed, for I am the eldest little girl, and more is expected of me. I have no organic disease . . . but in the light of the present I know that the cross of the Eurasian bore too heavily upon my childish shoulders" ("Leaves," 127). On its surface this passage would seem to endorse the prejudicial commonsense assumption that the mixture of Anglo and Chinese blood had produced weakened offspring, an assumption reinforced by Sui Sin Far's attributing her physical strength to her Anglo blood: "The white blood in our veins fights valiantly for the Chinese half of us" ("Leaves," 126). Yet its dominant image insists that Sui Sin Far's "weakness" be read as paradoxical. Not only does the cross remind readers that this woman cannot be classified as "heathen," but it also invokes the beatific paradox of strength in renunciation. Moreover, it reminds its white readers that obligations of Christian charity and brotherhood should overcome divisions of racial difference.

By her essay's conclusion, Sui Sin Far has convincingly demonstrated that her "spirit is more than [her] body," and that qualities not linked to race—including persistence, devotion, bravery, and filial respect—outweigh supposedly heritable physical advantages. As the "advisory head of the household" she has supported her family, helped raise her siblings, and sent money for their support long after leaving home.[24] Despite ill health, she has traveled coast to coast on the railroad, started her own businesses in Montreal, Boston, and Seattle, and worked as a reporter in the West Indies, San Francisco, and Los Angeles—this in an era when prevailing notions held that women of her class and intellect were not fit for such grueling tasks.

If such strength, loyalty, and family devotion are not purely heritable traits, the foolishness of domestic and political obsessions with pure bloodlines becomes apparent. Sui Sin Far's most compelling anecdote demonstrates this point, at the same time revealing how the claim to pure blood has been conflated with issues of class entitlement. One of the most poignant and ironic sketches of "Leaves from the Mental Portfolio" tells of a Eurasian woman who is finally able to force her white fiancé to break their engagement by threatening his devotion to race and class.[25] Driving with him behind "a pair of beautiful horses" while "trying very hard to imagine herself in love with him," she sees a "Chinese vegetable gardener's cart." She teases her lover by calling the "Chinaman" her "brother." She taunts, "When we are married . . . I intend to give a Chinese party every month. . . . As there are very few aristocratic Chinese in this city, I shall fill up with the laundrymen and vegetable farmers. I don't believe in being exclusive in democratic America, do you?" He counters weakly by asking her if it "wouldn't . . . be just a little pleasanter for us if, after we are married, we allowed it to be presumed that you were . . . a little Japanese lady" ("Leaves," 131–132). She immediately breaks the engagement.

The carefully chosen details of this sketch position it as characteristic of a society obsessed with breeding—both in the social and physical senses. We assume that the horses are a pair bred to match, unlike the couple who drives them. The relative status of the races is exposed in the Eurasian woman's insistence on claiming her kinship with the Chinese vegetable man who both is and is not her "brother." This is repellent to the fiancé, both because she has chosen to emphasize her Chinese heritage over the more socially advantageous white component of her genealogy and because the Chinese man she recognizes occupies a degraded social position. Finally, by allowing the fiancé to speak for himself, Sui Sin Far exposes the class biases underpinning his apparently rational suggestion that both partners would benefit were she to pass as Japanese: her enhanced social status as a "Japanese *lady*" would, in turn, make her a more suitable match for him. What he does not understand is that by asking his fiancée to "pass" as Japanese, he has demanded that she deny both sides of her "breeding."

Ultimately, "Leaves" demonstrates how preoccupations with class, ethnicity, and race determined literary and cultural politics in the nineteenth century. Sui Sin Far recounts that in California, "funny people" advise her to "'trade' upon" her "nationality." "They tell me that if I wish to succeed in literature in America I should dress in Chinese costume, carry a fan in my hand, wear a pair of scarlet beaded slippers, live in New York, and come of high birth" ("Leaves," 132). While she apparently resisted this advice and presented herself in photographic portraits as culturally assimilated, the magazines for which she wrote embellished her essays and sketches to emphasize her supposed exoticism, frequently using the very devices that she had ironically enumerated. For example, *The Century Magazine* illustrated "A Chinese Boy-Girl" with the image of a Chinese child in native costume standing in a dark and mysterious shop interior. Drawn by Walter Jack Duncan in a dark ink wash, this image repeats the photographic convention of the "oriental" business place. "The Chinese Woman in America" appeared in *Land of Sunshine* illustrated with photographs of exotically attired Chinese children and mothers surrounding a home altar and holding fans. It also features a photographic portrait, captioned, "A Chinese Bride in America," whose details match Sui Sin Far's ironic description of the exotic stereotype: a woman in Chinese attire sits placidly holding a fan; her beaded slippers peer from beneath her pleated underskirt. The elegant surroundings in which she is photographed assure the viewer that she is of high birth. Thus, in her lifetime, Sui Sin Far entered the literary world under the implicit assumption that her writing held interest because of its difference from the dominant national tradition.[26] The merit and argumentative content of her work are irrelevant.

Genre

Sui Sin Far's most significant challenge to the racist behaviors of a society fascinated with eugenics and class status arises from her choice of form. The title's figure of leaves suggests a family tree, as well as the interchangeable pages of a portfolio, at once incomplete and expandable. Attending to the significations of this form offers a new perspective on the purposes and accomplishments of "Leaves." Its vignettes claim for Sui Sin Far the genealogical and class entitlement requisite for middle-class Anglo citizenship while foregrounding the contingency of such identities through the instability of the form that contains them.

Sui Sin Far's appropriation and modification of the figure of leaves carry an implicit claim for her inclusion in mainstream histories of American literature. The title links the essay genealogically with Whitman's autobiographical and democratic anthem, *Leaves of Grass* (1855), as well as with Fanny Fern's collections of journalism—*Fern Leaves from Fanny's Portfolio* (1853) and *Fresh Leaves* (1857).[27] All three authors—writers of journalism, fiction, essays, and poetry—emphasize the personal in texts that are episodic and disjunctive. Such similarities align their writing with a new transgeneric form emergent in the United States in the mid-nineteenth century, an assemblage that Miles Orvell has called "the omnibus form"—one that includes not only literary productions, but also "daguerreotype galleries, . . . panoramas, and . . . exhibition halls."[28] These forms contain "an infinitely expandable number of parts in an encompassing whole," much like the omnibuses that moved individual and unrelated urbanites from place to place or like the railroads, which presented to their riders an ever changing panorama.[29]

Although "Leaves from the Mental Portfolio" has been classified as an autobiographical essay and is frequently used to establish biographical truth about Sui Sin Far and her family, it is riven by omissions, covering forty years in the space of approximately eight print pages. The essay might, then, be read as an exploration of the possibilities of the omnibus form, as signaled by its title, "*Leaves* from the Mental *Portfolio*" (emphasis added). Rather than a lengthy, seamless autobiography, or even a shorter coherent autobiographical sketch such as the one Sui Sin Far published three years later in the *Boston Globe*, "Leaves" is a collection of sketches—candid snapshots, as it were—comprising the textual analog to a family photograph album, or photodocumentary portfolio, a form that had wide popularity in the late nineteenth century.[30] Indeed, Sui Sin Far's writing has been characterized in adjectives appropriate to photographic images. Yin, for example, describes her stories as presenting "a panoramic view and a realistic picture of the Chinese-American community" and praises the "verisimilitude" of her Chinatown sketches.[31] Sui

Sin Far herself introduces her autobiographical sketch for the *Boston Globe* as a "mental gallery" filled with "radiant pictures."[32] The sketches collected in "Leaves" make up a corpus, a complete but fragmented and always expandable identity for this writer.

The advent of photography in the early nineteenth century had made self-representation available not only to the entitled, who could also afford to have portraits or miniatures painted, but also to the middle classes. By midcentury, photographic images, formerly unique artifacts, had become reproducible commodities to be circulated, exchanged, and collected in albums. With the advent of paper roll film and the hand-held Kodak camera in the 1880s, photography "thoroughly permeated [middle-class] family life."[33] At the same time that it made self-representation democratically available, photography offered a new and purportedly objective means of documenting lineage, genetic heritage, and social conditions of urban life.

The ladies' magazines of the period, the same magazines in which Sui Sin Far published, urged mothers to document family celebrations, family possessions, and leisure activities.[34] Their instructions helped would-be amateur photographers approximate the conventions of photodocumentary realism in the domestic arena. For example, these articles suggested that mothers collect photographs of the birth and development of children in pre-scripted baby books, albums that combined image, text, and anthropomorphic measurements to establish heritable genetic fitness. Physical resemblances between generations could be traced through illustrated pedigree charts, while written narrative recorded details of the mother's labor and baby's birth, first step, first word, and first sentence. Charts organizing vital measurements buttressed these images, mapping infant bodies onto informational grids that recorded progressions of height, weight, and circumference of head. Artifacts taken directly from the body—fingerprints, footprints, and even locks of hair—served as physical evidence of a child's genetic heritage.[35] Sui Sin Far's figurative album destabilizes these apparently empirical proofs of genetic entitlement by displaying the disconnected, ambiguous, and uncertain ethnic identities assumed by the several members of her family over the course of approximately forty years. The multiplicity of identity it displays unseats the notion of "family" as a self-evident unit, either as a description of a small group of people related by pure (or tainted) blood or a larger group of unrelated peoples united by ideology and geography—a nation.

Several members of the Eaton family were aware of the domestic possibilities of the photograph and were accomplished at constructing photographic images of themselves that matched the ethnic identities they had chosen. The ambiguity captured in their portraits demonstrates the fluidity with which they moved among the various ethnic groups constituting the family of nations at the turn of the century. George Eaton worked as an independent contractor for Kodak. Lillie Winnifred appears in the frontispiece portrait of her third novel, *The Wooing of Wistaria*, dressed "in a kimono with hair piled high in Japanese fashion, standing before a screen painted with wisteria and iris." In a later image, made in 1914, Winnifred kneels, again dressed in a kimono.[36] May Darling worked as a photo finisher for the Thors Photographic Company of San Francisco.[37] May is probably the sibling Sui Sin Far described in "Leaves" as a "half Chinese, half white girl. Her face is plastered with a thick white coat of paint and her eyelids and eyebrows are blackened so that the shape of her eyes and the whole expression of her face is changed. . . . It is not difficult, in a land like California, for a half Chinese, half white girl to pass as one of Spanish or Mexican origin. This poor child does, tho she lives in nervous dread of being 'discovered'" ("Leaves," 131). These phrases seem to describe a photographic portrait of May, in which her eyes are heavily made up.[38] Sui Sin Far, by contrast, represented herself photographically in more ambiguous terms, choosing clothing that suggests her assimilation and striking poses that signify an upper-class and educated identity.

The images collected in "Leaves" are not literally photographic portraits, but discrete, disconnected, highly realistic and evocative renderings of the chronological development of an individual child within a family unit. The album begins with a vignette in which the author is not more than four years old, follows her through adolescence and early adulthood, and, consistent with the unfinished and expandable omnibus form, leaves her in transit, "roam[ing] backward and forward across the continent" ("Leaves," 132). Its episodes are narrated in prose that echoes the eternal present of the photographic image, chronicling the incidents that formed—and that actively continue to constitute— Sui Sin Far as a racial subject.[39]

The scenes of "Leaves," like the images collected in family albums, have a predictable content. They record public and private rituals essential to constituting families (such as birth, confirmation, engagement, and marriage) and nations (such as Independence Day, Thanksgiving, and Christmas). These snapshots capture children at play, measure their growth, and record their rites of passage. They document family possessions—homes, cars, real estate, and gardens, as well as the less tangible possession of disposable income to spend on travel and leisure—all central themes in photographic images made by and/ or for recent immigrants anxious to document that they had succeeded in America. The vignettes of "Leaves from the Mental Portfolio" follow these commonplaces, presenting episodes whose album captions might read "Child-hood with Nanny," "Playing in a Garden," "At the Gate" ("Leaves," 125);

"At a Children's Party," "A Sleigh Ride in Eastern Canada" ("Leaves," 126); "School Days," "A New Baby" ("Leaves," 127); "Dancing Lessons" ("Leaves," 128); "Scenes in Jamaica" ("Leaves," 129).

Because family photograph albums most frequently preserve images of happy occasions, they are incomplete documents. They overlook "marital violence and infanticide, family strife and dislocation . . . adultery, divorce, mental breakdown, . . . juvenile delinquency[,]," or death.[40] They do not honor the "renegade, the wastrel, the outlaw. . . . The family pictures we like best are poignant—and optimistic."[41] Sui Sin Far's family album, however, does include some of these less pleasant moments, for she has merged the sentimentality of the private form with the objectivity of public photodocumentary. Unlike the earliest photojournalists, however, Sui Sin Far avoids the tendency of documentary to assume that its subjects, namely "the poor, the foreign and the injured . . . [have] no stake in the images they provide."[42] She emphasizes her position as the narrator within the portfolio, the photographer within the camera frame. Her vignettes in "Leaves" resist the easy fiction of a timeless present, a single representative photographic moment, with a textual narrative of cause and effect.

A comparison will demonstrate my point. The photographic images Jacob Riis made preparatory to writing *How the Other Half Lives* illustrate what he considered to be veracious accounts of tenement dwellers, ghettoes, and slums. His photograph of "Family Making Artificial Flowers" shows a mother with a baby in her arms, sitting at a round table with six other children, the oldest of whom appears to be no more than twelve.[43] This "family" is an index for all "respectable" poor immigrant families with dreams of social advancement. Calendar images decorate the wall; the worktable is covered with a serviceable cloth; a background table is draped with a more formal figured cloth and set with an ornate samovar; the room's wooden furniture is polished; the mother's and children's hair is dressed, and they are neatly attired. The products made by Riis's tenement family suggests that they are immigrants from a "cultured" country—flowers would not likely be associated with German immigrants, for example, whom Riis supposed to be stolid, lumpish, and without refinement.[44] Despite its realism, this is an incomplete photographic record. No father is present or alluded to; certainly he is not the photographer, for self-representation is not within the social or economic reach of this family. The photograph does not explain how the artificial flowers are marketed—whether they are sold to a contractor or whether, more likely, they are sold by the children on the street.[45]

In choosing to limn the less pleasant details of her family's life, Sui Sin Far echoes the Riisian documentary impulse. She chronicles the pain of childbirth and the shame of her family's indebtedness, not stinting on detail. However, the "Portfolio's" textual snapshots narrate cause and effect, before and after. Sui Sin Far narrates a vignette whose title, "The Little Chinese Lace Girl," might serve well as a Riisian caption. This incident demonstrates, however, how she presents racial subjects without reducing them to mere documentary instances. Speaking from the advantage of hindsight, Sui Sin Far reiterates a Riisian assumption—that "nationality, if I had only known it at that time, helps to make sales" ("Leaves," 128). It is probable that the stereotypical associations of Chinese women with delicate femininity did add value to the lace and paintings she sold. Yet Sui Sin Far also reminds her readers of what Riis's image does not suggest—that selling on the street constitutes "a dangerous life for a very young girl. I come near to 'mysteriously disappearing' many a time" (ibid.). This danger would have confronted the young women in Riis's image, as well. Riis, however, photographed only women street vendors who were old, toughened, and irretrievably déclassé, such as the "Stale Bread Vendor."[46] Most significantly, Sui Sin Far reports an ambiguity of feeling entirely absent from Riis's idealized image of the working poor: "The greatest temptation was in the thought of getting far away from where I was known, to where no mocking cries of 'Chinese!' 'Chinese!' could reach" ("Leaves," 128). Such narrative exceeds Riisian ideology. His photograph erases the danger—as well as the degradation—faced by women and children who peddled merchandise on city streets. Because Sui Sin Far narrates her own album, she can detail the effect of such traumas on the family and on herself. Thus the tone of her documentary resists the apparently objective detachment of photorealism and presents such scenes with engagement and empathy, challenging readers to think beyond momentary and stereotypical images.

Other snapshots in "Leaves" even more closely approximate public documentary. For example, Sui Sin Far shows her readers Chinese vegetable vendors and laundrymen and a particularly Riisian view of a "Chinese store" in Hudson City: "I have never seen a Chinese person. The two men within the store are uncouth specimens of their race, drest in working blouses and pantaloons with queues hanging down their backs. I recoil with a sense of shock" ("Leaves," 126). The apparently distanced rhetoric of this sketch is ambiguous, implying both ignorant racism and childlike naiveté. It demonstrates how powerfully verbal ("uncouth specimens") and visual ("queues") stereotypes essentialize racial difference, so much so that the child does not consider herself a member of the same "race" as these men. Riis, by contrast, adopts the moralizing, universalizing, and distancing tone of the urban guide, taking his titillated and appalled visitors through the slums of New York City. He informs his readers that "Chinatown as a spectacle is disappointing. . . . Mott Street is clean to distraction: the laundry stamp is on it."[47] He manages to make such tidiness into a sign and a threat: "It is the distinguishing mark of

Chinatown, outwardly and physically. It is not altogether by chance the Chinaman has chosen the laundry as his distinctive field. He is by nature as clean as the cat, which he resembles in his traits of cruel cunning and savage fury when aroused."[48] Riis endorses the cultural perception that evil lurks behind every foreign facade, pontificating, "There are houses, dozens of them, in Mott and Pell Streets, that are literally jammed . . . with . . . hapless victims"—"white slaves"—of opium.[49] Unlike the volitionless white men and women who have fallen victim to the cunning of Chinese opium dealers, Riis and his readers can escape from this fearsome scene and return to their homes and privileges.

Sui Sin Far, however, remains present in her narrative. She learns to identify with her subjects and to understand them. Her association with Chinese laborers is based on more than a single peep at them through the door or a glance at a photo in a documentary tabloid. She observes, "My Chinese instincts develop. I am no longer the little girl who shrunk against my brother at the first sight of a Chinaman. Many and many a time, when alone in a strange place, has the appearance of even a humble laundryman given me a sense of protection and made me feel quite at home" ("Leaves," 131). Ultimately, then, "Leaves" blends documentary photorealism with the sentiment of the family album, anticipating later efforts such as Edward Steichen's *The Family of Man* (1955) and, most recently, Hoobler and Hoobler's *The Chinese American Family Album* (1994), volumes that combine feeling and fact, aligning family lineage with national identification. Unlike these later examples, however, "Leaves from the Mental Portfolio" emphasizes paradox and critique and thus avoids the detachment of documentary, the sentimental elisions of album making, and their resultant uncomplicated claims to national or universal (if sexist) identifications.

In the end, one is led to ask why "Leaves from the Mental Portfolio" was not published with accompanying photographs of the Eaton family. In the first place, its images are more akin to candid photographs than to formal portraits. Candid snapshots of the family are virtually nonexistent, having been technically impossible to produce before 1880. It is more likely, however, that the absence of any kind of image in the first publication of this essay signals Sui Sin Far's sophisticated understanding of the uses—and misuses—of photographic images. For many of Sui Sin Far's contemporaries, photography was a discourse of truth and stood independent of its processes, its framing, postures, conventions, and narrative implications. Sui Sin Far, by contrast, adapts the form, composition, and subject matter of the family album into a documentary narrative that emphasizes the processes by which she came to understand, control, and sometimes exploit the social construction of her own "racial" difference.

Gender

Paradoxically, the writer who documented her racial descent and autobiography in the textual equivalent of a family photograph album left no direct descendants, effectively refusing to meet the cultural expectation that a woman's social, cultural, and sexual fulfillment came through motherhood. Sui Sin Far refuses this role, the essay implies, because she is convinced that children of mixed races are destined by be misunderstood and unhappy, strangers to both parents' cultures. Her children would be doomed to repeat her own estrangement from her parents. She confesses that she cannot confide in either her mother or her father, since "I am different to both of them—a stranger, tho their own child" ("Leaves," 128). Lest this seem an aberrant perception, she includes a family portrait of a Chinese scholar who has graduated from an American college and has married an American wife. Presumably their children would enjoy a more elevated social status because of their father's occupation and their presumed advantage of "white" blood. Yet, telling "of their experiences as Eurasians," these children ask, "'Why did papa and mama born us?' . . . . Why?" (ibid.)

Recollecting her childhood, Sui Sin Far tells of her estrangement from both Anglo and Chinese cultures. She overtly emphasizes her difficult relationship with her mother, the parent with whose race and gender she has chosen to identify. Thus it becomes apparent that her choice of Chinese identity, as well as her femininity, is purposeful rather than instinctive. Unlike her mother, she will be proudly, even aggressively, Chinese. She will find a feminine identity in nurturing activities that are not instinctively maternal, notably by producing texts, not children. By contrast, Sui Sin Far's relation to her white father is not overtly narrated. Yet he determines the structure of the entire reminiscence because his race and gender combine to establish him as an omnipresently absent determinant of the conditions of her life.

In "Leaves," men enjoy an unquestioned power to gaze and to measure. Sui Sin Far tells of an early instance of being called from a childhood party to be "inspected" by "a white haired old man . . . [who] adjusts his eyeglasses and surveys me critically. 'Ah, indeed!' he exclaims. 'Who would have thought it at first glance. Yet now I see the difference between her and other children. What a peculiar coloring! Her mother's eyes and hair and her father's features, I presume. Very interesting little creature!'" ("Leaves," 126). This man produces the child's "difference," by implication, from *all* other children, not just those present at the party. In the process, he reduces her to a specimen through the mechanically enhanced vision of his eyeglasses. His scrutiny is overt, a blatant demonstration of the power of his race, age, and sex to call attention to, to differentiate, to consume, to measure, and to classify.

The childhood incident is ironically repeated in Sui Sin Far's adulthood. In Jamaica, she is surveilled "at the races . . . and twice at King's House" by a white naval officer "several years younger" than she. Rejecting what he has been told about Sui Sin Far, and ignoring her protests, he evaluates her solely by what he thinks he sees, equating her with "the sweet little Chinese girls I met when we were at Hong Kong." His judgment that "They're not so shy!" exposes the inconsistency of ethnic and gender stereotypes ("Leaves," 130). "The" Chinese woman is at once shy and sexually available. The facts of Sui Sin Far's identity are immaterial, since a white man, an officer in the Queen's navy, a representative of the colonial power of Britain over Jamaica and Hong Kong, has classified her as a "little Chinese girl." His dictum assumes that the sexual availability of women of color is an inevitable component of their race.

These gender- and racially coded relations of visual power characterize the enterprise of photo-making as well, especially in the early moments of the twentieth century, when the photographic gaze—conventionally coded as masculine—dictates, arranges, and overpowers its feminized subjects.[50] "Leaves," however, resists these unequal relations of power. Sui Sin Far's textual eye/I is both inside and outside the picture frame. She is simultaneously spectator, analyst, and participant. Unlike portrait photographs or Kodak candids, both of which are anchored in a fixed point of view, Sui Sin Far's sketches are mobile, made by a *flâneuse*, a feminine observer of the spectacle of urban life. This feminine mobility, like the omnibus form, becomes possible only in the new urban spaces of museums, department stores, panoramas, and travel. Formerly, such a woman would have been considered a "carnal commodity. . . . The female *flâneur* was not possible until a woman could wander the city on her own."[51] Sui Sin Far moves through racial classifications, national locations, and temporal moments. She decides how her vignettes will be framed, rather than being placed in them by another representer. This is not to claim that she has total freedom in the process; rather, she manipulates the conventions of representation that her readers will recognize and accept as veracious.[52]

In "Leaves from the Mental Portfolio of an Eurasian," Sui Sin Far constructs multiple versions of herself, merging representer and representation. She begins her essay by announcing a doubled point of view: "*When I look back over the years I see myself*" ("Leaves," 125; emphasis added).[53] Having brought herself under visual scrutiny, she trains her eye on men, as well—both Chinese and white: "Chinese men . . . compare favorably with the white men of my acquaintance in mind and heart qualities. Some of them are quite handsome. They have not as finely cut noses and as well developed chins as the white men, but they have smoother skins and their expression is more serene; their hands are better shaped and their voices softer" ("Leaves," 128). Her multiple perspective simultaneously endorses "white" assumptions about racially coded and racially valued physiognomic features while suggesting that physical features other than the cranium can signify character and culture. Finally, she brings under scrutiny the racist behavior of even well-intentioned Americans. Joining some midwesterners at a dinner party, she observes, evaluates, and transcribes their ignorant dismissals of Chinese railroad laborers. Her "employer," for example, sees Chinese faces as "utterly devoid of expression." The "town clerk" confesses, "A Chinaman is, *in my eyes*, more repulsive than a nigger." Her landlady declares that she "wouldn't have one in my house." The episode concludes as Sui Sin Far courageously re-turns their gaze: "*I raise my eyes from my plate.* 'Mr. K.,' I say, addressing my employer, 'I want you to understand that I am—I am a Chinese'" ("Leaves," 129; emphases added). This scene's conclusion aptly demonstrates Annette White-Parks's observation that "Sui Sin Far's narrative stance forces her European-based audience to enter into dialogue with those they have customarily conceived as 'the Other' and even to see themselves, through alternative eyes, in a position of 'Other-ness.'"[54]

Consistent with her refusal to accept restrictions of gender by following an inappropriately feminine path, Sui Sin Far publicly appropriates signs of masculine authority and citizenship. Although "Leaves" does not include illustrative candid family photographs, it did appear under the authenticating sign of her photographic portrait, as did the poetic album of her predecessor, Walt Whitman.[55] "Leaves" first appeared in the *Independent* under the half-page photographic portrait of Sui Sin Far. In this portrait, as in others she published with her writings, Sui Sin Far adopts the conventions of pose and self-presentation associated with heroic portrait in photography's first public national uses. This "civic" pose is formal, not candid. It generally shows the head and shoulders of its subjects, who either directly address the camera's gaze or, more frequently, assume a three-quarter pose, gazing thoughtfully into the distance. Its subjects are formally attired, their costume signifying social entitlement. The physical props accompanying the portrait reinforce these codes of class privilege. Generally, the background is muted, although not blank. Drapes, columns, and landscapes may suggest the antique or British romanticism. Intellectuals and statesmen frequently hold props—books, pen and paper, gavels—that suggest their occupations. The sitters are bathed in a flatteringly diffused light or illuminated from above or behind their heads.

In her portraits, Sui Sin Far demonstrates her command of these conventions of class-based photographic self-fashioning. In the image accompanying "Leaves," for example, she assumes a pose that approximates that of the twelve solemn gentlemen featured in Mathew Brady's *Gallery of Illustrious Americans* (1850).[56] The purpose of this and similar volumes was to circulate and perpetuate the appearances and traits understood to constitute an American civic identity. As Marcus Aurelius Root explained in 1864 to the first viewers of such images, there was significant "moral benefit to be derived from viewing portraits of America's political and social elite—'the great and the good, the heroes, saints and sages.'" Adopting similar conventions of self-representation, Sui Sin Far joins herself to a visual tradition in which portrait sitters have learned to adopt similar poses and thus "present themselves as good Americans in a quest for upward mobility."[57]

At first glance, the photographic portraits of Sui Sin Far seem to be at odds with their accompanying texts. Whereas she presents herself textually as a laboring woman, wasted and emaciated from years of poor nutrition, illness, and a peripatetic lifestyle, her photographic portraits present her as a self-conscious Author.[58] Bust-length images of Sui Sin Far show her in three-quarter posture, often framed in the Victorian oval. Such "cultivated asymmetries of the aristocratic pose" are, according to Suren Lalvani, "a function of leisure, while frontality confirms the complete lack of it."[59] Her body is illuminated from above; she is dressed formally, even elaborately, in western clothing (in explicit contrast to the portraits of Onoto Watanna). She is often posed with a book against a plain background or a background of indistinct landscape, her status as a literary woman constituting her sole significance.

This disjunction between image and text echoes the episodic and non-linear structure of "Leaves" and the portfolio form generally. Such a refusal of coherence reinforces Sui Sin Far's effort to free herself from the limitations of gender and ethnicity. In her portraits, she has represented her body as a "symbolic text." Such a transformation is made possible, according to Lalvani, by "leisure, or that which signifies freedom from the necessity of reproducing the body." In the case of Sui Sin Far, such freedom has its literal referent in her refusal to marry and bear children. Her formal portraits separate her womanly body from its "brute facticity." Her body is thus "reconstituted and mediated by the photograph as text and posed as cultural value at some distance from itself."[60] Thus while Sui Sin Far is never entirely free of the conventions of self-representation, especially as a gendered subject, she does selectively emphasize those that remove her from the confining bounds of gender and ethnicity and that insert her, instead, into a larger narrative of the heroic. As she told the readers of the Boston Globe, she has discovered that "the true fathers and mothers of the world [are] those who battled through great trials and hardships to leave to future generations noble and inspiring truths."[61]

Sui Sin Far's textual and photographic self-fashioning mark her attempts to associate herself with a more abstract notion of parenthood. Rather than allow herself to be seen as a dead branch on the family tree, she asserts that her writings are her "dear children."[62] In figuring her books as her progeny she steps away from the typically feminine role and appropriates a trope that is more properly masculine. In assuming the civic portrait pose, she joins the genealogy of civic leaders whom she came to see as the "true fathers and mothers of the world." Thus her writings and photographs create a new fiction of gender, escaping the binary notions that assigned to women the limited roles of physical reproduction and reserved to men the more "elevated" work of intellectual, cultural, and political reproduction.

Conclusion

If, as Richard Rudisill suggests, Brady's *Gallery of Illustrious Americans* constitutes a "[conscious effort] to display the nation in her ideal character as defined by images of the men who determined it," Sui Sin Far's individual portraits constitute a photomontage of a new transnational face.[63] These portraits bear no resemblance to the Orientalist boudoir images that so titillated an earlier generation of Americans. Whereas those earlier images purported to unveil the mysterious women of the East, Sui Sin Far's portraits cloak her own identity in a mystery that has little to do with simplistic ideas of race. Nor do they resemble the engravings illustrating such magazine features as Sui Sin Far's "Chinese Women in America." Ultimately, they resist the putatively straightforward documentary function of genealogical photography whose apparent guarantee is racial entitlement.

Lest her portrait images be subsumed into whiteness, their captions and contexts insist that Sui Sin Far is "Half Chinese" or "our little 'Chinese Contributor.'"[64] Captions, however, cannot stabilize the photographs' ambiguous content. Nor can authorial photographs guarantee an unchanging coherence in their texts. Meaning oscillates among the genres of autobiography, portfolio, and image, reinforcing Sui Sin Far's final claim to "have no nationality" ("Leaves," 132). Image, genre, and text together follow the conventions of realism and middle-class respectability in the late nineteenth century but demonstrate, in the process, that endurance, character, and courage should take precedence over ideological notions of eugenics, properly gendered behavior, and racial/national entitlement in determining citizenship in a transnational republic of letters.

Notes

I am indebted to the Hellman Family Foundation for generous fellowship funding that aided me in preparing this essay. I also wish to thank the Chinese Historical Society of San Francisco for mailing me resources. Carolyn Haynes and Timothy Powell gave careful editorial responses that immensely improved the essay's argument.

1. Sui Sin Far, "Leaves from the Mental Portfolio of an Eurasian, *Independent* 66 (21 January 1909): 132. All subsequent citations to "Leaves" are from this source and will be noted parenthetically in the text.

2. Xiao-Huang Yin, "Between the East and West: Sui Sin Far—The First Chinese-American Woman Writer," *Arizona Quarterly* 47, no. 4 (1991): 49–84; see also Amy Ling, "Edith Eaton: Pioneer Chinamerican Writer and Feminist," *American Literary Realism* 16, no. 2 (1983): 287–98; Amy Ling, "Pioneers and Paradigms: The Eaton Sisters," in *Between Worlds: Women Writers of Chinese Ancestry*, ed. Amy Ling (New York: Pergamon Press, 1990), 21.

3. Literary historians have classified Sui Sin Far as a "Fictionist," a category that emphasizes her imaginative writing while scanting her journalism, documentary work, and autobiographical essays. S. E. Solberg, "Sui Sin Far/Edith Eaton: First Chinese-American Fictionist," *MELUS: The Journal of the Society for the Study of Multi-Ethnic Literature of the United States* 8, no. 1 (1981): 27–39; see also Amy Ling, introduction to "Short Fiction from Mrs. *Spring Fragrance*," in Mrs. *Spring Fragrance and Other Writings*, ed. Amy Ling and Annette White-Parks (Urbana: University of Illinois Press, 1995), 11. Yin declares, "Among the early Chinese immigrant authors, [Sui Sin Far] was virtually the only one who engaged in writing imaginative literature rather than social-anthropological works." Yin, "Between the East and West," 49. Ling and White-Parks endorse this distinction. Introduction to Mrs. *Spring Fragrance and Other Writings*, ed. Ling and White-Parks, 2.

4. Jeffery Paul Chan et al., "An Introduction to Chinese-American and Japanese-American Literatures," in *Three American Literatures: Essays in Chicano, Native American, and Asian-American Literature for Teachers of American Literature*, ed. Houston A. Baker, Jr. (New York: Modern Language Association of America, 1982), 204.

5. See Ann Douglas, for example, who condemns the ephemeral, and, in her opinion, self-deprecating, apologetic, "personal and subjective" tone of short essays and sketches. Ann Douglas, *The Feminization of American Culture* (New York: Alfred A. Knopf, 1977), 286–87. Elizabeth Ammons counters such evaluations, suggesting that Sui Sin Far "did not share the mid twentieth-century bias against short fiction, sketches, and vignettes as inferior 'sub-genres' of the novel." Elizabeth Ammons, *Conflicting Stories: American Women Writers at the Turn into the Twentieth Century* (New York: Oxford University Press, 1992), 117.

6. Solberg, "Sui Sin Far," 32; 35; 27.

7. Amy Ling, "Creating One's Self: The Eaton Sisters," in *Reading the Literatures of Asian America*, ed. Shirley Geok-lin Lim and Amy Ling (Philadelphia: Temple University Press, 1992), 309. Unlike the Chinese, the Japanese were admired. They had not migrated in great numbers to the United States. They did not threaten to compete with white laborers for scarce jobs, as did thousands of Chinese laborers laid off after the completion of the transcontinental railroads. Finally, in an era that valued bravery and militancy, Japan's wars against China (1895) and Russia (1905) were seen as a "noble embodiment of the samurai tradition." Ling, "Creating" 309.

8. Other discriminatory legislation in Canada included an 1896 law imposing "head taxes" of ten dollars per person on Chinese immigrants; by 1904 those taxes had risen to five hundred dollars per person. In 1914, Montreal proposed to segregate "Oriental schoolchildren." Ling, "Pioneers," 29.

   The United States pursued similar discriminatory legislation, beginning with the Foreign Miners Tax (1853), which forbade noncitizens to mine precious metals in California. Other legislation included statutes such as the California miscegenation laws, which prohibited white/"Mongolian" marriages (1880); the segregation of Chinese children from "white" schools in San Francisco (1893); and a series of Chinese Exclusion Acts, beginning in 1882 and not rescinded until 1943.

9. Quoted in Annette White-Parks, *Sui Sin Far/Edith Maude Eaton: A Literary Biography* (Urbana: University of Illinois Press, 1995), 64.

10. Richard H. Brodhead, *The School of Hawthorne* (New York: Oxford University Press, 1986), 59.

11. See, for example, Marion van Riper Palmer, "The Women's Patriotic Societies," *The Ladies' Home Journal*, July 1897, 35. This article describes ten such organizations, founded between 1890 and 1896. Sui Sin Far's "Engaged Girl in China" appeared in *The Ladies' Home Journal* in January 1902. Her sister Onoto Watanna published "My Impressions of American Women" in the *Journal* in April 1899.

12. Donald K. Pickens, *Eugenics and the Progressives* (Nashville, Tenn.: Vanderbilt University Press, 1968), 16.

13. Peter Thomas Conmy, *The Origin and Purposes of the Native Sons and Native Daughters of the Golden West* (San Francisco: Dolores Press, 1956), 9. The purpose of the Native Sons of the Golden West, founded in 1875, was to bring into being "a living, self-perpetuating monument in memory of [the pioneer] forebears of the gold rush era." Conmy, *Origin and Purposes*, 5. The date of birth required for membership commemorates "the raising by Commodore Sloat of the Stars and Stripes at Monterey," which "proclaimed California under American rule." Ibid., 9. The Native Daughters of the Golden West was founded in 1886.

14. Sue Fawn Chung, "The Chinese American Citizens Alliance: An Effort in Assimilation, 1895–1965," *Chinese America: History and Perspectives, 1988*, 32.

The Los Angeles Chapter of the Native Sons of the Golden State was incorporated in May 1915. Sui Sin Far was apparently aware of such societies and their nationalist and accommodationist agendas. She commented indirectly on the exclusionary effect of their work in the essays she published in California periodicals. For example, in "Chinatown Needs a School," written for the *Los Angeles Express* in 1903, she profiles the Sing family, one of the "most prominent" in Chinese Los Angeles. Mrs. Sing, "educated a Christian and Americanized," hopes that a government school will be established in Chinatown to serve children who refuse to or cannot afford to adopt western dress. All ten Sing children "wear the comfortable Chinese dress," but "speak . . . English fluently" and bear Anglicized names. They are, she stresses, "native sons and daughters of the Golden West"—well educated children of pure (albeit Chinese) breeding, elevated social class, born in California well after 1846. Sui Sin Far, "Chinatown Needs a School," *Los Angeles Express*, 14 October 1903, 6. Although the Sing children are citizens, they are excluded from the rights of citizenship, including education. Here Sui Sin Far's ambivalent stance toward assimilation becomes apparent. She advocates the right of children of mixed racial heritage to follow Chinese custom as well as to claim their rights as citizens. Yet her apparently intentional use of the phrase "native sons and daughters of the Golden West" emphasizes that Chinese who do not wish to assimilate have little or no claim to patriotic identity and to its political advantages.

15. "Trefusis" takes several spellings, among them "Trepesis" or "Trefusius." Ling, "Pioneers," 26; White-Parks, *Sui Sin Far*, 10.

16. White-Parks, *Sui Sin Far*, 12.

17. Yin contrasts the authenticity and Chinese signification of Sui Sin Far's name (Sui Sin Far=water fragrant flower=Narcissus="dignity and indestructible love for family and homeland") to Winnifred's fabricated Japanese pseudonym, Onoto Watanna. According to Yin, Winnifred traded "her birthright for recognition and popularity." Yin, "Between the East and West," 54. The biblical allusion is not Yin's, but echoes Winnifred Eaton's autobiographical *Me* (1915), where she laments: "Oh, I

had sold my birthright for a mess of potage [sic]." Ling, "Pioneers," 31. Ling removes the discussion of Winnifred's choice from the moralizing binary of resistance/accommodation and more productively classifies her as a "literary trickster." Ling, "Creating," 307.

18. Ling, "Pioneers," 36.

19. Ling, "Creating," 310. Of *The Diary of Delia,* Ling writes, "Thus, for the first, and undoubtedly only, time in literary history, we have a novel written in Irish American dialect by a Chinese Eurasian Canadian published under a Japanese name."

20. The mutability of Sui Sin Far's name suggests the range of her ethnic identification. According to Yin, "In contrast to the popular belief that Sui only adopted her pseudonym in publications, she also used it in real life. In an [apparently undated] autobiographical letter written to Harold Rugg, a Dartmouth College student and an admirer of her writing, she says: 'Perhaps I should say "they," as I have both an English and a Chinese name.'" Yin, "Between the East and West," 81 n. 7).Ling and White-Parks suggest that Sui Sin Far is a self-chosen pseudonym that signifies her choice of Anglo-Chinese identity. Ling, "Pioneers," 21, and *Mrs. Spring Fragrance and Other Writings,* ed. Ling and White-Parks, 189 n. 30. According to Ling, the choice emphasizes her matronymic over her patronymic. Ling, "Creating," 307. Ammons argues that "while the various flower translations of the words *Sui Sin Far* conform to [the Chinese custom of giving people positive names], the English words *sin* and *far* certainly do not. Add to them the meaning of *sui* in Latin, 'of herself,' and a cryptic phrase made up of western words hovers within the Anglicized Chinese name. The phrase might read, 'Of sin far herself.'" Ammons, *Conflicting Stories,* 120. Ammons's footnote explains that "at the time that Sui Sin Far wrote, she could have spelled her name any way she wished and thus avoided the words *sin* and *far*. . . . She did not have to encode the Chinese sounds in western words that have clear meanings." Ibid., 216 n. 19. Indeed, she used variants that include *Sui Seen Far* and *Sui Sin Fah.* White-Parks's traces the changes in how Sui Sin Far signed her publications, linking those changes with the changes in how she understood her racial identity. Annette White-Parks, "Naming as Identity, Sui Sin Far," in *A Gathering of Voices on the Asian American Experience,* ed. Annette White-Parks et al. (Fort Atkinson, Wis.: Highsmith Press, 1994), 73–80.

21. C. F. L., [Charles F. Lummis], "In Western Letters," *The Land of Sunshine* 13, no.4 (1900):336.

22. Ling, "Creating," 306.

23. Fourteen of sixteen children of Edward and Lotus Blossom Eaton "survived into adulthood." Ling, "Pioneers," 26.

24. Sui Sin Far, "Sui Sin Far, the Half Chinese Writer, Tells of Her Career," *Boston Globe,* 5 May 1912.

25. Ling assumes this is an autobiographical sketch. "Edith Eaton," 289, and "Pioneers," 29–30.

26. Sui Sin Far's writings entered a literary context whose Orientalist assumptions had been formed by dozens, if not hundreds, of books published in the last decades of the nineteenth century and the first decade of the twentieth, including Onoto Watanna's fictions. White women associated with missionary societies pandered to assumptions about "Oriental" behavior by publishing such sensational fictions as Lu Wheat's *The Third Daughter: A Story of Chinese Home Life* (1906); Helen Clark's *The Lady of the Lily Feet and Other Tales of Chinatown* (1900); Eliza J. Gillette's *Daughters of China* (1853); and Henrietta Shuck's *Scenes in China; or Sketches of the Country, Religion, and Customs of the Chinese, by the late Mrs. Henrietta Shuck, Missionary of China* (1852). For lists of such publications, see Joan Jacobs Brumberg, "Zenanas and Girlless Villages: The Ethnology of American Evangeli-

cal Women, 1870–1910," *Journal of American History* 69, no. 2 (1982): 368 nn. 70 and 71, and Solberg, "Sui Sin Far," 37 n. 10. White, entitled male writers took advantage of the Orientalist trend as well. Jack London, for instance, published a number of sinophobic texts, including a horrific short story, "The Unparalleled Invasion" (1906), which ends with the elimination of China by United States– initiated germ warfare. See Solberg, "Sui Sin Far," 37 nn. 14–16, for other such texts. Those who published books written by the Eaton sisters also took advantage of the public's fascination with the supposed exoticism of the Orient by printing them on delicate, decorated papers, embellished with calligraphy and ink sketches.

27. The image also prefigures the modernist poets' fascination with Oriental imagery. Ezra Pound's "In a Station of the Metro" (1916), in some ways a miniature analog to Sui Sin Far's "A Trip in a Horse Car," likens "faces in the crowd" to "Petals on a wet, black bough." Ezra Pound, "In a Station of the Metro," in *The Heath Anthology of American Literature*, 2nd ed., vol. 2, ed. Paul Lauter et al. (Lexington, Mass.: D. C. Heath, 1994), 1261).

28. Miles Orvell, "Reproducing Walt Whitman: The Camera, the Omnibus and *Leaves of Grass*," *Prospects* 12 (1987): 321–22. Textual cognates to the omnibus cultural spaces of museums, galleries, department stores, and panoramas include collections of loosely related short stories such as Sherwood Anderson's *Winesburg, Ohio* (1919) and Sarah Orne Jewett's *The Country of the Pointed Firs* (1896); magazines, diaries, and journals; catalogues, anthologies, and encyclopedias; and episodic travel writing.

   Benjamin's concept of "panoramic literature" is similar. Both he and Orvell link this genre to technological changes in the nineteenth century. According to Benjamin, "Contemporary to the panoramas is a panoramic literature. . . . They consist of isolated sketches, the anecdotal form of which corresponds to the plastic foreground of the panorama, and their informational base to its painted background." Quoted in Suren Lalvani, *Photography, Vision, and the Production of Modern Bodies* (Albany: State University of New York Press, 1996), 183.

29. Orvell, "Reproducing Walt Whitman," 342. Interestingly, Sui Sin Far's first published sketch, "A Trip in a Horse Car," is overtly such an omnibus form. It studies the riders who board a Montreal car, "a microcosmic gathering of human beings." White-Parks, *Sui Sin Far*, 65. Sui Sin Far also wrote promotional material for the railroads.

30. See, for example, Frances Benjamin Johnston, *The Hampton Album: 44 Photographs from an Album of Hampton Institute* (New York: Museum of Modern Art, 1966); Jacob A. Riis, *How the Other Half Lives* (1890; reprint, New York: Dover, 1971); and Arnold Genthe, *Old Chinatown: A Book of Pictures by Arnold Genthe*, text by Will Irwin (New York: Mitchell Kennerley, 1913).

31. Yin, "Between the East and West," 50, 58.

32. Sui Sin Far, "Sui Sin Far."

33. Philip Stokes, "The Family Photograph Album: So Great a Cloud of Witnesses," in *The Portrait in Photography*, ed. Graham Clarke (London: Reaktion, 1992), 194.

34. In 1897 and 1898, *The Ladies' Home Journal* printed the following articles: a four-part series entitled "Amateur Photography at Its Best" (January through April 1897); Frances Benjamin Johnston's "What a Woman Can Do With a Camera" (September 1897); "Getting Good Pictures of Children" (February 1898); and "Photographing Children at Home" (December 1898). During these same years, a number of advertisements touted Kodak cameras' portability and usefulness for capturing "Baby's Picture." I am indebted to Shawn Smith for increasing my interest in the uses of domestic photography in the late-nineteenth-century United States.

See Shawn Michelle Smith, "Superficial Depths: Visions of Identity in the Age of Mechanical Reproduction, 1839–1900" (Ph.D. diss., University of California, San Diego, 1994).

35. For a detailed study of how these same technologies of collection, photography, filing, anthropomorphic measurement, and fingerprinting operated in criminal discourse and national eugenic projects, see Alan Sekula, "The Body and the Archive," *October* 39 (1986): 3–64.

36. Ling, "Pioneers," 25; 50.

37. White-Parks, *Sui Sin Far*, 58 n. 77.

38. Sui Sin Far's grand-nephew, L. Charles Laferriere, who owns a photograph of May, believes that this anecdote refers to May. Ling, "Creating," 317 n. 5. The photograph in question is reproduced in White-Parks, *Sui Sin Far*, 38.

39. By contrast, the autobiographical essay Sui Sin Far wrote for the Boston *Globe* in 1912 is a linear and coherent narrative written in past tense. Its coherence suggests the teleological development by which a highly motivated writer has matured into an Author.

40. Julia Hirsch, *Family Photographs: Content, Meaning, and Effect* (New York: Oxford University Press, 1981), 32. The narrative content of photographic images does change over time. See, for example, recent studies of funeral, memorial, and death-bed photography in the nineteenth century by Cathy Davidson, "Photographs of the Dead: Sherman, Daguerre, Hawthorne," *South Atlantic Quarterly* 89, no. 4 (1990): 667–70; Jay Ruby, *Secure the Shadow: Death and Photography in America* (Cambridge, Mass.: MIT Press, 1995); and Stanley Burns, comp., *Sleeping Beauty: Memorial Photography in America* (Altadena, Calif.: Twelvetrees Press, 1990). For a complex and important consideration of the connection of commodity culture and memorial photography, see Karen Sanchez-Eppler, "Keeping the Loss: Reproduction and the Dead Child" (paper read at the Nineteenth-Century American Women Writers in the Twenty-first Century conference, Hartford, Conn., May 1996).

41. Hirsch, *Family Photographs*, 118.

42. Judith Williamson, "Family, Education, Photography." In *Culture/ Power/ History: A Reader in Contemporary Social Theory*, ed. Nicholas B. Dirks, Geoff Eley, and Sherry B. Ortner (Princeton, N.J.: Princeton University Press, 1994), 238.

43. This image was not included in the original edition of *How the Other Half Lives* but is reproduced in the Dover edition, which supplements Riis's first edition with photographs from the City Museum of New York's Jacob A. Riis Collection. These additional photographs have been captioned by the museum.

44. According to Horace Greeley's catalog commentary to the 1853 New York Crystal Palace exhibition, the manufacture of artificial flowers was the art that most nearly approached "the mimicry of nature." Greeley writes, "The Italians seem to have been the first European nation who attained any degree of excellence in the art, but they were soon surpassed by the French, who have ever since maintained their pre-eminence. . . . The flower-trade gives constant employment throughout the year to a large number of women and children . . . [whose] wages average from one dollar to six per week; and some children become so expert, after a short time, that they are enabled to contribute to the support of their families." Horace Greeley, ed., *Art and Industry as Represented in the Exhibition at the Crystal Palace*(New York: Redfield, 1853), 162, 163, 165.

45. Riis, *Other Half*, 123.

46. Ibid., 23.

47. Ibid., 77.

48. Ibid., 80.

49. Ibid., 78.

50. This gender coding occurs in nineteenth-century studio photography, in pornography, in documentary, and in anthropological/scientific photography. For some notable exceptions, see the work of U.S. photographer Francis Benjamin Johnston. See also Abigail Solomon-Godeau, "The Legs of the Countess," *October* 39 (1986): 65–105.

51. Anne Friedberg, "*Les Flâneurs du Mal(l)*: Cinema and the Postmodern Condition," *PMLA* 106, no. 3 (1991): 421. For a dissenting opinion, see Janet Wolff, who argues against the possibility of *flânerie* for women, positing that "the literature of modernity describes the experience of men" and overlooks feminine experience and points of view." Janet Wolff, "The Invisible *Flâneuse*: Women and the Literature of Modernity," *Feminine Sentences: Essays on Women and Culture* (Cambridge, England: Polity Press, 1990), 34.

52. Solomon-Godeau, for example, posits that a woman who controls her own photographic representation engages in an "individual act of expression [that] is underwritten by conventions that make her less an author than a scribe." Solomon-Godeau, "Legs of the Countess," 67.

53. Such doubling is a quintessentially feminine characteristic, and an important concept for feminist visual theory. The phenomenon is eloquently described by John Berger: "A woman must continually watch herself. . . . From earliest childhood she has been taught and persuaded to survey herself continually. And so she comes to consider the surveyed and the surveyor within her as the two constituent yet always distinct elements of her identity as a woman." John Berger, *Ways of Seeing* (London: British Broadcasting Company, 1972), 46.

54. White-Parks, *Sui Sin Far*, 151.

55. In the first edition of *Leaves of Grass* (1855) Whitman "[withheld] his name from the title page, and [instead presented] his portrait, neatly engraved on steel" by S. Hollyer following a daguerreotype by Gabriel Harrison. Charles Eliot Norton, quoted in Alan Trachtenberg, *Reading American Photographs: Images as History Mathew Brady to Walker Evans* (New York: Hill and Wang, 1989), 62. This image changed in the subsequent editions of the book, demonstrating both the organic growth of the poem and the bodily changes of its author. According to Trachtenberg, "In 1876 he replaced the cold typeface bearing his name with an engraved signature. All editions opened with a frontispiece portrait, never the same, all showing him as he looked contemporary with the book. Signature and image provided organic expressions of the living author. . . . Whitman imagined his book as if it were a living daguerrean image." 67.

56. Brady's *Gallery* is a perfect example of Orvell's "omnibus form," as well. Its publishers originally intended to issue twenty-four daguerreotype portraits, translated into reproducible lithographs by Francis D'Avignon. These would be sent "monthly to subscribers, with binding into a permanent volume optional at the end of the year." Trachtenberg, *Reading American Photographs*, 45. Because the publishers insisted on maintaining a high quality, both in the lithography and in the overall presentation of the images, the project became extremely expensive, and only twelve images were issued. Barbara McCandless, "The Portrait Studio and the Celebrity: Promoting the Art," in *Photography in Nineteenth-Century America*, ed. Martha A. Sandweiss (Fort Worth, Tex.: Amon Carter Museum, 1991), 57. See also John Plumbe's *National Plumbeotype Gallery*, published in 1847, a portfolio version of the Plumbe National Daguerreotype Gallery on Broadway, cited in McCandless, "Portrait Studio," 55. The textual cognate to such collections of civic heroes is Ralph Waldo Emerson's *Representative Men* (1850).

57. McCandless, "The Portrait Studio," 49.

58. Images of Sui Sin Far were reproduced and circulated in *The Chautauquan, The Land of Sunshine, The International Examiner, The Independent,* and *The Boston*

Globe. Recently, Annette White-Parks has prefaced her biography of Sui Sin Far with a variant of the authorial portrait, this one a full-length, three-quarter view that emphasizes Sui Sin Far's gender and class status and thus is more appropriate to a late-twentieth-century understanding of authorship.

59. Lalvani, *Photography*, 66.
60. Ibid., 66.
61. Sui Sin Far, "Sui Sin Far."
62. Sui Sin Far, *Mrs. Spring Fragrance* (Chicago: A. C. McClurg, 1912), vii.
63. Richard Rudisill, *Mirror Image: The Influence of the Daguerreotype on American Society* (Albuquerque: University of New Mexico Press, 1971), 229.
64. Sui Sin Far, "Sui Sin Far"; Sui Sin Far, "The Chinese Woman in America," *The Land of Sunshine* 6, no. 2 (1897): 59–64.

Chapter 11

Miscegen(r)ation or Mestiza Discourse?: Feminist and Racial Politics in *Ramona* and *Iola Leroy*

DIANE PRICE HERNDL

WHEN WE READ NINETEENTH-CENTURY women's novels about race, what do we hope to find? Why do we read such novels in the first place? Are we looking for texts that speak to or for a particular cultural moment, to give us an authentic view of the times? What would such an "authentic" view look like? Do we look at these texts as aesthetic objects? In her 1981 essay "Archimedes and the Paradox of Feminist Criticism," Myra Jehlen raised the problem for feminist criticism of coping with texts about which our aesthetic and ideological opinions conflict; she suggests that often we find ourselves recognizing the aesthetic quality of fictions that are nonetheless politically reprehensible, while finding some fictions whose ideological stances we find comfortable just not very aesthetically pleasing.[1] To my mind, the conflict she describes has yet to be solved, is perhaps insoluble. But the lack of a resolution to the problem is not reason to ignore it, to pretend that we can read historical, political fiction without an ideological—even an ethical—filter, or that we can teach such texts without any reference back to their aesthetics. This problem becomes acute, I think, when we read texts that deal with racial and gender questions, especially if we find ourselves torn not only between ethics and aesthetics but even between competing ethics when the racial politics and the gender politics conflict. This is particularly complicated when we read a text in terms of its political and social background, looking to fiction for evidence of historical reality—at its production of an "authentic" voice or vision, or its participation in constructing racial and gendered selves. Using two race novels from the late nineteenth century, both written by women, I want to suggest some ways we can cope with the problems of conflicting ethics and aesthetics by taking into account the novels' own heterodoxy and diversity.

Helen Hunt Jackson's 1884 *Ramona* and Frances E. W. Harper's 1892 *Iola Leroy, or Shadows Uplifted* themselves challenge a lot of ideas about race, authenticity, and genre.[2] The title characters are women of mixed race, women who face the choice, in fact, of the race to which they will belong. Both novels are simultaneously sentimental and antisentimental, are protest novels that nonetheless center on romance. They present narrative resolutions that do not resolve the problems at issue in the novels and offer visions of their heroines' success that challenge and accede to traditional ideas of success.

David Goodman Croly's tract, *Miscegenation: The Theory of the Blending of the Races, Applied to the American White Man and Negro*, written in 1863 to defend the idea of racial equality, begins with a definition: "*Miscegenation*—from the Latin *Miscere*, to mix, and *Genus*, race, is used to denote the abstract idea of the mixture of two or more races."[3] While both *Ramona* and *Iola Leroy* feature heroines who are of mixed race, the novels themselves feature a mixture of "genus" in a more literary context; both novels represent a mixture of *genres*, or at least subgenres. Both are, in one sense, sentimental tales, but Jackson's sentimentalism is blended with the social-problem novel, as well as with the "tragic, doomed Indian" novel, and Harper's is strongly influenced by the slave-narrative tradition.[4] The rather awkward neologism I'm using in the title of this essay—miscegen(r)ation—is therefore meant to call attention to both the mixing of races and the mixing of genres. By attending to these mixtures, this diversity of racial and literary backgrounds, I believe we can find a way not to resolve but to understand and perhaps use the difficulties facing readings of these books that would try to take into account feminist, multicultural, and aesthetic interpretations.

Racial Politics: Authenticity and Disharmony

One of the continuing problems in reading nineteenth-century literature has been the difficulty of identifying or defining an "authentic" voice for women and members of minority cultures. "True" slave voices (and languages) have been all but lost, Native American voices (and languages) are never fairly represented, and the freed African American is usually represented as either a stereotypical fool or a cultured orator, steeped in an Anglo tradition (sometimes even in writings by African-Americans). This problem is very often related to genre. It is perhaps most clearly outlined in Houston Baker's essay "Autobiographical Acts and the Voice of the Southern Slave," in which Baker raises the problem of authenticity and the construction of a black self through language, arguing that in the process of "transmuting an authentic, unwrit-

ten self—a self that exists outside the conventional literary discourse structures of a white reading public—into a literary representation" the ex-slave
loses an "authentic" self.[5] Similarly, James Olney, in "'I Was Born': Slave Narratives as Autobiography and Literature," examines the influence of the white
sentimental novelistic tradition on slave narratives; he concludes that the sentimental, abolitionist sensibility that sponsored the publication of slave narratives actually defined the slave's narrative for the slave. He suggests that in
narratives written under the guidance and control of abolitionists "the narrators show themselves more or less content to remain slaves to a prescribed,
conventional, and imposed form; or perhaps it would be more precise to say
that they were captive to the abolitionist intentions."[6] In contrast to Baker
and Olney's views, however, Claudia Tate, in "Allegories of Black Female Desire; or, Rereading Nineteenth-Century Sentimental Narratives of Black Female Authority," argues that African American women were not co-opted by
sentimentality but successfully adapted the form to accurately reflect both an
ambition for racial advancement and their own desires for familial stability.[7]
I suspect that as readers and, especially, as teachers of these novels, we need to
acknowledge the accuracy of all these views. The desire to find that "authentic"
voice, to "hear" the real character of the slave or the not-yet-dispossessed Native American is, after all, why we keep reading texts from the past, in the
hope of making some kind of human connection. And, surely, those writers
were as clever as we are in adapting forms to meet their needs, despite the
intervention of editors. But we also need to recognize the demands of those
forms in shaping not just what the writers were able to record but even the
framework through which those writers were able to recognize what was re-
cordable. In fiction that was as polemic as the slave narrative or the political
novel, especially, authenticity was probably never a real goal for the writer.
There were more immediate needs. Houston Baker, to be fair here, does not
advocate looking for authenticity in fiction; his subject is autobiography, and
he asserts that looking at the "truth-value of [an] assertion" in fiction is not
"a very fruitful analytical issue to pursue."[8] But both Jackson and Harper assert the "truth-value" of their fictions; both authors argue that we read their
texts for their cultural validity. I am, of course, raising the problem of "realism" in fiction generally; when we connect that difficulty with a sense of both
race and gender as *constructed* rather than given, then we've broached a very
large question of authenticity indeed. Reading these novels, we have to resist
being locked into an either/or position; we have to make room for a reading
that allows for accurate representation and polemic vision. This is what makes
Claudia Tate's reading of *Iola Leroy* so powerful: one has to temper any sense
of "reality" or "authenticity" in polemic fiction with a sense of the author's
vision, ambition, and desire.

Similarly, when Deborah McDowell examines the problem of racial "voice" in *Iola Leroy*, she urges contemporary readers to take into account the novel's social discourse and its circumstances of production. Written for a largely northern, white, female, and Christian audience, its goal was to induce those northerners to support reforms that would aid the homeless and displaced ex-slaves. In doing so, the novel represents black life with images that "[accord] with that audiences' horizon of social and literary expectations," rather than with anything that actually represents black life of the times.[9] Jackson's narrative, written for that same audience, addresses their attitudes and expectations in a similar vein in order to further the cause of racial tolerance and respect. But in making their heroines "just like" their northern white audience, do Harper and Jackson efface the very causes they were working toward? In making their heroines partially white by birth and mostly white by conventionality of attitude, do they enslave racial identities to "a prescribed, conventional, and imposed form," as James Olney argues, or do they open up the possibility of real intercourse between white women and women of color? In some ways, I think they do both, balancing a certain measure of realism with reformist rhetoric.

One way to understand the double consequences of these novels is to consider them as "mestiza" discourse, a mixed discourse, like the mixed-blood heroines. In her essay "*La conciencia de la mestiza*: Towards a New Consciousness" in *Making Face/Making Soul*, Gloria Anzaldúa explores the possibilities opened by a new "mestiza" consciousness and identity, one that, perhaps, will reveal all the strengths of the hybrid. She argues that this "new *mestiza* copes by developing a tolerance for contradictions, a tolerance for ambiguity. She learns to be an Indian in Mexican culture, to be Mexican from an Anglo point of view. She learns to juggle cultures. She has a plural personality, she operates in a pluralistic mode—nothing is thrust out, the good, the bad and the ugly, nothing rejected, nothing abandoned. Not only does she sustain contradictions, she turns the ambivalence into something else."[10]

If we look at the whole of these two novels—and not their narrative resolutions (to which I will return later)—I think we may see in them the hint of this very emerging mestiza consciousness. Iola is neither white nor black, but both, and thus embodies the racial unity that Harper envisions for society in her novel. Ramona, like the same mestiza Anzaldúa describes, is alternately Indian and Mexican in both Mexican and Anglo cultures; her tolerance and love for all good people, regardless of race, be they Indian, Mexican, or even Anglo serves as a model for the kind of peaceful coexistence Jackson urges in her pages. These two heroines of the nineteenth century achieve what Anzaldúa predicts will come: "The future will belong to the *mestiza*. Because the future depends on the breaking down of paradigms, it depends on the straddling of two or more cultures. By creating a new mythos—that is, a change in the way we perceive reality, the way we see ourselves and the ways we behave—*la mestiza* creates a new consciousness."[11] Jackson and Harper both work within this new mythos in creating mixed-race heroines who, in their consciousness of their own multiple racial identities, are indeed signs of a future racial harmony.

The novels, however, do not close on this note of racial harmony. Both heroines face prejudice, expulsion, rejection, and dislocation. The possibilities that Anzaldúa envisions do not materialize. She celebrates the "ambivalence" of *la mestiza*, her ability to be alternately from one race and then another, but she also recognizes that "she can be jarred out of ambivalence by an intense, and often painful, emotional event which inverts or resolves the ambivalence."[12] Anzaldúa envisions this resolution as a uniting of multiple consciousnesses into a new one. In *Iola Leroy* and *Ramona*, that intense, painful event does resolve the ambivalence, but by forcing the heroine to choose one racial consciousness over the other, not unite them. Anzaldúa imagines this new ambivalent consciousness as a blending, a hybrid consciousness that combines the best characteristics of both races. But in Harper's and Jackson's novels, the heroines face a choice not unlike Lacan's famous gender choice—it is as if there are doors marked "white" or "colored," "Indian" or "Mexican," that the heroines have to walk through. (Certainly, in the South Harper was writing about, these doors were literal, not metaphoric.) Ramona is Indian for a while, just as she had once been, and later becomes again, Mexican. Iola must choose whether to "pass" and renounce her black family and heritage or to become a black woman. There is no mestiza option for either of these women. And it is through this choice, in both novels, that the problems that Olney and Baker identify become apparent.

In the racially charged nineteenth century, the mixed-race heroines' existence is already problematic, and the authenticity of their voices as women of color is dubious since neither heroine is raised in the racial culture she finally chooses. Iola is raised as a white girl, goes to white schools, and knows other African Americans only as her slaves until she becomes, herself, a slave. Ramona, similarly, is raised in a privileged household, as an heiress in a wealthy Southern California hacienda, until she falls in love with one of the hired hands, a young Temecula Indian named Alessandro. Because of her love affair, she is disinherited by her aunt and discovers that she is not Mexican, as she had been raised to think, but the adopted, illegitimate child of a Scottish gold miner and a poor Indian woman. Both heroines also choose to follow in the "condition of their mothers"; each chooses a racial identity as a woman of color, a choice, again, being made by many women in our own time. What does it mean, though, for these nineteenth-century novels to represent those women as authentic voices for "their people"? In considering this, we confront the issues I raised earlier: this authentic racial self is a convention of a genre dominated by white, middle-class women.

This resolution of racial difference comes to a particularly troubling pass in *Ramona*. In this white-authored text, Ramona leaves behind her racial identity as an Indian after her husband's murder. In using two names for her heroine—the Spanish "Ramona" and an adaptation of a Temecula word, "Majella"—Jackson separates Ramona's "Indian self" from her "real" identity. When Ramona leaves her Mexican family with her lover Alessandro, she assumes the name Majella, but after Alessandro's death, she is reconstructed as Ramona when she reassumes her Mexican name and identity at her marriage to Felipe. In doing so she obliterates her Indian heritage, in a sense reenacting the cultural dislocation Jackson is writing against. When Felipe asks if she would like to leave California for Mexico, she confesses that her "most beautiful dream for [her daughter] would be, that she grow up in Mexico." This daughter, whom she had named Ramona, is three-quarters Indian by blood, but Ramona raises her as a Mexican in Mexico City, because she wants to "spare her daughter the burden she had gladly, heroically borne herself, in the bond of race" (*Ramona*, 359). This troubling narrative resolution raises not only the problems of authentic racial identity I have been discussing up to this point but also the problems of feminine/feminist individual success to which I will turn in a few pages.

The conclusion of *Iola Leroy* raises problems of its own—a kind of artificial racial identity and a "noblesse oblige" of the lighter-skinned African Americans ministering to the darker and more ignorant—but it does resolve the problem of racial identity by affirming the *value* of African American identity, however difficult it is in white culture to get jobs and housing, or just to live unmolested. It may be troublingly shaped by what one could call a white ethic or white conventions, but it is not, as one could argue that *Ramona* is, distorted against its own political sympathies by those forms.

These endings, I am suggesting, are finally determined by the hybrid genres they embody, rather than the hybrid race that their heroines do. If the heroines finally face a choice about which race they will claim, the authors, too, have to face the choice of what kind of novel they are writing: a sentimental romance? a social-protest novel? a kind of slave-narrative? a "doomed Indian" tale? That choice of genre determines the narrative resolution in ways that even the choice of race for the heroine does not, or rather, the choice of genre in some ways determines the choice of race itself, by forcing the writer to accede to certain ideas of realism and to shape certain of her desires and ambitions for her fiction.

Mixed Race / Mixed Genre

These two novels represent a very uneasy marriage of sentimental narrative and racial identity. Here, race becomes an issue of sentiment, and to the extent that the sentimental novel focuses on issues of love and marriage, race itself gets tied to that sentimental focus. The title characters face a very similar decision, and one faced by few other heroines of sentimental novels—the choice of the race to which they will belong. Ramona, who is half Native American and half white must choose whether to marry the Indian man she is in love with or the Mexican man who has been raised as her cousin and who loves her; the choice of husband becomes a choice of both racial and class identity—the Indian man is poor, the Mexican rich. But, like most heroines of sentimental romances, she makes her choice based on love and what the novel reveals to be her "natural" feelings, and chooses a life "with her people," despite its hardships and poverty. As do most sentimental writers, Helen Hunt Jackson has to come up with a "happy ending" for Ramona. Likewise, Iola Leroy, who is mixed African and white, is raised as a white girl (as a slave-owner, in fact) until she is betrayed and sold into slavery. In this Reconstruction-era novel, Iola must decide whether to live the postwar years as a worker among "her own people" or to marry a white man and attempt to "pass." Like Ramona's choice, Iola's is a choice of class as much as of race, and she chooses based on her "natural" feelings; she will follow her mother's condition and be black.

While both novels are sentimental, they are at the same time explicitly "protest" novels. Jackson, a white woman, had taken up the Native American cause several years before she wrote *Ramona* in the political tract *Century of Dishonor* (1881). She championed the rights of Native Americans, as she saw them; many of her "reforms" are now seen as in themselves regressive, but at the time, her crusades for *some* land—reservations—were better than the genocidal policies she was fighting against. Harper, an African American woman, was explicit about the fact that she was writing a novel with a "mission"; in her conclusion she expresses the hope that she will have "awaken[ed] in the hearts of our countrymen a stronger sense of justice and a more Christlike humanity" (*Iola Leroy*, 282).

Both novels employ the traditional narrative structure of the sentimental romance: a woman faces difficulties, but rises, marries, and lives happily. Both also temper that with strident and overt political commentary, however; they are more social commentary/protest novels than romances. This conflict of genre creates the novels' most serious problems: what happens to a narrative when romance becomes a vehicle for social commentary? One answer is that romance itself becomes political, and the politics of mixed-blood heritage and interracial marriage are foregrounded. Another answer is that, like the heroines who are forced into a choice of race, the writers are forced into a choice of novelistic conventions; rather than producing a hybrid, mestiza genre, they eventually give in to the forces of one genre. This conflict, rather than producing a harmonious blending, leads to the aesthetic problems to which I alluded earlier: disjunction in the narrative between its different parts, and endings that seem tacked on, that do not really resolve the deeper political issues that the narratives raise.

If, as Mikhail Bakhtin argues in *The Formal Method in Literary Scholarship*, genre is an ideological form, then the mixing of genres must of necessity mean a mixing of ideologies: "If we approach genre from the point of view of its intrinsic thematic relationship to reality and the generation of reality, we may say that every genre has its methods and means of seeing and conceptualizing reality which are accessible to it alone." Genre, according to this view, controls not just the way a writer can express ideas, but even what ideas can be seen:

> The process of seeing and conceptualizing reality must not be severed from the process of embodying it in the forms of a particular genre. It would be naive to assume that the painter sees everything first and then shapes what he saw and puts it onto the surface of his painting according to a certain technique. In real fact, seeing and representation merge. New means of representation force us to see new aspects of visible reality, but these new aspects cannot clarify or significantly enter our horizon if the new means necessary to consolidate them are lacking. . . .
>
> The same is true in literature. The artist must learn to see the reality with the eyes of the genre. A particular aspect of reality can only be understood in connection with the particular means of representing it.[13]

The blending of genres could, then, theoretically, afford precisely those new means necessary to consolidate new representations of reality. But if, as I have argued, the genres compete in a text instead of cooperating, the result can be that one "aspect of reality" wins out over another. This is what happens in *Iola Leroy* and *Ramona*.

The first half of *Iola Leroy* describes Iola's antebellum and Civil War experiences, her betrayal by a jealous uncle, her sale into slavery, her survival of slavery by her virtue and beauty, and her work as a nurse in a Civil War battle hospital. But the second half of the novel treats her postwar experiences of Reconstruction in a black middle-class elite; it is shaped by the conventions of a romantic genre that has to end with a happy marriage but dominated by the Reconstruction-era narrative genre of racial progress, perhaps most famously typified by Booker T. Washington's *Up From Slavery*. Iola is taken North, where she meets some of the best of abolitionist society, black and white, including a young white doctor who had fallen in love with her while she was working in the hospital. When he proposes to her and she refuses, he asks her to explain. She replies: "I feel . . . that there is an insurmountable barrier between us. . . . [it is] the public opinion which assigns me a place with the colored people" (*Iola Leroy*, 230–231). When she makes him see that there is prejudice against all African American people, he encourages her to "pass" as a white woman, since her eyes are blue and her skin is as white as his; to this she replies, "No, Doctor, I am not willing to live under a shadow of concealment which I thoroughly hate as if the blood in my veins were an undetected crime of my soul" (*Iola Leroy*, 233). Eventually, she meets Dr. Latimer who, like her, is of mixed blood, and, like her, has decided to devote his life to the cause of "uplifting" his brothers and sisters in the South. What characterizes both of these love relations, though, is not the typical love story of the sentimental romance; both seem a particularly bloodless and passionless courting and wooing. When Dr. Latimer proposes and Iola accepts, the words "sober," "seriously," and "earnest" appear more often than "laughingly" or "merry." As Iola accepts, Harper writes, "His words were more than a tender strain wooing her to love and happiness, they were a clarion call to a life of high and holy worth, a call which found a response in her heart" (*Iola Leroy*, 271). Romance in this novel becomes politics and is totally subsumed by it; love is translated into a "clarion call" to work.

The love relation in *Ramona*, too, is defined by the politics surrounding it. Ramona and Alessandro, despite being exiled by her Mexican family on the one hand, and the Anglo seizure of his village on the other, find themselves in one edenic setting after another, always loving each other, always loving the children who come. But, like the Adam and Eve they are figured as, they are continually cast out of Eden not by their own sin but by the evils of white land-grabbers who are systematically eradicating all of Alessandro's people. They face one white settler who has paper title to their land, only to be pushed off the land they later settle by another one, only to escape to a mountain hideaway where Alessandro is eventually killed by yet another. Throughout these episodes of horror and brutality, the love between Ramona/ "Majella" and Alessandro remains strong but is continually threatened by the forces of racism and the white settlement of the West. But despite Ramona's taking of her new name and her repeated exclamations, "Oh, I am glad I am an Indian!" (*Ramona*, 133) and her sense that she is becoming "like [the] true Indian woman [that] I am" (*Ramona*, 190), we never quite lose the sense in the novel that she is playing at being Indian the whole time she is with Alessandro.

It is on this point of characterization that the novel most reveals its allegiance to the conventions of the sentimental genre. Ramona's reactions are those of a privileged, individualized, bourgeois woman, her voice the voice of the traditional (almost always white) sentimental heroine. She engages the sympathies of the reader by being so, but she also distances the reader from the politics of the novel by never really embodying those politics, despite being, for many years, persecuted as a Native American. In fairness to Helen Hunt Jackson, I should note that she felt that the response to *Ramona* signaled that the novel was a failure; she was disgusted that her readership involved itself in the romance of the novel at the expense of the politics. She believed that she was writing a social protest novel, one that would bring the same attention to the oppression of Native Americans that Stowe's *Uncle Tom's Cabin* had brought to the plight of slaves.[14] But the fact that, after Alessandro's death, "Majella" returns to her life as the Mexican woman Ramona with her cousin Felipe seems to reinforce the sense that the romance is the real subject of the novel. When the romance is over, so are the politics. Whereas the politics of *Iola Leroy* seem to dominate and determine the romance, the romance in *Ramona* determines the politics. In finally taking her cousin Felipe for her husband, Ramona abandons racial controversy altogether.

Ultimately, the problems in both novels are a matter of form as much as they are problems of ideology or ethics; or rather, the problems of ideology *are* problems of form and vice versa. The narrative itself becomes fragmented. The two halves of *Ramona* do not cohere—the love plot (courtship and marriage) of the first half of the novel doesn't fit the social commentary (oppression, misery, and death) of the second. The conclusion of *Iola Leroy*—her marriage to Dr. Latimer—does not necessarily answer the problems of racial politics (the questions of integration and segregation) outlined so clearly in the novel and ignores totally the specter of southern lynching that underlies the real danger of Iola's final undertaking as a teacher in the Reconstruction-era South. The politics of race are converted into romance, and far from resolving them, the romance seriously clouds the questions.

Finally, both *Ramona* and *Iola Leroy* illustrate and even exaggerate the problems that Baker and Olney outline. Written for a white audience, conforming to "the conventional literary discourse structures of a white reading public," these "race-problem" novels are ultimately captive to that form. In offering individual solutions for their individual heroines, they construct a version of racial identity that must be questioned.

I have claimed that the ending to *Iola Leroy* is less problematic than the ending of *Ramona*, and that the choices the authors made may be tied back to race. Harper, writing about the problems of African Americans, had available to her the conventions of the slave narrative in a way that Jackson did not, concerned as she was with Native American problems. The two generic traditions that Harper could draw on then—sentimental fiction (open to women writers) and slave narrative (open to African Americans)—both at least shared the convention of the happy ending.[15] Harper could then resolve her narrative with the traditional happy ending for a woman—marriage to a good man—with the traditional happy ending for a slave narrative—finding real freedom and working for the benefit of the race—in a relatively harmonious way.

Jackson, on the other hand, had three narrative traditions to choose from, at least two of which were at real odds with her political purpose. She could write a sentimental novel, in which the heroine overcomes all odds, but that would obviate the need for any political intervention—if Indian women could cope with anything, including dispossession, then United States policies were fine. She could write a social-problem novel, like Rebecca Harding Davis's *Life in the Iron Mills*, where the reality of Indian life in California prevailed, where after Alessandro's murder, Ramona and her child starved, or died of illness, but she almost certainly would not reach as wide an audience, and the audience she reached might well have found the situation too hopeless to do anything about it. Such an ending would also have fit the third tradition Jackson could have used, of early- and mid-century fictions about Native Americans in which the Indian is a tragic figure, fated to fall victim to extinction. Unlike Harper, then, Jackson did not have generic conventions that could be easily blended; her choice to save Ramona and her daughter may amount to evading her real political question, but it also avoids a necessarily politically helpless ending.

I do not want to offer an apologia for Jackson, but I do want to suggest that we need to read her text in light of her desires and its discourse and circumstances of production, just as Tate and McDowell suggest we have to read Harper's. From that vantage point, *Ramona* may fit a new genre in which the goal is neither the "female domination" of the sentimental novel nor the "realism" of the social-problem novel but a vision of what will be gained or lost if political and social changes are not made. Perhaps sending Ramona away to Mexico is Jackson's attempt to let the American people know what they are losing or stand to lose if they completely dispossess the Indian people. Read this way, the figure of Aunt Ri—who dominates, really, the final quarter of the book—functions as a representative of the reader (that is, a white woman) in two ways: first, her opinion of Indians changes, as Jackson hopes the reader's will, and, second, when she mourns Alessandro's death and Ramona's departure, she models what the reader should be feeling. While Harper's ending represents not the reality of what Iola Leroy will face but, as Tate and McDowell have already suggested, a vision of what could be, Jackson's offers a warning of what will come unless changes are made.

Feminist Politics: Success, Individualism, and Racial Progress

The problem of reading ideologically that Myra Jehlen outlined in 1981 has, if anything, become more difficult for feminist criticism in the 1990s, when we cannot even be sure to which "feminist ideology" we are referring. Obviously, I cannot sketch out the whole range of feminist positions here, but I can describe some real dilemmas that arise in trying to read *Ramona* and *Iola Leroy* through a "feminist" lens, problems that are clearly related to the generic constraints on the novels, especially on the endings.

The problem of authenticity I raise with regard to race can equally apply to gender. But to raise the question of an authentic female voice in *Ramona* and *Iola Leroy* is to raise the question of whether the sentimental novel ever represented an "authentic" voice even for middle-class white women. Certainly, sentimental fiction—which usually features beautiful, blonde heiresses—never did represent a majority of women, not really even the women whose mores and values it most clearly reflected. Even though these novels center a certain amount of power in their heroines, those heroines do not accurately represent even middle-class white women, much less a majority of women, and therefore offer no more authentic voice for women than do other nineteenth-century narratives for African Americans or Native Americans. The sentimental novel did, however, represent a powerful tool for advancing a particular kind of female—if not feminist—power in the nineteenth century, a power only rarely granted to African American and Native American figures in literature. The debate over this female power was the centerpiece of the great Tompkins-Douglas debate of the early 1980s.[16] Was the power this fiction advocated an alternative form of power that does not urge domination, an effort to expand matriarchal values and to center cultural power in women? Or was it a position foisted on unsuspecting women by an anti-intellectual clergy to keep women at home and unclear in their thinking? This raises the question of authenticity: were women claiming their own variety of power, or were they puppets of patriarchal preachers?

Authenticity of voice is not the only question that such feminist critical debates raise. How should feminist criticism weigh female success in these novels, especially when we are reading them within the difficult framework of the racial dilemmas I describe? How is the feminist critic to read the happy marriage typical of sentimental endings? More troublingly, how do we read that marriage when it is so clearly tied to racial politics?

Certainly, one could take one position or the other in the Tompkins-Douglas debate: the marriages represent the reimposing of the sentimental sloppiness of thinking that was part of the problem in the first place, or the establishment of a kind of female realm, where women urge values of kindness and tolerance that serve as political models. Either of those readings, which I'm oversimplifying here in the interest of space, would require that we look at the individual woman's narrative outcome, that we value her success more highly than the success of the political position the writer is promoting. In other words, to be satisfied with the endings of these novels, at least ideologically, we have to read as individualist feminists, a perspective at odds with a multicultural, antiracist position that advocates group success.[17]

Harper's novel cannot, of course, offer an answer to the problems of racial difference, but it does offer a more coherent (if itself troubled) view of racial politics than does *Ramona*. Despite Jackson's own best intentions, the individualistic "solution" she reaches for Ramona enacts a kind of cultural genocide—the abandonment of the racial heritage she has only just embraced—that is more sympathetic, but not less devastating, than the genocidal dispossessions enacted in the novel by Anglo settlers. In embracing the individual's plight, in giving us a happy ending to that single woman's trials, she abandons the larger questions of white eradication of all Native American cultures. In suggesting that Ramona "pass" as a Mexican señora rather than stay to help resist domination by white settlers, she erases the very racial identity she has tried to validate during the whole novel. I do not mean to suggest that I think *Ramona* is an evil or even a bad novel—in fact, I think it is one of the great overlooked novels of the nineteenth century—but it is a troubled novel.

The narrative resolution that Jackson chose was the success—at least by middle-class, sentimental lights—of the individual female character. Harper, on the other hand, could combine that kind of individual success with promoting the success of the group. What Ramona has to sacrifice in order to live a healthy, happy life—namely, her identification with an oppressed racial group—is precisely what Iola can embrace to live hers. The contrast here may be one of generic demands, as I suggest, but it raises troubling conflicts for feminist and multicultural critical work. What can we do with a text that perpetuates the valuing of an individual woman's success over the needs of a racial group?

Reading Beyond the Binary

What we can do is use Anzaldúa's model to create in ourselves the mestiza reader, in all her ambivalence. Unlike Jackson and Harper, we have critical conventions that do not necessarily force us to choose one identity or another as readers—we can recognize the positive and negative aspects of their racial and gender politics as illustrating the complexities of the issues they represent. Ironically, the *inauthenticity* of these texts may be the testament to their authenticity; their problems may be their real strengths. If, by pushing the generic limits open to them Jackson and Harper created textual crises that cry out for other options, then they advanced the political and literary traditions for and in which they were writing. Their successes and failures open the way for later writers. By attending to their textual crises, we readers may also be able to push the limits of our own critical dilemmas, not just tolerating contradiction, but using it to create a new mestiza consciousness of reading.

Notes

1. Myra Jehlen, "Archimedes and the Paradox of Feminist Criticism," *Signs* 6 (1981): 575–601.
2. Helen Hunt Jackson, *Ramona* (New York: Signet Classics, 1988), and Frances E. W. Harper, *Iola Leroy, or Shadows Uplifted* (New York: Oxford University Press, 1988). All subsequent references are to these editions and will be cited parenthetically in the text.
3. David Goodman Croly, *Miscegenation: The Theory of the Blending of the Races, Applied to the American White Man and Negro* (1863; reprint, Upper Saddle River, N.J.: Literature House, 1970), ii.
4. The preeminent example of the doomed-Indian novel is almost certainly James Fenimore Cooper's *The Last of the Mohicans* (1826), but the inevitability of the Indians' demise or disappearance was a well-established literary and political trope, in such novels as James Eastburn and Robert Sands's verse epic *Yamoyden* (1820), Lydia Maria Child's *Hobomok* (1824), and Catharine Maria Sedgwick's *Hope Leslie* (1827). For an excellent consideration of this genre, see Nina Baym, "Putting Women in their Place: *The Last of the Mohicans* and Other Indian Stories," in *Feminism and American Literary History* (New Brunswick, N.J.: Rutgers University Press, 1992), 19–35.
5. Houston Baker, "Autobiographical Acts and the Voice of the Southern Slave," in *The Slave's Narrative*, ed. Charles T. Davis and Henry Louis Gates, Jr. (New York: Oxford University Press, 1985), 251.
6. James Olney, "'I Was Born': Slave Narratives, Their Status As Autobiography and Literature," in *The Slave's Narrative*, ed. Davis and Gates, 167.
7. Claudia Tate, "Allegories of Black Female Desire; or, Rereading Nineteenth-Century Sentimental Narratives of Black Female Authority," in *Changing Our Own Words: Essays on Criticism, Theory, and Writing by Black Women*, ed. Cheryl A. Wall (New Brunswick, N.J.: Rutgers University Press, 1989), 98–126.
8. Baker, "Autobiographical Acts," 259.
9. Deborah McDowell, "'The Changing Same': Generational Connections and Black Women Novelists," *New Literary History* 18, no. 2 (1987): 287. Marilyn Elkins argues that Harper's representation of minor characters is more realistic than her portrayal of Iola, and that characters like Linda and Lucille lend the novel a good deal of authenticity. Marilyn Elkins, "Reading Beyond the Conventions: A Look at Frances E. W. Harper's *Iola Leroy, or Shadows Uplifted*," *American Literary Realism* 22, no. 2 (1990): 44–53.
10. Gloria Anzaldúa, "*La concienca de la mestiza*: Towards a New Consciousness," in *Making Face/Making Soul: Haciendo Caras*, ed. Gloria Anzaldúa (San Francisco: Aunt Lute Foundation, 1990), 379.
11. Ibid., 379.
12. Ibid., 379.
13. Mikhail Bakhtin and P. N. Medvedev, *The Formal Method in Literary Scholarship:*

A Critical Introduction to Sociological Poetics, trans. Albert J. Wehrle (Baltimore: Johns Hopkins University Press, 1978), 133, 134.

14. Valerie Sherer Mathes, *Helen Hunt Jackson and Her Indian Reform Legacy* (Austin: University of Texas Press, 1990).

15. Elizabeth Young examines how Harper's novel also fits the genre of war fiction, in "Warring Fictions: *Iola Leroy* and the Color of Gender," *American Literature* 64 (1992): 273–97. For a discussion of the blending of sentimentalism and the slave narrative in Jacobs's *Incidents in the Life of a Slave Girl*, see Franny Nudelman, "Harriet Jacobs and the Sentimental Politics of Female Suffering," *ELH* 59 (1992): 939–64.

16. See Jane Tompkins, *Sensational Designs: The Cultural Work of American Fiction* (New York: Oxford University Press, 1985), and Ann Douglas, *The Feminization of American Culture* (New York: Knopf, 1977). For an excellent discussion of the Tompkins-Douglas debate, see Laura Wexler, "Tender Violence: Literary Eavesdropping, Domestic Fiction, and Educational Reform," in *The Culture of Sentiment: Race, Gender, and Sentimentality in Nineteenth-Century America* (New York: Oxford University Press, 1992), 9–38.

17. The problematic relation between individualistic and community-oriented feminisms is explored in depth by many of the writers in *This Bridge Called My Back*, ed. Cherríe Moraga and Gloria Anzald'a (New York: Kitchen Table/Women of Color Press, 1983), and in *Making Face/Making Soul: Haciendo Caras*, ed. Anzaldúa, and at length by Elizabeth Fox-Genovese in *Feminism Without Illusions: A Critique of Individualism* (Chapel Hill: University of North Carolina Press, 1991).

About the Contributors

Laura Browder is an assistant professor of English at Virginia Commonwealth University, where she teaches playwriting and American Studies. Her books include *Rousing the Nation: Radical Culture in Depression America* (University of Massachusetts Press, 1998) and *Slippery Characters: Ethnic Imposture and American Identities* (forthcoming from the University of North Carolina Press).

Michael Davidson is professor of literature at the University of California, San Diego. He is the author of *The San Francisco Renaissance: Poetics and Community at Mid-Century* (Cambridge University Press, 1989) and *Ghostlier Demarcations: Modern Poetry and the Material Word* (University of California Press, 1997). He is also the author of eight books of poetry, including *The Arcades* (O Books, 1998), *Post Hoc* (Avenue B, 1990) and *The Landing of Rochambeau* (Burning Deck, 1985).

Lennard J. Davis is professor of English and graduate director at the State University of New York, Binghamton. He is the author of *Factual Fictions: The Origins of the English Novel* (Columbia University Press, 1983); *Resisting Novels: Fiction and Ideology* (Routledge, 1987); *Enforcing Normalcy: Disability, Deafness and the Body* (Verso, 1996); *My Sense of Silence: A Memoir of a Childhood with Deafness* (University of Illinois Press, 1998); coeditor of *Left Politics and the Literary Profession* (Columbia University Press, 1991); and editor of *The Disability Studies Reader* (Routledge, 1997) and *"Shall I Say Kiss?" Love Letters of a Deaf Couple, 1936–1938* (Gallaudet University Press, 1999).

Professor Davis is currently working on *Novel Theory* to be published by Duke University Press.

Heather Hathaway is an assistant professor of English at Marquette University. Her writings include articles on African American and Caribbean literature, immigration history and culture, and the relationship between race, ethnicity, and identity. The essay included here is part of a larger study of Caribbean narratives of immigration to the United States.

Diane Price Herndl is an associate professor of English at New Mexico State University. She is the author of *Invalid Women: Figuring Feminine Illness in American Fiction and Culture, 1840–1940* (University of North Carolina Press, 1993). She is the coeditor, with Robyn Warhol, of *Feminisms: An Anthology of Literary Criticism and Theory* (Rutgers University Press, 1991; second edition 1997). She is at work on a book about women, apocalyptic narrative, and technology after the atomic bomb.

Sharon P. Holland is an assistant professor of English at Stanford University. Her book, *Raising the Dead: Death and Black Subjectivity in 20th Century Literature and Cultures* is forthcoming from Duke University Press. She works on a range of interests from African American to Queer and Feminist studies. Her next book project involves an examination of the modernist inheritance in late-twentieth-century writers.

John Lowe is professor of English at Louisiana State University and author of *Jump at the Sun: Zora Neale Hurston's Cosmic Comedy* University of Illinois Press, 1994); editor of *Conversations with Ernest Gaines* (University of Mississippi Press, 1995); and coeditor of *The Future of Southern Letters* (Oxford University Press, 1996). He is currently completing The *Americanization of Ethnic Humor*, a multicultural and interdisciplinary examination of changing patterns of comedy and culture.

David Mitchell is an associate professor of English at Northern Michigan University. He is coeditor of the "Corporealities: Discourses of Disability" series from the University of Michigan Press and coeditor of *The Body and Physical Difference: Discourses of Disability* (University of Michigan Press, 1997). Currently, he is completing a new book-length manuscript entitled, *Narrative Prosthesis: The Materiality of Metaphor in Literary Narratives*.

Rosemarie Garland Thomson is an associate professor of English at Howard University in Washington, D.C. Her essay on Toni Morrison won the 1989 Florence Howe Award for Feminist Scholarship, given by the Modern Language Association. She is the author of *Extraordinary Bodies: Figuring Physical Disability in American Literature and Culture* (Columbia University Press, 1997) and the editor of *Freakery: Cultural Spectacles of the Extraordinary Body* (New York University Press, 1996). She is currently writing a book about the cultural dynamics of staring.

Nicole Tonkovich is an associate professor of nineteenth-century U.S. literatures at the University of California, San Diego. She is author of *Domesticity with a Difference: The Nonfiction of Catharine Beecher, Sarah J. Hale, Fanny Fern, Margaret Fuller* (University of Mississippi Press, 1997).

About the Editor

Timothy B. Powell is an assistant professor at the University of Georgia; he specializes in nineteenth-century American and multicultural American literature. His articles have appeared in the *African American Review, Toni Morrison's Fiction: Contemporary Criticism*, ed. David L. Middleton (Garland, 1997), and *The Pre-Occupation of Post-Colonial Studies*, ed. Fawzia Azfal-Khan and Kalpana Seshadri-Crooks (forthcoming from Duke University Press). His new book *Ruthless Democracy: A Multicultural Interpretation of the American Renaissance* is forthcoming from Princeton University Press.

Index